MW00582877

Sinister Forces

A Grimoire of American Political Witchcraft

Book Two:

A Warm Gun

Peter Levenda

TrineDay
WALTERVILLE, OREGON

SINISTER FORCES—A GRIMOIRE OF AMERICAN POLITICAL WITCHCRAFT: A WARM GUN Copyright © 2006 Peter Levenda. All rights reserved. Artwork ©TrineDay

TrineDay
PO Box 577
Walterville, OR 97489

www.TrineDay.com
support@TrineDay.com

Levenda, Peter
    Sinister Forces—A Grimoire of American Political Witchcraft: A Warm Gun / Peter Levenda ; with forward by Dick Russell — 1st ed.
    p. cm.
    ISBN 0-9752906-3-0 (acid-free paper)
    1. Political Corruption—United States. 2. Central Intelligence Agency (CIA)—MK-ULTRA—Operation BLUEBIRD. 3. Behavior Modicfication—United States. 4. Occultism—United States—History. 5. Crime—Serial Killers—Charles Manson—Son of Sam. 6. Secret Societies—United States. 1. Title
    364.1'3230973—

FIRST EDITION
10 9 8 7 6 5 4 3 2 1

Printed in the USA

Distribution to the Trade By:
  Independent Publishers Group (IPG)
  814 North Franklin Street
  Chicago, Illinois 60610
  312.337.0747
  www.ipgbook.com
  frontdesk@ipgbook.com

For Vivica

"History, Stephen said, is a nightmare from which I am trying to awake."
-- James Joyce, *Ulysses*

BOOK TWO: A WARM GUN

TABLE OF CONTENTS

FOREWORD

BY DICK RUSSELL

Let us begin with a couple of quotes from Carl Jung. "The unconscious is the unwritten history of mankind from time unrecorded," Jung wrote. It "only becomes dangerous when our conscious attitude to it is hopelessly wrong. To the degree that we repress it, its danger increases."

In this, Book Two of his trilogy *Sinister Forces*, Peter Levenda walks us through that minefield, dredges up and weaves together considerable material that many would prefer stay buried. There have been, for example, many books about the decline and fall of Richard Nixon, and no few books exploring the bizarre world of Charles Manson. But, beyond their existence in the same chronological time-frame, no one has probed the parallel reality of their not-so-separate universes. "Power, to people like Manson and Nixon, is the only reality, the only absolute," writes Levenda. "Nixon *had* to proclaim Manson guilty to the press; he had to address the one other man in the country who understood power, and truth, and evil, and murder the way he did."

It may make certain readers uncomfortable, this pairing of a president and a pariah. Comfort, however, is not Levenda's intent. Consider as well: "But the demon in the smoke that crawled out of the God Struck Tower on September 11, 2001 bore the face of Charles Milles Manson, the bastard son of America and product of its institutions and—even more importantly—scion of its bartered Soul."

Heavy stuff. Heavier still, because Levenda strides here into a realm where good and evil are often not what they appear. Or, rather, what Americans fantasize they are. In today's America, where biblical literalism is the absolute truth for an increasing number of people, Levenda's tracing of an Islamic and Christian "underground" through the centuries—in the cults of the Nizaris and the Templars—may be seen by many as heretical, if not blasphemous or even treasonous.

Cut from there to the author's "Heart of Darkness" chapter—the terrifying relationship between the CIA's attempts to control human behavior and the "mass suicide" inspired by Jim Jones at Jonestown—and one can almost envision poor Peter at the stake for this heresy. But wait, we are not done with assassins "under the influence," not until we have investigated the Chapman (John Lennon), Hinckley (President Reagan), and Bremer (George Wallace) capers.

Levenda is perhaps, above all, a master of exploring mysterious synchronicities, or at least giving such events a context. To wit, the year 1947 saw the creation of the CIA and the discovery of the Dead Sea Scrolls, not to mention the Roswell crash and the death of Aleister Crowley. In *A Warm Gun*, we are awash not in the coincidental but in the subliminal, and the possibility that the mythic battles between demonic and angelic forces are yet being recreated on planet Earth (and even beyond).

How quickly we forget, and with what urgency Levenda would remind us! The author's initial expertise was in the occult realm of Nazi Germany (*Unholy Alliance*), and here he sweeps through post-war events with a rapier, exposing the unctuous underbelly of a national history whose inevitable denouement may now be occurring—under the radar—with the corporate Christocracy of George W. Bush.

The pace of contemporary life moves too quickly—all sound-bite and videogame lever—for many of us to reflect upon yesterday, much less upon the patterns that fuel our paranoia. This book, then, is an often-maddening (but not mad!) excursion beyond the pale, beyond what has come to be considered "normalcy." Indeed, Levenda seems to be telling us, we live in the most *ab*normal—even *para*normal—of times. And unless we heed the reality that underlies the everyday, our failure to connect the dots will allow our denial to persist. And increase the likelihood that, one of these godawful days, we shall either boil in our own carbon emissions or blow ourselves to smithereens in the name of righteousness.

"The bugle blows…" James Hillman writes in *A Terrible Love of War*. "Wake up, said Plato; we are all in a cave watching shadows on the wall, believing them to be reality."

So look down the barrel of Peter Levenda's *A Warm Gun*, and pay heed to the dark saga of how we came to our current "reality."

INTRODUCTION

Why this is hell, nor am I out of it.
   —Mephistopheles in *Dr. Faustus*, Part , I, iii, 76-80 by Christopher Marlowe

Welcome to Book Two of *Sinister Forces: A Warm Gun.* In Book One: *The Nine,* you were introduced to a thread of violence and bizarre belief—represented by violent and bizarre people—running, like Sherlock Holmes' "scarlet thread of murder," through American history up to and including the assassinations of the two Kennedy brothers. Strange priests, satanic rituals, political conspiracy, and the occult. Not the sort of thing one normally encounters during the course of graduate work in political science ... or during a walk down a dark alley in an American city at night. That all of these things happened is a fact; that these people committed these actions is a fact. That some very strange belief systems are at the heart of American policy, foreign and domestic, is also a fact.

That many Americans are not aware of this, or simply don't care, is another fact.

In this, the second book of a trilogy concerning American "political witchcraft," we will examine some of the more modern manifestations of this unsettling concourse of sinister forces. We will look at terrorism, true, but we will also discover the coincidence stream in full flow in the lives of men as disparate in social standing as Richard Nixon and Mark David Chapman, Jim Jones and Richard Mellon Scaife, David Berkowitz and Donald Cammell. It is a study of Washington ... and Hollywood. Of serial murder and mysticism. Of the straining of the American intelligence community towards a manipulation of the unconscious mind and of their transgression into the realm of the occult and initiation. We will look at the stories we all think we already know, and see—maybe for the first time—what the Renaissance

an Giordano Bruno meant when he wrote of "the links": the doctrine
rrespondences that is not only the province of ceremonial magic but of
emonial politics. That is why this trilogy is called a "grimoire."

There are times when it appears that world history is nothing less than the
story of warring secret societies, with all of the rest of humanity mere pawns
in what historian Ladislas Farago called "the Game of the Foxes."

The Rosicrucians of the 17th Century gave us a prototype of the secret
society: a band of brothers, bound together by mystical visions, which had
probably never existed in reality but was the romantic invention of an English
alchemist. It was an otherwise anonymous manifesto – a printed broadside
– that created the myth of the Rosicrucians and since then many individuals have sought to capitalize on the name and the glamour by proclaiming
themselves heirs to the Rosicrucian tradition.

What is Al-Qaeda, then, but another secret society: a band of brothers,
bound together by a mystical vision of the world, whose membership is
largely secret, where betrayal of the group's mysteries is punished by death,
and which is probably a very small organization with a larger-than-life profile
whose reputation is made on websites and videotapes ... and mass murder.
The same was said of the Illuminati and the Freemasons, upon whom the
blame for centuries of violent revolution was laid. That Al-Qaeda—"the
Base"—has more in common with the Assassins cult of Hassan i-Sabah only
reinforces this idea of a secret society at war with the world ... and with the
West in general.

Should it surprise us, then, that the putative opponents of Al-Qaeda should
be members of a Western secret society?

The secret society and occult affiliations of America's political and intelligence leadership is something that is never discussed on the open airwaves,
never investigated by the mainstream media. We have all heard of Skull &
Bones, and know that somehow President George W. Bush was a member of
this college fraternity while a student at Yale University. The story seems to
end there. No one delves too deeply into this aspect of Bush's life, even when
it is revealed that his father belonged to the same society, and that Democratic
presidential candidate John F. Kerry also belonged to Skull & Bones. The very
idea that, in 2004, the presidential election was a choice between two Bonesmen never seemed to make the headlines in America even when it was shown
that Skull & Bones membership is quite small (only *fifteen* new members are
initiated every year), very select, and depends upon a strenuous enforcement of
the rules of secrecy and deception. That the two presidential candidates were
both members of this same small and elite group should have raised warning
flags, and didn't. Yet, at a time when America was embroiled in the Iraq war
and in an ostensible "war on terror"—directed against Al-Qaeda—our only
choices for president were two members of the same secret society.

If that was all, it would be enough. But that's not all.

In 1833, the year after Skull & Bones was founded, another secret society was formed, this time at Union College in New York. This one was called Psi Upsilon, and was formed by seven students who signed a pact stating, "We, the undersigned, having determined to form a secret society, and having some conversation on the subject, do now and hereby pledge our sacred honors that we will keep all that has been done and said a most profound secret."

Psi Upsilon spread to many universities across America and even abroad. Its second, or Beta, chapter was founded at Yale University in 1840 and became known as The Fence Club in 1934.

In 1960, both Porter Goss, the George W. Bush-appointed Director of the CIA—and John Negroponte, the Bush-appointed Intelligence Chief–were members of The Fence Club at Yale, as was John Kerry, a Bonesman.

Porter Goss was also a member of the super-secret Order of Book & Snake, a seemingly associated society of Skull & Bones. The same year Goss joined Book & Snake he also joined yet another secret society: the CIA.

And let us not forget still another member of the Bush dynasty, William Henry Trotter (Bucky) Bush, brother of former CIA Director and President, George Herbert Walker Bush. William Bush was also a member of The Fence Club in 1960, along with Porter Goss and John Negroponte.

So, what do we have?

We have George Herbert Walker Bush, George W. Bush, William Henry Bush, John F. Kerry, Porter Goss, and John Negroponte all members of secret societies at Yale University. And let's not forget Prescott Bush, who was one of the directors of the Union Banking Corporation that was shut down by the US government in 1942 when it was discovered that Bush and his partner, E Roland Harriman, were "trading with the enemy": i.e., the Nazis. Prescott Bush was another member of Skull & Bones.

That's two presidents, one presidential contender, two CIA directors, and an intelligence czar who are all fellow-travelers in the world of rituals and sworn oaths, secrecy and deception, trained since their late adolescence and early adulthood in the environment of privilege and control. Dear reader, should I burden you with revelations that Averell Harriman as well as Roland Harriman—partners with the Bush family in "trading with the enemy" before and during World War II—were also Bonesmen? That the Psi Upsilon secret society abandoned its pretence of being a literary society early on and admitted its preference for members with a proven *ancestry?* That there is little to associate these Orders with the popular conception of college fraternities represented by such films as *Animal House?*

As members of Skull & Bones, Psi Upsilon and Book & Snake consolidate their control over America's wealth, intelligence agencies, and military power, they are also engaged in a war with Islamic secret societies that costs us thousands of lives and hundreds of billions of dollars. Conservative Americans were worried in 1960 that should a Catholic become President, then America would somehow be controlled by the Pope. Instead, we have an America that is in thrall to a handful of initiates in a few small secret societies that share a hidden agenda, a covert brotherhood, and a contempt for individual liberty … and no one is bothered by this at all except the crazies, the loonies, the militiamen, the conspiracy theorists, the paranoid schizophrenics.

As the eminent *New York Times* critic Anatole Broyard once said, "paranoids are the only ones who notice anything anymore."

There are around 700 members of Skull & Bones alive today. That represents less than .00001 percent of America's total population, or 1 per every 300,000 persons. Yet, somehow, they occupy a large percentage of top positions of our government. The attitude of our media, however, is to "pay no attention to the man behind the curtain."

The previous volume of *Sinister Forces* ended with a review of the strange world of secret societies, wandering bishops, psychological warfare, and mind-control programs that culminated in the assassinations of President Kennedy and his brother, Senator Robert F. Kennedy. This volume picks up where the first left off: a discussion of these same influences around the Republican Party of Nixon and Reagan, Watergate, the assassination of John Lennon, the Son of Sam cult, the Manson Family, Jonestown, terrorism, and the "vast, right-wing conspiracy." This is a look behind the curtain, an exposé of The Nine as they perpetuated the ultimate secret society at work beneath the surface of America's long political nightmare, through children especially selected as carriers of their message. It is *The Wizard of Oz* meets MK-ULTRA.

I'd like to end this by saying "We're not in Kansas, anymore." Unfortunately, might I say, paraphrasing Mephistopheles, "Why, this *is* Kansas. Nor am I out of it."

Peter Levenda
New York City

SECTION FOUR:
ALL THE PRESIDENT'S MEN

...Buzhardt told Haig that he could find "no innocent explanation," and concluded that the buzz had come from "some outside source of energy" rather than a malfunctioning of the tape recorder. Haig says he and other Presidential assistants suspected that night that the buzz had been caused by "some sinister force."
 —J. Anthony Lukas, *Nightmare: The Underside of the Nixon Years*[1]

Mike, the One-Armed Man: *"Don't turn on the overheads. The fluorescents don't work. I think a transformer's bad."*
FBI Special Agent Dale Cooper: *"We know that."*
Mike: *"Yes."*
 —Pilot Episode, *Twin Peaks*

Therefore with us there must be some accidental and particular cause preventing the human spirit from following its inclination and driving it beyond those limits within which it should naturally remain.

 I am profoundly convinced that this accidental and particular cause is the close union of politics and religion.
 —Alexis de Toqueville, *Democracy in America*[2]

We have had our last chance. If we will not devise some greater and more equitable system, our Armageddon will be at our door. The problem basically is theological and involves a spiritual recrudescence, an improvement of human character that will synchronize with our almost matchless advances in science, art, literature and all material and cultural developments of the past two thousand years. It must be of the spirit if we are to save the flesh.
 —General Douglas MacArthur, Sept. 2, 1945

MOSES AND AARON BEFORE PHARAOH

And Aaron cast down his rod before Pharaoh, and before his servants, and it became a serpent . . . (Exodus 7: 10)

CHAPTER NINE

FOR REBELLION IS AS THE SIN OF WITCHCRAFT

For rebellion is as the sin of witchcraft.
  —1 Samuel 15:23

[King] Unas devoureth men and liveth upon the gods, he is the lord of envoys, whom he sendeth forth on his missions.... Khonsu the slayer of the wicked cutteth their throats and draweth out their intestines, for it is he whom Unas sendeth to slaughter; and Shesmu cutteth them in pieces and boileth their members in his blazing caldrons of the night. Unas eateth their magical powers, and he swalloweth their Spirit-souls.... The old gods and the old goddesses become fuel for his furnace
  —Pyramid Text[3]

If the power of God comes into a person, don't we become like God?
  —Sirhan Sirhan[4]

By the conclusion of the first volume of *Sinister Forces, The Nine,* much had been made of political conspiracies, particularly those surrounding assassinations. There was also a focus on the Manson Family, as we walked with them through desert and canyon. But not so far as the Tate and La Bianca households. Not yet.

Furthermore, those events took place in a larger context. The pursuit of evil and the tracking of evil through the political and scientific machinations of intelligence agencies is ultimately unsatisfactory if we do not address an unspoken and normally unconscious assumption of our political leaders and particularly of our intelligence chiefs, and that is that their mission is in some way a divine one: that they represent the will of God.

The human assumption of divinity has been construed as evil—as a usurpation of the status of divine beings—for thousands of years. No organized religion of any size or amount of temporal power encourages or permits its followers direct access to divinity; the privilege of communicating directly to God has been reserved for the organized and socially approved priesthood. This is as true of ancient India as it is of modern Catholicism. Access to God is very tightly controlled, and is usually forbidden to certain elements of society, particularly women. Women may not become priests in the Roman Catholic Church, and are thus separated from the sacrament of ordination, a situation that calls into question the very nature of the soul. For it presupposes that the soul has a gender, since sacraments do not affect the body but only the soul. This is perhaps understandable in view of the etymology of the word "sacrament," which comes from the Latin and which originally meant a military oath, an oath of (male) soldiers. Women may not be ordained in the Eastern Orthodox churches, either.

In Orthodox Judaism, women may not become rabbis. Menstruating women, in fact, are considered unclean and may not enter the synagogue during their period. A man who touches a menstruating woman becomes unclean, and must bathe in the ritual bath—the *mikvah*—before going to worship himself. In the East, women are noticeably scarce in the lists of divine Hindu and Buddhist and Daoist figures.

Yet, in the West, it has traditionally been women who were charged with the practice of witchcraft, a phenomenon that has led some historians and anthropologists—such as Margaret Murray, Robert Graves and Erich Neumann—to develop the theory that witchcraft is the survival of an ancient goddess-oriented religion that was suppressed on a virtually global scale, from Europe to the Middle East, and to the borders of India. If this is true, and it was suppressed, then the reasons for the nearly perfect destruction of this religion had to be political.

Our most ancient artwork as a people has been that associated with magic and religion. The prehistoric cave paintings of Lescaux, for instance; the Venus of Willendorf; the many thousands of different varieties of goddess statues found all over the world. People did not venerate human leaders and etch their likenesses in stone and clay until civilization began to coalesce around villages and towns and away from field and forest. When they did, they did because their leaders partook of the divine essence, the divine nature; they were the representatives of the gods upon the earth.

And when this occurred, when state religions were established and associated with city-cults such as those of ancient Sumeria, Babylon and Egypt, then there grew up around them secret cults that worshipped older gods, the gods and goddesses that had been usurped by the newer, royally-linked deities. Even ancient Sumeria—arguably the oldest western civilization that has left any written record of itself—had its cult of witches, and various texts (such as the *Maqlu* or "Burning" Text) contain chants and prayers against the practice of witchcraft, some three thousand years before the birth of Christ. These witches were independent practitioners of ritual; in other words, they did not belong to the state cult, were not approved by the ruler (who was both secular and sacred ruler), and they worshipped beings that were not approved by the state cult. Thus, the Biblical phrase cited above, that witchcraft and rebellion were synonymous. Rebellion is a revolt against secular authority; the implication is therefore that witchcraft is a revolt against sacred authority. It puts access to God in the hands of the Great Unwashed. It creates an anti-church, just as rebellion creates an anti-government.

In a way, this is a logical extension of the Creation epics of all races. The Creation of the world (or the universe, or the cosmos, or just one race or nation) is always divine in nature. The First Man and the First Woman were created by God or Gods. Thus, society itself owes its existence to a deity of some kind. Following this chain of logic, then, the king—as the ruler of society—*must* have a special, sacred relationship with the divine. This is especially true in the West, where God is perceived as a King on a throne. (It may be argued therefore that the secularization of cosmology brought about by modern science could undercut any special claims to kingship, and render human rulers about as "special" as servers or routers on a computer network.)

The Cult of the Pharaoh in ancient Egypt was a religious as well as a secular cult. The Pharaoh was a representative of God; he was able to communicate directly with God, and after death he was guaranteed a continued existence as an Osiris, a resurrected god of the ancient Egyptians, after the performance of a long and complicated ritual which included mummification. The ancient Sumerian secular leaders would ascend to the top of their ziggurats and commune with their gods directly at certain times of the year. The Chinese Emperor was the "Son of Heaven" as was (and is) the Japanese Emperor; China was the "Middle Kingdom," at the center of the earth, and halfway between the earth and heaven. It is still called "Middle Kingdom"—*Zhong Guo*—to this day. The Dalai Lama is a political leader as well as a spiritual one; he is the incarnation of a god—*Avalokitesvara*, the God of Mercy—and when the Dalai Lama dies a search is undertaken to find his reincarnation. The leaders of the ancient Aztecs, Incas and Mayas had religious power. In Europe we had the Holy Roman Empire, and in England they talked of the "divine right of kings." Yet, in all of these cases, the composite religious-secular cult replaced an earlier one.

The older cults were buried, sometimes literally, and the new cults erected like shiny edifices on the bones of the old. In many cases, old cult centers were renovated and new cult centers built on their sites. This is true of Christian church construction in Europe, where many older sites of important pagan significance were co-opted by the new Christian leaders and turned into

Christian shrines. The Gothic Cathedral at Chartres is a good example of this, but there are many more including St. Peter's Basilica itself, which was built on the site of the old Tauroboleum, a Mithraic cult center where bulls were sacrificed in honor of the god, Mithra. In fact, the name of the ceremonial headdress of Catholic bishops is still called a "mitre" seemingly in his honor, from the Latin *mitra* or "Mithra." This retention of ancient sites and ancient gods in the structure of their replacements may simply be a social strategy—to ensure greater and faster acceptance of the new cult by old cult members—or it may have an additional purpose, which would be to retain the particular powers of the older cults, those powers which their worshippers cultivate in secret ceremonies in the dead of night.

The ruthlessness with which new religions persecuted old ones was absolute. There is so little documentation left with which to appreciate and understand the older cults. Most of the documents we have on the ancient religions of Mexico and South America were written by Spanish Catholic priests and monks, for instance, and are therefore not necessarily wholly reliable. Tibetan Buddhism has all but eradicated the earlier Bon religion that it replaced, subsuming remnants of that shamanistic cult under its "Black Hat" Lamaistic branch, along with the Dalai Lama's "Yellow Hat" and the Gyalwa Karmapa's "Red Hat" sects. Of the old cults of pre-Dynastic Egypt we still know very little; the god Set—considered evil, on a par with the Christian "Satan," in Dynastic Egypt—was a god in his own right before the coming of the Pharaohs, as were Keb, Hathor and many others. The "God of the Witches" according to Margaret Murray in her controversial research was an ancient, horned deity whose worship was aggressively exterminated by the Church. Satan himself is an enigmatic figure, treated rather ambiguously in the Bible: sometimes as an adversary of God, sometimes as God's lieutenant (as in the Book of Job).

To worship the "old gods" was to commit heresy and, in the old days, treason. The political leadership and the religious leadership were one and the same. To go outside the system was to be cast into the outer darkness, to lose one's soul; to become a worshipper of devils, a word that comes from *deva*, the Sanskrit word for "god."

There is an interesting etymological puzzle that confronts the English speaker and the speaker of the Romance languages, and which compels us to draw some interesting and sobering conclusions about what we know and what we think we know. It is a puzzle that is at the heart of this study, and which will lead us into the Tunnels of Set, into the very bowels of Evil itself. And it may help us to understand Evil for the very first time.

REALITY, WHAT A CONCEPT

The word "real" and the word "royal" are inextricably linked. Indeed, in some languages the word for "real" and the word for "royal" is the same, such as Spanish *real*. Reality is, in this view, linked with Royalty; what is real is what is part of the kingdom, the "real estate." What is outside the kingdom is, therefore, outside of reality. It is not "royal," hence it is not "real." This speaks to Robert Anton Wilson's concept of "consensus reality," mentioned in the previous volume. Reality is a shape-shifter, dependent as much on political decisions as it is on scientific observations. And these decisions and observations are not usually the prerogative of the individual citizen. An essential part—a fundamental part—of the social contract, and imposed from the top down, is a general agreement as to what constitutes reality. To deviate from that agreement is to deviate from society—the kingdom, the real estate, the state religion—itself. It is to become, in a sense, a Satanist, a worshipper of an adversary; or a witch, a worshipper of an unapproved God.

We can take this analogy one step further, to the political arena, and say that he who attacks the king is insane, i.e., out of touch with reality. That is why our most famous assassins have all been pronounced "crazed" and "lone": they are insane and not part of a social group, at least not a social group recognized as valid in the kingdom. An attack on the king cannot be seen to originate from within the kingdom, from within the king's "reality": it has to come from outside, from the realm of the unreal, the unholy, for if it came from within the kingdom it would partake of the logic of the kingdom.

The other social group that is both crazed and alone is the independent ascetic, the hermit, the yogin, the sorcerer, the shaman. While often providing value to the social group—divination, exorcism of demons, channeling of spiritual forces—this person lives outside the general social structure in isolation from everyday communication and social intercourse. It is necessary to do so, for the forces that are contacted are those from outside the kingdom. The hermit or ascetic is a kind of probe into the Other World, the world outside the walls of the kingdom of reality. At times, the counsel is valued; usually, though, the person is despised, even ridiculed. The independent ascetic is one who breaks the social tabus of the group and refrains from social contacts, from eating socially approved foods (or from eating at all), from sexual activity and thus from the gene pool. The non-sexual ascetic does not share in the transfer of property—of real estate—that is so dependent upon marriage and the production of heirs. Or the ascetic may use unconventional sexual practices to reach altered states of consciousness: forms of reality outside the social contract.

Professor Wendy Doniger O'Flaherty—in her important study *The Origins of Evil in Hindu Mythology*—describes how the ancient Sanskrit texts relate the history of demons.

> The belief is often expressed that the demons were not only the equals of the gods but their superiors—the older brothers, the original gods from whom the gods stole the throne of heaven.[5]

This, of course, is exactly how the Sumerian creation epic describes it, showing how Marduk and his Company of Heaven rebelled against the older gods, their parents, and destroyed them. It is also related in this text that humanity was created from the blood of the slain older gods and the breath of the victorious younger gods. In fact, the Sumerian myth goes even further and describes the creation of human beings a bit as if Marduk was building automata, destroying the first set as defective. This parallels a Qabalistic legend that all of creation as we know it is really only the second draft; the first draft was defective and broke, and the shells of that first draft became the demons—the *qlippoth*—of the second. The idea that demons represent a moral quantum—evil, which is supposed to be the opposite of good—does not develop until much later and, in some cultures, not at all.

The idea that we are living in a replacement universe is common among the myths of the world which show an earlier civilization being destroyed, and the ancestors of the present human race as the survivors of the former. The Biblical legend of Noah and the Deluge is a good example of this, a legend that has its parallels all over the world. Hindu mythology, of course, describes Ages of vast length that repeat endlessly throughout time, witnesses to the rise and fall of many civilizations, many different forms of life and consciousness.

To the Hindus, the demons and the gods are consanguineous; they come from the same family, the same genetic stock. They both attempt to use humans to serve them, but they are really at war with each other. The gods have established an earthly priesthood to serve them, and society is obligated to support this priesthood—this "ritual sphere"—and to pay for the sacrifices which keep the gods strong. To do otherwise, is to invoke disaster:

> ...it was in the interest of the Brahmins to convince these patrons that the gods regarded powerful human beings of the nonritual sphere as demons and treated them accordingly.... Those mortals who aspired to religious power outside of the ritual sphere inherited the role of demons in the cosmic masque.[6]

and again:

> ...a priest might legitimately emulate the gods, but an ascetic should not. An ambitious priest was like a god; an ambitious ascetic was like a demon.[7]

The ascetics were those who *interiorized* the rituals and the myths of the Vedas, the sacred Hindu scriptures, and who sought unity with godhead through their practices. Professor O'Flaherty makes particular reference to this system—which many readers will recognize as Kundalini Yoga—in the following passage:

...Sumeru ("good Meru"), the world-mountain at the center of the earth, was now given a demonic counterpart, a mirror-image in the under-world—Kumeru ("bad Meru"). The world-mountain, which had provided access upwards, now extends down as well—and the gods oppose human and demonic ascetics who, by interiorizing these pillars within the spinal column, would mount to heaven.[8]

This anatomization of the world-mountain as the spinal column is known to the Jewish Qabalists as well. In fact, in Qabalism it is referred to as a "pillar," of which there are three. On these three pillars is drawn the glyph of the Tree of Life, and contemporary occultists have shown a relation-ship between the Ida, Pingala and Sushumna *nadis* or channels of the human body in Kundalini Yoga and the Right, Left and Middle Pillars of the Jewish Qabala and the body of Adam Kadmon, its ideal human. The important line in this citation is that the gods do not want either human or demonic ascetics to climb the pillar or mountain and so reach heaven. It is perceived as an attack on divine authority—to show up without an invitation—and the rituals and other practices designed to activate these powers in humans are prohibited by organized religion which is, certainly, the human representation of divine authority; organized religion becom-ing, in a sense, a colonial power on earth representing the home country on Mount Olympus or on Sumeru.

The interesting phonetic similarity of the world-mountain as "Sumeru" and the name of the ancient Mesopotamian culture "Sumeria" is, of course, noted. The Sumerians were famous for their stepped pyramids, the ziggurats, and many have conjectured that the Biblical Tower of Babel was in reality a ziggurat being built at Babylon by the Sumerians or by their successors, the Akkadians or Babylonians. The ancient Egyptians also revered mounds, and believed that the world was created when a Primeval Mound rose and separated the waters. This ancient belief may be related to the prevalence of mound cultures in ancient Europe, the British Isles and the Americas, just as the Egyptian pyramids have their counterparts in Mesopotamian ziggurats and Aztec, Maya and Inca pyramids in Latin America. While it is outside the scope of this book to go into further detail, it is tantalizing to speculate that there might have been significant communication between ancient Indian and ancient Sumerian cultures, representing general agreement on such things as a creation myth, a world-mountain myth, and the existence of evil and of demonic beings. They do, however, obviously agree on certain points whether they were ever in contact or not, and the abhorrence of individuals practicing religious—i.e., mystical or magical—rituals alone, outside the "ritual sphere" of the approved priesthood, is evident in both cultures.

Since the relationship of the society with God was all-important and communication with God deemed appropriate only for the highest levels of society (for reasons of national security!), we have to look for a motive for this. Obviously, survival of the society was dependent on the good graces of a powerful spiritual being who was considered to be omniscient and omnipotent (or, at least, more knowing and more powerful than the king). There was believed to be a channel of power or energy that emanated from that being and which was bestowed on the king, who then bestowed it on his kingdom. Thus, power and survival, the king and the god, formed the mechanism by which a society was identified and prospered. In a time when natural disasters—drought, flood, disease—could spell life or death for the tribe or the city-state, it was considered essential that someone in the kingdom have a direct line to the forces that controlled these disasters, since society itself could obviously not do so on its own.

Independent ritual-performers, therefore, must have been viewed with horror, for they were going directly to these forces and enlisting their aid in projects that did not have the blessing or approbation of society, that is, the king. It was a usurpation of the king's power, and it could spell catastrophe for the kingdom. Further, if the independent ritual-performers—let's call them sorcerers—contacted supernatural forces that were allied against the king's god, then a state of spiritual warfare existed in which sacrifices were being made and resources of the kingdom exhausted in propitiation of the *wrong* gods, the *older* gods, the spiritual adversaries of the king's god. It is easy to see why sorcerers and witches would be considered traitors or rebels. We can also see that the very fabric of reality itself was threatened when witches were allowed to practice their craft, since their successes with spells and potions and the shamanistic channeling of supernatural forces were more spectacular—and more convincing—than the elaborate ceremonial of the state religions that relied more on the maintenance of the status quo than on the expansion of consciousness or the direct apprehension of the Godhead by a normal citizen. The witch or sorcerer had access to a level of knowledge about the world that was not available to the general public and perhaps not even to the priesthood itself. This practice was especially attractive to women, as they were usually excluded from the state priesthood or from direct participation in their rituals, except perhaps for purely sexual purposes as ceremonial concubines or temple prostitutes.

The author believes that the political implications of witchcraft are rarely addressed in the literature, and hopes that the present work stimulates more in-depth research on this subject, especially now when the relationship between religion and politics is becoming more important, more pronounced in the world arena. One of the problems in addressing these issues, however, is the lack of a vocabulary for expressing some basic concepts. The literature of witchcraft—i.e., of shamanism, sorcery, "black magic" and the like—is such that it resists easy classification; but if we view witchcraft from both a psychological as well as an existential (perhaps an ontological) viewpoint, and politics from a psychological and religious viewpoint, we may be able to provide a convincing and workable political metaphor.

Why bother to concern ourselves with such an arcane task? Because modern science in the twenty-first century is on the verge of a major breakthrough in the physics of consciousness as we will see in the final volume of this work, and we as a race have demonstrated that we do not understand consciousness itself; we don't understand the forces with which we are dealing. We have so far left this responsibility in the hands of politicians, generals … and sorcerers. And they have used their knowledge to commit murder and other outrages, and have covered up their crimes by destroying evidence, shredding documents, and vilifying their accusers … or by couching their discoveries in such esoteric terms that the layman has no hope of ever understanding what they have accomplished, or what dark forces have been loosed upon the earth.

THE HIDDEN FORCE

It is useful to look at contemporary beliefs and practices concerning witchcraft and the "black arts," and the influence they have over the political lives of the people. In the West, such practices are, on the one hand, suppressed and devalued by a kind of media assault aided and abetted by such professional skeptics as the late Carl Sagan, James Kreskin, Martin Gardner and others, while, on the other hand, subliminally encouraged by Hollywood offerings such as *The Believers; Rosemary's Baby; Charmed; Sabrina, the Teen-Aged Witch; Buffy, the Vampire Slayer;* and *Angel.* In the East, these practices are tolerated *and accepted* to a degree unheard of in modern Europe or North America. Asian religions are—compared to their Western counterparts—a rich amalgam of mainstream religious practice and theological discussion mixed with indigenous occult practices and beliefs. Chinese Daoism (often spelled "Taoism") is a very good example of this. It had been suppressed in the People's Republic of China, of course, and only lately have a few of the ancient Daoist temples been renovated and re-opened, including the famous White Cloud Monastery in Beijing while, at the same time, Falun Gong has been brutally put down, its members imprisoned and dying during "questioning."

The practice of what is loosely called Daoism is a survival of very old pagan practices of the Han Chinese, mixed with elements of imported Indian Buddhism and yogic and Tantric practices. At its heyday, it was the state religion of China, much as Shinto is the state religion of Japan, where the Japanese emperor is an embodiment of indigenous Japanese Shinto beliefs. A study of Daoist occult literature—specifically in reference to what is known as "Daoist alchemy"—will show very clear correspondences with Tantric ritual as well as elements familiar to students of European alchemy; it is thus a valuable source of information on a very old system of beliefs and practices that predate Christianity, Buddhism and all the other monotheistic faiths in the world. It may have come from the same fountain of belief that provided the underpinning of the Vedic and pre-Vedic practices of India as well as of the religion of ancient Mesopotamia, of which we have only the sketchiest knowledge. As discussed in the previous volume, the jury is still out on whether the "diffusionists" or the "independent inventionists" have the better explanation for these similarities, but let's leave that discussion open for now.

While Daoism has had its ups and downs in China, it has flourished within the Chinese communities outside China: in Taiwan, Singapore, Malaysia, Hong Kong, and in the Chinese communities of the West. What many non-Chinese do not know, however, is the prevalence of spirit possession as a divinatory practice in the temples. It is common for a Chinese desirous of knowing about the future to go to a Daoist temple (or, perhaps, a Chinese Buddhist temple; it is sometimes difficult to tell the difference between the two!) and ask for guidance from a medium. The medium goes into a trance, is possessed by a spiritual force, and gives answers to questions. This is all within the precincts of the temple and is supported by the temple, its monks and the people; thus, one would be hard put to categorize it as an "alternative" practice. It is obviously, however, a clear survival of Asian shamanism, a practice that was already ancient when the Buddha was born.

In Asian Muslim countries there is a corresponding cult of spirit possession, shamanism and what can only be called a type of "witchcraft." In Malaysia and Indonesia particularly (and to a lesser extent in Singapore and the Philippines), Islam has permitted the existence of a kind of witch doctor-cum-medicine man, known in Malaysia as a *bomoh*. This is a phenomenon that predates the arrival of Islam to these countries in the fifteenth century, and has been sturdy enough to survive as a reliable occult entity alongside the usually theologically intolerant Muslim faith for almost five hundred years; and it has had tremendous influence on not only the grass-roots political structures of the *kampung* (the Malay word from which we get the English "compound," and usually used to refer to a village or a "neighborhood" of houses in a village) but also on politics at a national level.

Indonesia is the largest Muslim nation in the world. Located in Southeast Asia, south of the Philippines, it includes a share (with Malaysia) of the large island known as Borneo; all of Sumatra, Java, and Sulawesi; West Timor; the part of New Guinea known as Irian Jaya; as well as the captivating paradise of Bali and literally thousands of other islands in the archipelago. Indonesia is home to over 200 million people, most of whom are at least nomimal Muslims, but which include some Hindus (principally on Bali), Chinese of various faiths, and people known as *orang asli* or "original people": animists and jungle-dwellers whose ancestors go back on these islands for thousands of years. Indonesia's most notable ancient architecture is the temple at Borobudor on Java, which is a Hindu masterpiece.

An essential element of Indonesian culture and especially of the Javanese is something known as *kebatinan,* loosely translated as "inner dimensions of life." It comes from the Malay root *batin* which means "inner feeling," a kind of mystical sense and sentiment wrapped up in one. (This concept of *batin* actually comes from Islamic mysticism, and is an Arabic word meaning "esoteric" or "hidden," as we will see in a later chapter.)

Anthropologist Dr. Neils Mulder, in his *Mysticism in Java: Ideology in Indonesia*, describes it this way:

> Things are not what they appear to be, but have a hidden core which fascinates them.... They speculate about hidden forces—whether spirits, or secretive political manipulation.... They are fond of explaining the symbolism of the ritual meal, of religious practice, of chance occurrences, of chronograms, and suchlike. In brief, the symbolic—and the mystical—dimensions of life constitute an important field of interest.[9]

In one paragraph, Mulder sums up the essential elements of this entire study: the hidden forces which are either (or both) spiritual forces and political ones; the symbolism of chance occurrences, religious practice, and the mystical dimensions of life. Western societies today do not consciously live in such a world; but they do so unconsciously, as it is hoped this study goes far to prove. However, Eastern societies *do* live consciously in a world where the "hidden force"—to borrow a phrase from both Neils Mulder and Dutch novelist Louis Couperus—penetrates and permeates all existence, and is a component of reality that cannot be ignored. *Kebatinan* is one way of describing this force. Couperus gives us another:

> Under all the appearance of tangible things the essence of that silent mysticism threatens, like a smouldering fire underground, like hatred and mystery in the heart.[10]

And:

> He would never know that, lurking under the simple life, there are all those forces which together make the omnipotent hidden force. He would have laughed at the idea that there are nations that have a greater control over that force than the Western nations have. He would shrug his shoulders—and continue on his way—at the mere supposition that among the nations there are a few individuals in whose hands that force loses its omnipotence and becomes an instrument.[11]

Couperus lived in Indonesia for a while when it was a Dutch colony, and was intimate with both the Dutch expatriate community there as well as the local population. It is impossible to live in Southeast Asia for any length of time and not become aware of this "hidden force" ... or, at least, of the belief of the people in its existence, for they conduct their lives in accordance with its myriad manifestations. The longer one spends in Indonesia, Malaysia, Singapore and environs the more one becomes accustomed to the operation of this force; this is especially true of those who spend time outside the major cities and in the smaller towns, where the rule of the *bomoh* is stronger, and where *kebatinan* is thick in the atmosphere against the backdrop of the mosque and muezzin's cry; the lavish Hindu temples with their colorful statues of thousands of deities crammed together like a cocktail party of the gods; the mysterious Chinese temples in clouds of incense, strange heiroglyphic characters painted on scrolls representing the signatures of invisible forces. It almost takes a novelist's sensitivity to grasp the essential nature of this hidden force, as science has provided us with no intelligible language to describe it; or, perhaps, our very nature as Europeans and Westerners has imposed upon us a certain way of looking at life that is somewhat at odds with those of the East, and as well with those of our own Native Americans, our *orang asli*. As ethnographer of the Navajo culture Sam Gill writes,

> As I have come to think of it, when the facts of history come together for someone in a way that reveals their meaning or in a way that enables their fuller understanding to be sought, a story is born. History lacks meaning without story. Story lacks substance and relevance without history.... For the European-American story tradition the authority is history, even though the story is not strictly historical; for the Native American story tradition the authority is religious and outside of history, even though the story reflects history.[12]

Thus, for European-Americans, the facts are obvious—historical data—even though they may be treated in a novelistic manner in order to extract as much meaning as possible. For Native Americans—according to Gill—the facts are not necessarily obvious from a European-American perspective: the underlying structure, the "authority," is "religious and outside of history," which is comparable to Mulder's take on *kebatinan*, and which represents a force essentially religious (or, at least, mystical) and outside of what we understand as history, *outside the linear flow of time*, as much Navajo tribal legend is expressed.

Mulder's study of Javanese mysticism is simultaneously a study of Javanese politics. He begins by describing traditional Javanese concepts of kingship:

> Kings were thought to be among the most powerful mystical elements on earth, to be receptacles of cosmic potency. Their worldly power reflected their charisma, that is, their receiving of a supernatural mandate to rule, known as their wahyu .... Such wahyu was a clear sign of their association with and

concentration of kasekten (cosmic potency), which was thought to radiate as a beneficial magical force from their persons to the populace ...[13]

As Mulder goes on to describe, even their palaces reflected this concept, designed as microcosms, pictures in miniature of the entire universe with the king as the center, or "axis mundi."[14] Thus, the spirituality of the king represents an interplay between the visible and invisible worlds, and thus affects the peace and prosperity of his kingdom.[15] Although this seems like perfect superstitious mumbo-jumbo to modern Western ears—especially in the postwar era of atomic energy, space travel and the Internet—if we were to suspend disbelief for a moment and apply this notion to a European or American ruler, we might see that some of these same beliefs apply.

No matter how good a president Bill Clinton may have been, for example, he was pilloried over his supposedly private sex life: something that has no relevance to how well or how poorly he did his job. This suggests strongly that some significant portion of the American electorate feels that a President should be the moral equivalent of a minister of religion, even though there is no such provision in the Constitution which, to the contrary, mandates a separation of church and state. The viciousness of the attacks on Clinton over this issue—and the maneuvering of his friends and Party members away from openly supporting him in light of the revelations concerning Monica Lewinsky—demonstrates a clear (if somewhat hypocritical) connection in the popular mind between the President's behavior as an individual and the state of the nation, much like the old legends of King Arthur and the Holy Grail. This is so for a political leader who is democratically elected and who serves a maximum of two terms of four years each. How much more so for a leader who attains his or her position by virtue of genetics or marriage, such as a king or queen?

In Malaysia the king was viewed as a kind of shaman, as Sir Richard Winstedt points out in *The Malay Magician,* in a way very similar to that of Indonesia.[16] Winstedt, in fact, sees a close association between Malay magic and that of ancient Babylon, going so far as to suggest that the creation myths of the pre-Hindu Malays—recited as part of ritual by Malay shamans—are an echo of the Sumerian legends of Marduk and Tiamat.[17] The facts may be somewhat the reverse of appearances, as Stephen Oppenheimer suggests in his *Eden In The East.* Oppenheimer, a doctor specialzing in tropical pediatrics and based out of Hong Kong, believes he has found genetic markers and other evidence in the tribes of Malaysia and Indonesia to suggest that the peoples of the ancient Middle East originated in ... the Malay archipelago. His arguments are persuasive for a Southeast Asian "Garden of Eden," from which civilization sprang at the time of a great deluge eight thousand years ago. Winstedt was writing in 1951; Oppenheimer in 1998. It is a strange theory, from the point of view of traditional anthropology and archaeology, but the medical evidence in Oppenheimer's case and the internal evidence of Malay myth and ritual in

Winstedt's case make for a compelling story. The idea of the king as high priest is also consistent with ancient Sumeria, and it is still understood as such by some contemporary Malays regardless of the influence of traditional Islam.

For example,

> In the eighteenth century Perak had a state shaman, who was of descent fully royal and bore the title of Sultan Muda or Junior Sultan.... The holder of this office (which still exists under the title of State Magician) is head of all the magicians in Perak and he is expected to keep alive the sacred weapons of the regalia, to conduct an annual feast and séance with libations for the royal drums and to make sacrificial offerings to the genies of the state. Such offerings are still made as part of the ceremony of installing a Sultan of Perak.[18]

As mentioned above, Winstedt was writing in 1951, but these citations are from a revised 1960 edition, i.e., after Malaysian independence in 1957. Perak is a Malaysian state on the west coast of penninsular Malaysia, on the Straits of Malacca (Melaka), north of Kuala Lumpur and south of Georgetown (Pulau Pinang). The point of this geography lesson is that the State of Perak is not a strange, isolated little community deep within the rain forest, but on the contrary is an important part of Malaysian history and has seen Hindus, Buddhists, Muslims, Christians, Chinese, Indians, Dutch, English, Arabs and every sort of trader, missionary, soldier and politician along its coast.

Again:

> The Malay shaman ... and the Malay ruler both own familiar spirits. The familiars of a sultan are the genies who protect his state.... At a famous séance held in 1874 to discover if Mr. Birch, the first British Resident, would be wrecked on the bar of the Perak river, Sultan Abdullah himself was a medium and was possessed by nine spirits in succession.[19]

For the interested, the much-unloved Mr. J.W.W. Birch did not survive. A typical example of English colonial arrogance, he considered himself superior to the Sultan and thus to everyone else in Malaya and conducted himself accordingly; and accordingly, he was the victim of an assassination.

More than merely a medium or shaman, the Malay ruler was also believed to be the incarnation of a god; something that is no longer discussed in polite Malaysian company, but which survives in some of the pomp and ceremony that attends the installation of a sultan. This belief is thought to have occurred among the Malay people via India and Tantric Hinduism.[20] Hinduism has affected every layer of Malaysian society, even though it is often not recognized as such and its evidence merely accepted as being "traditionally Malaysian." The wedding ceremony of the Malay people, for instance, is virtually a carbon-copy of the Indian wedding ceremony, in which the bride and groom sit on a throne or raised dais and are told to look solemn.

The installation of a sultan in some states, however, particularly in Negeri Sembilan and Perak, is replete with even more Hindu and Buddhist ceremonial, although much of it has been sanitized and Islamicized to be in accord with the state religion. There is a limit to how much one can sanitize or Islamicize an ancient ritual, however, and the procedures involving lustration, circumambulation, the sacred weapons, the blessing of the four cardinal directions, etc. remain as very strong and incontrovertible evidence of both Malaysia's Indian heritage as well as its native, animist, shamanistic culture. Even more, it is evidence of a global preoccupation with the identity of king and magician, and the idea that a political ruler is also a kind of medium, a channel for the hidden force.

In Malaysia today, kingship is a revolving door. The king or "agong" of Malaysia is chosen among the sultans. The sultans are, of course, hereditary rulers of their specific states, and as such are believed to have an equal claim to the throne. The investiture of a king is ritualistic and involves (among other things) the bestowal of the ceremonial sword and the *kriss*, a wavy-bladed dagger that is a mystical weapon similar to the *athame* of modern witchcraft (traditonally, a double-bladed knife with a black handle), or the magic wand of European ceremonial magic. Spiritual forces are believed to reside in the kriss, and there are a tiny handful of people in Southeast Asia whose specialty is their manufacture, a process complicated by elaborate ritual requirements.

The king serves for a limited period of time before he is replaced by another of the thirteen sultans, making this a unique type of constitutional monarchy. The king in Malaysia has very little political power as such, this being invested in the Prime Minister (who is elected) and his Cabinet, after the British parliamentary fashion. Yet, the *authority* of the king is extremely important and sacred to the Malay people. His position is a ritual one, yet that does not diminish its power but rather enhances it. The king of Malaysia is the repository of its *kebatinan*, a tangent point between this world and the hidden force that underlies it. This is not seen as a philosophy antagonistic to Islam, for the sultans are all Muslims and hold a position of authority where the practice of Islam is concerned in their respective states. It is viewed as a philosophy that runs parallel to that of Islam, involving concepts of power, spiritual harmony and social integration that are deemed to co-exist with the teachings of the Prophet. There is the same co-existence, albeit with local variations, in Indonesia as in Malaysia; and other Islamic nations are not immune to flirtations with cosmic forces.

Indeed, in devoutly Muslim Pakistan, former Prime Minister Benazir Bhutto expressed a belief that the trials and tribulations of her father's regime were a re-enactment of the life of the Prophet, Muhammad. Blending religious imagery with political realities, Bhutto exploited the supposed similarities between the two men in an effort to crystalize her own role in the affairs of her country, and to demonize her father's opponents.[21] Elsewhere in Southeast Asia, yellow-beribboned Corazon Aquino expressed a belief that the spirit of her martyred husband, Ninoy Aquino (who was assassinated by men loyal to then-dictator of the Philippines, Ferdinand Marcos) entered into her to help her win the Philippine presidential elections on the "People Power" ticket.[22] Cory Aquino is a Catholic, and for a Catholic the idea that a spirit of the dead could enter into you and help you win an election is pure and unadulterated witchcraft; but in Asia, it is politics as usual.

Although mystical beliefs and their influence over politics in Indonesia go back for more than a thousand years, and can be traced in the Hindu–Buddhist pantheism that is unique to the country (after all, the national art form of this largest of all Muslim nations is the famous shadow-puppet theater in which scenes of the Hindu epics the *Ramayana* and *Mahabharata* are enacted) as well as in local legends about the sanctity of various sites, trees, stones and so forth, the codification of these beliefs into a coherent system only began in the days after the end of World War II. Nationalism in the wake of the Japanese invasion and liberation, the end of Dutch colonial rule, the rise of Javanese political parties and a more orthodox approach to Islam as a result of greater communication with Arab countries all contributed to the creation of a national identity. This artificial Indonesian man is a spiritual *homunculus* born of a need to create a homogeneous national character out of the thousands of islands, races, religions and tribes that compose the archipelago. Rather than emphasize Islam as the unifying force, since many Indonesians were lukewarm Muslims at best, it was necessary to dig deeper into the beliefs that form the bedrock of consciousness, not only for the Javanese but for all the peoples of the new country.

It was against this background in 1945 that Indonesian strongman Sukarno came up with a spiritual paradigm for citizenship, called *pancasila* or the "five principles": belief in one God, a just humanity, Indonesian unity, democracy, and social justice.[23] (This was copied virtually verbatim by the Malaysian government as their *Rukunegara*: Articles of Faith of the State.) The development of these principles (which eventually became a full-fledged government program requiring acceptance by every citizen) took place only after warring mystical sects in Indonesia began to threaten national unity. It is perhaps not realized by contemporary commentators on Indonesian affairs that the people of the country were by no means unified in their Muslim beliefs. Amidst the open hostility between traditional and modern Muslim factions there was, in fact, a strong and vocal anti-Islamic movement in Indonesia in the 1950s. Opposition to Islam did not come only from the Hindu island of Bali, but from mystical sects—such as the Permai—that based their ideology on what they perceived to be indigenous religious and mystical practices that predated the arrival of Hinduism from India. Permai was both a mystic cult and a political party, and thus shared some features with other cults abroad in the land that were forming themselves into action groups.[24] These groups were a threat to political stability, and the relatively new government of Indonesia saw an urgent necessity to codify religion and "approve" only certain faiths while proscribing the rest. Thus, once again, political rebellion and religious divergence became synonymous.

Indonesia provides us with a laboratory case of how nationalism is manufactured in any society. The German experience with Nazism gave us one case, but as it was a European example it may, paradoxically, be difficult for Europeans to understand it fully. The Indonesian example has all of the elements necessary to create the same type of nationalism, and the exotic nature of Indonesia to Westerners may enable us to see the action in more relief.

The country now known as Indonesia is in reality an amalgamation of many different cultures, including the Javanese, which seems to be dominant at this time, but also the Sumatran, Sulawesian, Balinese, etc. Once the Dutch left the "East Indies" at the end of World War II—and the British left Malaya and Singapore—the entire region went into a period of ideological self-discovery. Nationhood was a fragile thing; the territories that comprised the new country of Malaysia fell apart into Malaysia, Singapore and Brunei. The presence of a large number of Chinese in Malaya helped to consolidate Malay identity as the Malays banded together to show a united front against the non-Muslim, non-Malay Chinese. This resulted, however, in largely Chinese Singapore breaking away from the new Malaysia and forming its own, independent country while retaining Bahasa Melayu as their official language. Indonesia had a much smaller Chinese population, but itself has had trouble holding onto East Timor (which was predominantly Portuguese-influenced and Christian), and as of this writing that tiny piece of real estate is now independent.

In any nationalist state, language is supremely important and it is necessary to elevate one language above all others; it is also the most practical approach for any country. The decision on which language to use, however, is fraught with political consequences. In the case of Malaysia, it was easy to adopt Bahasa Melayu as the official state language while also recognizing Chinese and Tamil as important local tongues. The Communist victory in China, however, galvanized the Malaysians in a struggle against what they perceived to be Chinese Communist insurgents in their own country. The struggle against Chinese Communism became, unfortunately, a struggle against their own, indigenous Chinese and any Chinese opposition to Malaysian government policies was interpreted as evidence of Chinese Communist agitation, much as opposition to US government policy in the United States during the McCarthy Era was seen as evidence of Communist "sympathy" if not outright treason. The Chinese were deliberately isolated from the rest of society for a time—during the so-called "Malay Emergency"—and placed in what were euphemistically called "New Villages," but which were only a step away from concentration camps. Thus, in Malaysia, race, religion and politics became inextricable one from the other. This has led to increasing states of tension over the years, and the equally increasing measures taken by the government to quell any outward signs of opposition, resulting in the famous "incident" in May of 1969, in which hundreds of Chinese were slain by rioting Malays.

In Indonesia, which shares a basic language in common with Malaysia, language was not as large an issue as religion, especially in a land where national culture is so closely identified with religion. The ringing tones of the *gamelan* orchestra, the almost furtive shadow figures of the *wayang* puppet shows, the massive Hindu structure at Borobudur ... these have nothing to do with Islam but everything to do with Indonesia. This is why the Sukarno concept of pancasila was so necessary for national unity, because it did not elevate any religion or culture above another but sought to create a new Indonesian citizen, tolerant of all, as opposed to a primarily Javanese or a Balinese citizen. In this way, individual cultures were allowed to retain their special identities while still contributing to the nation as a whole. On paper, this seemed like a very workable concept; but in action it allowed the proliferation of occult beliefs and practices among both the educated classes as well as the relatively uneducated mass of people who could not decide whether Islam—as a foreign import—was inimical to their nation, or if it provided a healthy alternative to the mystical belief in *kebatinan*. It was the pancasila program that, in its attempt to incorporate the entire Indonesian cultural experience, managed to adopt the mystical attitudes of the people into a general cultural gestalt. Thus, to survive as a nation, Indonesia had to recognize the value of *batin*, the inner spiritual side of what it means to be human, that side of oneself that is in contact with the hidden force. Indonesia has had to legitimize the occult power of *kebatinan*.

Much the same has occurred in Malaysia. There is a concept there known as *badi* which is as resistant to translation as the Indonesian *batin* and which may represent the same term (the differences between Indonesian and Malaysian languages are slight; they are virtually the same language but have developed some local terminology), but which in Malaysia has a more sinister connotation. *Badi* is considered to be an "evil principle" by Skeats, who is one of the acknowledged authorities on Malay mysticism.[25] The catalogue of what has and does not have *badi* is very long, and seems to be much more specific in nature than the relatively amorphous *batin* of the Indonesian shamans. The ability to control the *badi* of animate and inanimate objects is the province of the *bomoh*. The power of the *bomoh*, the local village shaman, is recognized—albeit unofficially—by government and industry. Bomohs are widely believed to have power over the weather, for instance, and they can be called upon to ensure a sunny day for important political and cultural events and for open-air speeches by the Prime Minister. Some bomohs have been accused of much worse, however, including rape, sexual abuse of children, theft, and murder. In the year 2002, a bomoh—a woman accused of murdering a client—was executed in Malaysia. It is said she went smiling to her death.

The practice of extreme forms of occultism occurs with astonishing regularity in Malaysia, although most of the reporting on them usually takes place in Singaporean newspapers. In one case, a group of occultists had been murdering Caucasians in rituals designed to give them winning numbers in the lottery. The skulls of the murdered men and one woman were found in a hut in the forest, alongside ritual paraphernalia. Cases that would have made national news in the United States for months are treated with a kind of bland distance that is the result of both a desire to suppress the uglier aspects of Malaysian society and the contempt born of familiarity, and the cases are lost quickly from the media and never heard of again.[26]

Religious deviance is punished in Malaysia. The country has embraced the Sunni form of Islam, which means they view Shi'ism as a heresy. Shi'ism is not permitted in Malaysia, and its practitioners can be arrested by the Islamic courts (which are not, strictly speaking, government or secular courts) and imprisoned. More than Shi'ism, however, any form of theological deviation from strict Sunnism is frowned upon and can result in arrest and imprisonment. As in Indonesia, religious deviation automatically implies political rebellion; fundamentalist Islamic sects in Malaysia have been known to accumulate weapons and to call for an end to the domination of the main political alliance, UMNO (United Malays National Organization) and its creature, the Barisan Nasional. Strongest opposition to UMNO comes from PAS, which is a fundamentalist Islamic political party and which has, in the Malaysian states where it has won the majority, instituted the *shariyah*—Islamic law, such as obtained in Afghanistan under the Taliban and does yet in Saudi Arabia. Thus, supermarket check-out lines are divided into male and female; swimming pools at resort hotels are to be equally separated by sex, as are movie theaters and any public place; the sale and consumption of alcohol is not allowed, nor is even the presence of a pig much less the consumption of pork. PAS would like to see all of Malaysia—especially the capitol, Kuala Lumpur—under the rule of *shariyah*, creating, in essence, a theocracy. Fundamentalist forces in Indonesia and in the province of Mindanao in the Philippines are looking forward to the same goals; in fact, a goal of the local terrorist organizations allied to Al-Qaeda is the creation of a Muslim state that would encompass Malaysia, Indonesia, and the Philippine island of Mindanao.

None of this would matter to most Westerners, except that now the question of religion—and especially the unholy alliance of religion and politics—has become a major issue whose solution has profound implications for American and European national security. While Americans like to think that their

Constitution protects them from state sponsored religious bigotry and fundamentalism, the threat from outside and inside their borders is very real.

When Western intelligence services analyze the political, economic and cultural situations in Asian countries for their leaders, they naturally do so from a perspective that is the end result of thousands of years of cultural conceit (much the same way Eastern intelligence services view Western political developments). Much nuance is lost in the translation. Mistakes that were made in Vietnam are repeated endlessly in American foreign policy decisions, for instance; no one has the time or the inclination to become expert in the delicate cultural infrastructure of these societies and, anyway, we can always "bomb them into the Stone Age." United States presidents have only four years to succeed in their position and have to run for re-election a year before even that term is complete. This means they look for easy solutions, fast solutions to every problem. That is dangerous in any organization, but when the president is the leader of the most militarily and economically powerful nation on earth, such a fast fix invites catastrophe. Those citizens who oppose American foreign policy towards the developing nations, however, tend to swing to an extreme position and often hold up the beliefs, practices and social organizations of these societies as something exemplary, something to emulate. Both are examples of a perverse kind of racism that does nothing to ameliorate the situation, and both are wrong.

The psychological warfare experts of the 1950s came closest to understanding how to manipulate and exploit national *weltanschauung*. Their studies of African witchcraft, discussed in Book One, for instance, should be taken out and dusted off by their modern counterparts and improved upon with what is known now by academics, field engineers, social workers, Peace Corps volunteers and anyone else who has spent years in developing nations becoming accustomed to local beliefs and practices. Much has been made of the FBI profilers who must train themselves to think like their prey in order to capture them; men like Ressler and Vorpagel and Douglas have all written books about this process. The same approach is necessary for those intelligence services who wish to understand their target countries and to predict political developments with any kind of accuracy. This type of information is not always easily quantifiable—the hidden forces frustrate logical description. The United States has very few experts available on the cultures, the languages, the histories and the native beliefs of the people living in developing countries; yet, these are the same people who have become, in some instances, America's greatest enemies. It is this type of institutional racism that is causing a serious security problem in the United States. American political and military leaders have, in many cases, listened too long to Sagan and Gardner and Kreskin; it is time they paid more attention to Roscoe Hillenkoetter, Douglas MacArthur, Claiborne Pell, Carlos Castaneda, Jack Parsons ... and the witches. Unfortunately,

American foreign policy has been largely "anti-occult," as can be seen by its vociferous campaign against voodoo in Haiti.

THE COMEDIANS

Although there have been many examples of theocracies in ancient history (and a few in modern history, such as Tibet), there are perhaps even fewer "cultocracies" in the world, but when they do occur they offer evidence of the way cults operate even when they do not control an entire nation. In my previous work, *Unholy Alliance*, I attempted to show how the Third Reich was just such a cultocracy. Here, in North America, we have had another: the Republic of Haiti, under the dictatorships of Papa Doc and Baby Doc Duvalier.

Haiti is perhaps a unique example of a nation that was created out of the *houngans* and *hounforts* of the Voudon religion, normally spelled "voodoo." A survival of Dahomeyan, Nigerian, and religions from other parts of Africa's west coast, within the outer façade of Roman Catholicism, Voudon is a dynamic and energetic faith that unites racial identity, spirituality and what may be called "witchcraft" or "sorcery" into a single, all-encompassing practice. Voudon has always attracted other Americans and Europeans because of its exotic sensuality and aura of the mysterious, even the sinister. When the author was a child, his father had a "voodoo doll" in a box, imported from Haiti. The word was out to destroy the dolls because they contained poisonous berries for eyes. The doll was a black female, dressed in Haitian costume, and I was shown the doll once, and never saw it again, presumably to ensure that I did not consume one of the poisonous eyes ... or did not become possessed by the desire to know more about the Haitian cult and its numerous *loa*, or gods.

Even Watergate co-conspirator and CIA agent E. Howard Hunt fell back on voodoo for his novel *The Coven*, having a young woman go to Africa on a research scholarship and come back as an initiate of the mysteries. She goes on to try to supplant another African priestess since she has had more direct contact with the original faith, but is murdered instead. The other priestess is referred to as a *mamaloi*, which is a Haitian term—and not an African one—for a priestess of the faith. Of course, practitioners of voudoun do not collect themselves into "covens," which is more appropriately a term used to refer to a gathering of European-style witches.

Voudon (or voodoo) is also the setting for a novel by another former intelligence officer, Ian Fleming, in *Live and Let Die*, the James Bond book that was made into a movie starring Roger Moore as 007. This story also centers on a beautiful priestess, and a voodoo cult based in the Caribbean as well as in New York City. The mixture of magic and eroticism—particularly of the interracial kind—is a hallmark of popular fantasies about voodoo. The controversial film *Angel Heart* also develops this idea, and once again we have a beautiful priestess (played by Lisa Bonet) who captivates a New York City detective (played by Mickey Rourke), and the voodoo cult is once again at the center of the action, along with a European-style Devil (played by Robert DeNiro). The action takes place in both New Orleans and New York City, and involves a ritual of European ceremonial magic in New York on the one hand, and voodoo rites in the swamps outside New Orleans on the other. The incestuous relationship between the Rourke and the Bonet characters, as well as the amnesia and consequent identity confusion of the Rourke character is perhaps a metaphor for something much deeper taking place, but this is thankfully beyond the scope of the present study!

What most audiences never realize, however, is that the relationship between magic and politics in Haiti is very strong, virtually inextricable. Papa Doc Duvalier was a powerful voudon practitioner, and bragged that it was his magic that resulted in the assassination of his enemy, President John F. Kennedy. This is not as much of an anomaly as it may appear, since the Haitian republic itself was born out of both political revolt and voudon, rebellion and witchcraft.

On the night of August 14, 1791 at Bois Caiman in Haiti, near the town of Morne-Rouge, a secret voudon ceremony was held in the midst of a storm of thunder and lightning. Amid that theatrical setting the god of war, Ogun, was invoked in the presence of legendary leader Boukman Dutty. Slaves from plantations all over the northern plain of Haiti were present, and swore allegiance to Boukman and to his lieutenants, Biassou, Celestin, and Jean-Francois. A black pig was decapitated in the midst of the ritual, and the Revolt of the Slaves was baptized in its blood.

From that moment on, Haiti was in the midst of terrible turmoil. Plantations were burned to the ground, and thousands of white settlers and plantation owners were slaughtered. Towns fell to the rebels, known as Maroons to the French, and with the advance of a Spanish force from the neighboring Dominican Republic and its alliance with the Maroon armies, the days of French colonial supremacy on the island were numbered. France made several treaties with the slave leaders, some of whom betrayed their leadership and became almost as bad as the white slavers themselves, but in the end France (and Napoleon) could not prevail against Haiti, losing some thirty- to sixty-thousand troops in a futile effort to retain control over the colony and use it as a base to attack the southern part of the United States. Boukman became a national hero, a Haitian slave who, with the energy and passion of the voudon cult, organized a slave revolt against the French and won, dying in the process. Voudon priestesses danced in the streets of the towns they would capture, and the sound of the conch shell horns and the pounding of the drums drove terror into the hearts of the slave owners. These children of the Slave Coast had vanquished the strongest European force in the world at that time, using a mixture of politics, military strategy, and African faith that had never before been seen.

The revolt took twelve long years before the streets were finally peaceful and the people returned to the land. Haiti has been betrayed by enemies both internal and external over the years since, but voudon itself has never died. When Harvard ethnobotanist Wade Davis went to Haiti in 1982 in search of the secret of zombification, he found the voudon cult vibrant and alive under Baby Doc Duvalier's regime. When the author himself visited a year later little had changed in Haiti: the politics were still the same, the violence had not abated, the poverty and sickness unsurpassed in the entire western hemisphere; but the people were still proud and beautiful, and the *houngans* and *bokors* still strong and still politically powerful.

The grand old Hotel Oloffson was still there, made famous by Graham Greene in his novel of Duvalier-era Haiti, *The Comedians,* and a favorite of celebrities and movie stars such as Marlon Brando, who had one of the Olofsson's private cabanas named after him. White people were still trying to squeeze out of Haiti whatever they could, and Haitian political leaders were squeezing back. One of these white, European post-colonialists in an ice-cream suit and Panama hat was George de Mohrenschildt, the friend of both Lee Harvey Oswald and Jacqueline Bouvier Kennedy, some-time spy, petroleum engineer, and world traveler, who went to Haiti only months before the assassination of President Kennedy. De Mohrenschildt would know that Papa Doc Duvalier had bragged about his magic spells that killed the President. Papa Doc rode around in a black limousine with the license plate "22," a number of tremendous occult power in the voudon cult, and the number of the date when Kennedy was killed in November, the 11th month. To Duvalier—and to other priests and practitioners of voudon—the combination 11/22 is a potent one, and seemed like mortal evidence of the vicious old politician's powers.

Papa Doc was born Francois Duvalier, one of the sons of the elite, intellectual class of Haitian society, but with strong feelings of identity with the Haitian people as opposed to the French society to which the elite normally swore cultural allegiance. At a time when an American occupation of Haiti was a festering sore of humiliation and shame, Dr. Duvalier—who had by this time become a medical doctor as well as an ethnologist specializing in Haitian culture—decided to do something about it. He gathered around himself a clique of like-minded souls who saw in Haitian identity—as opposed to the imported French variety—a source of national pride, and this included the popular folk religion of voudon.

In 1915, the United States had invaded Haiti. It was the start of World War I and the US Government was concerned over the security of the Panama Canal. French and German interests were present in Haiti, and had the local government decided to allow their country to be used as a base of operations against the Canal, it could have been disastrous for the newly-opened sea lanes. The US stayed in Haiti for long after the end of the war, however, which resulted in anti-American protests and an active resistance movement, aided and abetted by Haitian secret societies, all of them representing a mixture of mystical and political agendas. The US military finally left Haiti in 1934, after nearly twenty years of attempting to suppress the practice of voudon, since it was perceived to be a factor in fomenting rebellion, and tried to replace it with the more staunchly pro-American Roman Catholic Church. Books that were published abroad about Haiti around this time tended to paint the culture in satanic and depraved colors, thus legitimizing American military occupation of the "heathen" nation. This strategy was supported by first one Haitian political group and then another, as the culturally pro-French, mixed-race mulatto elite tried to suppress voudon in favor of the European style religion, Catholicism, embarrassed by the popular accounts of voudon that had exploded in the world press.

A former professor at the University of Pittsburgh—a zoologist and author of a number of books on the fauna of North America—visited Haiti in the late 1940s, some ten years before the start of the Duvalier regime. Samuel H. Williams, in his *Voodoo Roads* (oddly enough published in English by an Austrian firm in 1949) relates that "our American Marines had long been engaged in breaking up their voodoo practices in the length and breadth of the island under the mistaken idea that these practices were responsible for the lack of law and order there."[27] He further relates that the neighboring Dominican Republic took the opportunity of the departure of the Marines in 1934 to massacre some ten thousand Haitians on the Dominician border, an atrocity that was not answered by the Haitian government.

Although Williams' work reflects the racial biases of its author, particularly in its lingering descriptions of nubile, naked young Haitian women wherever he finds them, it is also politically sensitive, and the outrage of the academic at the atrocities perpetrated by the Haitian government against its own people is evident on many pages. He also states that Caucasians who fall under the spell of the voodoo rituals are "emotionally abnormal,"[28] although a few pages later he writes, "Voodooism is more than a religion. It is the embodiment of *all* the activities and psychological manifestations of the people. *Few religions can claim as much*" (Williams' emphasis).[29] These two sentiments seem to contradict each other, but perhaps they don't.

In the 1950s, as voudon was still being actively suppressed by the government and the sacred drums and flags of the religion were still being burned, Duvalier and his group represented a political, intellectual and cultural alternative, and Duvalier—seen as a "black" candidate as opposed to a supporter of the mulatto elite—won the presidential election in 1957. For the first time in over a hundred years, voudon priests, or *houngans,* were invited to the presidential palace and given government positions. On one particularly historic occasion, Duvalier invited *all* of the houngans in Haiti to a special meeting in Port-au-Prince, the capital of the country. His allegiance to voudon was no secret, and the allegiance of voudon to Duvalier was cemented. The rumors in Haiti (and abroad) were that Duvalier was, himself, a houngan or perhaps even a black magician, a *bokor*.

Things were not easy for Duvalier, however. The first few years of his administration there were numerous attempts at military coups and assassinations, and in reaction he formed his own personal bodyguard, the dread Tontons Macoutes. With their sinister sunglasses and small arms, they were everywhere in Haiti for about thirty years. They wore no uniforms, but their presence was pervasive in every town, on every street corner. It was a huge organization, and the secret behind it was peculiarly Haitian: an occult society known as Bizango.

The roots of Bizango are not a matter of historical documentation, but of Haitian tradition and legend which places Bizango at the beginning of the slave revolt, and even earlier. According to an informant of Wade Davis, the word *bizango* was "of the Cannibal,"[30] and therefore Arawakian, the language of the Native American people all but wiped out with the advent of Columbus to Hispaniola in December of 1492—the same people that gave us Tituba, the "witch" of Salem, Massachusetts. The same informant also relates *bizango* to the name of a spirit found in a famous medieval grimoire known as the *Red Dragon* (*Le Dragon Rouge*), which was the title of the first book in Thomas Harris' Hannibal "the Cannibal" Lecter series, and also the name of a tile in the Chinese game of Mah Jong. (The reader may also remember the Red Dragon video game parlor in West Virginia encountered by the author on his way to Ashland, Kentucky, and described in Book One.) Another medieval grimoire that is frequently mentioned in association with voudon is the French *Le Petit Albert* which, we are told, was once banned in Haiti in the pre-Duvalier era. This is hard to believe, for the "Little Albert" is hardly a work of demonic character but contains chapters on palmistry, herbalism, and—of course—a bit on summoning spirits and spells for success in love and money.

Whatever the origin of Bizango, it has developed into a secret society that exists in every part of Haiti, and with whom its followers claim the Haitian government must cooperate if it wishes to stay in power. The Bizango cult has murdered its enemies, and has worked its voudon magic against them as well using a mixture of herbal poisons and drugs as well as incantations and spells. It is believed that Duvalier's Tontons Macoutes were soldiers of the Bizango society, or that, at least, their memberships overlapped considerably (as implied in the Wes Craven film very loosely based on Wade Davis' research in Haiti, *The Serpent and the Rainbow*). Upon coming to power, Duvalier relaxed the hold of the Catholic Church over the Haitian people and the practice of the native religion came into greater flower than ever before. Duvalier himself was widely believed to be a channel for the typically and uniquely Haitian god, the dread *Baron Samedi* ("Baron Saturday"), and Papa Doc went out of his way to cultivate this identity, dressing in the Baron's typical black suit, black hat and sporting a cane. Baron Samedi is the Lord of the Crossroads, and thus is the Guardian of the path into the Other World. The Baron is usually invoked before most rituals that have to do with summoning power from beyond. His empire is in the cemetery, and for this reason he is sometimes also called the Baron of the Cemetery. Although there are many important deities in the Haitian religion, the Baron is the one that Hollywood has fixated upon the most, as he is the most sinister in appearance. The Baron takes several bows in the James Bond film aforementioned—*Live and Let Die*—replete in skull and skeleton costume and top hat, as well as *Erzulie*, who is the flirtatious goddess most associated with love and sex (it is, of course, both Baron Samedi and Erzulie who also make an appearance in the Wes Craven film, mentioned above, evidence of Hollywood's fascination with death and sex).

Regardless of Hollywood's interpretation, however, the story of Haitian independence has much to tell us about the relationship between rebellion and witchcraft. The Duvalier regimes, on the other hand, have much to teach us about how politics, religion and the occult can come together as a powerful, and terrifying, force. When Duvalier dissolved the bicameral legislature of the government in 1961, the US government under President Kennedy suspended aid to Haiti in disapproval, and from that point on Duvalier—the personification of Baron Samedi, the Lord of Death, and at least the repository of the Baron's *kebatinan*—targeted Kennedy as an enemy of the state.

Haitian voudon has much to teach us about such things as possession and temporary madness, as well as about modern European ceremonial magic and the practices of some of the more interesting—and dangerous—cults extant today, and we will return to it later. For now, its strange syncretistic structure and its identification with the Haitian people and their nationalism are what compel us. Never in modern times has one nation been so identified with what we think of as the "occult"; the exception possibly being the short-lived Third Reich, with SS chief Heinrich Himmler playing the role of Baron Samedi in his black uniform with the death's head insignia. Of all the Nazi leaders, probably Himmler comes closest to being a "Baron of the Cemetery," as the SS officers in charge of the death camps were under his command.

In America, there is a specific division between the affairs of state and the affairs of religion; freedom of religion is protected by the Constitution, and the government may make no laws concerning the practice of religion. Thus, a colonel in the US Army, such as Temple of Set founder Michael Aquino, can have his religion listed as "Satanist," on a par with Catholic, Jew, Methodist, Buddhist, Muslim, etc. (God forbid anyone in the armed services should openly proclaim his or her homosexuality, however!)

Yet, this division is in a sense artificial. American coinage is minted with the slogan "In God We Trust," and the Pledge of Allegiance states—since the 1950s—that America is "one nation, under God." The United States is largely viewed as a Christian nation, and there have only been Christian presidents so far. No provision is made for government funding for churches, however; and prayer in the public schools has been proscribed as violating the Constitutional separation of church and state. Individual presidents have been very open about their religious affiliations, however, and many Americans are alternately charmed and relieved to see their elected officials attending Sunday services. The electorate may be forgiven if they are not aware of the depth of religious feeling of some of their officials; presidents rarely express these beliefs openly for fear of alienating some voting bloc or another. However, some of them have had … strange beliefs, and dangerous ones. One would not wish a man with apocalyptic visions formed by an idiosyncratic interpretation of the Bible to have his proverbial finger on the proverbial button to ignite a nuclear holocaust, but that is just what America had in the 1980s; and he was married to a woman who consulted an astrologer on a regular basis, organizing her husband's schedule on the basis of planetary transits.

The author has covered the occult aspects of the Third Reich in some detail in his previous work. Although he followed the progress of the Nazi ideologues and war criminals to Latin America via the Vatican's "rat lines" after the war, he did not focus too much on the presence of Nazism in the United States and its influence on post-war twentieth century American politics. While the presence of Nazi war criminals in the United States came to the attention of the public only gradually in the 1970s and 1980s, they had, after all, been in the country since 1945. The scientists of Peenemunde and Nordhausen were discussed in Book One; but the political influence of Nazism on the development of the post-war Republican Party has remained virtually unexamined, except when some particularly egregious blunder has exposed the presence of the Dark Lords in an embarrassing way. These cult leaders have wielded a disproportionate amount of influence over the Party since the early post-war years, mostly as a reflection of the Cold War mentality of the United States and its terrified reaction to the rise of Communism in Eastern Europe and the Asian landmass. Protection and support of Nazis—including war criminals—by the Republican Party remains as one of the biggest under-reported scandals of American politics, regardless of the *realpolitik* justifications and secret agendas of the intelligence agencies and the New Right, and it is evidence of a moral stand that is at best debatable and at worst deplorable.

These influences boiled over temporarily during the Watergate scandal and subsequent investigations—perhaps epitomized by the "sinister force" behind the erasure of a crucial eighteen-and-a-half minutes of a secret Oval Office tape recording—and it is to this strange and paranoid episode of American history that we now must turn.

Endnotes

[1] J. Anthony Lukas, *Nightmare: The Underside of the Nixon Years*, Viking Press, NY,

1976, ISBN 0-670-51415-2, p. 460

[2] Alexis deToqueville, *Democracy in America*, HarperPerennial, NY, 1988, ISBN 0-06-091522-6, p. 300

[3] E.A. Wallis Budge, *The Book of the Dead*, Gramercy Books, NY, 1960 ed., ISBN 0-517-12283-9, p. 94

[4] Robert A Houghton with Theodore Taylor, *Special Unit Senator*, Random House, NY, 1970 p. 230

[5] Wendy Doniger O'Flaherty, *The Origins of Evil in Hindu Mythology*, Motilal Banarsidass, Delhi, 1988, ISBN 81-208-0386-8, p. 66

[6] Ibid., p. 80

[7] Ibid., p. 89

[8] Ibid., p. 81

[9] Niels Mulder, *Mysticism in Java: Ideology in Indonesia*, The Pepin Press, Singapore,1998, ISBN 90-5496-047-7, p. 9-10

[10] L. Couperus, *The Hidden Force*, The University of Massachusetts Press, Amherst, 1985, ISBN 0-87023-715-2, p. 129

[11] Ibid., p. 142

[12] Kelley & Francis, p.3; from Gill, *Mother Earth*, 1987 pp 67-68

[13] Mulder, op. cit., p. 30

[14] Ibid., p. 30

[15] Ibid., p. 32

[16] Richard Winstedt, *The Malay Magician*, Oxford University Press, Kuala Lumpur, 1993, ISBN 0-19-582529-2, p. 9-13

[17] Ibid., p. 8-9

[18] Ibid., p. 10

[19] Ibid., p. 11

[20] Ibid., p. 157-166

[21] Ian Buruma, *The Missionary and the Libertine*, Vintage Books, NY, 2000, ISBN 0-375-70537-6, p. 118-130, "Bhutto's Pakistan"

[22] Ibid., p. 131-140, "St Cory and the Evil Rose"

[23] Mulder, op. cit., p. 18

[24] Ibid., p. 19

[25] Endicott, op. cit., p. 66

[26] See, for instance, P. Chandra Sagaran, "Three Charged With Murder," *New Straits Times*, July 28, 2001, p. 9; Kuldeep S. Jessy, "Trio charged with murder of American woman," *The Star*, July 28, 2001, p. 6; and similar cases in Lam Li, "Woman's body exhumed, hands and toes missing," *The Star*, December 19, 2001, p. 6 and Sim Bak Heng, "Body Snatchers," *The Malay Mail*, December 19, 2001, p. 2

[27] Samuel H. Williams, *Voodoo Roads*, Verlag fuer Jugend und Volk, Wien, 1949, p. 37

[28] Ibid., p. 12

[29] Ibid., p. 16

[30] Wade Davis, *The Serpent and the Rainbow*, Warner Books, NY, ISBN 0-446-34387-0, p. 309

CHAPTER TEN

WALLOWING IN WATERGATE

But the accusations are enough to show what thoughts worked under the surface of all that belligerent orthodoxy. We seem to see men half aware of their hallucination, and proportionately angry with those who do not share it.
    —Allen Upward, *The Divine Mystery*[1]

Neurosis and initiation are the same thing, except that neurosis stops short of apotheosis, and the tremendous forces that mold all life are encysted—short circuited and turned poisonous.
    —Jack Parsons[2]

L'amant dit a la belle:
Ou est la verite?
La verite, dit-elle,
Qui donc s'en fut doute,
La verite, dit-elle,
Est morte et enteree.
    —Maurice Maeterlinck, *The Cloud That Lifted,* Act III, Scene 3

Religion, like Watergate, is a scandal that will not go away.
    —Victor Turner, *Revelation and Divination in Ndembu Ritual*[3]

In 1968, America turned a corner politically and, some would say, spiritually as well. In January, the Tet Offensive showed America that the war in Vietnam was nowhere near over. The author and millions of his fellow citizens sat in stunned silence in front of their television sets as Walter Cronkite, in a state of shock over the dramatic attacks that occurred on the Vietnamese New Year, said, "I thought we were winning this thing." By April, Martin Luther King had been assassinated, and by June so had Robert F. Kennedy. It looked as if both the peace movement and the civil rights movement had been dealt serious, mortal blows. The Days of Rage during the Democratic National Convention in Chicago represented the frustration and anger of the anti-war movement, as Mayor Daley called out the troops and had Lincoln Park cleared of demonstrators with Walter Cronkite, again on television, visibly upset at what was happening to our country.

And in November, Richard M. Nixon was elected President of the United States.

When dawn broke on the first day of January, 1969 seventeen-year-old Marina Habe's lifeless body was lying at the bottom of a ravine off Mulholland Drive, like a human sacrifice on the first day of the first year of Nixon's first term as president, a young victim whose father worked for US intelligence and psychological warfare operations in Europe during the War; a young victim who was slaughtered in Nixon's home state, a few miles from the town where he was born, a few miles from the town where he was first nominated by his party. Nixon, a lawyer by profession, would later go on to proclaim the alleged perpetrator of this atrocity to be "guilty" while his trial for other murders was still in progress, thus threatening a mistrial.

And in March, less than two months after his inauguration, President Nixon ordered the bombing of Cambodia.

In the months that followed in that first year of Richard Nixon's first term as President, the Manson Family gathered guns, vehicles, drugs and additional members and headed out to the Mojave Desert and Death Valley in preparation for a long-term siege. Manson's dream of becoming a rock star was not materializing, but his nightmare of race war and armageddon was taking shape. There had been the JFK/MLK/RFK assassinations, the race riots in Los Angeles in 1965, and earlier George Wallace had stood in the doorway of University of Alabama, staring down the National Guard that had been sent at Bobby Kennedy's insistence to force the desegregation of that college. Even earlier, Nazis had been welcomed with open arms into the United States to help with the space program, and in July of 1969—a bare two weeks before the Tate killings—American astronauts had set foot on the Moon.

Evil had an Asian face, not a European one. Korea. Vietnam, Laos, Cambodia. China. Even Russia was Asiatic, except of course for the "White Russians," i.e., "our" Russians, the aristocratic Russians with German blood. When the Romanov family had been led to its murder by the Soviets in 1917, one of them left behind a swastika swabbed on the wall, a last desperate plea to the Gods of the noble White Europeans to protect them, to protect Holy Mother Russia. Is it any wonder, really, that Charles Manson—poor, white trash from

Ashland, Kentucky; Moundsville, West Virginia, and various penitentiaries on both coasts and points in between—would have adopted Scientology, the Process, and eventually Nazism as a solution to his own problems as well as those of the world? He would not support the war in Vietnam, but he wasn't a hippie, either. He believed in violent action, in the use of force, in the disruption of society, in race war. The drugs and sex of the Sixties were only fringe benefits. And he would one day carve a swastika into his forehead. Observers are mistaken if they believe that Manson was a creature of the Summer of Love, of Haight-Ashbury be-ins and Grateful Dead "experience" concerts, although that is what commentators have desperately tried to prove in order to discredit and devalue the anti-War movement and the sixties youth culture in general.

Manson was a creature of the Right: raised by the State, formed by the State, brutalized by the State since he was a child, Manson was the Right Wing in America, taken to its logical conclusion, in an environment in which Nazis were protected and coddled, in which the Church itself collaborated in some of the worst crimes that century had ever seen, and in which the American State Department, the CIA, the military, and other institutions fought among each other for the spoils. The cynicism of Manson was conceived as he watched this duplicity unfold in his own life. In "brainwashing" his followers he was only doing to perfection what the men of MK-ULTRA were trying to do with a larger budget and a lot of paperwork. The fact that he was convicted of the Tate/La Bianca murders and is still in prison to this day is testament to his success, since it is acknowledged that he did not pick up a knife or pull a trigger or in any way actually participate at the Sharon Tate crime scene. He was, as he said, "convicted of witchcraft in the twentieth century."

With the assassination of Dr. King in April, racial tensions were as high as they had ever been. Bobby Kennedy had the credentials with the black community as well as the anti-war community to make a difference, but he was gunned down as well. The Beatles came out with the White Album in 1968 (on November 22, the fifth anniversary of the assassination of President Kennedy), and Manson thought they were speaking directly to him about *Helter Skelter*, *Revolution 9* (understood by Manson as a Biblical reference to "Revelations 9"), *Piggies*, and *Happiness is a Warm Gun*.

This is a phenomenon that will be analyzed by academia one day: the replacement of traditional religious figures and texts by rock star celebrities, movie stars, and song lyrics. Anyone who has seen how young people reacted to the physical presence of the Beatles—screaming, shaking, fainting, hysteria—must have wondered if this was a kind of religious ecstasy taking place. Biblical figures never actually appear to the faithful, except in visions and then only to a few; but television and motion pictures made it possible to create new figures of Biblical proportions and to give the masses direct access to their every move, glance, strut, pout, or moue. And when they appeared in person—at a rock concert or movie premiere or book signing or supermarket opening—the impossible would take place: the Biblical figure was in the very flesh, corporeal, present and breathing the same air, walking in the same space. For many, this was as close to a mystical experience as they would ever get. In the case of the Beatles, they came with their own sacred texts: their songs. The music, the lyrics, the beat of Ringo's drums, the immediate reaction of conservative Christianity against them resulting in the destruction of records and the burning of their albums by religious groups; and the origins of rock 'n' roll itself in the black music of the South, the devilish blues of men like Robert Johnson, provided white America with a kind of voodoo cult of its own, shrink-wrapped and hi-fi. The package was complete, and thus John Lennon could be forgiven for having said—albeit cynically—that the Beatles had become more popular than Jesus Christ.

The backlash to all of this was the election of a right-wing Republican president to replace all those murdered or disgraced Democratic candidates. The tension in the streets of America rose exponentially. For the first time in the postwar era, America had become polarized into an Us and a Them. One could tell who was whom by such simple matters as a haircut (or lack of one), a clothing style, or a method of employment. It was not so simple to deduce a person's allegiance on the basis of age; many young Americans were also Young Republicans. Many older Americans had marched on Washington to protest the war in Vietnam. The polarization was cutting across all demographics.

When the author was a high school senior in the Bronx in 1968, the Students for a Democratic Society were busy trying to engage and organize the student body, but all they managed to organize were tedious meetings full of quasi-political discussions that did not advance the cause or stop the war in Vietnam; enter the Weather Underground.

The Weathermen believed in taking action to "bring the war home." They bombed Army recruiting stations, banks, and any other targets that were understood to be supportive of the war effort. One day in 1969, the author was on the telephone to the headquarters of the Presbyterian Church which was, at that time, located on the edge of New York City's Greenwich Village. At one point during the phone conversation, there was a deafening blast and the sound of breaking glass. A terrified voice on the other end shouted, "I have to go! There's been a bomb!" and hung up.

The Weathermen had been making bombs in the basement of a West Village brownstone across the street from the Presbyterian Church, and accidentally blew up the building and themselves. Several people died, and some Weathermen escaped, including one woman who would turn herself in twenty years later after a lifetime spent underground.

During that same period, the author had the opportunity to meet many Weathermen, Black Panthers, members of the Irish Republican Army, NORAID, the Palestine Liberation Organization, and other underground groups plotting all sorts of mayhem in the United States and abroad. He once shook the hand of Bernadette Devlin, the fiery young woman who was a Member of Parliament from Northern Ireland, the woman who wrote, "I was not born a Socialist; life has made me one." He also met Pete Seeger, Oscar Brand, Milos Forman, and a host of other counter-culture celebrities and activists. He visited the offices of the *East Village Other* (the EVO Eye) and, of course, the *Village Voice,* handing out press releases and placing ads announcing meetings of various subversive groups at the basements of radical churches throughout the City, including Judson Memorial in Manhattan and Spencer Memorial in Brooklyn Heights. He also became acquainted with the surreptitious movement of young men to Canada to avoid the draft, via an underground railroad that stretched from New York City anti-war churches and temples to coffee shops like The Yellow Door in Montreal. And all of this to the sensory backbeat of marijuana fumes, acid trips, day-glo posters, lava lamps, Peter Max and black light; the music of Leonard Cohen, Janis Joplin, Joni Mitchell, Joan Baez and the entire *Forrest Gump* soundtrack; rock groups like the Grateful Dead and Led Zepellin and the Rolling Stones; movies like *The Strawberry Statement, Joe,* and *The Revolutionary.* Bobby Seal; Abbie Hoffmann and *Steal This Book;* R. D. Laing and *The Politics of Experience.*

This was the atmosphere in the United States of America in the late sixties.

I had grown up in the 1950s thinking that at any moment the Russians or the Chinese would bomb the bejesus out of us; I was taught how to protect myself in the event of a nuclear strike, how to lean over with your head between your knees and—in the joke of the day—"kiss your ass goodbye," as the air raid sirens wailed periodically over the South Side of Chicago where I first attended school. Then the Cuban Missile Crisis. Then the Kennedy assassination. Race riots. Freedom marches.

In 1968, this was followed by the horror of the Martin Luther King, Jr. assassination, only to be intensified by that of Bobby Kennedy. Many historians look back on that period from a safe distance and try to explain it all in terms of dialectical materialism or some other force of history; we knew differently. We knew that there was a war between two opposing forces in America, and that one side was winning.

There were other forces at work in the world than those I learned of in my high school physics classes. Forces of darkness, surely, but of tremendous power as well. We had to identify them and, if possible, tame them, or at least protect ourselves against them.

Heady stuff for a high school student in 1968; but, after all, we were all of us involved in greater things. Marches on Washington, the Students for a Democratic Society, the Black Panthers, the Weathermen. Hippies, free love, pot and LSD. The Beatles, the Rolling Stones, Led Zeppelin. Hard rock, acid rock, folk rock. Beads and beards and peasant blouses and blue jeans. There was a war on, and at any moment any of us could be called up, and at that point we would have to make the most important decision of our lives.

By August 1969 I had not been drafted but was in need of money and took a job with a Presbyterian Church in Brooklyn Heights. That month, on August 9th, disciples of Charles Manson slaughtered Sharon Tate and her house guests, and then went on to hack Leno and Rosemary La Bianca to death the following day.

I worked for the Church for almost a year, and the following year got a job at a lingerie company in New York's Garment District. It was exactly a year after the Manson killings, and on my first day at work I heard a disturbing story. The son of one of the owners of the firm had committed suicide in a New York City hotel room, fleeing from Los Angeles where he had worked as a gossip columnist. Steve Brandt killed himself because he was afraid the Manson Family was coming for him. Because he knew too much. It was while working for this highly unlikely firm that I also heard—from another co-worker—of a plan to kidnap Howard Hughes. More of that later.

If I needed any evidence that sinister forces were at work in the world, subtly manipulating reality in ways we could not predict or defend against, then my two years of work at Stardust, Inc. provided all the reinforcement I required. Charles Manson was arrested on October 12, 1969 (the birthday of Aleister Crowley; Columbus Day; and the birthday of President Eisenhower), and the trial and its aftermath lasted through much of 1970 and into 1971. During the trial, President Richard Nixon proclaimed that Manson was guilty; as a lawyer he should have known better, and as a president he should have kept his mouth shut. It threatened a mistrial if the jury had heard of it. Manson knew this, and brought a newspaper to the courtroom with him, waving it in front of the jury. Incredibly, the judge allowed the trial to continue after being assured by the jury that they would not be swayed by the President's remarks.

Readers of Book One will find familiar the odd coincidence that one of the jury was an employee of Ashland Oil.

President Nixon would resign in the wake of the Watergate investigation on August 9, 1974: the fifth anniversary of the murder of Sharon Tate and, incredibly, the fifth anniversary of the day that Disneyland inaugurated their "Haunted House" ride.

Walt Disney had once owned the house where Leno and Rosemary La Bianca were slain.

It is amusing to note that President Nixon was, after all, a Quaker. It is amusing for the very reason that Ruth Paine was also a Quaker, as was Whittaker Chambers and even the wife of Alger Hiss: a tight little circle of plain speech and affirmations. If the Paines had something material to do with the assassination of President Kennedy, who was heartily and energetically despised by Nixon, then we have the very rudiments of a Quaker conspiracy theory! The reader may be grateful to learn that we will not go down that particular road.

What we will discover, however, is something considerably more serious. It is a theme of this work that sinister forces were evoked by American political, military and intelligence leaders in the twentieth century, and that one of the traces of this is the support of Nazism by prominent Americans, and the involvement in occult and extremely bizarre religious practices and beliefs by still others. This support of a heinous political and mystical philosophy was ongoing from the very end of World War II and has continued—in one form or another—through to the present day, thus contributing to a politico-occult malaise that has manifested in such atrocities as the Manson murders, the revival of the Ku Klux Klan and other racist organizations, and the laying of the famous wreath at the SS cemetery at Bitburg.

We will leave discussion of the author's own life for a while, and continue this investigation with the life of Richard Nixon himself.

It Didn't Start With Watergate

Soviet penetration of the Nazi networks were not only a threat to Allen Dulles' reputation, their exposure would have ruined the political career of Richard Nixon, the Republican candidate for President in 1959. Nixon authorised Dulles' covert projects during Eisenhower's illnesses in 1956 and 1957.
-- Aarons and Loftus, *Unholy Trinity: The Vatican, the Nazis, and Soviet Intelligence*[4]

I am being the devil's advocate ...
-- President Nixon, White House tapes, March 13, 1973

Richard Nixon occupies a unique place in American history. It is probably safe to say that no political leader—certainly no president—attracted so much vitriol, so much absolute disgust, in his opponents as did Nixon. He was vilified not only by Democrats, such as Eleanor Roosevelt, Harry Truman, Edmund Brown, and others but also by members of his own party, such as Eisenhower and even Nixon's own running mate, Henry Cabot Lodge, as well as his longtime staff members, such as Haldeman (who, of course, could be expected to have an axe to grind considering how he was treated during the Watergate crisis). Those who did support him and actually seemed to like him were mostly villains in their own right, people like Murray Chotiner, Bebe Rebozo, and Howard Hughes, or people with other secrets to hide, such as Allen Dulles, with whom Nixon had an improbable, lifelong friendship, and disgraced Attorney General John Mitchell. The forces of a contentious evil gathered around Nixon like blue-bottle flies on a day-old summertime corpse, and to this day there are still those who consider him to be a great president, and one much maligned by the same evil forces themselves arrayed against him. To be sure, no one is moderate when it comes to Richard Nixon.

Nixon's career takes us into the very belly of the Beast; there is virtually no aspect of his adult life that is not tainted somehow by associations with the vilest of men, as if somewhere in his distant past this hungry, ignored, socially-uncomfortable small-town lawyer signed a pact with the Devil, and the rest of his life was simply the logical conclusion of the contract. We look, in vain, for signs of redemption; a signal that he found an escape clause in his Faustian bargain and relaxed, finally, into the arms of his Quaker Savior.

It was not to be.

Nixon found his political legacy in his foreign policy successes, principally with China; which is ironic for a man who led the charge against Communism from his earliest political days. His foreign policy disasters—Vietnam and Chile come immediately to mind—are not regarded as such by his admirers. A casual observer may be forgiven if it seems strange that a man who held the line against Communist North Vietnam and the Socialist administration of Chile's Salvador Allende with an almost hysterical zeal would then toast Communist hero Mao Ze Dong with *mao tai* in the Great Hall of the People in Beijing, and welcome him into the United Nations against the wishes of staunchly loyal (if slightly fascist) ally Taiwan. This is because Nixon's political life—although polarized in the extreme—did not depend on such mundane concepts as left-wing and right-wing, capitalism and Communism, democracy and totalitarianism, but on deeper divisions in the human soul. Nixon had been making pacts with devils since 1946 at least, and he was less a man in control of his own destiny than a creature of other powers, other forces; a kind of political homunculus, a golem that could not be destroyed except by its maker.

The origins of Richard Milhous Nixon are not exactly shrouded in mystery like those of a Marvel Comics character, but they might as well have been. Like high school geek Peter Parker, who would become Spiderman, Nixon's background was modest and unassuming, his personality nerdlike and awkward. There was no sign that he would evolve into a super-hero to some, a super-villain to others. Yet, there was one element—the crucial one, as it turns out—that molded his future forever and it *was* mysterious. It was his selection as a Congressional candidate after the end of World War II by a group of businessmen ... businessmen with intelligence backgrounds and Mafia connections.

Nixon was born on January 9, 1913 in southern California, not far from Los Angeles. He had four brothers, two of whom died while quite young, leaving Richard and his brothers Donald and Edward. (Readers will smile when they learn that Richard himself was named after King Richard the Lionhearted, of Crusader fame.) The Nixon family was by all accounts middle-class and relatively prosperous, even though Nixon himself would later claim (for political spin) that he had a childhood full of suffering and hardship.

As a student, Nixon applied himself diligently, and won a scholarship to Whittier College (not difficult, as it was the Milhous Scholarship and only awarded to members of the Milhous clan). While at Whittier, he was involved in setting up a fraternity to rival the existing—more prestigious—one. The initiation rituals devised by Nixon and his colleagues for this "anti-frat" involved going at night, naked, and digging up a dead animal and feasting on its decaying flesh. It is said that Nixon, as the one who created the fraternity, did not have to go through this repulsive, Jeffrey-Dahmer-like, hazing ceremonial.[5] Nixon would go on to create spurious orders throughout his career, such as the Order of the Hound's Tooth (after the "Checkers speech" that saved his political career amid allegations of financial wrong-doing). Interest in secret societies, espionage capers, and all the other hallmarks of a paranoid personality (or, simply, a suspicious one) would characterize Nixon as both a man and as a politician in the eyes of an increasingly nervous electorate.

Nixon went on to Duke University for a time to get his law degree, and eventually wound up married to Pat Ryan. The woman who would become known as Pat Nixon was born Thelma Catherine Ryan on March 16, 1912; she acquired the nickname "Pat" because her father called her that, as her birthday was so close to St. Patrick's Day. Nixon did not even know his fiancee's birth name until almost the time to fill out the marriage license; and Nixon would later make political hay out of obscuring her real birth date so he could claim she was as Irish as Paddy's pig, born on the one day possibly more sacred to the Irish than Christmas or Easter Sunday (Easter Monday excepted). Pat Nixon had been a sometime actress in Whittier, and Nixon met her when he was auditioning for a role there as well. It seems odd, somehow, that the *next* elected Republican President and First Lady—the Reagans—would also meet the same way and would also have been (somewhat more successful) actors. Pat Nixon (before her marriage) had even worked as an extra in a few Hollywood films.

She also spent some time in New York City in the 1930s before meeting Nixon, working in a hospital that treated patients suffering from tuberculosis. Then three years after her return to California she was working as a teacher and acting on the side, where Nixon discovered her on the set of *The Dark Tower* by George S. Kaufman and Alexander Woollcott, and began to pursue her with sullen determination.

The script of *The Dark Tower* contains references to a play by the same name that—according to the storyline—is enjoying some success in Greenwich, Connecticut and sparking plans to take it to Broadway. (We must assume that the name of the play is a reference to that famous line, "To the dark tower the Childe Rolande came," which has been such an influence on Stephen King, among others.) In the Whittier production, Pat played the role of Daphne, and Nixon of Barry: a cynical, hardboiled actress and a boyish, idealistic playwright who are eventually thrown together and become lovers towards the end of the play. They are supporting roles rather than central characters, but the play still deserves another look, as it deals with a man believed to be dead who returns, only to be killed again (as apt a metaphor for Nixon's career as any), and themes of hypnosis and possession.

The resurrected man, Stanley Vance, was a career criminal who had caused one wife to commit suicide through hypnosis, and thus inherited her estate. He is on his way to doing the same with his current wife, when his brother-in-law kills him, first with chloryl hydrate and then finishing the job with a knife, while impersonating a Viennese investor in a room at the Waldorf Hotel. Thus, the young Nixon is introduced to the idea of hypnotic control of individuals to further criminal ends, pretty much what the CIA's MK-UL-TRA was all about. The doctor who is examining the young woman under the influence of Stanley Vance's hypnotic powers claims that the only doctors who would be able to help her had died during the Middle Ages: in his estimation, she is possessed by an evil spirit. Her brother, Damon, had been dating the Daphne character, but when Stanley Vance—who was believed to be dead—returns at the end of the first act, Damon loses interest in Daphne (whom he had been treating shabbily even earlier in the play, ordering her about like a recalcitrant schoolgirl) and Daphne eventually winds up in the arms of Barry, the worshipful, puppy-like playwright. Oddly, this is what happened in Pat Nixon's own life, as she was dating other men when Nixon was pursuing her with totally-focused determination after meeting her on the set of *The Dark Tower*.

Psychohistorian Bruce Mazlish has studied Nixon's personality from the point of view that this brief association with the theater when young had influenced his political life.[6] Nixon as vice president and president is always talking about playing a role, about acting, and criticizing those whose ability to play a role (politically) are amateurish. Nixon clearly felt that he was a better actor than most of his fellow politicos—including the Russians—and it is obvious that he understood that an ability to act, to perform, *to pretend* was essential to the success of every politician. In the course of the action in *The Dark Tower*, one character is certain that the hypnotized wife—who is an actress—is only acting and that she is not genuinely "possessed" or under hypnotic influence, but only pretending to be so to enable the murder plot against her hideous husband to go forward. In the end, the "resurrected" husband is killed and his murderer goes free; such is the moral of the tale. *The Dark Tower* originally opened in New York City on November 25, 1933 at the Morosco Theater, almost thirty years to the day before the assassination of President Kennedy.

Nixon, in his earnest, steadfast wooing of Pat even acted as her chauffeur when she went out on dates with other men. Imagine the silent resentment, the self-loathing Nixon must have felt during this time. Humiliation of one kind or another would always dog his life and his career; self-abasement could be viewed as romantic idealism, though, with enough spin, and Nixon would get his own back in later years as he consistently humiliated Pat in public and, it is claimed, even beat her on occasion. For a long time Pat Ryan avoided Nixon, not finding herself particularly attracted to him, but by 1940 she finally relented to his barrage of love letters and constant attention, and they were married on June 21, 1940 (the summer solstice) in a Quaker ceremony near Whittier, California, Nixon's home town. (She would die almost exactly fifty-three years later, on June 22, 1993 in New Jersey.) It's an interesting fact that the Nixons' youngest daughter, Julie, married President Eisenhower's grandson, Dwight David Eisenhower II, on December 22, 1968, which happens to be the winter solstice.

When war broke out in December 1941, Nixon took a job working in Washington, D.C. for the Office of Emergency Management. Tiring of that, he enlisted in the Navy in 1942 and—after a short posting to Quonset, Rhode Island—was sent to the Pacific theater, where he served the remainder of the war, becoming a Lieutenant Commander in the process. This is where it gets interesting.

In 1937, he had gone job-hunting in New York City at two firms that had strong intelligence connections: Donovan, Leisure, Newton and Lombard, of which General William "Wild Bill" Donovan was the founding partner, and Sullivan and Cromwell, which had John Foster Dulles as a senior partner. Donovan, of course, was the genius behind the OSS; John Foster Dulles was a statesman of world renown and brother, of course, to Allen Dulles, who would one day become Director of the Central Intelligence Agency. At this time, Nixon also applied to the FBI but was turned down. The reasons are a little vague.

In 1945, at the war's end, Nixon—still in uniform—was back on the East Coast, and this time we know even less of what he was doing and for whom. There is one tantalizing reference to the "Bureau of Aeronautics," which is suggestive of a Jack Parsons link, but alas there is nothing else there to work with. What we do have, however, is evidence that Nixon had been involved— however briefly, however peripherally—with Operation Paperclip.

Mark Aarons and John Loftus, in *The Secret War Against the Jews*, refer to interviews with former Counter Intelligence Corps personnel as well as the Central Intelligence Group (the forerunner of the CIA), who claim that Nixon had seen documentation that Allen Dulles wanted kept secret, and that Dulles in return offered to help finance Nixon's run against incumbent California Congressman Jerry Voorhis in 1946. (This claim is repeated in their *Unholy Trinity*.) As Dulles had contacts and business associations with Nazis going back long before the start of the war, it is possible that the documentation Nixon saw implicated Dulles in some ugly relationships. However, it might have been even more complicated than that.

As is discussed more fully in *The Nine*, Operation Paperclip was a US Government program to bring over as many Nazi scientists and medical personnel as possible to the United States to assist in the space program which was, at that time, a purely military program. The Army and the Navy were both involved, both fighting over the intellectual spoils (the Air Force at this time was still part of the Army). Allen Dulles was running OSS operations during the war from Switzerland, and was in a position to influence the selection process. At the same time, Nazi spymasters such as Reinhard Gehlen were offering their services to the Americans in their new war against the Soviet Union. President Truman had disbanded the OSS in October 1945, but had created the Central Intelligence Group in January 1946; the CIA was created in 1947. It was during this interregnum reshuffling of experienced intelligence personnel that Richard Nixon found himself on the East Coast, in some mysterious capacity concerning a review of captured Nazi records and documents, ostensibly for the Navy. And it was this experience that gave Nixon some very valuable connections, for when it came time to go after alleged Communist spy Alger Hiss, he had the Dulles family on his side, providing him with sensitive intelligence information that would confirm Hiss' Communist sympathies.

The Dulles family had long and extensive ties to the Nazi underground, and had been laundering Nazi money for decades. They were not alone in this. As Aarons and Loftus demonstrate, the Bush family was so heavily involved in "trading with the enemy" that some of their company assets were seized by the US government in 1942. Nixon had stumbled on to the Dulleses' own dirty laundry, and Allen Dulles took Nixon under his wing, grooming him for a position of power in Washington. Somehow, this information never makes its way into the authorized biographies.

This exposure to Nazism—Nixon's war was, after all, in the Pacific against the Japanese—was not to be Nixon's last. As the years went by, Nixon would find himself involved in protecting known Nazis in the United States, and using neo-Nazis in anti-Democrat "dirty tricks." And when the axe fell on Chile on September 11, 1973, it was once again Nixon calling the shots, with assistance from his Nazi admirers at Colonia Dignidad.

In the meantime, however, he was being groomed (and financed) by a consortium of businessmen, right-wing activists, intelligence agents, and Mafia dons, from the very beginning of his political career. It all started with a letter from California, urging Nixon to run against Jerry Voorhis.

In September 1945, the manager of the Whittier, California branch of the Bank of America—Herman Perry—contacted Nixon by mail and asked him if he would consider running against a five-term Democratic veteran, Congressman Jerry Voorhis. Voorhis seemed unbeatable, a shoo-in for the Democrats in 1946 for a sixth term. The Republicans had no one with any serious chance against him in southern California, and Nixon—as a lawyer, and a veteran, someone well-known to Perry and the people of Whittier—seemed like a possible candidate to support. At least, that is the story.

This author finds it difficult to believe that the Republican Party of California would have reached so far, to an inexperienced young lawyer just returned from the war, a political non-entity really, to run against such a popular candidate as Voorhis. It's true he had some political experience before the war, making speeches in support of local Republican candidates and trying to get a state assembly seat, but nothing came of his efforts and the war interrupted everyone's lives. If what Loftus and Aarons say is true in *The Secret War Against The Jews*, that Nixon was privy to some unwholesome secrets about Dulles as early as 1945, then the scenario becomes tighter, if more sinister. It also explains the friendship between Dulles and Nixon, which is otherwise inexplicable.

Dulles was urbane, sophisticated, cosmopolitan, multilingual, the very type of Eastern Establishment figure that the socially-awkward Nixon despised. Dulles on his part should have found very little to admire or find likeable in Nixon. According to Nixon biographer Anthony Summers, "they shared the same worldview,"[7] which evidently was enough to overcome their personality differences. In any event, Dulles seems to have pledged support to Nixon, and support did arrive: from companies such as Standard Oil and other big business interests who felt threatened by Voorhis. Voorhis himself was aware that money was flowing into Nixon's coffers from a "New York financial house" in an effort to remove him from office.[8] Dulles would play further roles in Nixon's career, giving him the intelligence information he would need to go after Alger Hiss. The partnership between Allen Dulles and Richard Nixon was truly a Faustian bargain, but it is hard to tell just who is Faust and who is Mephistopheles in this scenario.

Further investigation also revealed another twist to the mystery of Nixon's anonymous backers, this from longtime mobster and associate of Meyer Lansky, Mickey Cohen. As early as the 1946 election, Nixon had been in the pocket of organized crime. Cohen confessed during his incarceration at Alcatraz to what had already come to the attention of US government officials as well as Democratic party leaders, that he—on Mafia orders—had supplied funds for Nixon's first campaign against Voorhis, in a meeting arranged by Nixon's "campaign manager," Murray Chotiner. Then, for the 1950 Senate race, Cohen came up with an additional $75,000 from a group of "associates" in the rackets. The sum of $75,000 in 1950 is equivalent to $660,000 today.[9]

Mickey Cohen was Los Angeles' answer to Bugsy Siegel in Las Vegas, and indeed the two had worked together to consolidate the West Coast rackets for the Lansky operation, while Lansky busied himself with his casinos in Cuba. When Cohen was eventually convicted and sent to prison, he at first refused to confirm or deny the allegations about Nixon, Chotiner and the Mob, because that would be "like ratting," but he eventually signed a statement full of details regarding names, dates, places and amounts that could have served as Nixon's rapsheet. What is even more worrisome, however, is Mickey Cohen's relationship to another character who would figure prominently in American history: Jack Ruby.

While Jack Ruby's connections to organized crime are well known and beyond any reasonable doubt, what is perhaps not so well-known is his relationship to a former girlfriend of Mickey Cohen's, a stripper whose stage name was Candy Barr but whose real name was Juanita Slusher Dale Phillips Sahakian. Candy Barr had been the object of Mickey's passionate attentions until she got sent up for marijuana possession, doing four years in a Texas prison and out on parole at the time of the Kennedy assassination. Ruby was phoning her and visiting her from her release in April of 1963 right up to a week or so before Dallas. It seems clear that this was not to get her to resume her career in one of Ruby's clubs, since she was under strict orders by her parole board not to go back to her old job. We may never know the real reasons behind Candy Barr's importance to Ruby; the assumption is that he was interested in what underworld connections she might have made while in prison,[10] but that does not explain the many phone calls, especially those leading up to the assassination. Ruby was chronically short of cash, though, always on the verge of bankruptcy, so it is quite possible that he was looking for a Mafia "loan" and was hoping Candy could lead him to the right people; indeed, remarks he made to associates in the days before the assassination led many to believe that he was on the verge of a windfall. He had met with various organized crime figures in the weeks preceding Kennedy's visit to Dallas, and spoke to many more by phone. None of this explains Candy's role, since Ruby certainly had his own connections to organized crime including all manner of loan sharks. Candy's importance to Ruby was probably due only to her long affair with Cohen, and it is possible Ruby was using Candy to communicate with Cohen. These circumstances may be totally irrelevant to the assassination and its aftermath, but we will probably never know for sure. What Candy Barr, Mickey Cohen and Jack Ruby did eventually have in common, however, was the same lawyer: Melvin Belli. Beyond that, the documentation is slim; but if we put Mickey Cohen together with Murray Chotiner and Richard Nixon on the one hand, and with Candy Barr and Jack Ruby on the other, we have a personality who knew where the bodies were buried. Literally. When he confessed to financing Nixon's early career, and when Warren Commission investigators uncovered Ruby's connections to Cohen, alarm bells should have gone off somewhere, but they didn't.

No matter the identity of the secret backers of Richard Nixon, he entered into the Voorhis campaign with complete focus. He developed his patented form of slanderous accusations and Red-baiting at this time, attacking Voorhis as a Communist when he knew that it was a completely unfounded allegation. According to Nixon's official platform, Voorhis was an instrument of the radical left; this, even though Voorhis was a member of the House Un-American Activities Committee (HUAC) and had an anti-Communist act named after him! To be fair, however, Voorhis *was* viewed as an ultra-liberal by many; his involvement with HUAC included hauling American Nazis such as George Moseley and George Deatherage (he of the reformed Knights of the White Camelia) before the Committee as early as 1939, criticizing their virulent anti-Semitism.[11]

The other real problem Republicans had with Voorhis, and probably the single most important reason they had to take him out in 1946, was of a piece. Voorhis had called for an overhaul of the American monetary system and "the purchase of the Federal Reserve System."[12] To American conspiracy theorists, there is probably nothing more sinister than the Federal Reserve System, which is viewed as a creature of the Illuminati, the Rothschilds, and mysterious foreign interests that use the Federal Reserve—which is an independent institution and not technically a part of the US government—to control America's financial destiny (and that of the rest of the world). For Voorhis to come out against the Federal Reserve was tantamount (in the eyes of the conspiriologists) to an attack on the Illuminati themselves. He had also attacked the oil industry as well as the insurance industry, not to mention the liquor industry. After that, there wasn't much left to go after except maybe your mother and her apple pie. It seemed as if Jerry Voorhis was going after all of business' sacred cows, all at once. He had, in effect, signed his own political death warrant and it was up to Tricky Dick to deliver it.

A combination of smears, lies, dirty tricks, anti-Communist hysteria and even anti-Semitism took the day. Registered voters in California would get phone calls from anonymous callers, asking, "Did you know Jerry Voorhis was a Communist?"—the same tactic that was used in 2000 against Democratic candidate for president, Al Gore in Florida (in Spanish this time). Leaflets were printed characterizing Voorhis as a tool of "subversive Jews" bent on destroying "Christian America." This, in 1946: only a year after Nazism was crushed in Europe at a terrible cost of human life, including those of Americans. It is important to realize from this episode how many Americans still distrusted Jews, even with the newsreel footage of the death camps fresh in their minds. Perhaps especially in face of the death camps. It was General Patton, after all, who claimed that during the war the Allies were aiming their guns in the wrong direction and should have sided with the Nazis against the Soviets. It was Patton who put captured SS officers back in charge of the temporary DP (Displaced Persons) camps, filled with their former prisoners.

Dr. Carl Goldberg, a psychiatrist and psychotherapist of some renown who has held posts at the Albert Einstein School of Medicine and at New York University, has discussed this phenomenon in his *Speaking With The Devil: Exploring Senseless Acts of Evil.* In Chapter Twelve of that work, he discusses the case of "Emil," a Serbian man married to a prosecutor with the US District

Attorney's office. Emil had participated in an atrocity in the former Yugoslavia before his emigration to the United States. His father had witnessed the horrors of World War II firsthand and had seen the selection process take place at one of the death camps. He watched as prisoners, hopeful to the end, were taken to be executed. The lesson he learned from this?

"It is better to be a Nazi and survive than to be one of those people who are so helpless and naïve that they have no choice but to pray to God that the Nazis are there to deliver them from harm!"[13]

Emil was taught to hate Jews by his father, to hate what his father saw as their weakness and victim mentality. As much as his father hated the Nazis who invaded their country, he hated their helpless and unresisting victims more. Emil went on to emulate this attitude, murdering civilians during raging ethnic strife in his own country. This may be a valuable perspective for understanding the flawed spirituality of people like Nixon, and of the party he represented for so many years.

In the end, Nixon won the election against Voorhis and went on to greater glory in the campaign against Helen Gahagan Douglas, who was the victim of even worse Red-baiting and racial slurs. The wife of actor Melvyn Douglas, a man whose Jewish father was born Hesselberg, Helen Douglas was attacked for the mere fact that she was married to a Jew. (Strictly speaking, Merlyn Douglas was not Jewish; according to the rabbis, Jewish heritage is passed down through the mother's side.) Both she and Nixon were fighting over a US Senate seat in 1950. Douglas, a New Deal Democrat, was a former opera singer and had been an actress on Broadway. Douglas had also appeared at the National Conference on the German Problem, held at the Waldorf-Astoria Hotel in New York City in March 1946. This Conference—arranged by Eleanor Roosevelt—was attended by such anti-Nazi luminaries as Albert Einstein and Henry Morgenthau, Jr. The Conference had targeted Operation Paperclip, demanding an end to Nazi immigration to the United States and a more aggressive prosecution of war criminals.[14]

But there was more to it.

As *Los Angeles Times* political correspondent Ronald Brownstein points out in his *The Power and the Glitter: The Hollywood-Washington Connection,* Helen Douglas had first-hand experience of Nazism. Douglas came from a conservative, Republican background, but was changed by the idealism of F.D. Roosevelt's New Deal and switched parties as early as 1932. An opera singer and sometime film actor (she played the lead in the first film made of the Ryder-Haggard novel, *She*), she was traveling through Europe for a concert tour in 1937. In Salzburg, Prague and Vienna she saw anti-Semitism, Nazism, and fear of the Nazi ideology firsthand.

The experience changed Helen Douglas' life. Against the great upheavals wracking Europe her passion for her career suddenly seemed shortsighted, insular, selfish.... She returned to the United States committed to finding ways to express herself politically. Her husband, who had seen the same dangerous signs while accompanying her on part of the trip, followed suit. In the years leading to the war, both Douglases would devote as much energy to politics as to the movies, becoming pivotal figures in the struggle between liberals and Communists to define the agenda for the emerging Hollywood left.[15]

In June, 1936 the Douglases—along with Gloria Stuart, Frederic March and many others—formed the Hollywood League Against Nazism which later became the Anti-Nazi League for Defense of American Democracy. In 1944, Helen Douglas was elected a Representative from the State of California, and she threw herself wholeheartedly into the work of a political figure and one of the few women in the House. A dedicated anti-Nazi, she could never have been legitimately confused with a Communist or even having Communist sympathies. She frequently voted against the "Hollywood left" in favor of the Marshall Plan, for instance, and against the candidacy of Henry Wallace. But she was an outspoken anti-Nazi and was completely against the importation of Nazi war criminals under Operation Paperclip, and she made her position abundantly clear.

This type of activity was an attack on the heart of the Dulles/Nixon agenda, of course. Although she was as anti-Communist as Nixon, she also took a leaf from the Voorhis book on big business and especially oil business, attacking the oil companies for their rape of southern California. For this reason alone, the Republicans knew she had to be stopped, as they had stopped Voorhis before her. Nixon could not effectively attack her on policy, but that was never his strong point anyway. Instead, he began a vicious smear campaign which portrayed Douglas as a Communist, and a whisper campaign—again by phone—reminding voters that she was married to a Jew. This bugaboo combination of Communist and Jew was precisely that used by the Nazis in their hate campaigns against the rest of the world; all that was missing to make a Heinrich Himmler proud would be a reference to the threat of global Freemasonry.

Nixon—and his anonymous backers—got their way, and he beat Douglas in the 1950 election, thereby winning his seat in the US Senate. At thirty-seven, Nixon was a Senator in Washington and within striking distance of the Presidency.

Victor Lasky, a Nixon crony and political hack who worked for Nixon's campaign and who was friendly with mob fixer Murray Chotiner, wrote a book entitled, with unintended irony, *It Didn't Start With Watergate*, in which he defended Nixon at the expense of the Kennedys and other Democrats. He had a long history of this sort of thing, and had written *JFK: The Man and the Myth* and the equally lugubrious *Robert F. Kennedy: the Myth and the Man*.

The author has to agree with Lasky on one point, and that is that "it" truly didn't start with Watergate at all. Nixon's low cunning not only comprised the manipulation of the electorate in 1946, 1950, 1952, 1960, 1962, 1968 and the bugging of Democratic National Committee headquarters at the Watergate complex in 1972. In fact, it started in 1945 and continued throughout his career; but the crimes for which he was not impeached or held accountable during his life were, if anything, more heinous than even Lasky could imagine, and may have resulted in the loss of thousands of American lives.

Unholy Trinity

In Rome itself, the transit point of the escape routes, a vast amount was done. With its own immense resources, the Church helped many of us to go overseas. In this manner, in quiet and secrecy, the demented victors' mad craving for revenge and retribution could be effectively counteracted.
    —Nazi Ace Colonel Hans Ulrich Rudel, Kufstein 1970[16]

According to Charles Colson, the aide who later turned to God and became a lay minister, Nixon had considered converting to Catholicism before the 1972 election, having come to be convinced that Catholics represented "the real America."
    —Anthony Summers, *The Arrogance of Power*[17]

While much of the story behind the Dulles-Nixon partnership has been sanitized, and sensitive material remains classified to this day, there is enough in the public record concerning Nixon's support of Nazi war criminals to afford us an honest gaze at this aspect of American history. Most Americans have had little exposure to the Byzantine machinations of the postwar émigré community in the United States. Many would be scandalized to learn of American support for men who caused death and atrocity during the war on the side of the Nazis; many more would be outraged to realize that the Catholic Church was a major factor in the escape of fugitive Nazis to countries all over the world. Still others would be confused by the plethora of Eastern Orthodox churches, idiosyncratic priests, spies and double agents, former SS officers, Republican Party flacks, South American political movements, captains of industry, Middle Eastern intelligence operations, multinational corporations and unorthodox banking practices that form the real structure of a network of resurgent fascism, a kind of Nazism *nouveau*, equal in everything but swastika armbands and Furtwaengler conducting *The Ring*. It is impossible to go into all of this in any great detail here; there are a number of books, however, for the interested reader who wants to pursue this story further, such as Christopher Simpson's essential *Blowback*, his *The Splendid Blond Beast*, and the equally important *Unholy Trinity* by Aarons and Loftus. What we will do is give a brief outline of what was going on after the war, and how Nixon and other Republican Party leaders became enmeshed in an unforgiving web of collaboration with the most despicable enemy the Twentieth Century had to offer.

The Nazi Party was a cult. Anyone who believes that the Nuremberg rallies, the speeches by Hitler, Rosenberg, Himmler, Hess and the others, and the swastika itself are all emblems of a traditional political party has not looked too carefully or too deeply at the phenomenon. In fact, with the swastika—a mystical, religious and occult glyph with ancient associations all over the globe—the Nazis were telling the whole world what they were about; it is a sad fact that no one really listened. The nationalist policies of the Third Reich were a manifestation in the mundane world of a philosophy that was transcendent—incorporating race, religion, architecture, astronomy, medicine, war, and politics only as a continuation of war by other means. The Holocaust had no political purpose; the tremendous expense in terms of time, money and personnel to keep the ovens burning had no political or military advantage to the Reich. It was a crusade against a race, a religion and a philosophy that the Reich found abhorrent.

Fascism is the elevation of one's own country above all others, and the elevation of the state above the individual. It is, in essence, an assault on the rest of the world and is more easily sustained if national policy assumes a racial superiority over all other races, coupled with a belief in its own structural superiority: i.e., its economic system, its system of government, perhaps even its geographical location. In countries which enjoy a mix of races, this idea of superiority is more difficult to sustain, since its own citizens have come from other countries and have some—if only sentimental or cultural—allegiances there. In that case, it is important to disregard—officially—any hint of racial superiority and instead focus on economic and political (i.e., ideological) differences. In any event, the concerns of one's own state are of absolute importance on a cosmic level, and the rights and concerns of the citizens of one's own or other countries become negligible. Thus, a foreign policy which undermines the sovereignty of other nations is acceptable.

In the days of Nazi Germany, race and nationalism went hand-in-hand. There was no way to separate the two. All other races were deemed inferior to the pure-blooded German. Attacks on other countries were considered normal and justified. In fact, Germans considered themselves *spiritually* superior to Jews and members of other races. Judeao-Christianity was viewed as a spiritual aberration, a disease that had to be eradicated. If a woman slept with a Jewish man, as an example, she was considered tainted by some sort of mystical Jewish essence and was therefore lost to the race. The Nazis were thus in the midst of a spiritual war of light against darkness, of the Aryan versus the Semite and the Slav, of the German against the Jew, the Arab, the African, the Asian, the Latin. The war was elevated to that of an astral conflict, a cosmological struggle for survival.

With the defeat of Nazi Germany at the end of World War II, fascism did not go away. How could it?

It was strong enough in Italy and Germany (and Austria, and many other countries) to cause tremendous physical dislocation, the murder of millions of civilians, the deaths of millions of combatants, and the redrawing of the map of Europe. It was tantamount to a religious faith, a mystic belief in national superiority and racial purity. It took anti-Semitism to its logical conclusion, redrawing the spiritual and genetic map (in the eyes of the Nazis, the same thing) of Europe as well. A military defeat was not enough to discredit the faith in the eyes of its true believers. In fact, to some it made Nazism even more romantic. The Nuremberg trials were considered a sham and a hoax by the Nazi war criminals fleeing along the rat lines into South America and other havens, a spiteful and vengeful exercise on behalf of the "demented victors," with no moral or ethical message worth taking away, no lesson to be learned. The Allies were preaching to their own choir; the sinners were still plotting in the basement. It would take more than bullets to kill off Nazism and fascism. After all, Christianity itself lived underground for almost three hundred years before it became a state religion.

Thus, in the damp and overheated postwar world, Nazism mutated, virus-like, and became confused with—one could say it "infected"—patriotism. What began as a war of Aryans versus Semites and sub-humans became the West versus the East, Capitalist versus Communist. The Communists were "godless" and therefore evil in a very real moral and spiritual sense. Stories were told of the persecution of religion in Communist nations, such as the Soviet Union and the People's Republic of China. The Catholic Church went underground in these countries; Masses were celebrated in secret. Priests were hunted down and imprisoned, tortured, executed. Membership in any religious organization was grounds for expulsion from the Communist Party, and consequent penalties in terms of housing, wages, education, etc.

The Vatican, therefore, was under attack in Eastern Europe and China. At the same time, its underground network of priests was a potentially valuable intelligence asset. The Church found itself cooperating with Western intelligence services against Communist countries. This meant that, in order to cooperate with the United States Central Intelligence Agency, they had to cooperate with the Nazis. The Gehlen Organization became a creature of the CIA in Europe, and once again the Vatican and the Nazis were in agreement according to both philosophy and tactics. The Vatican ran interference for war criminals escaping to less hostile nations on the one hand, and worked with resuscitated Nazi intelligence organs on the other. The Cold War had started, and every political leader in the West made sure that it was painted in Manichaean terms of Light versus Darkness, of Good versus Evil. After all, the Soviet Union was, according to President Reagan, the "Evil Empire," and not merely a sovereign nation with whom we disagreed on matters of economics, human rights and foreign policy. The Soviet Union was evil; it represented the forces of Satan on earth and had to be destroyed.

To those who believe the author is indulging in hysterical hyperbole, it is only necessary to refer to the speeches made by a long line of postwar Republican presidents and presidential candidates on the issue. Since they can be construed as "spin," however, the skeptical can review the record on support for Nazi individuals and political organizations in the United States by Republican leadership as they girded their loins for battle with the Communists.

(This is not an attack on the Republican Party itself; not every Republican is a closet Nazi, and it is not the intention of the author to suggest this. Probably very few Republicans are even aware of the extent to which their Party has embraced the politics of war criminals in their midst. However, as other authors have pointed out with mountains of documentation and rivers of primary source material, the Republicans seem to have embraced the Nazi underground with much more zeal and commitment than the Democrats, both as individuals and as a Party. There is a reason for this, and as we delve more deeply into America's political subconscious we may reveal it in all its ugliness and satanic glory.)

To understand the degree to which resurgent fascism and refugee Nazism have influenced the political direction of the United States (including its foreign policy), it is necessary to examine the role that Eastern European ethnic groups have played in the postwar years, forming voting blocs on the one hand, and making themselves essential to Western intelligence operations on the other. It is also necessary to examine the political allegiances and philosophies of these groups before they came to the United States. In many cases, these were nationalist organizations that had actively resisted Soviet Communism and, in the process, turned to fascist, extreme right-wing support, adopting anti-Semitism and other racial ideologies from the Nazis. The fact that Eastern Orthodox churches—the dominant religious group in Eastern Europe—are also intensely nationalistic and to a certain extent anti-Semitic (at least, no less than the Catholic Church in that era) made the alliance between Nazism and Orthodoxy inevitable. The Nazis welcomed the political and military support of these militias, even though the Slavs were considered "sub-human" and their religions anathema, and ripe for the ovens one day once the war was over and Nazi hegemony assured. This type of cynicism was comparable to that of Richard Nixon, for instance, whose anti-Semitism did not preclude him from supporting Israel or hiring Henry Kissinger. Power, after all, has its own ideology.

The split between the Eastern Orthodox churches and the Roman Catholic Church took place on July 16, 1054. The then Patriarch of Constantinople, Cerularius, rejected the claim of Pope Leo IX to universal leadership of Christendom. Until that time, all national Christian churches had been autocephalous, i.e., with their own head, or patriarch. There had been no universal ruler to whom all churches owed their allegiance regardless of the country in which they were located. Leo, in an attempt to consolidate political power over all Christian countries, was demanding allegiance from the Greek Patriarch, which would have given him the East. Instead, as a result of Cerularius' refusal to kow-tow to the Pope, he and his entire Church were excommunicated.

Christianity at that time was already geographically and culturally divided. The first important political leader who embraced the Christian faith was the Roman Emperor Constantine, who elevated Christianity to the status of a state religion, while moving the capitol to the ancient city of Byzantium, renamed Constantinople (what is now Istanbul). It retained this status for well over a millennium, throughout the illustrious history of the Byzantine Empire. As political power in the West in the centuries after Constantine, however, switched from Constantinople back to Rome, so did the emphasis on purely "Western" interpretations of Christianity.

Until the Catholic Church became dominant in the West, the religious services of the Church had always been held in local languages. Thus, the Greeks celebrated Mass (called the "Divine Liturgy") in Greek; in Eastern Europe, Greek missionaries Cyril and Methodius developed the Slavonic alphabet and a language called Church Slavonic: a brilliant attempt to provide a unified language for the many disparate ethnicities to be found in what is now Russia, Ukraine, Poland, Hungary, Romania, Czechoslovakia, Serbia, etc. The alphabet of this language was based on the Greek alphabet and called "Kyrillic" after Cyril who invented it. The language itself was a kind of Slavic Esperanto, in which much of the service could be understood by everyone, and all of it by no one! The emphasis on local language (vernacular) celebration of the Church services is a hallmark of Eastern Orthodoxy, and to this day one can experience this spirituality in Greek, Arabic, Serbian, Russian, Ukrainian, and many other languages. The local churches were also permitted to add cultural details of their own, such as the Easter eggs which are always red in Greece but which are multi-colored and fantastically designed in the Eastern European countries, etc. In addition, the leader of the Russian Orthodox Church, for example, is a Patriarch. So also is the leader of the Greek Orthodox Church and all of the various national Orthodox Churches. The Greek Orthodox Patriarch is considered "first among equals" but the emphasis is on "equals." Each national church conducts its own affairs internally, without reference to the "spiritual headquarters" in Greece. Thus, Eastern Orthodoxy was always nationalistic, from the very beginning, and this provided a potential recruiting ground for more extreme forms of nationalistic political expression, such as Nazism.

By contrast, Roman Catholicism was ... well, just that. *Roman* Catholicism. The official language was Latin, no matter in what country one found oneself. And the leader was the Pope, in Rome. Whereas Eastern Orthodoxy was a "distributed system" of leadership and ritual, Roman Catholicism was strictly hierarchical, with the Pope at the top, followed by cardinals and then bishops, down to priests and the faithful. In 800 A.D., when Charlemagne proclaimed himself Emperor of the "Holy Roman Empire," the handwriting was on the wall. And, as successive Muslim invasions of Turkey and Eastern Europe weakened the Byzantine Empire, the political power of the Eastern Church in Europe also waned.

The Byzantine Empire fell to Sultan Mohammed II in 1453. Oddly, though, the Sultan made the Greek Orthodox patriarch the *ethnarch* of all the Greeks in the Ottoman empire, in effect making him a civil authority as well as a religious one. This enabled the survival—if not the flourishing growth—of Greek Orthodoxy. Possibly the Sultan thought of using the Eastern Orthodox churches as a tool against his ultimate enemy, the Holy Roman Empire. After all, the Eastern Orthodox Churches had suffered from invading Catholic armies during the Crusades, which had witnessed the sacking of Constantinople, the burning of Orthodox churches and the murder of Orthodox priests: a campaign as ruthless as that against the Muslim enemies in the Holy Land; and thus the Sultan could make a case that the sympathies of the Orthodox should rest with the Ottomans. It would not be the last time the Eastern Orthodox churches were politically manipulated this way.

The Orthodox churches are called "Orthodox" because they follow the form of Christianity as it was practiced since early times. The Divine Liturgy of St. John Chrysostom is about three hours in length, no matter in which language it is celebrated. The Catholic Mass is an abbreviated form of this same Liturgy, cut down to about forty-five minutes. There are many other differences, including the strange pre-Liturgy ritual in which the crucifixion of Christ is re-enacted with loaves of bread and wine, and a golden knife: a somewhat Gnostic survival perhaps reflective of the Church's eastern origins.

Catholicism, on the other hand, modified its rituals considerably through the years. Whereas Eastern Orthodoxy seems frozen in time circa 1000 A.D., the Roman Catholic Church has undergone many transformations and has constantly evolved since the break with Orthodoxy. Ironically, however, the changes they have made—and contemplated—would bring the Church back to where the Eastern Orthodox already exist. The Vatican II decision to permit local churches to celebrate Mass in the local dialects—considered a major concession at the time—is merely what the Orthodox have been doing since the beginning. The Orthodox also have a married priesthood (which the Catholics also had for hundreds of years), and a form of confession in which priest and penitent face each other rather than in a confessional box, among many other practices that would be considered modern and "enlightened" today.

The Catholic Church, in an effort to attract Orthodox laity to the Papal fold, accepted what is known as Uniate or Eastern Rite Catholics. In this hybrid form of Catholicism, the beliefs of the people—including the all-important allegiance to the Roman Pope—are Catholic. The rituals, however, are Eastern Orthodox. Thus, with the Uniates, the Church enjoys the allegiance of some Eastern European and Middle Eastern Christians while the latter can keep the rituals with which they are the most familiar. Using this method, the Church extends its political power into these otherwise impenetrable countries. This became an important issue during World War II, when the Uniates were utilized as a kind of Vatican intelligence network against the Reds.

The groups most openly hostile to Communism and most open to Nazi support were Ukrainian, Croatian, Romanian, and Hungarian nationalists. The Hungarians and Croatians were, by and large, Roman Catholic and received tremendous support from the Catholic Church both in their actions against Soviet Communism as well as in intelligence operations and political action in support of Intermarium and other pan-Slavic cabals, support that would eventually earn these Nazi and pro-Nazi criminals safe haven in North and South America. The Ukrainians and Romanians were largely Eastern Orthodox or Eastern-Rite (Uniate) Catholics. The Russian Orthodox churches themselves were divided between those who supported the Moscow Patriarchate (largely seen, and with reason, to be an instrument of the Soviet government) and those whose bishops fled Russia at the time of the 1917 revolution and who wished to distance themselves from any dominance by the Moscow hierarchy (a group of bishops known, loosely, as the Synod or more formally as the Russian Orthodox Church Outside Russia or ROCOR). Whereas this latter policy seemed reasonable from a political perspective, it raised doubts about the canonicity (ecclesiastical legality) of these break-away groups, a problem that need not concern us here at the moment, but which has caused many dislocations of those Eastern churches based in the United States and Canada, especially after the fall of Soviet Communism. In New York City, where the two Russian churches have their American headquarters, the Moscow Patriarchate is known to insiders as "Ninety-Eighth Street" and ROCOR is known as "Ninety-Third Street," due to the locations of their respective cathedrals.

In addition, groups like the Serbian Orthodox churches were actively suppressed by the Croatian Catholics operating in what would become Yugoslavia, their parishioners forced to convert to Catholicism or be killed, and sometimes both. Testimony has come down to us of entire Serbian Orthodox congregations being forced through a conversion ceremony in a Croatian Catholic church, and then machine-gunned outside the church's walls moments later. Catholic priests and monks were responsible for hideous atrocities in Serbia and Croatia during the war; in one case, a Franciscan priest was enthusiastically in charge of a concentration camp. Croatian Catholics also perpetrated gross atrocities against the indigenous Jewish populations of Croatia under the banner of the dread Ustasch, the rabidly pro-Nazi political and military organization of World War II Croatia. It would be the Ustasch that would benefit greatly from Vatican support both during and after the war, as Father

Draganovic ensured that his countrymen would never stand trial for the war crimes for which they had been indicted, but would instead flee to the four corners of the earth, where they would take up their banners again.

Further, countries such as Slovakia—which were mostly Roman Catholic—actively supported Hitler during the war. In Slovakia's case, Hitler promised the people independence from the Czechs, with whom they had been artificially mated after the end of World War I. The Slovak leader during the war was Monsignor Tiso, a pro-Nazi Catholic prelate who was responsible for pogroms against the Jews in his own country.

In the Ukraine, the situation was, if anything, even more complex. Two rival religious institutions vied for the loyalty of Ukrainian Christians: the Ukrainian Orthodox Church and the Ukrainian Uniates. In both cases, the Nazis used their hatred of Soviet Communism to enlist their aid as militia against Russia: providing training, uniforms, weapons and leadership, just as they did for the Croatian Ustasch and the Romanian Iron Guard. The Nazis effectively unleashed the violence and rage against the Russians that had been building since the Revolution, when the Soviets had made every attempt to eradicate both the religion and the culture of the indigenous peoples of the region. They also unleashed Ukrainian anti-Semitism, and they did all this using the collaboration of the Vatican.

> ...the debacle had been predominantly the responsibility of the tsar, his ministers, the whole state apparatus, and their policies over many years, which had Russia involved in a war for which it was not prepared and that it could not win. And so the search got under way, as it did in Germany one year later, for the "sinister forces," the "hidden hand," that had administered the "stab in the back" that had led to the catastrophe.
> —Walter Laqueur, *Black Hundred: The Rise of the Extreme Right in Russia*[18]

By early 1943, virtually every one of the 800,000 Ukrainian Jews had been killed by the Ukrainian Nazis. Members of the Ukrainian SS—largely composed of Uniate Christians who owed their spiritual allegiance to Rome—were enthusiastic in their support of the Final Solution; the Nazis had promised to overlook both their religion and their race in order to enlist their aid against their common enemies: Communists and Jews. Under other circumstances, being both Christian and Slav was enough to be considered sub-human and unworthy of the SS uniform. Forty thousand Ukrainians volunteered for duty in the specially-created SS Galicia Division—twice the number required, overwhelming the SS leadership. In the end twenty thousand were accepted, trained, and armed. Then, as the troops passed by in review, Archbishop Szepticky blessed the SS Division, urging them to glory.

They would follow in the footsteps of the Organisation of Ukrainian Nationalists (OUN) under Stephen Bandera and Yaroslav Stetsko. The OUN organized the pogrom of the Jews of Lvov, where six thousand were murdered in three days and three nights of savagery in 1941. Stetsko would later become president of the Anti-Bolshevik Bloc of Nations (ABN), a merger of the OUN and White Russian Nazis, with Mikolai Abramtchik (the Byelorussian Nazi Minister of Intelligence) as vice president, along with war criminal Stanislav Stankievich and many other renegade Nazi leaders. The ABN was being run by British Intelligence, under the supervision of Kim Philby; Philby would later be revealed as a double agent, working in reality for Soviet intelligence, which had penetrated the ethnic anti-Communist émigré groups since the earliest days of the Revolution.

And let us not forget the Croatians.

Let us look at the example of Bishop Ivan Saric, known as the Hangman of Sarajevo, whose slaughter of Croatian Serbs was legendary; or Father Josip Bujanovic, who—as the Ustaschi leader of Gospic—presided over the massacre of Serbian Orthodox peasants, before escaping to Australia at the end of the war, courtesy of the Vatican rat lines. Or Father Vilim Cecelja, a lieutenant colonel in the Ustaschi militia who was named war criminal number 7103 by the Yugoslav government, but who also emigrated to Australia, where he became important in the creation of Nazi and Ustaschi cells. Or Father Dragutin Kamber, the concentration camp commandant of Doboj, who slaughtered Serbian Orthodox priests and incited the wholesale massacre of Serbs in Bosnia.

Thus, the religious and political tapestries of these Eastern European countries are varied and their histories complex and interrelated to a great degree. Even Ukraine's status was always a matter for debate, since Ukraine was considered to be part of Russia from early times, though large parts of Ukraine had been annexed by Poland, thus causing some political wrestling over the issue of the Ukrainian Waffen SS Division "Galicia." Were the Ukrainians captured at the end of the war, serving in German uniforms under German officers with German training really Ukrainians and therefore Russians to be deported back to the motherland, or were they in reality Polish citizens and therefore not part of the Yalta agreement which would have surrendered them to the Soviets?

Regardless, the SS Galicia Division was responsible for pogroms and atrocities the equal of any other SS division during the war, and it was only due to a complicated arrangement between the Catholic Church on the one hand and Western intelligence agencies on the other that they were given over to the protection of the British via General Pavlo Shandruk, who had commanded the SS Galicia Division in its final months. Shandruk emigrated to the United States after the war, and was buried in the cemetery adjacent to Ukrainian Orthodox Church headquarters in Bound Brook, New Jersey … as a war hero.

Many fleeing Ukrainian Catholics had switched allegiance to the more fiercely nationalistic Ukrainian Orthodox Church, and it was this same church that consecrated renegade Romanian Iron Guard commandant and instigator of the 1941 pogrom of Bucharest, Valerian Trifa, as a Bishop of the Romanian Orthodox Church in America in 1952—even though he had no qualifications whatsoever as a bishop, had never been a priest or even an altar boy, and had no theological training at all. Trifa went on to create cells of Romanian Nazi "priests" under church cover throughout North America and in other countries, right up to his eventual deportation from the US in 1984.

When the Eisenhower-Nixon campaign of 1952 was successful in depicting the Democrats as "soft on Communism," it attracted the political and financial support of these émigré groups all across the country. A special "Ethnic Division" was created at campaign headquarters to ensure that the Ukrainian, Romanian, Slovak, Croatian, etc. vote was turned out in support of the former World War II Commander-in-Chief of Allied forces in Europe and his Red-baiting, anti-Semitic vice-presidential candidate. The Republicans had cornered the market on Eastern European hatred of Communism, and had promised a vigorous campaign to win back the motherlands from Soviet domination.

It is vitally important to understand that this was not a post-World War II aberration. This was *policy* and had been in place since the *first* World War, which is when the Dulles brothers cut their eye teeth on foreign affairs and found themselves agitating for a strong postwar Germany to stand as a buffer state against the Bolshevik Revolution that had taken power in Moscow and assassinated the royal family of Nicholas and Alexandra, and which was then struggling with *volkisch* groups such as the *Thule Gesellschaft* for dominance in Germany. Allen Dulles was already in an intelligence position in Switzerland during the *first* World War, developing the contacts and networks he would need as the years went by. John Foster Dulles was already in the State Department during World War I. Their uncle, Robert Lansing, was President Woodrow Wilson's Secretary of State, an ultra-conservative when it came to assigning blame for war crimes in World War I, who insisted that individual countries be responsible for prosecuting their own war crimes; from Lansing's point of view, the right people to judge what was and was not a war crime—what was and was not necessary for the preservation of the state—was the military leadership of each individual nation! In other words, the fox should guard the hen house. He objected to the idea of atrocities and "crimes against humanity"; it smacked too much of internationalism, which he opposed. Thus, if the German Army had committed atrocities then let the German Army prosecute their own troops. It should be an internal matter, of no concern to other nations.

Thus, Allen Dulles, John Foster Dulles, and their uncle Robert Lansing had already formulated a geopolitical strategy that they would implement not only at the end of World War I, but consistently through the postwar years, through World War II and beyond. It involved strengthening Germany as a guardian against the spread of European Bolshevism and Communism, and the creation of a *cordon sanitaire* composed of Eastern European countries to hold back Russian expansionism. The Dulles brothers actively courted Nazi officials in the 1930s—as did such American concerns as the Ford Motor Company and IBM—with no scruples about the type of institutionalized anti-Semitism that Hitler and his colleagues were planning for Germany and the Occupied Territories. While the Democratic president, Franklin D. Roosevelt, saw Nazism as an evil that had to be confronted and covertly plotted ways to bring America into the war against Hitler, the Republicans in Congress were talking about isolationism and appeasement: the continuing evolution of the Dulles strategy that had begun in 1917.

Thus, when, as we shall see, Nixon began taking bribes from the Greek military junta and ran interference to get President Johnson's peace initiative with Vietnam scuttled in time for the 1968 election, it was business as usual for the Republican Party. When he commanded that the socialist Allende regime in Chile be overthrown, and provided the financial support to the truckers' strike necessary to cripple Chile's economy and create instability that would pave the way for General Pinochet and his junta, it was business as usual once again.

In the case of the Greek military junta, we can assume that the primary motive was to get as much funding as possible for Nixon's election campaign; in other words, perhaps it was not ideologically motivated. In the case of Vietnam, we can assume that it was simply more important to Nixon to win the election than to halt the bombing and save human life; in other words, his tactics were not motivated by any desire to crush the North Vietnamese Communist forces but once again were purely to win an election. But when we discuss the overthrow of Allende's regime—in 1973 after Nixon had been twice-elected and thus could go no further politically—then we have to assume that ideology was the only motivating factor.

It does no good to give the benefit of a doubt in one case or even two cases when the overwhelming majority of instances of support for right-wing dictatorships had no other intrinsic value to Nixon or the Republicans in general except to promote a way of life, a political philosophy that was more allied to a kind of misguided German Romanticism—the icily ethereal fascist and Nazi ideal—than it was to a purely economic or pragmatic political policy. Like the Holocaust itself, which had no military value to the Reich and which diverted vital resources unnecessarily during the height of the war, the Republican policy of support for fascists, Nazis, war criminals, and neo-Nazis was (and is) a *mission*. When we embrace men who have committed unutterable atrocities and shake the hands of men that have been bloodied with the gore of Jews, of women and children, of Muslims, of Orthodox Christians, of Slavs, of homosexuals, of Gypsies, then we have bartered the soul of the nation for a handful of votes, a few million dollars, and a dubious place in history.

Was it worth it? Are we truly any safer now than we were at the end of World War II?

As for the public record, the following chronology may serve as evidence of the existence of a pro-Nazi cabal lurking in America's corridors of power.

Item: 1945. Operation Overcast and Operation Paperclip bring hundreds, some say thousands, of Nazi scientists (many of them—such as General Walter Dornberger, the future boss of Michael Paine at Bell Aerospace—considered war criminals by the Nuremberg Commission as well as by the rest of the world) to the United States to assist in the space program, much against the express wishes of Democratic President Harry Truman. Other Nazis, including an entire division of Ukrainian Waffen SS, are assisted out of Europe and into safe havens in North America, South America, Australasia, and the Middle East by the US State Department, British Intelligence, French Intelligence and the Vatican. This operation will be aided, abetted and covered up by the CIA in the post-war years, and especially beginning in 1953, when Allen Dulles becomes CIA Director. Dulles' Chief of Counter Intelligence, James Jesus Angleton (later the CIA's Vatican liaison), and Frank Wisner are particularly involved, along with thousands of former Nazi "freedom fighters." What is variously known as *Die Spinne, Die Kamaradenwerke*, and *ODESSA* is born, but it is in reality even more of a Vatican operation than an organization of former SS officers, who are its primary beneficiaries.

In 1945, Dulles—along with his OSS agent Hans Bernd Gisevius, a former Gestapo officer—was accused by the US Treasury Department of laundering Nazi funds from Hungary into Switzerland (where Dulles was based). The investigation was dropped when the US State Department claimed jurisdiction. Gisevius himself was working for the massive intelligence operation being run by a White Russian, General Turkul, and known as the Black Orchestra, a Vatican-linked Nazi intelligence network that was in reality a miracle of Soviet penetration into the Western intelligence services, something that Dulles would not have known at the time. Gisevius, from his position with the Reichsbank, also had excellent connections in the Nazi intelligence services and had been used by Dulles to communicate with Admiral Canaris of the Abwehr during the war.[19]

Richard Nixon was brought in on the money laundering secret by Allen Dulles in 1945 or early 1946, of which the Treasury Department investigation had only revealed a small portion. Nixon, in examining captured German documents as a Navy officer after the war, is presumed to have come across evidence of this money laundering effort, and of other links between German industrial and banking firms, OSS officers, and Dulles in particular. This was at the same time as the US Treasury Department investigation, so it is reasonable to assume that Nixon uncovered elements of a paper trail that would implicate such firms as Chase Bank, Morgan Bank, ITT and other companies that have since been revealed to have operated freely in Nazi territory, and often with

Nazis on the local board of directors (such as Nazi Intelligence chief Walter Schellenberg, who kept his board position with ITT throughout the war). Dulles, in return, promised to assist Nixon in his California congressional campaign if he buried the data. A life-long partnership was born.

In this context, it is worthwhile to note the research of Charles Higham who, in his *American Swastika*, speaks of captured SS documentation which clearly shows that Dulles gave voice to extreme anti-Semitic views in several conversations with Max von Hohenlohe, a Nazi agent and intimate of Schellenberg, who himself was acting on instructions from SS leader Heinrich Himmler. (Higham's research was further corroborated by Christopher Simpson in *The Splendid Blond Beast*.) Hohenlohe had first cleared Dulles' credentials with the Spanish Ambassador to the Vatican, who proclaimed Dulles reliable.[20]

Dulles met with Hohenlohe in Geneva in January 1943 and is recorded—by the SS, remember, in their documents—as stating that in Europe "there must be no toleration of a return of the Jewish power positions" (Higham's paraphrasing) and that "the Americans were only continuing the war to get rid of the Jews and that there were people in America who were intending to send the Jews to Africa."[21] We may choose to give Dulles the benefit of a doubt here and assume that, if these remarks are correct, he was only trying to win the cooperation of the anti-Hitler Nazis with whom he was negotiating. This is basically what Simpson is saying. Dulles told Hohenlohe that the Allies would not accept Hitler as a leader, but that he was more interested in creating a buffer zone between Russia and the rest of Europe, and that a reconstructed, postwar Germany was central to the scheme. The extermination of the Jews was a fringe benefit. Even the eventual resolution of Czechoslovakia was immaterial to the Allies. In other words, the key to this geopolitical problem was anti-Communism, which was code for Russia. The Allies, according to Dulles, had no interest in the eventual disposition of European Jewry, understanding that Europe would not tolerate a "return of the Jewish power positions." The Nazis could do as they liked.

But were such anti-Semitic remarks necessary in order to win the cooperation of men like intelligence chief Schellenberg and Himmler, on whose behalf Hohenlohe was meeting Dulles? By accepting Himmler as a future leader of Germany, Dulles had already played any cards he needed. He could have saved countless lives if he had made it clear to the Nazis that the United States was firmly against the Holocaust, thus threatening Himmler's future career if he persisted in genocide. He would have at least made Himmler and Schellenberg stop and think and perhaps slow down the ongoing mass murder, perhaps using it as a bargaining chip if nothing else. By giving tacit approval to Himmler for the Holocaust—indeed, by saying that America was only continuing the war to collaborate (there is no other word) in Hitler's extinction of the Jews—he gave the green light to the SS to go ahead with the Final Solution.

Dulles had a wide and deep circle of business contacts, friends, and personal allies in Europe long before the war began. His business interests included Schroeders Bank, of which he was a director, and his law firm represented many other German organizations both before and during the war. He had even met Hohenlohe in the years before the war. Was it really necessary to give voice to such loathsome anti-Semitic sentiments? Or was it, perhaps, a reflection of Allen Dulles' genuine feelings in the matter, feelings that would influence decades of American intelligence activity and possibly open up the CIA to foreign penetration?

Further, were the records of these conversations with Dulles among the captured German documents that fell under Nixon's jaundiced eye during those sensitive postwar months when Operation Paperclip was being openly condemned by the Democrats? If so, it is clear why Dulles would have been desperate to have them "deep sixed" and to enlist Nixon's aid in doing so. A few phone calls from Dulles to business partners on the East Coast would have been enough to get the young lawyer's career off on the right track.

Later, the World Commerce Corporation is formed, ostensibly to "rebuild German-South American trade networks."[22] The directors are Sir William Stephenson ("Intrepid" of British intelligence fame) and General William Donovan, the creator and leader of the OSS. Allen Dulles served as counsel for the corporation, along with Frank Wisner. Both of these men would, of course, become much better known in their positions at the CIA. It is only one of many fronts for American intelligence activities that use former Nazis—many of them accused war criminals—in important leadership positions. These will include the Anti-Bolshevik Bloc of Nations (ABN), the World Anti-Communist League (WACL), of which US Army General and self-professed "black" psychological warfare expert John Singlaub of Iran-Contra fame was director, and many others. The Republicans were regrouping the Nazis: hiding them, recruiting them, using their networks and contacts, giving them visas and citizenship, hailing them as patriots. And pointing them at Russia.

Item: 1946. September 29. Nikolae Malaxa, Romanian Nazi financier and industrialist, arrives in New York as part of an official Romanian trade mission ... and doesn't leave.

Item: 1946. November. Nixon's attack on Jerry Voorhis characterizes him as a Communist and his campaign uses anti-Semitic smears, saying that Voorhis is a tool of "subversive Jews." Nixon is financed from a mysterious East Coast cabal of oil industry executives and industrial tycoons on the one hand (via Dulles), and by organized crime figures around Meyer Lansky and Mickey Cohen on the other (via Murray Chotiner). Nixon wins the election.

For those mindful of events discussed in *The Nine*, this is the same year—and the same place, Pasadena—where Jack Parsons and L. Ron Hubbard had conducted the occult operation known as the Babalon Working. It was at the California Republican Assembly (CRA) in Pasadena in 1946 that Richard

Nixon was selected to run against Voorhis. The President of the CRA at that time was Meyer Lansky's "mouthpiece," Murray Chotiner. For those really titillated by bizarre linkages, Pat Nixon's birth name was Thelma. The FBI, in investigating the Parsons occult lodge in Pasadena, had mistakenly called it the "Order of Thelma." (Was Pat Nixon ... Babalon!?!)

Item: 1947. The CIA is created, and organizes anti-Soviet intelligence networks in Western and Eastern Europe utilizing former Nazis under Third Reich intelligence chief General Reinhard Gehlen. This will become known as the Gehlen Org, and forms the backbone of anti-Soviet CIA operations in Europe, coordinating its efforts with Vatican officials friendly to the CIA. It will be years before it is known how deeply this operation was penetrated by Soviet intelligence, due in part to the cabal of Soviet agents within British Intelligence, including Kim Philby (the "third man"), Guy Burgess, Donald MacLean and Anthony Blunt. Nixon and Dulles tour Europe together, Dulles showing Nixon the importance of holding the line against Communism using any means necessary, including the use of "Freedom Fighters" taken from the ranks of pro-fascist organizations in Eastern and Central Europe, and led by former Nazis and SS officers.

Item: 1948. Prior to the November elections, Dulles—in Operation Bloodstone—authorizes his deputy Frank Wisner to maintain the Vatican's rat lines of escaping Nazi fugitives and "freedom fighters" using false paperwork to hoodwink Immigration officials.

Item: 1948. There is an attack on Alger Hiss, a suspected Communist in the State Department. Nixon, the youngest member of the House Un-American Activities Committee (HUAC) is given confidential information on Hiss by Dulles as well as by the FBI, via Republican presidential hopeful Thomas Dewey. A key figure is Catholic priest Father John Cronin, who had reported to the FBI on Communist penetration of American labor unions during the War. Cronin receives information on Hiss from the FBI and then leaks it to Nixon. One of the HUAC investigators on the Hiss case is FBI agent Lou Russell, who would become involved in the Watergate break-in more than twenty years later.[23] The CIA had known of Hiss for years, and had once considered him for a position as general counsel with the Agency until they came up with information linking him to Communist activities in the United States. Dulles and former OSS chief William Donovan trade information on Hiss, and then leak it to Congressman Nixon, thereby ensuring that Nixon's political star will rise.

Item: 1948. November. Republican candidate Thomas Dewey does not win the US presidential election, much to the dismay of Dulles and the other intelligence officers working the Nazi rat lines and building Nazi intelligence networks in Europe. Truman remains in power, and remains a problem, as he is not in agreement with covert efforts to save Nazi war criminals. Nixon also remains in power, winning reelection as Congressman.

Item: 1949. Cardinal Mindszenty's show-trial is televised, in which the Roman Catholic prelate robotically confesses to the Hungarian Communist regime's outlandish charges against him, leading the CIA to opine that "some unknown force" is compelling him to act this way, the result of some mysterious Russian interrogation technique.[24]

Item: 1949. Wisner's Nazis begin arriving in the United States. Some find work as broadcasters at Radio Liberty and the Voice of America, both fronts for CIA activity and black propaganda.

Item: 1950. February. Wheeling, West Virginia. Senator Joseph McCarthy makes his famous speech claiming Communist penetration of the State Department, using lines lifted verbatim from a previous Nixon speech on Alger Hiss.

Item: 1950. June. The Korean War begins. Nixon's senatorial campaign against Helen Gahagan Douglas uses the same Red-baiting and anti-Semitic tactics as in the Voorhis race, and he keeps referring to her husband's birth name of Hesselberg as an attempt to remind voters that she is married to a Jew. Nixon wins the election and enters the US Senate.

Item: 1950. July 19. Viorel Trifa arrives in New York. Trifa had been commandant of the Romanian Iron Guard student movement and responsible for the January 1941 attempted coup and resulting pogrom in the Jewish quarter of Bucharest, in which one thousand Jews were killed, including more than two hundred who were taken to a slaughterhouse and butchered in a grim parody of koshering. During the pogrom, Trifa himself visited the cells where Jews were being held and murdered them personally. He was a member of the Iron Guard General Staff, along with only two others. He was tried and sentenced *in absentia* by the Romanian government, but was living in protection at the German Embassy in Bucharest. At war's end, Trifa sought asylum in Italy and obtained a position as a history teacher in a Catholic college. In 1950, he manages to emigrate to the United States by disguising his Nazi past.[25] He will take over the Romanian Orthodox Church in the United States by force,[26] become an Archbishop, and in 1955 open a session of the US Congress by invitation of Vice President Richard Nixon.

Item: 1951. Soviet moles in British intelligence, Burgess and MacLean, defect. Kim Philby, the "third man," is recalled from his post in the United States. Soviet penetration of Dulles' espionage network of former Nazis is in danger of being exposed, but Dulles remains oblivious.

Item: 1951. Nixon introduces a private bill to allow Nikolae Malaxa to stay in the United States. Malaxa is a Romanian émigré and financier of the Iron Guard, and hence of Trifa's pogroms against the Jews in which thousands were tortured and murdered. Malaxa had been a business partner of Hermann Goering, the Nazi Reichsmarschall, and his factories "integrated" with Germany's during the war. The arms supplied to the Iron Guard came from Malaxa's factories. Malaxa then hired the Nixon law firm in Whittier, California to represent him, and funneled (illegally) $100,000 to the Nixon campaign fund.[27]

Malaxa is allowed to remain in the United States. Other beneficiaries of Malaxa's business included the law firm of Sullivan and Cromwell (the law firm of the Dulles brothers), the law firm of Pehle and Loesser (John Pehle, of the Treasury Department, had frozen Malaxa's assets during the war), and former US Immigration commissioner Ugo Carusi, whom Malaxa hired, as well as a former OSS officer stationed in Romania, Grady McClaussen, with whom Malaxa had other business dealings and signed contracts.[28]

Item: 1952. July 4. Viorel (now "Valerian") Trifa takes the Romanian Orthodox Church by force, using a team of former Iron Guardists in a violent assault on church headquarters in Grass Lakes, Michigan. Trifa, now calling himself a bishop, had never even been ordained a priest; he is thus the epitome of the "wandering bishop," and his consecration is performed by bishop of the Ukrainian Orthodox Church, Ioan ("John") Teodorovich, who himself fled Soviet secret police in the Ukraine and came to the United States in 1924 to organize the Ukrainian Orthodox Church. (While the history of the Ukrainian churches—as well as Ukrainian history itself—is complex and beyond the scope of this work, it suffices to say that many pro-Nazi Ukrainian nationalists are considered heroes to this church, and some are even buried in the Church's cemetery in New Jersey, including one of the organizers of the rescue of the SS Galician Division, General Pavlo Shandruk.) In his career as Romanian Archbishop, Trifa will bring many more Iron Guardists into the United States and ordain them as priests, even though they have had no theological or religious training at all. Instead, under Church "cover," they establish Iron Guard operations in the United States, South America and Europe.

Item: 1952. The Republican campaign against the Democrats in the presidential elections includes a call for the liberation of Eastern Europe: those countries that had become "satellites" of the Soviet Union or which had been invaded and occupied by the Russians, such as the Baltic states of Latvia, Lithuania and Estonia, as well as Poland, Hungary, Romania, Bulgaria, Albania, Yugoslavia, and Czechoslovakia, in addition to the Ukraine and Belarus.

The Republican Party at this time creates its "Ethnic Division" to handle concerns of these minorities in the United States and to bring out the ethnic, i.e., Eastern and Central European, vote. It is also a way to earn campaign contributions from wealthy donors who have a vested interest in keeping up American pressure on the "captive nations." Many of these émigrés had been Nazis in their native lands, members of the Romanian Iron Cross and the Hungarian Arrow Sword, for instance. They go on to achieve leadership positions within the Ethnic Division and in other groups formed in the 1950s in Europe and the United States to combat Communism. The Republican ticket of Eisenhower and Nixon wins the election with Nixon campaigning for Joe McCarthy as well. John Foster Dulles is named Secretary of State; his brother Allen Dulles becomes Director of the CIA.

Item: 1954. Nikolae Malaxa meets with Otto Skorzeny and Juan Peron in Buenos Aires, Argentina, according to CIA documents.[29] Skorzeny—the famed Nazi commando—has eluded a Nuremberg indictment and, as an international arms dealer, is now running an informal worldwide SS underground operation. Juan Peron, of course, is the President of Argentina and a supporter of Italian and German fascism. Most escaping Nazis wind up in Argentina at some point during their exile, and Peron profits financially as well as politically from the arrangement. Skorzeny is based in Franco's Madrid, where he oversees a resurgent Nazi renaissance. The other Iron Guard leaders are still active at this time, soliciting funds from Romanian exiles worldwide and publishing Guardist newspapers.

Malaxa, Trifa and others are eventually implicated, but no action will be taken against them except for sporadic attempts to deport Malaxa and Trifa, which fail due to the interference of Vice President Nixon and other Republican leaders.

OCTOBER SURPRISE

We've just seen some very terrible forces unleashed. Something bad is going to come of this.
—Richard Nixon in 1968, speaking of Robert Kennedy's declaration as a Presidential candidate [30]

Most people remember the term "October Surprise" as being linked to a purported deal between the Republican Party and the elements holding American hostages in Iran. The year was 1980, and forces loyal to the Ayatollah Khomeini had taken the American Embassy in Teheran the previous year and were holding fifty-two Americans prisoner. A deal with the Carter administration which would have had the hostages released before the end of the year suddenly went awry; some witnesses came forward, stating that George Bush, Sr. had asked the Iranians to hold the hostages for a few more weeks until after the November election, to ensure the victory at the polls of the Reagan-Bush ticket. This was in return for certain concessions. Carter, who believed he could have had a deal with the Iranians, suddenly found himself without one. The American electorate, tired of the long ordeal and the humiliation of the first American rescue attempt which foundered in the desert, elected Reagan, and the rest is history. The hostages were released on the day of Reagan's inauguration.

What most Americans do not know, however, is that this was not the first time American lives had been bartered for power. In an earlier October, it had cost many thousands of Vietnamese lives as well. As revealed in the Anthony Summers work on Nixon mentioned previously, Richard Nixon had performed the same deplorable maneuver in a desperate attempt to ruin upcoming peace talks, arranged by outgoing President Lyndon B. Johnson. It was in the final weeks of the 1968 election and could have been the template for the actions of 1980.

Although confirmation of this event comes from various, well-informed and well-placed sources, perhaps the most damning revelation comes from the woman who helped arrange the deception: Anna Chennault, the Chinese-born wife (and widow) of Claire Chennault, the commander of the famous Flying Tigers of World War II. Mrs. Chennault was used as the go-between in a deal that involved Nixon, John Mitchell, South Vietnamese Ambassador to the United States Bui Dem and, ultimately, South Vietnamese President Thieu. The deal was simple: torpedo Johnson's peace initiative and Nixon (once elected) would prop up Thieu's regime with guns and money and a more aggressive stance against the North. Had Thieu gone to the peace table with Johnson, it is not certain that he would have left with anything more substantial than an uneasy truce and a Demilitarized Zone à la North and South Korea.

It would have meant peace, it would have meant the end of war and atrocity and the suffering of civilian and soldier alike, but that is obviously not what either Nixon or Thieu had in mind. Thieu agreed, and in the eleventh hour, only days before the election, he announced that he would not be a party to the peace initiative for various reasons. Nixon beat Vice President Humphrey at the polls, and the war in Vietnam continued for American forces for five more years, with the deaths of thousands of American troops and hundreds of thousands of Vietnamese casualties. Saigon finally fell over two years later, on April 30, 1975: *Walpurgisnacht*, and the thirtieth anniversary of Hitler's suicide; a day heavy with sinister correspondences.

That was not all, however.

Once he had won the election, betraying America in the process, he then proceeded to betray Thieu. President Johnson had discovered what Nixon was up to in the last hours of the campaign but was afraid of exposing it until he had concrete proof in hand. When he did, it was after the election and Nixon's narrow victory. He then forced Nixon to support a peace initiative in the remaining days of the Johnson administration, lest Johnson himself blow the whistle on what Nixon had been doing. Nixon, fearing what the exposure of his machinations would do, accepted the terms. He then asked Mrs. Chennault to go back to Thieu and press him to agree to Johnson's peace initiative. Chennault was furious, of course, and the whole affair was in danger of falling apart, but Chennault retired behind closed doors and refused to speak to the press or to expose her role in the affair until many years later; relevant FBI documents became declassified in 1999, and the story slowly leaked out anyway.[31]

Nixon's program in Vietnam did go on, however, regardless of the empty posturing for peace. Hundreds of American soldiers died while Nixon was running interference in October and November of 1968; tens of thousands more would die before America's role in the war was over. Hundreds of thousands of Vietnamese soldiers and civilians would also die. All of this was defended by Henry Kissinger, who believed that Nixon's "constituency" supported the war and would abandon him if Nixon worked too hard for peace. In other words, Nixon's domestic political future outweighed any consideration of the cost of life. Nixon knew the war was not winnable; Kissinger knew it. Like something out of *The Seventh Seal*, they coldly decided to use it as a chess piece in a cynical gambit that had nothing to do with the war, but everything to do with winning. Yet, the Vietnam affair was only one element of the Nixon "game plan" in 1968. The second phase involved supporting yet another corrupt military government.

At the same time as Nixon was jockeying for position against Johnson on Vietnam, he was also cutting a deal with the Greek military junta, and illegally accepting huge cash contributions from the generals. This is also covered in detail in Summers' book, and it deserves summarizing here.[32]

Only the year before, in 1967, the generals took over Greece and turned it into a police state overnight. Their reign was dramatized in the Costa-Gavras film *Z*, which boasted a memorable score by Mikis Theodorakis, who had to compose the music in secret to avoid being arrested ... or worse. One of the strangest episodes of the Nixon campaign was the selection of Maryland Governor Spiro Agnew as his running mate; George Bush had been put forth as a logical vice president, but Nixon stunned the convention by choosing the Greek-American Agnew instead (much, one imagines, to Mr. Bush's great relief years later!). This is now believed to be directly linked with events in Greece and Nixon's friendship with the enigmatic Thomas Pappas, who is mentioned in the Oval Office tapes as "good old Tom Pappas," a guy who was raising hush money for the Watergate burglars. Pappas was a self-made millionaire who started in the grocery business and later wound up with a small empire of his own in oil and chemicals. He funneled large cash contributions into the Nixon war chest, and when Agnew was selected as candidate for vice president it appeared to be due to Pappas' influence.

More than that, however, was the willingness of the Greek military junta to finance the man they saw as their ally in Washington: Richard Nixon. The Democrats, who traditionally made human-rights issues a campaign platform, could be expected to give the generals a hard time. They knew they would get support from a right-wing Republican ... particularly if that Republican had been paid off. According to Summers, the sum of $549,000 had been transferred to Nixon's campaign in three separate payments between July and October of 1968, an amount equivalent to millions of dollars today. The money originated not with rank-and-file Greek citizens—illegal as that would be in any case—but from the Greek Central Intelligence Service, KYP. The cash would go to Thomas Pappas in Greece, who would then carry the funds himself to the United States.

In other words, the Greek military junta added their very healthy contribution to the Nixon war chest to ensure a victory over Hubert Humphrey.

Naturally, this was a gross violation of American law. It turned Nixon into an unregistered lobbyist for a foreign power, and it violated US campaign contribution regulations, which forbid any American politician from receiving any kind of financial contribution from foreign governments or their agents. This did not faze the candidate, however, since he had been receiving contributions from arms dealer Adnan Khashoggi for years. It would seem that in 1968 the Greek military government bought themselves a Vice President of the United States, with an option to buy the President. They had to stand in line, though, because Vietnamese President Thieu had the same idea.

It seemed as if Nixon could not get enough of dictators and mafia bag men. As the years went by, we saw time and again how the Nixon White House supported military governments and coups all over the world, in every hemisphere, from Vietnam to Chile to Greece. The list of secret financial contributors to Nixon's political career was maintained by his longtime secretary, Rose Mary Woods, and was known informally as "Rose Mary's Baby," certainly a characterization more apt than they realized. As Nixon added a second term, the bodies continued to pile up. The line stretched back through the days he spent as vice president under Eisenhower, when he began work to assassinate Fidel Castro and return Cuba to the control of the Lansky mob, and at least as far back as the time he worked with Dulles on the Nazi spy networks that had been "seconded" to the CIA, covering up Soviet penetration of western intelligence services in Europe that dated back to the earliest days of the Russian Revolution.

As information has come to light in recent years, we now know that the Soviets were well aware of anti-Communist agitation among the White Russians, as well as among the various disenfranchised ethnic groups living in the West. They began penetration of these groups shortly after the Revolution, and never abandoned their intelligence networks in the West. By the time Dulles and his British counterparts began using Ukrainian, Hungarian, and White Russian émigré groups against the Soviet Union, they had been so compromised by Russian intelligence as to be virtually useless. Worse, they acted as agents against the West and did untold damage to the Western intelligence services. Dulles and his men, in their hubris, did not suspect that the White Russians on their team were agents for the KGB and Soviet military intelligence. By the time they did, the damage had been done.

THE COVEN

Although we have come to know E. Howard Hunt, G. Gordon Liddy, Donald Segretti, James McCord, Chuck Colson and the entire mixed media collage of anti-Castro Cubans, CIA officers, FBI agents, White House aides, Mafia bagmen, and Nazis-on-the run as "the Plumbers," or "the President's Men," or even "the finest public servants it has been my privilege to know," perhaps another designation is in order, one that is suggested by the title (and subject matter) of one of Howard Hunt's occult novels: *The Coven*.

Hunt himself lived in a white, wood frame house in suburban Montgomery County, where a sign near his mail box read, "Witches Island," and he wrote several occult novels as well as a number of spy-type thrillers under various pseudonyms. His background with the CIA was extensive, going back nearly to the beginning of the Agency's existence; he began his career with the OSS during the War and was very fond of Allen Dulles, whom he met at that time. His admiration of Richard Nixon also went back to the earliest days of Nixon's career. He met Nixon sometime in 1952 at a restaurant in Washington, D.C. He spoke with him awhile, and gave him a calling card on which he wrote, "My wife and I want to thank you for the magnificent job you are doing for our country."[33] The card named Hunt as an attaché at the US Embassy in Mexico City, where he had been stationed since 1949, taking up for the CIA where the FBI left off after the CIA's creation in 1947; Nixon at that time was running for Senator. Twenty years later, Nixon was President and Hunt—retired from the Agency—was masterminding the break-in at the Watergate Hotel on his behalf.

E. Howard Hunt was the inspiration for the Cigarette Man on Chris Carter's television series, *The X-Files*. According to Carter's mythology, the CGM was responsible for everything from the Bay of Pigs invasion, to the Kennedy assassination, and just about every dirty trick and dirty deed in American history of the past fifty years. He was also a failed novelist, and the bitterness of a frustrated career behind the typewriter led the CGM to a hard-bitten, cynical approach to life. This very nearly parallels Hunt's own career. Hunt—in his "Eduardo" persona—had been involved deeply with the Bay of Pigs operation, as was then-Vice President Nixon. He was suspected of involvement in the Kennedy assassination, and for years photographs of a derelict who had been arrested close to the assassination site was believed to have been a photo of Hunt in disguise.

Hunt later retired from the CIA during Nixon's tenure as president—on April 30, 1970, the most infamous day on the European witches' calendar: Walpurgisnacht in Germany or Beltane in the British Isles, something the occult-oriented Hunt (resident of Witches Island) would have known—and took a job at Robert Mullen & Company, a public relations firm that did extensive work for the Howard Hughes empire, on the very next day. One of his colleagues—Douglas Caddy—was the first lawyer called when the Watergate burglars were arrested. He is depicted in the book (and film) *All The President's Men* as the man who sat in quietly at the burglars' arraignment and refused to answer any of Woodward's questions, saying simply, "I'm not here. I have nothing to say."

Another colleague at Mullen was Arthur Hochberg, a mysterious individual who virtually disappeared after Watergate. Hochberg was a CIA action officer who was stationed variously in Brazil and the Far East, and who was based in Singapore in the early 1970s, setting up and running an overseas office for Mullen. Not much PR work was done at the Singapore Mullen or at another Mullen operation called Interprogress, as Hochberg's job had more to do with debriefing Chinese defectors and running agents against the People's Republic of China. (His Mandarin Chinese was fluent, as was his Brazilian Portuguese.) The author has tried in vain to obtain corporate records of Hochberg's operation in Singapore, visiting government offices there and discovering that the files have been sanitized: no record was kept of corporate officers or anything else, beyond the dates of the opening and closing of the offices. Attempts to learn more were firmly discouraged; this, thirty years after the offices were closed. Thus, after all this time, there is still sensitive information connected to this obscure, Vietnam-era CIA operation in Singapore.

Hochberg later went on to work for a company in Queens, New York that sold transmission systems for trucks and buses, and wound up traveling extensively to Africa on various business deals, principally to Mauritania: not exactly on one's list of prime export markets. When the author met him, as a co-worker in 1980, Hochberg seemed a little wistful about the good old days at the CIA and was disappointed in the action taken by Admiral Turner, who was Director of the CIA for a short time, in firing all the old hands in a post-Watergate house-cleaning maneuver. Experienced intelligence personnel were suddenly without work all over the country; one wonders what they got up to in the years since Watergate.

G. Gordon Liddy is also an obvious member of the Watergate Coven. A lifelong admirer of German culture, who was smitten by hearing Hitler's speeches over a radio when he was a child, he is known to start singing the Horst Wessel song at the drop of a microphone. While known to the media as the Plumbers, Liddy had named his team for stopping leaks and disrupting the Democratic presidential campaign "ODESSA," after the fabled organization of former SS officers:

> It appealed to me because when I organize, I am inclined to think in German terms and the acronym was also used by a World War II German veterans organization belonged to by some friends of mine, *Organisation Der Emerlingen Schutz Staffel Angehoerigen:* ODESSA.[34]

Liddy had inured himself to pain since he was a young man, even going so far as to hold his arm over a flame and gritting his teeth against the intense hurt, giving a whole new meaning to the concept of "burn." He would turn this into a kind of parlor trick in the Watergate era, holding his hand over a flame, and when people asked him what the trick was, he would reply, "The trick is not minding." Few seem to remember that this is a direct reference to the film *Lawrence of Arabia*, in which Peter O'Toole, playing Lawrence, extinguishes lit matches with his fingertips. He is asked, "What's the trick, then?" and he replies, "The trick is in not minding that it hurts." *Lawrence of Arabia* was a favorite film of the author's youth, and I believe I could easily trade quotations from the movie with Liddy, who obviously watched it about as many times as I did.

He also grew up a Roman Catholic, attending schools in New Jersey run by German Benedictines and then by Jesuits, both of whom he admired. It was perhaps logical that Liddy would eventually wind up at the FBI, and in 1958 getting posted to Gary, Indiana: the Chicago suburb and center of the steel industry. The author's father, brother and sister were all born in Gary, Indiana, and the author's father went on to some notoriety in Gary in the immediate postwar period. I cannot help but wonder if Liddy had reviewed my father's files.

Gary was considered to be a target of Soviet espionage in the 1950s, when both Liddy and the author and his family lived in the area. My father had been prominent in something called the Gary School Strike in the fall of 1945, and had been investigated by the FBI as a possible shill for the Communists. This story is referenced in *The Sinatra Files*, edited by Tom Kuntz and Phil Kuntz, which is a summary of FBI files on Frank Sinatra throughout his career. My father's name comes up in this collection because of an incident in the crooner's life, in which he visited Gary in an attempt to calm the racist fever that was threatening to erupt into something even uglier.

High school students in Gary—including those at my father's alma mater, Froebel High—were boycotting classes over a plan to desegregate the schools. I am not proud to say that my father was considered the leader of the boycott and, thus, a segregationist. His parents had come to America from small mining towns in eastern Slovakia, escaping the Austro-Hungarian Empire and coming to the promise of a better life in the United States. My grandfather truly disliked no one except the Poles. (Polish gangs would raid Slovak towns along the border, stealing and raping, with numbing regularity.) His youngest son, however, found himself involved in a high school debate over the question of segregation, and—winning the debate—became an overnight celebrity and an ad hoc segregationist. I never knew if my father had truly been a segregationist at the age of seventeen, or if he had just found it irresistible to be the center of attention. Whatever the case, he remained politically conservative and right-wing for the rest of his life.

The Gary School Strike became national news. Other schools were following Froebel's lead, and it threatened to become a test case for desgregation legislation. Frank Sinatra—at that time enormously popular with young people—decided he would do what he could to defuse the situation, although no one had actually asked him to do so. He arrived in Gary on November 1, 1945 (the Catholic "Holy Day of Obligation": All Saint's Day) and addressed a meeting that night in the school auditorium. In his address, he claimed that my father, Leonard Levenda, had refused to meet with him, but my father said otherwise, saying that he met briefly with Sinatra before the singer's address, when he informed Sinatra that two men the latter had singled out as instigators of the strike—men who had attempted to form an all-white PTA and who were active in segregationist circles—had nothing to do with the strike, which was a spontaneous action of the students themselves. One of the men singled out for Sinatra's attack was Julius Danch, characterized by a Gary police captain as a staunch anti-Communist.

These were Eastern Europeans, for the most part. Danch was the president of the Hungarian Political Club in Gary. (And the reader will remember that Hitler had made Slovakia an independent country during the war, and that Catholic Monsignor Tiso had been put in charge.) Put anti-Communism and racism together in a single package and it is easy to believe that Nazi sympathies were close at hand. The FBI, however, believed that Sinatra's appearance had been arranged by Communist sources, at least in part; indeed, after his appearance at Froebel High School, Sinatra became an idol to the Left and was forever afterwards identified with liberal forces in American politics. My grandparents, however, once proudly showed me a clipping of the front page of a local Gary newspaper from that period which reported that my father had thrown Sinatra out of his house for making disparaging comments about their ethnicity.

It was my father's fifteen minutes of fame. From there, he went on to New York City to attend the American Academy of Dramatic Arts with classmates Jack Palance and Grace Kelly. He once acted on the stage with Palance, in *A Silver Tassie* and also performed in *Rope* (the stage play, not the film). But his acting days were over by 1950 when I was born and the young family moved back to Gary before eventually winding up in Chicago. But that is another tale.

Liddy, in 1958, would have been familiar with the Gary School Strike, and with the FBI's concern that Gary was a target of Soviet espionage. The FBI maintained an S.I., or Security Index: a list of those individuals believed to be a threat in the event of war with Russia. Did the Bureau believe my father was a threat, or an ally?

Liddy went on to greater glory. It is well known that he raided Timothy Leary's estate at Millbrook in New York, when Liddy was an assistant District Attorney. Liddy and Leary years later put together a kind of comedy routine, in which Liddy debated Leary on drugs, altered consciousness, alternative politics, and the like. It was popular for a short time on the college circuit. Liddy is far better known, however, for the role he played in the Watergate affair.

Another member of the Coven would have been E. Howard Hunt's boss at Mullen, Robert Bennett. A Mormon, Bennett had lucrative contracts with the Howard Hughes empire. The Mullen Company itself had been a front for the CIA since its inception in 1959, and Bennett—who later bought the company—was close friends with such Watergate luminaries as Chuck Colson. In fact, a close look at Robert Mullen & Company reveals a rich lode of CIA (and Mormon) involvement in the Watergate affair, and it has become apparent to many that Bennett's role was to divert attention away from the CIA and over to the White House. The Mullen operation also had very close ties to the J. Walter Thompson advertising agency, which was itself a source of many Watergate personalities, as we will see.

Bennett personally handled campaign contributions for Nixon and set up dozens of phony committees to collect funds for the President. He had also worked on Nixon's election campaign in 1968. In fact, much of the plotting of the Watergate break-in took place at Mullen's offices, which were across the street from Nixon's CRP: The Committee to Re-Elect the President, more commonly known as "CREEP." E. Howard Hunt would meet Gordon Liddy there, as well as James McCord and other conspirators. Although Hunt's ostensible role at Mullen was as a writer—he held the title of vice president at Mullen—he seems to have spent more time on White House and CIA business than anything else, which is appropriate when you review Mullen's long history as a CIA front both at home and abroad. When the Watergate story broke, Bennett spent a lot of time criss-crossing the United States, giving interviews to the press that effectively pointed them in the direction of the White House and away from the CIA. We may believe he did the same with Woodward, as he was undoubtedly a source for many of Woodward's stories—the fact that they were acquainted and met frequently is not denied by either man.

Howard Hughes was surrounded by Mormons as bodyguards and servants. He apparently trusted the Mormons because they did not drink or smoke; their clean-cut appearance was appealing to the decrepit billionaire who had a horror of germs and contagion, and whose personal appearance was—if we are to believe press reports after his death—quite horrifying itself. The lank, unkempt hair and the long, yellowing, fingernails; the gaunt physique and ghostly pallor.... It seemed unbelievable that a man with so much wealth and so much power could have lived for years in total isolation from the outside world, except for his Mormon bodyguard. That is, until the Clifford Irving affair, when either Howard Hughes or someone pretending to be Howard Hughes made an historic phone call to a group of reporters telling them that the Irving book—*The Autobiography of Howard Hughes*—was a hoax and making other accusations that rattled the Hughes empire.

Strangely, the author himself was peripherally involved in the Irving/Hughes affair. In the summer of 1970, I joined a firm in Manhattan's garment district that supplied budget-conscious housewives shopping at Woolworth's, Kresge's, and Alexanders with knock-offs of designer lingerie. A co-worker—a tall, slender former model with an offbeat sense of humor—and I became fast friends. She was living with a singer/songwriter on the Upper West Side, a pretty common combination in New York City at any time, but especially in those days. As we became better acquainted, and I spent some evenings at their apartment listening to music and discussing everything under the sun—her companion was a Vietnam veteran with post-traumatic stress disorder to the extent that he would awaken in the middle of the night and throw his girlfriend to the floor, shouting "Incoming!"—she eventually came to confide in me concerning her past.

She had worked for the J. Walter Thompson agency in some capacity as a fashion model. (That same agency gave us Dwight Chapin, Ken Cole, Ron Ziegler, Larry Higby and Bob Haldeman: all of Watergate notoriety.) She only got out of the business due to their increasing demands for her to lose even more weight and the consequent beginning of a dependence on diet medication. They were also rather secretive, keeping her isolated in hotel rooms in New York and plying her with drugs to keep her weight down to Twiggy levels. She finally had enough and managed to leave; but not before attending a strange meeting with a client of J. Walter Thompson.

This meeting took place—if memory serves—at the offices of the agency, and several mysterious individuals were in attendance. One she knew only as "the Cowboy," and he indeed did wear a Stetson and dressed in Western attire; another was an aloof, quiet sort that was never identified by name, but who had an intelligence background; still another was a man who would stay friendly with her long after she left the agency, a man known to me only by the name Ackerman. The model was there evidently as some kind of window dressing, and she was kept busy refilling glasses and looking attractive. Not much of significance was discussed at the meeting, which was conducted with a lot of code words and other jargon, but the importance of the event was summarized for her later by Ackerman.

As she related it to me, Howard Hughes had been kidnapped.

My mind raced through different scenarios of what might have taken place. The theory that made the most sense to me was that Gay and Davis had taken the Man against his will.
-- Robert Maheu[35]

The gist of the story was that CIA had kidnapped Hughes. This was due to the fact that Hughes was enormously wealthy, enormously powerful, but a psychological basket case. He was believed to be a national security risk; he was involved heavily in politics and had contributed huge sums to both Democrats and Republicans, mostly to ensure that his personal projects would be approved with a minimum of fuss and red tape; but he saw no one, took no meetings, and had not been seen in public—or even by his own second-in-command, former FBI agent and Castro assassination co-conspirator Robert Maheu—at all. With the exposure of the Glomar Explorer affair and the revelation of a "special relationship" between the CIA and the Hughes empire, the intelligence agency had decided that Howard Hughes was a threat, a loose cannon that had to be neutralized in the interests of national security.

According to the story, Hughes had been kidnapped and was being held offshore, in the Bahamas. The Mormons were essential to this operation, as Hughes trusted them, which made the "snatch" even easier. Watergate had not taken place yet (that was two years in the future) and the main players were largely unknown to the public. The Clifford Irving episode was also unknown, it having been put into action no earlier than January 1971, and had not been announced until December 7, 1971 in a press release by publisher McGraw-Hill. Having the Mormons involved, however, became more significant to me as the Watergate affair unfolded and we learned of the existence of the Robert Mullen agency, for whom both CIA agents E. Howard Hunt and Arthur Hochberg worked and which had contracts with the Hughes organization ... *specifically regarding damage control over the Clifford Irving affair.* Hunt's boss at Robert Mullen was Robert Bennett, a Mormon with important connections back in Salt Lake City, who became a United States Senator, as was his father before him.

No one knew any of this back in 1970 or 1971, unless they were involved. I begged the model to go public with her information, or to let me report the story somehow. She adamantly refused, fearing for her life. When she realized that my reaction was to tell the story to the press, she suddenly would not discuss the story with me any further. Although we remained friends, the subject of Hughes and Ackerman was off limits.

Then, the Clifford Irving affair broke in late 1971 and early 1972. The Watergate break-in was in June 1972. I have often wondered if the Nixon administration—and especially E. Howard Hunt, one of the Watergate burglars—was interested in knowing how much the Democrats knew about the Hughes kidnapping, if in fact such did take place. We have Hunt working for both the CIA and the Mormon Robert Bennett; we have Mormon bodyguards around Hughes in the last years of his life; we have the Clifford Irving affair, which may have been intended to publicize the fact that Howard Hughes was well, at large, and *compos mentis* at a time when he was very probably none of those things, or perhaps not even alive. In fact, when Clifford Irving and his collaborator, Richard Susskind began work on a tell-all book about the hoaxed autobiography of Howard Hughes, the Mullen firm was on top of it. They had been approached for a quote on what it would cost to put Irving and Susskind under surveillance; Watergate burglar James McCord provided the quotation, which was judged to be too high. Instead Intertel, the private intelligence agency and security firm, was hired to spy on Irving and Susskind and keep them on around-the-clock surveillance to determine what information they were planning to reveal in their book. This seems unusual, to say the least. The Irving book had already been exposed as a hoax, and Irving a fraud. What value was there to the Hughes organization in maintaining a very expensive surveillance on Irving after the fact? What could they possibly reveal in their own story of the hoax that could be damaging to Hughes?

During the series of revelations about Irving and Hughes, several other interesting names came up. One was Ackerman. In this case, it was Marty Ackerman, Clifford Irving's lawyer (in civil, not criminal, matters), and I wondered if this was the Ackerman mentioned by my model friend. Ackerman acted as a kind of literary agent for Irving, and I could not help theorizing that Ackerman would have been perfectly placed to suggest the hoax autobiography to Irving at the request of other, interested parties, if Ackerman was working for one or another contingent in the Maheu-Hughes conflagration. Another name that would come up was that of Jim Phelan.

Phelan's name was familiar to anyone who had followed the Jim Garrison trial in New Orleans. Phelan had an agenda where Garrison was concerned, and was part of the effort by the media to discredit him entirely. He then turned his sights on Clifford Irving and McGraw-Hill in an aggressive maneuver to prove the Irving book a hoax. Although Phelan is a journalist and reporter—a "freelance investigative reporter" is how he is usually described—he always seems to have a secret agenda of his own. The Irving case was no exception, since he had already collaborated on a book about Hughes by longtime Hughes associate Noah Dietrich. When the Irving book was announced, Phelan smelled a rat and took it upon himself to dig a little deeper. In so doing, he discovered that the Irving book was based largely on his own, unpublished manuscript of the Noah Dietrich memoirs. It was the final nail in the coffin, as Phelan rushed to McGraw-Hill and proved the truth of his allegations.

Recently declassified material on Phelan raises some other, more distressing, questions. It is now known that Phelan was an FBI informant of long standing, and that during the Garrison investigation into the Kennedy assassination, Phelan was taking files from the District Attorney's office and giving them to the Bureau.[36] It has been further revealed that Phelan was a friend of Bob Maheu, which certainly puts a different wrinkle on the Hughes affair, especially as there is no mention of Jim Phelan in Maheu's own autobiography.

At the end of one investigation of the Clifford Irving affair—*Hoax*, by Stephen Fay, Lewis Chester and Magnus Linklater—these journalists reveal an interesting fact which has never been explained. They say that at a dinner in November 1970 in New York, Edith Irving (Clifford's wife at the time) revealed to her guests that her husband was considering a proposition "that could be worth upward of $500,000. It would, she said, be a dangerous one to undertake, since it concerned people 'who would stop at nothing to achieve their own ends—even murder.'"[37] The authors go on to state that the phrase she used about men who would stop at nothing was identical to the way in which she would later "describe the Hughes organization." Of course, Marty Ackerman's offices were in New York City; the Irvings had been living in

Ibiza, Spain for years. According to Irving's own account, published in his *The Hoax*, he came up with the idea to write a fraudulent Hughes autobiography in Spain in December of 1970, one month and three thousand miles away from New York City, an idea prompted by an article in *Newsweek*. There is no mention of a visit to New York the previous month.

But it was November of 1970 when the model was telling me about the purported Hughes kidnapping by the CIA.

Was the Irving/Susskind book—the "tell all" story of the Howard Hughes hoaxed autobiography—suspected of revealing this piece of information, information that would have led back either to the CIA or to the Hughes organization itself … or both? In any case, it didn't. When Irving's book finally hit the stands, it contained little that was not already known.

Hughes disappeared from his Las Vegas Desert Inn eagle's nest in November 1970, on Thanksgiving weekend. This, in spite of the fact that he was quite ill, suffering from anemia complicated by pneumonia, and "on the verge of heart failure."[38] It became obvious in later years that Hughes had been forced to sign the proxy which eventually resulted in the firing of Robert Maheu, and did so while under the influence of painkillers and other drugs. In fact, Hughes' doctors forced him to approve all sorts of deals by threatening to withhold the codeine on which he had become increasingly dependent. This included the hiring of the Mormon bodyguard, among other things. When Maheu became a problem, his handlers then forced Hughes to leave the country so that Maheu could not personally confront him, and so that Hughes would not have to appear in court to defend his actions. Thus Hughes had, in effect, been kidnapped indeed.

That same month, the Irvings were approached by a sinister cabal that offered them "upwards of $500,000" for an important and dangerous project. The hoaxed Howard Hughes autobiography was in the works the following month. The Mormon Robert Bennett then supposedly took charge of anti-Irving strategy in the months that followed, which eventually resulted in the famous phone call on January 7, 1972 from Hughes in the Bahamas to a group of reporters in California, in which he "proved" he was alive and well, and that Maheu was evil and had been deliberately fired by Hughes. One feels that Irving knew all along what he was getting himself into, and that the entire scenario had played out just as it was supposed to have done. To complicate matters even further, it appears as if President Nixon ordered the IRS to attack Robert Maheu with a full audit going back three years (as mentioned in Maheu's autobiography). If so, it would appear that Maheu was a threat to more than just the Hughes "palace guard." Maheu certainly knew where the bodies were buried in the Hughes/Nixon relationship, and would later testify to the Watergate Committee that he had personally handled the illegal campaign contributions between Hughes and Nixon's sidekick, Bebe Rebozo.

The Hughes affair is important to an understanding of the sinister forces surrounding American politics in the late twentieth century. Howard Hughes inherited a great deal of money from his father, who had invented a special type of drill bit that was heavily used by the oil industry and thereby made his fortune. Hughes himself was something of a playboy in his earlier years. He was a pilot, and was always trying to improve the airplane, acting as his own test pilot and nearly getting himself killed in the process. He also dabbled in Hollywood, and squired a number of famous actresses, such as Ava Gardner, Ginger Rogers and Ida Lupino, and even marrying Jean Peters. He discovered the curvaceous Jane Russell, and had a hand in creating a special brassiere to support and display her most obvious qualities.

Money, the military, oil, and Hollywood.

The ceremonial magician, self-proclaimed AntiChrist and invoker of Babalon, Jack Parsons, once worked for the Hughes empire; but then so did Wilford Brimley, the plump and grizzly character actor who would later appear in such films as *Heaven's Gate, Cocoon, Death Valley*, and *The China Syndrome* (as well as a series of commercials for Quaker Oatmeal). I guess it was the "right thing to do." After all, the Hughes organization was a dominant player in California—both in the film industry and in the military-aviation industry—as well as in the Texas oil industry, and in Nevada casinos, Hughes bought up hotel after hotel in a bid to consolidate his power there and run the entire state. He was active in trying to halt atomic testing (at least in Nevada) and threw money around in an attempt to buy off whatever politican he had to in order to get the job done. He also enlisted the services of Intertel, a private security and intelligence-gathering operation so well-documented in Jim Hougan's *Spooks*. It was Intertel which would eventually go after Clifford Irving, and eventually after Bob Maheu when he was "fired" by Hughes ... or perhaps fired by Chester Davis and Bill Gay, the men who created a Berlin Wall of Mormons and medicine around the eremitical billionaire.

Another, perhaps honorary, member of the Coven would have been the psychic Jeane Dixon.

A Gift of Prophecy

Jeane Dixon was familiar to many in the 1960s as a psychic who was said to have predicted the assassination of President Kennedy. The American-born daughter of German immigrants, she also made some startling predictions about a world war that was supposed to take place in the final decades of the twentieth century, as well as the birth of a Savior somewhere in the Middle East in the early 1960s. Most of this was included in the book about her, *A Gift of Prophecy*: a blue and white bound paperback that was ubiquitous in bookstores and magazine racks throughout the United States for years. What most people did *not* know, however, and which would have horrified them if they did know, was that Jeane Dixon was actively working on behalf of the FBI, tailoring her predictions to emphasize the danger of the Soviet Union!

It is a phenomenon which seems pecular to the right wing, this dependence on soothsayers, astrologers, entrail-readers and the like. The administration of Republican President Reagan would surprise everyone with revelations that his wife, Nancy, consulted an astrologer regularly and arranged the President's schedule according to transiting planetary positions. In fact, Jeane Dixon also provided consultation to the Reagan White House. This was a president who believed firmly in an apocalyptic interpretation of Christianity and the "end times," and who viewed foreign relations and foreign policy through a scrim of the Book of Revelations, sharing this at least in common with Charles Manson. Yet, in Nixon's case, the soothsayer was also as much of a political front as Radio Free Europe.

Nixon believed in the prophecies of Jeane Dixon, according to John Ehrlichman. Nixon's psychotherapist, Dr. Arnold Hutschneker, was also a believer.[39] According to Ehrlichman, Nixon was getting premonitions from both Billy Graham and Jeane Dixon that his life was in danger in late 1972. Recently declassified FBI files—released after the psychic's death in 1997—show a comfortable relationship between Ms. Dixon and the FBI, to the extent that the Bureau supplied her with information on groups they considered subversive so that she had ammunition for her speeches around the country. She volunteered to help the FBI erode popular support for the Left, by making speeches with material that could not be traced to the Bureau.

In 1969, Dixon accused the Soviet leadership of instigating and controlling race riots and student revolt in the United States; in 1971 she went so far as to say that there was a high-level spy in the US government who was reporting back to the Soviets. Her fear of the Left in general and of the Soviet Union in particular was consistent, and was exploited by the FBI for its own purposes. One angry correspondent wrote to Hoover demanding an investigation of the psychic, accusing her of trying to create an environment in which Democratic Party leaders would be assassinated, in particular Teddy Kennedy, about whom Dixon had always had dire things to predict. The accusation was that Dixon was consciously using her prestige as a diviner to suggest that Ted Kennedy ought to be killed. Her staunch support of Republican politicians, the FBI, and anti-Communism lends some credence to this point of view.

Nixon, himself was not totally unaware of occult forces. His own law firm, Nixon, Mudge, Rose, Guthrie and Alexander, based in New York City, had handled a volatile labor dispute in Puerto Rico in the 1960s. This dispute involved the practice of witchcraft—probably *santeria*, the Hispanic version of Haitian *voudon*—and the law firm wrote a brief discussing the practice of Puerto Rican occultism in some depth. The brief was, appropriately enough, thirteen pages long.

Finally, the presidency of Richard Nixon came to an ignominious end. The existence of an Oval Office taping system was revealed, and Nixon stonewalled as long as possible to avoid giving sensitive conversations over to the investigating committees. In one case, one particularly important tape recording was found to have eighteen-and-a-half minutes missing, that section of the tape either erased or recorded over. The buzzing sound could not be identified. According to Al Haig, it seemed as if the tape had been altered by some "sinister force." And thus the germ of an idea for this book was born.

As members of his staff all went off to prison on various counts of burglary, conspiracy, perjury, etc., many eventually becoming born-again Christians in the process, Nixon himself resigned from office on August 9, 1974. The previous year, he had warned the Joint Chiefs of Staff of the evil machinations of the "Eastern Establishment," and, according to Admiral Zumwalt, "It was clear that he perceived himself as a fighter for all that was right in the United States, involved in mortal battle with the forces of evil."[40]

But it was to no avail. As Nixon left the White House with his family for the last time that day—standing in the entrance to Air Force One raising his arms above his head in his familiar gesture and giving what the Golden Dawn would have understood as the sign of Typhon, the Destroyer—a crowd outside the fence was singing "Ding Dong, the Witch is Dead."

Evangelist Billy Graham, with whom Richard Nixon had prayed and agonized so often throughout the Presidency, once said, "I think there was definitely demon power involved. He took all those sleeping pills, and through history, drugs and demons have gone together."[41] According to Graham, the drugs opened a door in Nixon's soul and the demons flew in. This author believes that Nixon's pact with the demons had been signed much earlier, when he agreed to cover for Dulles, for the Nazis, and for the Mafia in return for the most powerful position in the most powerful country in the world.

Endnotes
[1] Allen Upward, *The Divine Mystery*, Ross-Erikson, Santa Barbara, 1976, ISBN 0-915520-01-x, p.xxxii
[2] Letter from Parsons to Marjorie Cameron, dated 27 January 1950
[3] Victor Turner, *Revelation and Divination in Ndembu Ritual*, Cornell University Press, Ithaca, 1975, 0-8014-9151-7, p. 32
[4] Mark Aarons & John Loftus, *Unholy Trinity: the Vatican, the Nazis, and Soviet Intelligence*, St Martin's Press, NY, 1991, ISBN 0-312-09407-8, p. 270
[5] Anthony Summers, *The Arrogance of Power: The Secret World of Richard Nixon*, Penguin Books, NY, 2000, ISBN 0-14-0267078-1, p.16
[6] Bruce Mazlish, *The Leader, the Led, and the Psyche*, Wesleyan University Press, Hanover, 1990, ISBN 0-8195-5220-8, p. 198ff
[7] Summers, op. cit., p. 63
[8] Ibid., p. 63
[9] Ibid., p. 55

[10] Seth Kantor, *Who Was Jack Ruby?*, Everest House, NY, 1978, p. 54-55

[11] Charles Higham, *American Swastika*, Doubleday, NY, 1985, ISBN 0-385-17874-3, p. 85

[12] Summers, op. cit., p.46

[13] Carl Goldberg, *Speaking with the Devil: Exploring Senseless Acts of Evil*, Penguin, NY, 1997, ISBN 0-14-023739-9, p. 214

[14] Higham, op. cit., p. 250

[15] Ronald Brownstein, *The Power and the Glitter: The Hollywood-Washington Connection*, Pantheon, NY, 1990, ISBN 0-394-56938-5, p. 57

[16] Simpson, op. cit., p. 179

[17] Summers, op. cit., p. 12

[18] Walter Laqueur, *Black Hundred: The Rise of the Extreme Right in Russia*, HarperCollins, NY, 1993, ISBN 0-06-018336-5, p. 15

[19] Aarons & Loftus, op. cit., p. 277-278

[20] Higham, op. cit., p. 190

[21] Ibid., p. 191

[22] Aarons & Loftus, op. cit., p. 278

[23] Summers, op. cit., p. 62-66

[24] John Marks, *The Search for the Manchurian Candidate*, Times Books, NY, 1979, ISBN 0-8129-0773-6, p. 21

[25] Howard Blum, *Wanted! The Search for Nazis in America*, Quadrangle, NY, 1977, ISBN 0-8129-0607-1, p. 91-102

[26] Ibid., 109-111

[27] Summers, op. cit., p. 130-135

[28] Blum, op. cit., p. 117-119

[29] Ibid., p. 121

[30] Summers, op. cit., p. 274

[31] Thomas Powers, *The Man Who Kept the Secrets: Richard Helms and the CIA*, Knopf, NY, 1979, ISBN 0-394-50777-0, p. 197-200; Summers, op. cit., p. 297-308

[32] Summers, op.cit., p. 284-287

[33] Ibid., p. 142

[34] G. Gordon Liddy, *Will*, Dell, NY, 1980, ISBN 0-440-09666-9, p. 203

[35] Robert Maheu & Richard Hack,, *Next to Hughes*, HarperCollins, NY, 1992, ISBN 0-06-016505-7, p.233

[36] See for instance FBI Airtel dated 4-12-67 from Hoover, entitled ASSASSINATION OF PRESIDENT JOHN FITZGERALD KENNEDY NOVEMBER 22, 1963 DALLAS, TEXAS concerning information from Garrison's office provided by Phelan to the Bureau to be "closely held" and "not disseminated."

[37] Stephen Fay, Lewis Chester, Magnus Linklater, *Hoax: The Inside Story of the Howard Hughes-Clifford Irving Affair*, Viking, NY, 1972, ISBN 670-37430-X, p. 309

[38] Maheu, op. cit., p. 265

[39] Summers., op. cit., p. 89

[40] Ibid., p. 463

[41] Ibid., p. 318

CHAPTER ELEVEN

NIGHT OF THE LONG KNIVES

In the colonial period, when religious creeds, institutions, and communities exerted a major impact on life and work, there was bound to be some spillover into politics. Because the contribution of religion to American political culture covers such important beliefs as obedience, the design of government, and the national mission, the religious roots of American political culture merit close investigation.
    —Kenneth D. Wald, *Religion and Politics in the United States* [1]

When I begin I try to follow the money, as they say in All The President's Men, up the evil ladder, past the businessmen, past the Mafia, past the leaders in the state, I ask, "Who is doing the stuff, who is pulling the cords?" It looks an awful lot like God. It's the big fascist in the sky. But all of this religion, government, and civilization bending towards God is dangerous.
    —Ken Kesey [2]

No, men were afraid of murder, but not from a terror of justice so much as the knowledge that a killer attracted the attention of the gods; then your mind was not your own, your anxiety ceased to be neurotic, your dread was real.
    —Norman Mailer [3]

Sharon Tate was eight months pregnant when she was stabbed to death by members of the Manson Family on August 9, 1969 at her home at 10050 Cielo Drive in Los Angeles. *Cielo* is Spanish for "heaven" or "sky." It is the domain of the Egyptian goddess Nuit, to whom one of the three sections of Aleister Crowley's *Book of the Law* is dedicated. Nuit is a form of Babalon, the Scarlet Woman of the Apocalypse, the mystical bride of the Great Beast, whom Jack Parsons had invoked in the Mojave

Desert. It is she who gives birth to the Magickal Child, the promise of the New Age.

In Sharon Tate's case, the child—her perfectly-formed unborn son—was killed along with his mother.

The ancient Egyptian analogue may appear gratuitous, but there are grounds for looking that deeply at the matter. In Book One, we discussed the seances of Andrija Pujarich, Arthur Young, Ruth Paine Young, etc. which resulted in contact with something called "The Nine." (These were the same individuals that were linked to the Kennedy assassination, and specifically to accused assassin Lee Harvey Oswald, as well as to American military and intelligence circles and, via Arthur Young and Michael Paine, to Operation Paperclip.) According to ancient Egyptian religion, there was such a Council of Nine—known as the Ennead of Heliopolis, called by Egyptologist R. T. Rundle Clark the "Divine Company"—which was made up of the major deities of that time, including Atum, Geb, Tefnut, Nut (or Nuit), Shu, Osiris, Isis, Nephthys, and Set (or Seth). Probably their most famous function was to act as intermediaries between the battling Horus and Set. Horus, the son of the slain god Osiris, was out to avenge his father's death; Set, as the murderer and as the embodiment of "blind force and unregulated violence,"[4] was Horus' target.

The war between the two—as recounted in the *Contendings of Horus and Set*—goes on so long and is so wasteful that the Council decides it must be stopped. They decide in favor of Horus; the powers of Set are thus curtailed; and the kingdom of Egypt is at peace at last. Egypt was divided into two kingdoms in ancient times, Upper Egypt (in the south) and Lower Egypt (in the north). Upper Egypt was said to be the realm of Set, and Lower Egypt the realm of Horus. The Pharaoh was king of both Upper and Lower Egypt, and wore two crowns to symbolize this fact, thus acting as representative of both Horus and Set. Of both Order and Chaos. Of both Peace and mindless Bloodshed.

This duality was also an important—if not central—feature of the Process Church of the Final Judgment, which preached the unity of both Jehovah and Lucifer, of both good and evil, with Satan thrown in for good measure a little later in the cult's development. This was also, of course, the main "rap" of Charles Manson: that he was both Jesus and the Devil, and that good was evil, and evil, good. The possibility that the Process may have strayed a bit too enthusiastically over to the Dark Side is evidenced by the Fear and Death themes of their publications, as well perhaps by their adoption of a stylized swastika and the German shepherd as cultic symbols. A dog-like creature was the emblem of Set, and dogs have been associated with the dark side of human consciousness for thousands of years. The dog is considered an unclean animal in Islam, for instance, for it is coprophagic: it eats the dead. The association of dog sacrifice—specifically of German shepherds—with satanic cults in the United States cannot be ignored, with numerous cases from coast to coast, especially in relation to the presumed Son of Sam cult (which incorporated the Manson Family). In addition, Jeffrey Dahmer, one of the twentieth century's most horrific serial killers, began his career by sacrificing dogs and putting their skulls on stakes around a ceremonial area behind his home in Ohio.

According to Rundle Clark, writing in 1959, "Seth is the essential enemy. He is the personification of blind force and unregulated violence.... Wherever there is a manifestation of blind force, Seth is in his element.... He is the desert wind, dryness and death."[5] There is perhaps no better description of the spirit of the Manson Family, born as it was in the Mojave Desert and reaching its apotheosis in "blind force and unregulated violence." Manson was perceived as the "essential enemy," and he reinforced this concept by carving a swastika into his forehead and by preaching race war and Armageddon.

In January 1969, shortly after the discovery of Marina Habe's body in a gulley off Mulholland Drive, several events occurred which are relevant to our study.

CIA Operation OFTEN was initialized by Dr. Sidney Gottlieb, based partly on documents which came into his possession after CIA agent William Buckley (who would later be tortured and murdered by Arab terrorists) tossed the premises of the late Dr. Ewen Cameron, he of the "sleep room" and "psychic driving" experiments in Canada. Initially, Operation OFTEN was a joint CIA/Army Chemical Corps drug project, based out of Edgewood Arsenal in Maryland and using inmates of the Holmesburg State Prison in Philadelphia as test subjects. It came under the aegis of the CIA's Office of Research and Development (ORD), which was concerned with parapsychology and the application of supernatural powers for military purposes.[6] Later, OFTEN would become a kind of grab bag of CIA investigations into the paranormal, and would include everything from séances and witchcraft to remote viewing and exotic drugs. Agents of Operation OFTEN would consult with such occult luminaries as Sybil Leek, the famous English witch who was interviewed constantly in the late 1960s on radio and television talk shows, and who had published a few books on the occult, astrology and associated themes. Although the CIA had been investigating ESP and the paranormal, and infiltrating occult groups, since 1952,[7] when Andrija Puharich began contact with The Nine, someone at theCIA evidently felt that the occult underground in 1969 might have access to special techniques for the manipulation of consciousness and memory, and they took to their study with renewed vigor. In some cases, university students who had been part of special controlled experiments in occultism later became occultists themselves; just as an earlier crop of drug experimenters became passionate advocates of LSD, mescaline and psylocibin. The CIA had opened the door, and all sorts of things were flying in and out.

When the powers that be had allowed the Nazi spy and science networks into the United States, it was with the understanding that *they* would control *them*, and not vice versa. As it happened, American hubris probably led to Soviet penetration of American intelligence systems, as Nazi/Soviet double agents found they had unfettered access to US government channels. In addition, by bringing over so many Nazis—many of whom were war criminals—they had unknowingly reinstated a Nazi underground in the United States, South America and Australia, not to mention the Middle East. The same was now happening with the CIA investigation of the paranormal and the occult: it was a two-edged sword, and the occultists were starting to develop under CIA tutelage and create their own networks. We will see evidence of this—especially with regard to the Stanford Research Institute, remote viewing, Uri Geller, and Andrija Puharich of The Nine—a little later on.

Also in January 1969, the Condon Report on UFOs was released, and immediately attacked as biased and basically worthless. The Condon Report had been contracted to the University of Colorado by the Air Force; its project leader, Dr. Richard Condon, proclaimed himself an agnostic on the issue of UFOs, but later documentation by Condon committee members—including the controversial Low memorandum—would prove otherwise, showing Condon to have been antagonistic towards the whole idea of UFOs and to have used the project as a forum to discredit the theories about space aliens, secret government aircraft, etc. According to a CIA article on the subject, published in the agency's *Studies in Intelligence*, the Condon report had been contracted as a means of showing the public that the Air Force had nothing to hide concerning UFOs; it was not an attempt to prove or disprove the existence of flying saucers, etc. Regardless of the ultimate purpose of the Report, it was embraced by those who were already skeptics and denounced by those who believed in the existence of flying saucers.

A few months earlier, Jim Garrison had subpoenaed Fred Crisman to testify before the grand jury he had convened in New Orleans in the matter of the President Kennedy assassination. Crisman, as was related in Book One, had been present at the birth of the twentieth century's UFO phenomenon, along with Kenneth Arnold and a number of FBI agents, including another assassination suspect, Guy Banister. Crisman was interesting to Garrison for a number of reasons, not the least of which was that Clay Shaw is said to have phoned Crisman immediately upon learning he had been arrested. Garrison's other interest in Crisman stemmed from the latter's knowledge of right-wing militia movements; the New Orleans District Attorney was evidently wondering what certain individuals in these movements had been doing in and out of New Orleans around the time of the assassination.

By the time the Clay Shaw trial was over, however, it was all moot. He had been declared "not guilty" on March 1, 1969. That same month, Nixon ordered the bombing of Cambodia, which began in earnest on March 18. The film *Goodbye, Columbus* was released, and Roman Polanski, Sharon Tate, and Jane Fonda attended the Directors Guild screening.

Shortly thereafter, Bruce Davis returned to California from London, where he had been staying for some months with the local Scientologists and, as some (including LAPD homicide detectives) insist, meeting with the Process Church of the Final Judgment.

Bruce Davis had been sent to London by Charles Manson in November 1968, shortly after the murders of Clida Delaney and Nancy Warren (the latter, like Sharon Tate, eight months pregnant) near Ukiah, California. They had been beaten, and then strangled to death "with thirty-six leather thongs,"[8] on the evening of October 13. Nancy Warren was married to a Highway Patrol officer, Clida Delaney was her grandmother. The Manson group was quickly suspected of having committed these murders when they were arrested the following year and more information about their criminal history came to light. Several members of the Manson clan were known to have been in the area on the day of the murders, and Manson moved his base of operations from the Spahn Ranch (near Chatsworth, just outside of Los Angeles proper) to the Barker Ranch (in Death Valley, on the other side of the Mojave Desert, many more miles away from Ukiah) about two days after they occurred.

Davis returned from London on April 25, 1969, and then flew to London again in November that same year, after the murder of a pair of Scientologists in California in which he was later considered a suspect, and in time for the murder of Manson Family associate Joel Pugh in London. (Joel Pugh was the husband of Sandy Good, who later teamed with Lynette "Squeaky" Fromme to create the Manson cult ATWA.) According to British Immigration officials, Davis had given as his address in the UK the address of Scientology headquarters.[9]

Since Davis was regarded by California investigators as "Manson's second-in-command," this constant traveling back and forth between California and London—specifically to either Scientology or Process headquarters, or both—is evidence of a larger plot. Davis was later convicted for his role in the murders of Gary Hinman and Donny Shea, the two "bookend' murders that took place before (Hinman) and after (Shea) the seven Tate/La Bianca killings, during the period July 26–August 26, 1969. He reappeared in February 1970 at the Spahn Ranch and then disappeared again when he was indicted for the Gary Hinman murder, only to reappear in Los Angeles in December 1970, when he turned himself in to authorities. He has since become a born-again Christian (like so many of the former Manson family members, as well as "Son of Sam" killer David Berkowitz) and a minister, although still in prison.

The Gary Hinman murder was as savage as the Tate and La Bianca killings. Hinman was a jazz musician with a master's degree in sociology who was friendly to the Manson clan, but when Manson needed money, he sent some of his followers to visit Hinman and extort cash from him. Hinman was making mescaline in his house, and Manson claimed that one batch of the drug was bad. The story has it that the bikers to whom Manson sold the hallucinogen had become ill and blamed Manson's mescaline, and Manson in turn blamed Hinman. Hinman was due to fly to Japan in two weeks on a religious pilgrimage (he was a follower of the Nichiren Shoshu sect of Japanese Buddhism); it seemed he also had come into some kind of an inheritance, or at least that is what the Family had heard.

Hinman did not have any cash in hand beyond about twenty dollars, but under threats of violence—including being pistol-whipped by Bobby Beausoleil—he signed over two of his cars. That still did not satisfy the Mansonites. Phone calls back and forth to Manson, giving updates on the ongoing cash extortion, resulted in Hinman's death at the hands of Bobby Beausoleil, Mary Brunner, and Susan Atkins, with Davis and Manson as co-conspirators. He was stabbed repeatedly by Beausoleil, after his ear had been chopped in half by a sword brandished by Manson, who had left the Hinman residence before the actual murder, but who is said to have ordered it by phone when Hinman was still not coming across with the money. Hinman is said to have died with the chant "Nam Myoho Renge Kyo" on his lips, the famous prayer of the Nichiren Shoshu sect.

His death occurred on July 27th, Beausoleil writing "Political Piggy" and making a crude drawing of a cat's paw on the walls in Hinman's blood, in an attempt to put the blame on the Black Panthers. This was a tactic that would be repeated in the Tate and La Bianca killings, as one of the purported motives for the killings was to instigate a race war between blacks and whites.

In another eerie chain of coincidence, as the reader of *The Nine* will recall, Aldous Huxley had his first hallucinogenic experience *with mescaline* and *in Hollywood*, after which he wrote *The Doors of Perception*. Jim Morrison named his rock band—the Doors—after this book, and became initiated into witchcraft in 1970, shortly before his death in July 1971. His 1968 release "Five to One" seemed like an eldritch prediction of the Manson slaughters with its tag line, "No one gets out of here alive," and his reference to "five to one and one to five": the address of the Tate residence on Cielo Drive was 10050.)

A YEN FOR MAGIC

The same day that Hinman was being tortured and killed, an occult lodge was being raided in southern California in an effort to rescue six-year-old Anthony Gibbons, who had been imprisoned inside a packing crate on May 23 and had yet to be released a full two months later, except when he was allowed outside the box to work. He had been accused of burning down a building (accidentally) and this was his punishment. Local police received reports of child abuse, and thus the raid on this supposed lodge of the Ordo Templi Orientis.

It is not clear at this time whether the police informants in the case were telling the truth or, as one commentator and apologist for the OTO insists, were embellishing a story for its sensationalistic value and to inflate their importance to the local police. That a young boy was kept chained in a wooden building by himself at the Brayton "ranch" is beyond dispute, however; what is controversial is the length of time he was kept there and under what conditions. The FBI report of August 15, 1969 is detailed and contains much corroborating information that does not appear in the OTO apologist's summary of the events, making a clear case for felony child abuse. In the final analysis, however, it didn't matter. The Solar Lodge of the OTO was raided, and its leaders scattered over the desert to avoid arrest and prosecution, some winding up in Mexico as fugitives from justice: a strange reaction from a supposedly benign organization that was not guilty of serious criminal activities.

The so-called Solar Lodge of the OTO was primarily the creation of one Georgina Brayton, and its story is rife with rumor, innuendo, false leads, and disinformation. The American branch of the OTO that was run by the late ex-Army officer Grady McMurtry has consistently disavowed any connection with the Brayton lodge, but information recently available in the wake of numerous McMurtry-OTO lawsuits against all and sundry suggests otherwise. Predictably, the author himself has been attacked by various individuals claiming OTO affiliation for references he made in his previous work, *Unholy Alliance*, which linked the Solar Lodge with the McMurtry OTO and with Charles Manson. Unfortunately for the Order, the link between Georgina Brayton's OTO and the McMurtry OTO is definite.

Ray and Mildred Burlingame were members of the Agape Lodge of the OTO, the one in Pasadena that was being run for a while by Jack Parsons, and had been in direct communication with Alistair Crowley in the 1940s when Parsons was being considered for a leadership position with the Lodge. After Parsons' death, the Burlingames—who were friends of Georgina Brayton and her husband, a lecturer at the University of California, Richard Montgomery Brayton—began working the rituals of the OTO in an informal way; they were unaffiliated with the main body of the OTO, which was in disarray anyway after the death of Crowley in 1947, the closure of the lodge in 1953, and the subsequent death of Crowley's nominated successor, Karl Germer, in 1962. The Burlingames were veteran initiates of the OTO, and there is some controversy over whether or not Georgina Brayton could be considered initiated. The Burlingames did not possess the requisite authority from an OTO hierarch to start their own lodge or to initiate new members; but, then, neither did Grady McMurtry, the Army officer who had been initiated at Agape Lodge in the days before America entered World War II, having been introduced to Crowley's religion of Thelema by Jack Parsons himself. Although McMurtry had attained the highest operative degree of the Order, the Ninth Degree, he was not an Outer Head of the Order, or OHO (although he would claim this distinction in later years). What is certain is that Georgina Brayton was initiated into the OTO by the Burlingames; what is in dispute is the "validity" of that initiation, given the lack of an OTO charter.

The author does not want to spend a lot of time going over what is a tedious example of how occult lodges fight among themselves, especially where legitimacy and "apostolic succession" are concerned. Suffice it to say that both the Brayton "Solar Lodge of the OTO" and the subsequent McMurtry variation—the "Caliphate"—seemed equally legitimate or equally illegitimate as the case may be. There was nothing intrinsically different about either organization to guarantee that it had legal standing from the point of view of the OTO's original charters and by-laws. Obviously, when the Solar Lodge got into trouble over the case of the "boy in the box," it was up to McMurtry and those loyal to his faction to distance themselves as much as possible from the Solar Lodge, and McMurtry did this ... especially with respect to correspondence he had with the FBI and the police in the wake of the Solar Lodge revelations.

The Solar Lodge had become somewhat notorious in Southern California in the late 1960s, and it was in the process of building a power center of its own in the Mojave Desert, near the towns of Blythe and Vidal. The reader may recall that the Manson Family was also relocating to the Mojave, but Blythe is far to the southeast of where Manson was setting up his operation, being roughly on the Arizona border. Regardless, the rumors of Manson's knowledge of the Solar Lodge and his attendance at some of its recruiting parties are quite persistent. It was this association, as well as the scandal over the "boy in the box," that, according to published accounts, brought Grady McMurtry out of occult retirement, and he traveled from Washington, D.C. to California to salvage what he could of the OTO (the Agape Lodge had been dissolved in 1953, but it had had the most active and serious members in the United States).

However, evidence shows that McMurtry arrived in California in April of 1969, which meant that he was in place months before either the "boy in the box" incident or the Manson killings. It is McMurtry's long military background (service in both World War II and Korea as an officer), coupled with his position at George Washington University (where he seems to have taught political science), that has raised the possibility that he went to California—leaving a paying job and security in Washington—to conduct an intelligence operation on behalf of ... someone. If the Scientology people are correct in insisting that their founder, L. Ron Hubbard, a former Naval officer in World War II, was involved with the OTO on behalf of either the FBI or ONI in an effort to break up a "black magic ring" that had attracted scientists with high level security clearances, then it seems equally valid to put forward the idea that a former Army officer in World War II and Korea was involved with something similar.

For those readers who find it frankly incredible that the US government would have attempted to infiltrate occult organizations, I add the following piece of evidence to the published documentation showing a CIA interest in occult phenomena already referenced. On November 21, 1968 an FBI Special Agent in Charge in Philadelphia wrote a memo to FBI Director J. Edgar Hoover under the infamous COINTELPRO program. COINTELPRO was the domestic intelligence, surveillance, infiltration and disruption program of the FBI designed to attack the anti-War movement in general, and the Communist, socialist, Black Panther, Native American and other domestic US political groups in particular.

The memo states,

> "The emergence of the New Left on the American Scene [sic] has produced a new phenomenon—a yen for magic…. Self-proclaimed yogis have established a following in the New Left movement. Their incantations are a reminder of the chant of the witch doctor…. Philadelphia believes the above-described conditions offer an opportunity for use in the counter-intelligence field. Specifically, it is suggested that a few select top-echelon leaders of the New Left be subjected to harassment by a series of anonymous messages with a mystical connotation."[10]

A few days later, on December 4, 1968, Hoover approved the strategy, with the caveat that specific individuals be chosen for this treatment, based on recommendations of FBI informants close to them, and the symbolism of the messages carefully selected and interpretations made available to the targets by the informants, thus reinforcing the "sinister" messages.[11] Thus, we have documentary evidence based on declassified COINTELPRO files that demonstrate the Bureau's attitude towards cults and their presumed involvement with political subversion. McMurtry's correspondence with the FBI in the Solar Lodge case (see below) would have only served to reinforce the Bureau's suspicion and paranoia of occult groups. This identification of occultism with political dissent—the New Age with the New Left—is fascinating. The fact that many mainstream churches and religious organizations were active in the anti-War movement—one thinks of all the religious leaders who marched on Washington, for instance—did not figure into this equation. The Bureau was concerned with the influence of cults over the rise of American political opposition to the Vietnam War. *For rebellion is as the sin of witchcraft.*

In April of 1969, Bruce Davis had just returned to California and the sticky embrace of the Manson Family after having spent more than five months with either the Scientologists, the Process, or both. His lengthy mission in England is still a mystery, as is the funding for this junket. Documents seized by the US Government after a raid on Scientology headquarters in 1977 show considerable anxiety over the alleged connection between the Manson Family and Scientology; the Scientologists sent emissaries to try to find Steve Grogan (who was later convicted of the murder of Donny Shea), a Family member who had information concerning Manson's Scientology background (they were unsuccessful). Then, an informant came to them with information on Manson's 150 hours of Scientology auditing sessions in prison. The picture painted is frightening, for it shows a Manson at turns extremely enthusiastic about his training… and terrified to the point of demanding to be put into solitary confinement so he could escape his auditor. It was after the Scientology cell was broken up at the prison by the warden that another inmate after his release began sending Manson books on hypnotism and "black magic."

Beginning in January of 1969, the CIA's Operation OFTEN quickly expands to include occult research and interviews with occult leaders and cult members. Several months after OFTEN becomes operational, McMurtry leaves the D.C. area and reheats his occult career with the same organization (the OTO) and the same lodge (Agape) that L. Ron Hubbard had allegedly been trying to infiltrate and destroy. At this point, McMurtry had not been active with the OTO since the early 1950s at the latest. According to official OTO sources, he did this latter turn at the instigation or request of Phyllis Seckler, an OTO member in California who was trying to contact all the old Agape Lodge members in the aftermath of a series of robberies of OTO books and documents, including two at the home of Mildred Burlingame (her husband had died a few years previously), robberies that were at first laid at the door of the Solar Lodge. Crowley follower and Mary Ferrell friend Israel Regardie had been burglarized as well, as had Karl Germer's widow, Sascha. It appeared to be a well-organized campaign that lasted from 1965 to 1967, and which was believed to be the work of Georgina Brayton who, having been rebuffed by Mildred Burlingame in her plan to start up a new OTO lodge, decided to obtain as much "classified" Crowley material as possible to enable her to start up a lodge on her own. McMurtry—who was recently divorced—decided to move to California and assist Phyllis Seckler with revitalizing the Order; we do not know what contact, if any, he had with Georgina Brayton. His contact with Ms. Seckler, however, resulted in their marriage a short time after.

A few months later all Hell broke loose, with revelations about the Solar Lodge of the OTO and then, in the wake of the Manson killings, rumors that Manson may have visited the Solar Lodge on at least one occasion, adding the OTO to his list of occult connections (Scientology, the Process, the Church of Satan, the Fountain of the World sect, etc.). McMurtry cooperated with the police and the FBI in an effort to create legal distance between the OTO and the Solar Lodge; this obfuscation has had repercussions down to the present day. Truly, it is of little importance whether or not Manson visited the Solar Lodge; there is no evidence at all that he was a member, or that his actions in any way reflected the philosophy of the Solar Lodge. However, the involvement of both Manson and Bruce Davis with the Scientology and Process organizations, which have a pedigree that goes back to the OTO, is suggestive of something more than sixties-style religious eclecticism. Further, the Solar Lodge had degenerated into an apocalyptic, end-of-the-world sect that practiced a subtle form of racism with a thin veneer of Thelema and Crowleyism as window-dressing for something that was turning more sinister. The philosophical similarities between Manson's occult vision and that of the Solar Lodge (as well as the Process) bear consideration; they are not, however, equivalent to the official OTO philosophy, and it is this more than anything else that justifies McMurtry's distancing of the Crowley cult from that of Georgina Brayton.

Another OTO offshoot that was active in the United States and in southern California especially at the time was the Gardnerian Wicca movement. Although largely underground, it was growing in numbers and in visibility due to the missionary work of Raymond and Rosemary Buckland, a Gardnerian high priest and priestess who were active in the New York City area. Raymond Buckland had appeared on several talk shows—one with CIA consultant Sybil Leek—in the late sixties. Gerald Gardner had received an OTO charter from Aleister Crowley, and Gardner's *Book of Shadows* contains much that was derived from Crowley, the Golden Dawn, and the OTO.

Both Gardnerian and Alexandrian Wicca were popular in the United Kingdom and the United States, and we have seen the influence of Alexandrian Wicca on the career of doomed actress Sharon Tate. Like Scientology—and the Process Church which derived from Scientology—the Wicca movement was a direct descendant of the OTO. Thus, we had witches, satanists, Thelemites, and an entire ragtag band of magicians and occultists whose origins all go back—in one form or another—to Aleister Crowley and the occult Order he "inherited" from German Masons and magicians in the early days of the twentieth century. At the same time, we had alleged American intelligence agency involvement in the penetration and control of these groups, particularly in the 1960s, when the objectives of both the CIA's MK-ULTRA mind control programs and the FBI's domestic intelligence gathering programs on potentially subversive secret societies dovetailed; both of these programs were motivated by fear of Communism.

And in that climate of fear and paranoia, Richard Nixon and Henry Kissinger—in May of 1969—authorized FBI domestic wiretapping of American reporters and government officials. At this time, Richard Nixon had been President of the United States for less than four months. (That same month, Manson's uncle—Darwin Scott—was savagely hacked to death in Ashland, Kentucky. Like the murders of Delaney and Warren in April, it is a case tied to Manson that has never been solved.)

It is worth noting in this context that, in one lawsuit against Nixon concerning the wiretapping of Morton Halperin (a National Security Council staff member), the Federal Court of Appeals in 1977 stated, "The President is the elected chief executive of our government, not an omniscient leader cloaked in mystical powers."[12] An interesting choice of words, considering our theme.

THE OMEN

There is no past. There is only now in this infinite time.... We are all one member—one force.
—Charles Manson to his Family[13]

With the premiere of *Rosemary's Baby* in 1968, America was on the way to a spate of films dealing with the subject of the incarnation of evil. In *Rosemary's Baby*, of course, an innocent young woman is impregnated by Satan in order to bring about the birth of Satan's child on earth, in a blasphemous recreation of the virgin birth of Christianity. Rosemary brings the baby to term, but it is taken from her at birth, and she is told that the baby died; she later hears chanting and the baby crying through the thin apartment walls and discovers the truth for herself. This idea—of a satanically-engendered or satanically-possessed child—is reprised in *The Exorcist*, in which the young Regan is possessed by an evil spirit, an emanation of the ancient Sumerian demon Pazuzu. Again, a child is the focus of evil; again, evil has became incarnated in human flesh rather than remaining merely a phantom or ghastly illusion. Even more frightening, this film was based on events that had actually occurred. A few years later, and the American public would be presented with yet another demonic presence, this time in *The Omen*, in which a young boy has the mark of 666 on his scalp: he is the Devil incarnate, again (and, like Crowley, in England again!). The 1990s film *Lost Souls*—starring Winona Ryder as a formerly possessed young woman on the trail of Satan—is another attempt to show the impending incarnation of Evil, although this time the vessel is a grown man (appropriately enough, a lawyer). Perhaps one day we will address this issue of why—from the late 1960s through the 1970s—we feared our children so much that we identified them with Lucifer himself; what concerns us here at this time however is the idea that Evil could be incarnated, could be "made flesh" and "dwell amongst us."

Charles Manson has become the ultimate example of the belief that a person—a human being born of woman—could be wholly, irredeemably, evil. Rightly or wrongly, we have characterized Manson this way. Some of the objections to Manson are quite valid, of course. Others are based on Manson's personality and style, an image that he cultivates that seems focused entirely on scaring the living daylights out of people. We know he was present during part of the time that Gary Hinman was being tortured to death, and that he ordered Hinman's murder; we know that he brought the ropes to the La Bianca house and tied up the victims; we know—at least we think we know—from the testimony of members of his "family" that he ordered the killings at the Tate household on Cielo Drive. We also know that he shot a drug dealer named Bernard Crowe in the stomach, leaving him for dead. All of that is bad enough, of course; but Manson was convicted for something darker, more sinister.

He was convicted of murder in the case of the Tate and La Bianca killings because of his psychological power over the men and women he sent to perform murder. The viciousness of the attacks on Sharon Tate, Jay Sebring, Abigail Folger, Voytek Frykowski, Steven Parent, Leno La Bianca and Rosemary La Bianca was not the work of Manson himself. He wasn't there when the victims were killed. Some of the victims were shot, but most did not die of the gunshot wounds. All were stabbed repeatedly, over and over again in a violent frenzy of homicidal passion, by two women and a man, a man—Tex Watson—who proclaimed upon entering the Tate home, "I am the Devil, and I'm here to do the Devil's business." These were young people who had never fired a shot in anger in their lives, nor stabbed helpless victims to death, nor written slogans on the walls of the abattoirs in the victims' blood. But Manson made it all possible, even probable.

As the events of that summer of 1969 began to percolate, Manson became more and more manic. Death was in the air. Everyone at his headquarters, the Spahn Ranch, was talking about death. Spahn Ranch had been a movie set for a slew of westerns that came out of Hollywood over the years, and now served as a horse ranch for weekend riders. Oddly enough, it was used as the set of *The Outlaw*, the Jane Russell vehicle that was produced by Howard Hughes. Hughes had even spent some time on the set at Spahn Ranch, but it was not used for filmmaking much any more. Now it was the headquarters for Helter Skelter.

Many observers (including Maury Terry in his controversial best-seller *The Ultimate Evil*) have proposed that Manson was a contract killer, taking contracts in exchange for drugs or money, or some other consideration. Indeed, the La Bianca killings were the most anomalous of all the murders; both Manson and Tex Watson knew the Tate residence since they knew its previous occupant, Terry Melcher, the son of actress Doris Day, and Manson had visited the Tate residence on Cielo Drive a few months before the murders, ostensibly looking for Melcher who had promised to help him land a recording contract. Yet no case could be made for the La Biancas, except that there was a Mafia connection and the rumor of bad blood between Leno La Bianca and the Mob. The La Bianca killings *could* have been a Mafia hit, contracted to the Family. The Tate killings, on the other hand, seemed motivated by something entirely different. Some authors have wondered if the La Bianca killings were the real focus of the horror that week and that the Tate killings were designed to confuse the issue and throw the police off the scent, or vice versa. A motiveless crime is the most difficult to solve and, indeed, it might never have been solved had not one of the Manson women confessed to the crime to another inmate while she was in prison on an unrelated offense.

Satanism and Nazism were very much part of the Manson philosophy. He avoided Spahn Ranch employee Donny Shea because he was married to a black woman; Shea would eventually wind up dead and buried in the desert. He planted the stolen La Bianca identification and credit cards in a gas station in a black neighborhood, hoping that someone would find them and use them, and thus pin the murders on the Black Panthers. Convicted murderer Bobby Beausoleil had actually played the Devil in a Kenneth Anger film, opposite Church of Satan creator Anton Szandor LaVey; he also played a homicidal Indian in the soft-porn flick *Ramrodder*, killing a helpless man the way he killed Gary Hinman a few years later. Convicted murderer Susan Atkins belonged to the Church of Satan before she ever met Charles Manson, and played the part of a vampire in a publicly staged Black Mass at LaVey's church. Convicted murderer Tex Watson claimed he was the Devil, to frighten the Tate residents. Convicted murderer Charles Manson claimed to be both Jesus and Satan. Convicted murderer Patricia Krenwinkle doodled satanic glyphs and the Church of Satan's Goat of Mendes during her trial.

The barter America made for its protection and defense in the 1940s and 1950s—selling its soul to the Nazis; creating a program to open the Pandora's Box of human consciousness to develop the perfect weapon: the mindless assassin—was a bill that had to be paid. The sacrament of choice was LSD, that golem of the CIA mind-control program: it provided the "material basis" for the evocation of sinister forces. The Manson Family—according to eyewitness testimony, published in many sources but most noticeably in *The Garbage People*—were constantly strung out on acid in the weeks and months leading up to the Tate and La Bianca killings. Tex Watson was said to be so deranged from constant use of the drug that he forgot his own mother's address and phone number. Manson consciously used the drug as a tool in his arsenal, along with sex. In one instance, he told an interviewer that he would make a woman exhausted with physical work before he would have sex with her, so that she was in no mood to have sex at all. Then he would approach her and gradually work on her until the point where she began to respond to his sexual ministrations; at that point, Manson believed he had control of her mind and could convince her to do anything. That combination of sex and drugs and a kind of perverse operant conditioning are the basic working parts of what Ed Sanders calls "The Manson Secret." It was what CIA psychiatrist Ewen Cameron was working on until virtually the day he died, except that Manson was much more successful. As documented in *The Nine*, Cameron created zombies; Manson created assassins.

Another aspect of the Satanic and Nazi elements of Manson's philosophy was the apocalyptic. Manson was seen carrying a Bible and constantly referring to the Book of Revelations, also known in the Catholic Douay Rheims translation as *Apocalypse*, where he pointed to messages and omens that he felt were referring to him, his mission, and the general state of the world.

Just as Fundamentalist Christians are concerned with the "End Times" and are only in debate as to when and how the End Times begin, so was Manson. Manson believed that he would be the engine of Armageddon, the last battle that would usher in a Golden Age. He believed that the End was imminent. In this, he was no different from Fundamentalist Christians, but also had a lot in common with his other predecessors: the Thelemites.

Those who follow the scriptures of Aleister Crowley agree that a New Age dawned in April of 1904, when Crowley received *The Book of the Law* in Cairo. It was the beginning of the Age of Horus, the Crowned and Conquering Child, the New Aeon that would replace Christianity. Crowley perceived himself to be the engine of that transformation, and called himself *To Mega Therion*, a Greek phrase that means "the Great Beast," the Beast of the Apocalypse known by his infamous number, 666. Crowley believed that he, himself, was the Beast prophesied in the Bible, and that the women he took as consorts were all "Scarlet Women," Whores of Babylon as mentioned in the Apocalypse.

Crowley's take on all of this was not that he was the personification of Evil, but that new Gods—when replacing old Gods—are rejected or resisted at first, until gradually they assume global acceptance, and the old Gods then become demons. Crowley identified the New Age with Horus, the Lord of Lower Egypt who avenged the murder of his father, Osiris, by Set. Jack Parsons, in pursuing his own spiritual path in the Mojave Desert, began to identify with the Antichrist, inasmuch as he was invoking the presence of the Whore of Babylon herself, spelled in Crowley's system "Babalon." Thus, the initial impetus of Thelema was as apocalyptic and millenial as that of Fundamentalist Christianity. The "End Times" were upon us, for Thelemites and Christians alike.

It was basically a time to choose sides and may the best God win. While Manson looked forward as eagerly to the Apocalypse as later President Ronald Reagan would do, he saw his own role differently. As both God and Devil, he was uniting the opposing forces within himself (thus being assured that he would remain victorious regardless of which side won the Final Battle). Like the pharaohs of ancient Egypt, he was both Horus and Set. Thus, whatever he did was permissible. There was no evil, no good. There was only Manson.

And murder.

The events that led up to the slaughter on Cielo Drive are still very much in dispute. The only witnesses to the gradual build-up of violence among the members of Charles Manson's entourage in 1969 are the killers themselves and their accomplices: in most cases young renegades so strung out on dope, sex, mystical vibes and California dreams that their testimony reads like Old Testament prophets on angel dust, and with bad cases of tinnitus from sitting a little too close to the speakers.

Part of the problem with Manson was that he found himself suddenly in the midst of all of these "beautiful people," and he had a hard time dealing with the reality *they* lived with, and the reality *he* lived with. He was walking between two worlds, one filled with Dennis Wilson of the Beach Boys, John Phillips of the Mamas and the Papas, Deana Martin (daughter of Dean Martin), Terry Melcher, Peter Falk, Nancy Sinatra, Jane Fonda (whom he despised for her "race mixing"), even little DiDi Lansbury, daughter of actress Angela Lansbury, who gave her daughter a note to carry saying it was all right for her to be hanging out with the Manson Family! In fact, Manson even had one of his songs recorded by the Beach Boys. Pretty heady stuff for an illiterate, fatherless drifter who had spent most of his life institutionalized in reform schools and prisons.

But rather than making him grateful for the turn his life was taking, it made him bitter and angry. Lists of famous people—show business celebrities mostly—were drawn up as a Family "hit list" that included Frank Sinatra, Elizabeth Taylor, Tom Jones and many others. No one knows exactly why the residence of Sharon Tate was picked for the first night of "Helter Skelter," except that Manson possibly still held a grudge over the way he was treated by Tate's housekeeper on his previous visit. Or perhaps it was as a kind of message to Melcher, the man who had disappointed him in his quest for fame and fortune as a rock star: an unveiled threat? (Manson had threatened Dennis Wilson, sending messages to Wilson that he would harm Wilson's young son, when Wilson did not come across with cash that fateful weekend.) Or perhaps there was another aspect to it, a connection with drugs that has bothered investigators for some time.

A few nights before the Tate slaughter there was a strange event at the house on Cielo Drive. A dope dealer from Canada was punished for selling Jay Sebring bad dope. According to actor Dennis Hopper, twenty-five people were invited to watch the dealer get whipped and to participate in the whipping. They videotaped the event, as they had other events involving—again, according to Hopper—"sadism, masochism and bestiality."[14] Hopper claims that LA police informed him about some of this information. The tapes have never surfaced, but rumors in the Hollywood underground have always insisted that they exist. Some say that the LAPD has them in a safe place, much like J. Edgar Hoover's famous "secret files," to be used when necessary to coerce or persuade a celebrity to cooperate.

This event cannot be considered in isolation from the Tate killings. According to Hopper, the public humiliation of the dealer took place three days before the murders at Cielo Drive, which would make it on or about August 5th. Manson had complained to Gary Hinman about a bad batch of mescaline on July 26th. The burn was worth two thousand dollars. Hinman was killed. Hairstylist to the stars (and former lover of Sharon Tate) Jay Sebring had complained about getting burned to the tune of the same two thousand dollars. He would die in the Tate house. Only the type of drug is in question: was Sebring talking about cocaine or mescaline? According to Ed Sanders, Sebring's burn—and the subsequent whipping of the drug dealer—involved cocaine.[15] That there were two dope burns for the same amount of money in each case, less than two weeks apart, is probably coincidence; but it got Gary Hinman murdered, got a dope dealer whipped on Cielo Drive in front of twenty-five eyewitnesses including many celebrities, and led up to the horrific murders in the same house only three days later.

Police and prosecution officials are naturally reluctant to discuss this case's peculiarities even now, more than thirty years after the events in question. On one side, this is because—as Vincent Bugliosi has admitted in his own book on the Manson murders, *Helter Skelter*—the police investigation of the Tate and La Bianca killings was shoddy, to say the least; but it is also because the perpetrators are still alive, still behind bars, and no one wants to jeopardize that. New evidence could be used in a new trial, or at least to get some of the convicted murderers out on parole. It could also embarrass a lot of people in Hollywood. Thus, we are forced to rely on informants, independent investigative journalism, police snitches, and the like.

Or, when more murders take place that have a ring of similarity to the Manson killings, we can begin to see connections where there were none before. Maury Terry has been criticized for his book, *The Ultimate Evil*, because it discusses the existence of a nearly unbelievable nationwide Satanic conspiracy in the United States involving drugs, Hollywood, and murder. However, Terry's book managed to get the Son of Sam case reopened in the State of New York due to the evidence he presented showing that more than one person was involved in the Sam murders ...something of which many of us who lived in New York City at the time were convinced. In addition, Terry's information on the occult scene in Brooklyn Heights and Manhattan in the 1970s is detailed and accurate, as the author himself can attest from personal experience. Terry's information regarding the drug dealer punishment on Cielo Drive is therefore important.

According to Terry,[16] the pistol-whipping of the Canadian drug dealer—who is likewise named "Billy Doyle" in the first edition of Ed Sanders' book *The Family*—took place on the same night as a party for French film producer Roger Vadim, who was married at the time to actress and anti-War activist Jane Fonda. Billy Doyle was well-known to the Cielo Drive crowd, since Abigail Folger and Voyteck Frykowski (both Manson murder victims) had lived on Cielo Drive before Tate and Polanski moved in, and Frykowski was heavily involved in the drug trade, being largely financed by his girlfriend who was the Folger Coffee heiress. Frykowski was running LSD and MDA, along with whatever else was going down. Doyle and several of Frykowski's friends had crashed Roman Polanski's house-warming party on Cielo Drive in March 1969 and were thrown out, much to their irritation. After the Polanskis left for England in April, however, Frykowski moved back into Cielo Drive with Abigail Folger, and the visits by Doyle, et al. resumed.[17] Jay Sebring, who would become a murder victim a few days later, brought some film that had been shot that night at Vadim's party to a developer for processing; it is suggested that the whipping of Billy Doyle was on that film.

It is important to note that Roman Polanski himself, in his autobiography, disputes this characterization of his friend Frykowski very strenuously, as he disputes other stories that have made the run of the press.[18] Whether this was out of loyalty to his friend, or a simple statement of fact, is impossible to discern at this remove. Polanski also implies that there was no cult activity of any sort at Cielo Drive[19] without ever specifically denying it, blaming it on a reporter's discovery of a Ouija board in his home; a conclusion that is difficult to accept. Instead, he says that *the police* "gave no credence whatsoever to tales of stray pickups, orgies, drug excesses, and black magic."[20] His explanation of the "hood on Jay Sebring" is that a police officer draped a cloth over Sebring's head because the victim's wounds were so grisly.[21] We know from other sources that Manson himself placed the towel around Sebring's head, just to throw off the investigation; much in the same way he planted an old pair of eyeglasses at the scene that had investigators running around for months trying to identify their owner. One of the strangest omissions from Polanski's autobiography is any mention of the poor doomed gossip columnist Steve Brandt, who was, after all, one of the witnesses to his wedding to Sharon Tate. Brandt does appear, however, in John Phillips' autobiography, and his account reflects what everyone else has said about Brandt's relationship to Sharon Tate.

Informants close to the case have insisted that the Tate killings had a motive that went beyond Manson's Helter Skelter philosophy. They insist that the target of the killings was Frykowski, and not Sharon Tate. That the killings were contracted to Manson. As were the La Bianca slayings the next night. Polanski believes that Manson chose the Tate household as a target because he believed that Terry Melcher still lived there and blamed Melcher for his failure to succeed as a rock star.[22] The La Bianca murders, according to Polanski's theory, were only to throw off the investigation. Using a kind of circular logic, Polanski implies that since no one has ever accused the La Biancas of orgies, drugs, and black masses that these could not have been factors in the Tate killings, either. And so it goes.

Maury Terry raises an important point in his observation of the killings, one which cannot be easily ignored: if Helter Skelter was the true motive, then why did the killings stop after La Bianca? There was no evidence linking the Manson clan to any of the killings; they were still in the clear on Tate and La Bianca, although Bobby Beausoleil had been picked up for the Hinman murder. They could have continued their Helter Skelter murder spree much longer before being stopped. Why only that one weekend in August? Why only the five victims at the Tate house (six, if you count Sharon

Tate's unborn son) and two at La Bianca? The only reason that makes sense is that both murders were contract hits, and that Manson dressed it up in Helter Skelter for the benefit of his young female assassins. (It is presumed that Tex Watson knew of the real motive, or had a suspicion anyway, as it was he who drove the car to the Tate residence specifically; it was not a random selection.)

Helter Skelter was Manson's "program" for the brainwashed murderers; it provided a context, and it also influenced their choice of bloody graffiti at each scene, thus attempting to lay the crimes off on the Black Panthers. For Manson, it was two birds with one stone, so to speak. He could spread the evil message of Helter Skelter while meanwhile getting paid—in *some* form, since money seemed to be in short supply in the days immediately preceding and succeeding the murders—by the drug dealing establishment to rid them of some problems. Once Frykowski's drug connections were known, then a motive for his killing could be understood. And once Leno La Bianca's indebtedness to the Mafia was known, another motive presented itself.

The brilliance behind these crimes had nothing to do with Manson himself. The brilliance was in *selecting* Manson and his assassins as the hit team, for it obscured the real motives and thus the real powers behind them. Further, due to the sensitive nature of the victims involved and their incestuous relationships with Hollywood, occultism, drugs, and "alternative" sexual practices—much of it captured on videotape—there was very little danger of their friends running to the police with information that could get the real masterminds into trouble. The Tate killings spread tentacles into the very highest reaches of Hollywood. Beginning with Terry Melcher and Dennis Wilson, and extending outward to the Mamas and the Papas, Jane Fonda, Roger Vadim, Jack Nicholson, Dennis Hopper, and so many others whose names were household words, the blood had splattered all over Benedict Canyon in an aerial spray that reached Mulholland Drive, Beverly Hills, Bel Air, North Hollywood, Malibu, and the back lots of studios all over town. Drugs, murder for hire, sadomasochistic sex on videotape involving celebrities, and satanic rituals ... is it any wonder LAPD had a hell of a time trying to extricate one strand of nastiness from another? The "scarlet thread of murder" never ran so red as it did on August 9, 1969 at 10050 Cielo Drive.

Since the trial, more information has come to light concerning the Manson Family and its connections to the murder victims. There are witnesses who insist that Manson knew Abigail Folger from the "Summer of Love" days in San Francisco in 1967, shortly after Manson was released from prison. According to these sources, Folger had invested in the Straight Theater in the Haight-Ashbury section of the city, only blocks from where both Manson and the Process set up shop. The Straight Theater, on September 21, 1967, had staged a performance by The Magick Powerhouse of Oz in honor of the "Equinox of the Gods," and Kenneth Anger was in attendance filming the event, as was Bobby Beausoleil, Manson, Folger, and many others including—according to sources close to the events—former members of the OTO Agape Lodge of Pasadena and the Process. It was a virtual occult convention, and Manson was able to "network" with a lot of people who would become notorious in the years to follow.

Information that became available to Maury Terry long after the killings shows that Manson had become involved with the Process after the Straight Theater performance in 1967, and through early 1968, at the famous Spiral Staircase house in Topanga Canyon (not far from where Bobby Beausoleil and Catherine Share were filming *Ramrodder*), which was a kind of occult headquarters and sex club combined; this information came from one of the convicted Manson killers, and was confirmed by Manson in his "autobiography."[23] In a further development, Manson—in a letter written in 1989—claimed to have met with Process leaders (naming names) at the Tate residence![24] Clearly, the relationship between Manson, Abigail Folger, Terry Melcher, Dean Moorehouse, Dennis Wilson, John Phillips, the Process, Scientology and 10050 Cielo Drive is much more convoluted and involved than the trial ever revealed. While Manson had become involved with occultism and "black magic" while in prison, this interest was kicked into high gear during the Summer of Love and beyond.

Another startling piece of information concerns Donald "Shorty" Shea, the Spahn ranch hand and would-be actor who was murdered a few weeks after the Tate killings, allegedly because he "knew too much." In this scenario, attested by informants to Terry and Sanders, Shea had known both Manson and Folger in those halcyon days in San Francisco. Shea had later come down to the Spahn Ranch when Manson and his group moved in. Something went awry between the two diminutive persons and Shea was eventually murdered, his body found in the desert long after the trial, homicide detectives led there by Steve "Clem" Grogan, who was also a putative source for Scientology officials concerning Manson's involvement with the Hubbard cult. Thus the attack on the Tate residence and some of the murders that would follow seem linked to events that transpired and connections that were made in San Francisco two years earlier, with the somber drapery of ceremonial occultism drooping menacingly over the *mis-en-scene*. In that case, perhaps Donny Shea knew too much after all.

What follows is a brief description of what we know transpired that night of August 9, 1969. It is necessary to demonstrate to the reader the sheer savagery of the attack as compared with the mental and emotional state of the perpetrators. It goes to motive, as they say in murder trials. The author apologizes in advance for the graphic recreation of the event.

Susan Atkins (age 21), Linda Kasabian (age 20), Tex Watson (age 23) and Patricia Krenwinkle (age 21) left in an old white and yellow '59 Ford for the

Tate residence, Watson driving. Manson had been at the Tate residence at least twice before, once when Terry Melcher was dropped off after a meeting and again on his own, a few months after Melcher moved out, when he was supposedly looking for Melcher. The last time he actually saw Sharon Tate was through a doorway when her housekeeper answered the door. Melcher, the son of Doris Day, had been living at the house with his girlfriend, the actress Candace Bergen, before Sharon Tate and Roman Polanski moved in. (Additional information emerging since the trial indicates that Manson may actually have spent much more time at the Tate residence with Melcher and company in the days before the Tates moved in, and thus knew the layout of the house quite well, data which he may have communicated to Tex Watson who, among all the killers, would have been the one that Manson entrusted with sensitive information.)

Watson was armed with a handgun, and two of the women carried knives. They brought a change of clothes with them, so that they could switch to their dark-colored "creepy crawley" outfits on the way to the death house. This was also in order to rid themselves of what would become clothing drenched in blood by the time the holocaust was over.

They parked down the street from the Tate residence. Tex Watson cut the telephone lines to the house, and the four of them crawled over the fence surrounding the lot and made their way to the house.

There is a rumor that Manson thought that Sharon Tate would not be there that night. She actually had plans to visit a friend, but changed these plans at the last moment. Her husband, Polish film director Roman Polanski, was in London at the time working on *The Day of the Dolphin*, a film inspired by the true story of the Navy's training of dolphins for military purposes. (When the film was finally released, the trailer described the plot as involving a nefarious scheme using dolphins to assassinate the President of the United States. When the author saw the trailer in a Manhattan movie theater, the audience laughed and applauded. Well, it *was* New York. And Nixon *was* President.)

But that month Polanski was frustrated with the way the screenplay was going, and was making plans to return to California early. His friend, the brilliant and quirky novelist Jerzy Kozinski, was also on his way to California. His luggage had been lost, though, so he decided to wait in New York City until they found it. It was the luckiest decision of his life. Had he arrived on time, he would have been at the Tate residence that night.

Voytek Frykowski was there, of course, along with his girlfriend Abigail Folger. Sharon Tate, eight months pregnant, was sitting in her bedroom talking to Jay Sebring. Sebring had been Sharon's lover before Roman Polanski arrived on the scene and broke that up. Friends in Hollywood claimed that Sebring still carried a torch for Ms. Tate, and he had remained good friends of her family. When Sebring opened his new salon that summer, the Tates were in attendance: Doris Tate, Sharon's mother who later started a fund for crime victims, and Sharon's father, Colonel Paul Tate, an intelligence officer with the US Army who had been serving in Vietnam. Colonel Tate would go underground in California after the murders, hunting for his daughter's killers.

A young man, Steven Parent, was just leaving the Tate residence by car. As he was going down the driveway, a man stood in front of the car and waved it to stop. He told Parent to get out of the car, but the boy refused. His body would later show defensive knife wounds, but it was the bullets that killed him. Tex Watson fired four times into the car, killing the eighteen-year-old and leaving him there.

The killers then proceeded to the house.

Linda Kasabian, recently arrived in California from her home in Milford, New Hampshire, pregnant and with an infant daughter, stayed behind at the fence to watch for unwelcome visitors. She says she had no stomach for the killing, and was horrified by the shooting of Parent. Things were spiralling out of control. The women went up to the house with Watson, knives at the ready. Watson also carried a length of rope with him. The idea was to hang the victims from the rafters of the living room, and then gut them.

Susan Atkins was known to the Family as "Sadie" or "Sexy Sadie" (after the Beatles song on the White Album) or "Sadie Mae Glutz." Patricia Krenwinkle was known as "Katie." Virtually all of the Manson Family members had aliases, but these were not aliases in the criminal sense of the word (although they would often be used that way); these were names they adopted upon joining the Family. This action suggests a process that Robert Jay Lifton calls "doubling," or the creation of an alter ego or dissociated identity to enable the individual to become a killer responsible for acts of unbelievable savagery, and then re-enter society as if there had been no effect on the individual's personality, psyche, or soul.

Manson, meanwhile, remained behind at Spahn Ranch. Before the killers left on their mission, he told them, "Now is the time for Helter Skelter." He gave Watson some specific instructions, directing them straight to the Tate house with the ostensible reason that they were going to steal whatever money was there to bail some Family members—Mary Brunner (the mother of one of Manson's children) and Sandy Good—out of jail, having been arrested that day after trying to use some stolen credit cards. According to Watson's later testimony, Charlie had told them to go to the next house if they didn't get enough money there, and the one after that if necessary, until they had amassed the six hundred dollars bail money they would need. That was the cover story, anyway.

Manson, who was no stranger to crime, knew the risks of ripping off people who knew him. There were a lot of houses in Los Angeles to rob that night; they could have picked one with no one home, where no one could identify them later. Instead, he chose the one house in LA, outside of Dennis Wilson's home, where his merry band would be familiar to the residents. That theft was not the principle motive for the murders is clear from the overkill at the Tate household, and the elaborate preparations, including the rope and Manson's instructions to the girls to "Leave a sign. You girls know what to do. Something witchy."[25] In the Tate homicides, as in the La Biancas, nothing of any value was stolen, even though—especially in the case of the La Biancas—there was a lot of jewelry, a coin collection, etc. that would have been easy for Manson to fence. In any case, they did not follow these alleged instructions and would return to Spahn Ranch immediately following the carnage.

The girls had gone to a common arsenal and selected the knives they were going to use. Watson carried a nine-shot .22 revolver, and took a few hits of amphetamine for the road. Susan Atkins had been snorting amphetamine for days before the murders, and was on a perpetual high from the speed. Patricia Krenwinkle was just coming down from an LSD trip, and was groggy from lack of sleep. Linda Kasabian had a valid driver's license, so she was elected to go along with them as the designated driver in case they were stopped by police, even though Watson would be doing all the driving that night. Squeaky Fromme, who would later attempt to assassinate a President, helped her find the license, which was kept in a communal cache under the close supervision of the pixie-ish Fromme.

When they entered the house, slashing through a mesh screen with their knives, it was Frykowski who saw them first. The stereo blaring, and Frykowski himself in the midst of a ten-day "mescaline experiment" (once again, echoes of Aldous Huxley and the Doors) he struggled to get up from the couch where he was lying, to focus on the strange-looking man suddenly standing in the living room.

"Who are you?" he asked.

"I am the Devil, and I'm here to do the Devil's business," Tex Watson replied.

Susan Atkins was ordered to look in the other rooms and find out how many people were in the house. She saw Sharon Tate and Jay Sebring in one room, talking, and Abigail Folger in another, reading, bringing the total to four people in the house. The body of Steven Parent was still in his car in the driveway outside, shot in the upper chest, left forearm, left cheek, lower chest. Abigail Folger looked up and saw Susan Atkins smile at her; she smiled back, a little uncertain. Strangers were always coming and going at Cielo Drive, friends of Sharon's, friends of Jay's or Voytek's. Drug connections, actors, musicians, mystics ... who knew? On the piano's music stand in the living room, two compositions were open: one, Elgar's "Pomp and Circumstance," the standard for high school graduation classes everywhere, and a melody used to ironic purpose in Stanley Kubrick's masterpiece, *A Clockwork Or-*

ange, the second, more ominously, by John Phillips, from the first album of The Mamas and The Papas: "Straight Shooter."[26] In another building on the estate, caretaker William Garretson was oblivious to the shooting and other sounds coming from the Tate residence; he was listening to The Mamas and The Papas and the Doors.

It was about half-past midnight in Los Angeles on August 9, 1969. The following day would be the thirty-fourth anniversary of Robert DeGrimston's birth in Shanghai. One wonders how the Process Church of the Final Judgment celebrated their founder's birthday. Devil's food cake? Black candles? Doggie bag?

That same day, Disneyland opened their Haunted House ride.

That night, Steve Brandt—former press agent for Sharon Tate, legal witness at her wedding to Roman Polanski, and columnist for Photoplay *magazine—was having dinner at a Japanese restaurant in Los Angeles with John Phillips of The Mamas and The Papas.[27] For a brief time he would be a suspect in the murders even though he cooperated with police, and gave them "voluminous" information on Tate, Polanski, Frykowski, and the LA drug scene, before committing suicide in New York City after several other failed attempts. He was afraid he was on a hit list. Why?*

Many more thousands of miles to the west, across the Pacific Ocean in Japan, it was four-thirty in the afternoon of the same day, the twenty-fourth anniversary of the atomic bomb attack on Nagasaki. There had been peace demonstrations throughout Japan but especially in Hiroshima and Nagasaki, the two towns devastated by the blasts of "Little Boy" and "Fat Man," respectively, while in Vietnam in the summer of 1969 the war went on without a break: more soldiers died, more civilians died, flames and chemicals and bombs destroying the landscape and maiming its inhabitants, and Nixon—who cut the deal with President Thieu to sabotage the peace process and prolong the war until after his election—saw everything that he had made and, behold, it was good. And the evening and the morning of the first day.

And no one got out of there alive.

Susan Atkins herded Sharon Tate, Jay Sebring and Abigail Folger into the living room, where Frykowski—a survivor of the Nazi invasion of Poland—was already bound with towels. Patricia Krenwinkle did not have a weapon, and rushed outside to where Linda Kasabian was waiting, took her knife, and then rushed back to the house.

Although Tex Watson had brought a long length of rope, Frykowski was tied up very inefficiently with towels they found at the Tate home. This was obviously a very poorly-planned robbery. In the end, they took less than eighty dollars from the scene, leaving jewelry, electronic equipment, and credit cards behind. Again, robbery as a motive doesn't play.

Tex ordered the three newcomers to lie on their stomachs on the floor. Sebring objected, saying that Sharon Tate was pregnant and that she should be allowed to sit. Tex ignored him and ordered them all on the floor again, at which point Sebring lunged for the gun in Watson's hand. Watson fired, and Sebring was down. The women screamed. Watson then kicked Sebring in the face. He demanded money once again; this time Abigail Folger said she had some cash in her bedroom. Susan Atkins led her there at the point of a knife. The take was seventy-two dollars. Total. For the night.

Tex then ordered that all of the victims be tied together with the length of nylon rope that he brought with him, tied around their necks. Abigail Folger and Sharon Tate had the rope tied around their necks, and then one end was tossed over a ceiling beam and down to where Jay Sebring lay, unconscious from the gunshot wound, and tied around his neck. Tex ordered that the lights be turned out, and the rest of what transpired took place in relative darkness. He told the assembled victims that he was the Devil once again, and then he told them that he was going to kill all of them. The women began screaming again; Sebring was still unconscious; Frykowski was struggling to free himself of the towels.

Watson ordered Susan Atkins to kill Frykowski. She came up on him with her knife. The towels did not hold him. He got loose and jumped at Susan, pulling her down by her hair as they struggled over the knife. Getting her arm free, she began stabbing Frykowski over and over again. The slaughter had begun.

Susan stabbed Frykowski in the legs and then aimed for his chest, hitting his lung, but he still struggled, and she lost her knife in the chaos. It would turn up later, long after the killers had returned to the Spahn Ranch, stuck in a chair cushion. Susan jumped on his back, yelling, as Frykowski crawled to the door. Tex Watson aimed his .22 at the escaping man and shot him several times, but to no immediate avail. Finally, Watson began clubbing him to death with the butt of the gun, breaking it in the process.

During the attack on Frykowski, Abigail Folger managed to break free and ran for the rear of the house. Patricia Krenwinkle gave chase, and the two fought, as Watson turned to see that Jay Sebring was regaining consciousness. Watson then began stabbing Sebring repeatedly. Krenwinkle screamed she was having problems with Abigail Folger, who by this time had been stabbed in the arms as she tried to defend herself against Krenwinkle's blade. Finally, though, Abigail gave up, exhausted and bleeding. Watson slit her neck, and then stabbed her repeatedly in her abdomen after smashing her head in with the gun butt.

Frykowski, meanwhile, had managed to escape outside the house to the front lawn, where he began screaming for help. The Tate house was in Benedict Canyon, and the echoes carried far. No one responded to his desperate plea for life. William Garretson in his caretaker's cottage was listening to the Doors and ignoring whatever was going on outside his four walls. "This is the end…" Watson ran out of the house and jumped on Frykowski, dragging him to the ground and stabbing him a total of fifty-one times.

At the same moment, Abigail Folger—still alive after having been stabbed and having her throat slit—made her way, step by bloody step, to the rear of the house and freedom. Krenwinkle gave chase, leaving a bloody fingerprint on the door in the process, but Abigail had managed to almost reach the fence in the rear of the house past the swimming pool when she collapsed onto the ground and died.

Sharon Tate was alone in the house, with the body of Jay Sebring. She started to walk towards the front door when Krenwinkle entered the house through the back at a run. She stopped Sharon's escape, and held her in a headlock. Sharon began crying, begging to be left alive so she could have her baby. It wasn't to happen. Watson and Atkins entered the house, Susan Atkins holding Sharon's arms and Patricia Krenwinkle her legs. Sharon turned to Susan and begged for her life once again, or at least the life of her baby.

Tex told Susan to kill her. Susan declined. He told Patricia to kill her. She also declined. Then Tex began to stab Sharon Tate, and eventually all three stabbed her a total of sixteen times. Her baby died a few minutes after his mother. Susan Atkins, in recalling the murder to another prison inmate, said, "It felt so good, the first time I stabbed her."

Tex ordered the women out, and then he went around to all the corpses in a frenzy, stabbing them all again for good measure and kicking their heads. They then ran down to where they parked their car, looking for Linda Kasabian. Their clothing was drenched in blood.

Linda had tried, a little ineffectually, to get Atkins and Krenwinkle to stop. Still horrified by the corpse of Steven Parent, she wanted nothing more to do with killing. When the screams and the shots resounded all over the Canyon she hid, terrified, in some bushes and later made her way to the car. The killers began looking for her, but couldn't find her on the estate; so they made their way back to the Ford, where they found Linda at the wheel, starting the car.

They jumped in, Tex taking over the driving, and they changed their clothes, making a bloody bundle for Linda to toss over a cliff. This bundle would be found later, as well as the broken gun Watson had used to kill Parent, Sebring and Frykowski.

(There were a total of 102 stab wounds over the five victims. When the Spahn Ranch was raided—seven days later on August 16, 1969—and Manson arrested on auto-theft charges unrelated to the Tate and LaBianca killings, there would be a total of 102 law enforcement personnel involved.[28] Three days later, the murderers would all be freed).

The killers returned to Spahn Ranch, to find Manson sitting outside, waiting for them. When he got the story of what happened, he shook his head and demanded to be taken to the scene of the crime, where he would add a few touches of his own, such as draping a towel over Jay Sebring's head. The important point to remember is that Manson did not go to any other houses that night; he did not rob anyone else, and there was no further attempt that day to raise any money for Mary Brunner's bail. In fact, he let Brunner stay in jail for quite some time, when it would have been easy enough for him and his crew to raise the bail money through their usual methods. Once again, money was not the issue, and robbery was not the motive.

Manson knew the house well. He had been there with Terry Melcher. He saw Sharon Tate on one visit to the house after Melcher left. He knew Abigail Folger from his days in San Francisco. It's possible he knew Frykowski as well, since Frykowski was Abigail Folger's lover and also because Frykowski was running drugs in Los Angeles, much to the discomfort of some long-standing dealers. He would have been the perfect person to use to take care of Frykowski, since the dealers would have known of Manson's relationships to the house and its inhabitants.

But other things went on at the Tate house, any of which could have provided a motive for murder. Witnesses have come forward to say that hokey satanic rituals took place there, some of which were filmed. Was this only some Hollywood Halloween kinkiness, a bunch of people dressing up in robes and chanting nonsense for fun? Or was there actual cult influence on Cielo Drive? As for film, police did confiscate one film from Cielo Drive showing Sharon Tate and Roman Polanski making love, which they then returned. Another witness has insisted that group sex was a feature of the Tate residence, sex that involved numerous celebrities, but which would also include strangers picked up in the clubs or along Sunset Strip or Santa Monica Boulevard. Jay Sebring was known to have a predilection for kinky sex, and was found to be in possession of bondage equipment. Dennis Hopper, as noted above, claimed LAPD told him of the existence of bondage, sado-masochism and bestialty films connected with the case. And, of course, they were all doing all sorts of drugs.

None of this is grounds for slaughter, certainly. Today, much of what was just described could be found in thousands of homes across America; but in the pre-VCR days, average citizens did not videotape each other having sex. There was no such equipment available to the general public. What did exist was extremely expensive and hard to come by, and required at least some training in its use. Further, the films taken would have to be developed at a film lab, so one needed pretty good connections to get "questionable" material processed, although that was usually not a problem for those already in the film industry (as this author can himself attest). Once the VCR and the video camera became ubiquitous in America, however, people began filming each other in various sexual states with reckless abandon, even selling the product on the open market as "amateur" films; this has only increased with the easy availability of basic desktop computer equipment, digital video cameras and multimedia software. Imagine, however, the heady intensity of those days in 1969 when only a handful of people had the capability to film each other, people associated with the film industry itself. The temptation to do so was overwhelming.

The author has no doubt that numerous "private" films were made in those days, films of sex, certainly, and possibly of torture and murder as well. The FBI has consistently reported that there is no evidence for the existence of "snuff films," that it is an urban legend, and we have to respect their statements on this. If anyone should know, the FBI should know. However, it is simply untrue that no one to date has filmed a murder.

The Son of Sam investigation has revealed—according to Maury Terry— that some films were made of specific killings. We also know for a certainty that serial killers Leonard Lake and Charlie Ng of northern California in the 1980s *did* videotape the torture and death of their victims, of which twenty were found buried around their cabin in Calaveras County. Leonard Lake—a former Marine who had served in Vietnam—considered himself a pagan, a worshipper of Odin, and was involved in creating the famous "unicorn" exhibit at the Barnum and Bailey Circus in 1984. With sexual tastes that were exclusively sadistic, he was involved in the pornography business, making films of women who were tied up and tortured. Later, he turned his pornographic fantasies into reality, and wound up killing his victims on camera and taking still photos of their corpses before burial. (He committed suicide with a cyanide capsule while in the custody of the San Francisco Police Department in 1985, before the police even knew his real name.)

Thus, "snuff" films *do* exist; whether they exist in the marketplace as a commodity is, of course, highly doubtful. Whatever does exist may be held either as blackmail material (real or potential) or for viewing by selected individuals. With the advent of the video camera, everyone can share in the magic of Hollywood; horror has become democratized, and the only question is whether your filmmaker neighbor is the future Wes Craven, John Carpenter... or Leonard Lake.

News of the Tate homicides broke later, after housekeeper Winifred Chapman arrived and found the bodies. The story of the hideous crime made instant headlines all over the United States and the rest of the world. Many individuals with guilty consciences immediately went into hiding, believing themselves next on the hit list even though the police had no leads and did not know the motive for the crime. The drug trade in Hollywood and the rest of Los Angeles was severely affected, as drugs were the first thing on everyone's mind, and homicide detectives began leaning on their informants all over town. Cult murder was not ruled out, either, nor were starlets, studio executives, and movie stars with connections to Polanski, Tate, Frykowski, and Folger. Due to Sharon Tate's husband, some people were of the opinion that the murders were somehow related to Polanski's film *Rosemary's Baby*, perhaps in reprisal by some offended coven or secret lodge. There was also the possibility that John Phillips of The Mamas and The Papas was involved; Polanski had once slept with Phillips' wife, the singer and now actress Michelle Phillips, and Phillips was angry over that. Polanski actually considered John Phillips the prime suspect and investigated him on his own, coming up empty. Then there was a substantial rumor pointing to what Ed Sanders calls a "voodoo cult" operating from Jamaica. Polanski went down to Jamaica to check it out, and again came up empty.

The Jamaican angle is interesting because Canadian drug dealer Billy Doyle, who was beaten at the Tate house only days before the killings, was known to have flown drugs into the United States from Jamaica specifically. The idea was that Doyle had arranged the killings as retribution for the treatment he received on Cielo Drive, and contracted a cult of killers from Jamaica to do the deed. This only fits what we know of the crime if we maintain that the Jamaican cult then sub-contracted the hit to a known local cult, the Manson Family. There is no evidence to support this, of course, and one suspects it would have been easier for Doyle to go direct to Manson with the contract.

Manson himself has said that the real motive behind the Tate killings would never be revealed (by him), but that it was so explosive it would rock the establishment. One tends to believe Manson in this instance, perhaps because of his personal code of honor which stipulates that one never rats or informs on another criminal, and perhaps because he has never tried to use this information to get himself better treatment in prison. Of course, the reverse may also be true: that Manson has no information to trade;. But Manson's own public self-identification with Robert Moore deGrimston of the Process Church of the Final Judgment—and the Church's subsequent visit to Manson, after which Manson no longer said a word about the Process—has opened a can of worms, a deep and unsettling suspicion that just won't go away.

More murders were committed in the coming weeks and months, as the police investigation went nowhere. The day after the Tate killings, Leno and Rosemary LaBianca were killed in their home after being tied up by Manson, who then left and ordered his minions to perform the actual homicides. Again, if robbery was the motive then they were pretty poor thieves, since they left jewelry and valuables worth many thousands of dollars all over the house, including a coin collection. Leno LaBianca's phone had been tapped, as it was later discovered by police, and the supposition is that the wiretap was federal and somehow connected to a famous bookie—known as The Phantom—who lived on the same street as the LaBiancas. Were the LaBiancas killed because the mob believed they were giving information to the Feds, when actually the information came from a wiretap? This doesn't seem likely, as the Phantom did not move from his home until *after* the LaBianca killings, indicating he did not have foreknowledge. Yet, he *did* move, and soon after the murders, indicating he at least knew the LaBiancas and was afraid of being dragged into the investigation, or that he had a snitch inside the police department who told him of the phone tap and its implications.

The LaBianca killings were the most cultic. It was at LaBianca that the police first came across the term "Helter Skelter" used in connection with the murder spree, as this phrase was written on the wall in blood, along with the word "Rise." The word "War" was carved into Leno LaBianca's stomach; and a serving fork was stuck into it as a final touch. Leno was killed first, within range of his wife; when they found him later, the police noticed a knife stuck in his neck along with the serving fork in his stomach.

That night, August 9th to August 10th, Manson, Tex Watson, Linda Kasabian, Susan Atkins, Patricia Krenwinkel and Steve Grogan had all piled into the car. Manson was going to show the murder crew how it was done. This time, they drove aimlessly through Pasadena for a long time, up and down streets, until finally Manson stopped in front of one house, got out of the car, and then returned a few minutes later having decided not to "do" that house, making the whole thing look random. (One wonders if they passed the house where Sirhan's family lived; or Jack Parsons' old neighborhood.) He next stopped at a church, which was locked.

Then, they drove directly to the Los Feliz section of Los Angeles, to a house on Waverly Drive. Incredibly, Linda Kasabian had been to the house next door back in June of 1968 for a "peyote party."[29] She panicked, thinking that Manson was going to break into that house. Instead, Manson said "No, the house next door." The one at 3267 Waverly Drive.

This was the real target.

Manson went into the house first, armed with a sword. He tied up Leno and his wife with leather thongs, took Mrs. LaBianca's wallet, and then left the house. He went back to the car, and ordered Tex Watson, Patricia Krenwinkel and Leslie Van Houten into the house to kill the two people; kill them, but don't frighten them.

He would leave in the car with Susan Atkins and Linda Kasabian; the others, when they were through with the slaughter, would hitchhike back to Spahn Ranch.

The three killers went into the house, saw the terrified couple tied up in the living room, and then went into the kitchen to select a long serving fork and a serrated knife. They separated the two people, and the girls took Rosemary LaBianca into a bedroom while Tex Watson kept Leno LaBianca in the living room. The girls placed a pillow case over her head and tied her neck with a lamp cord, shoving her face down on the bed. Then her husband began to scream.

Tex Watson had ripped off Leno LaBianca's pajama top and began stabbing him repeatedly. Leno's hands were still tied behind him, and he couldn't maneuver himself away from the berserk killer. He was stabbed four times in the throat and four times in the abdomen with the serrated knife from the kitchen, with a pillow over his face to muffle the screams. The kitchen knife was stuck in his neck in a brutal recreation of the murder of Manson's uncle, Darwin Orell Scott, a few months earlier in Ashland, Kentucky. Blood was everywhere in the living room.

Rosemary LaBianca heard the screams and struggled with the two women, dropping to the floor and crawling to the living room. The women stopped her, and began stabbing her, severing her spinal cord. She bore forty-two stab wounds when it was all over, mostly from Patricia Krenwinkle at first and later from Tex and Leslie Van Houten.

Tex then returned to the body of Leno LaBianca and carved the word "War" into his abdomen. Patricia Krenwinkle took the serving fork and stabbed both bodies with it, leaving it finally in the stomach of Leno LaBianca. Then, in his blood, they wrote "DEATH TO PIGS" on one wall, and "RISE" on another. In the kitchen, on the refrigerator, they wrote "HEALTER SKELTER," a rather strange misspelling.

They wiped down the house for fingerprints, took a communal shower to wash off the blood, then they went back to the kitchen to get something to eat. They were hungry.

Meanwhile, Manson, Steve Grogan, Susan Atkins and Linda Kasabian drove to a gas station to place Rosemary LaBianca's wallet in the rest room, hoping that a black person would find it and use the credit cards, thus placing the blame squarely on the Black Panthers. It would be months before the wallet was ever discovered, however.

In the meantime, there was a spontaneous plan to kill someone else that night, an actor living in Venice who had portrayed the role of Lebanese poet Kahlil Gibran in a movie, a person known to Linda Kasabian. They stopped in front of his apartment house, and Manson handed her a pocket knife after showing her how to use it to kill someone. Then he left in the car.

Kasabian, not willing to kill anyone, pretended to knock on his door, but she knew it was the wrong apartment. When the actor did not show up, she went back to Atkins and Grogan with the news and they continued on their way, hitchiking back to the Spahn Ranch.

Watson, Krenwinkle and Van Houten also hitchhiked back to the Ranch. Their only spoils from the murders: a handful of foreign coins not worth more than a few dollars they found in a small bag. Once again, robbery was not the motive. Mary Brunner in jail for stolen credit cards was not the motive. Bobby Beausoleil in jail for the murder of Gary Hinman was not the motive. These were either contract hits, taken on by Manson for reasons undisclosed to this time, or we have to believe that they were the opening salvos in Manson's dream of igniting a race war.

If the latter, then why did the high-profile murders suddenly stop? While many more murders were committed in the days and weeks to follow, they were low-profile attacks on members of the Family who knew too much… or on Scientologists for some strange reason also yet to be divulged. Steve Grogan, who had been to the LaBianca residence with Manson, was pursued by the Scientologists, who believed he had information on Manson of value to them, according to an internal Scientology memo dated 22 June 1970, just after the start of the trial. The memo does not state why the Church was interested in Manson, but it does go on to report on the conversion of Manson to Scientology while in prison with Lanier Raimer (called in the memo "Lafayette Raimer") at McNeil Island. The memo confirms that Raimer's wife was "in training here at the L.A. Org in 1965-66; she had disconnected from Raimer." Obviously, if Manson was involved with Scientology, then the Church of Scientology was very eager to find out how, and to what extent, so that they could perform some damage control.

But was Manson—through his famous "Family"—behind the series of killings of Scientology members and others close to the investigation that began in 1969 and which extended to the deaths around the Son of Sam killings in the late 1970s, murders that were variously described as "retaliation" killings or even as damage control?

Item: October 31, 1969. Halloween. Sharon Tate friend Steve Brandt attempts suicide in Los Angeles, over fear of a hit list with him on it. He survives, only to succeed a month later in New York City.[30]

Item: November 16, 1969. At almost the same location where the body of Marina Habe was discovered on January 1, 1969, the body of another young woman was found. She had been stabbed 157 times. She was identified as "Sherry" by Ruby Pearl, a horse wrangler who worked at the Spahn Ranch. Nothing else is known about her, or who killed her so brutally, leaving her roughly where Marina Habe, similarly stabbed, had been left.

Item: November 21, 1969. Los Angeles. The bodies of two teenagers were found in an alley; they had each been stabbed more than fifty times. The eldest, Doreen Gaul (19) was a Scientology "clear" who had been living at the Church of Scientology. The boy, James Sharp, was only fifteen, but also a Scientology member. They had been killed with a long knife or bayonet (or sword) somewhere else and dumped in the alley. The crime has not been solved. It was claimed that Doreen Gaul was a former girlfriend of Scientologist and convicted Manson Family killer Bruce Davis, but this has never been confirmed. It is known that Davis flew to London that month and did not surface again until the following year.

Item: December 1, 1969. The anniversary of Aleister Crowley's death. Charles Manson—captured by police on the anniversary of Crowley's birth,

October 12, 1969—has now been publicly associated with the Tate/La Bianca murders in a press conference given on this day in Los Angeles. On the same day, in London, Sandy Good's former husband—Joel Pugh—is found naked and dead in a hotel room where he had been living since that October. His wrists had been slashed, as had his neck. He was living on the ground floor, with window access to the street. The police cleared the incident as suicide and did not investigate further, even though there was writing on the mirror and other written materials in the room. They didn't even bother taking fingerprints. The possibility that this was murder cannot be ruled out. Bruce Davis was in England at this time, and was naturally acquainted with both eminent Family member Sandy Good and her husband. Was Joel Pugh another man who knew too much?

As we will see later, more murdered Scientologists turn up in the Son of Sam investigation.

These killings took place in an atmosphere of reprisal and damage control—murders committed *by* Family members or *on* Family members—after the Tate and LaBianca killings. One of these was of Donny Shea, who was murdered and buried at the Spahn Ranch on or about August 25, 1969; it was Steve Grogan (aka "Clem") who eventually led police to the site. Shea is believed to have known Manson and Abigail Folger as early as 1967, when Manson was first released and living in San Francisco. It is believed he was killed simply because he knew too much of Manson's past and his links to the Tate residence. The murder was made easier because Shea had been agitating to get the Family moved from Spahn Ranch, as they were bad for the Ranch's business of renting horses.

On November 5, 1969 Family member John Philip Haught (aka "Zero") was killed playing Russian roulette with a loaded gun in a house in Venice, California. When the gun was examined by police, it was discovered that it had no fingerprints. Bruce Davis was present at the time, but an informer stated that one of the women had killed Haught. No one believed that Haught killed himself while playing Russian roulette with the loaded revolver, but the case was carried as a suicide as there were many witnesses—all Family members—who insisted that this was the case.

Without going further into all the minutiae of the case, it is enough to report that the Manson Family was raided on October 12, 1969 for reasons unrelated to the Tate and LaBianca killings. As noted, this is Aleister Crowley's birthday, a day celebrated by many of the cults that adhere to his teachings. It is also, of course, Columbus Day. Yet, it would not be until December 1, 1969—the anniversary of Crowley's *death*—that the Los Angeles police would come to the conclusion that the people they had in custody were responsible for the Tate and LaBianca killings, a conclusion based largely on jailhouse talk by

Susan Atkins to another inmate, as well as corroborating testimony by people close to the Family …and by Linda Kasabian, who turned state's evidence and told in detail about both the Tate and La Bianca killings.

One interesting detail—noted almost in passing in Polanski's autobiography—is that someone at LAPD suspected the Manson Family in the Tate killings long before any such suspicions were made known, and had indeed connected them to the Hinman killing. Lieutenant Bob Helder had made it known to Polanski (soon after Sharon Tate's funeral, and therefore sometime in August) that they were looking at "a possible lead involving a bunch of hippies living in the Chatsworth area under a commune leader, 'a crazy guy who calls himself Jesus Christ.'"[31] Had this lead been followed up immediately, they might have saved Donny Shea. As it was, Manson was rousted again and again that month on unrelated charges and let go every time.

The trial would begin June 15, 1970 and would last until January 25, 1971, with the penalty phase not over until March 29th of that year. During that time the trial itself would become a microcosm of insanity, as lawyers were hired and fired, as the antics of the accused and their supporters disrupted the courtroom constantly, and as Richard Nixon would proclaim Manson guilty, on August 9, 1970: the first anniversary of the Tate killings *and four years to the day* before he would resign as President in the wake of the Watergate investigation. No matter. When the trial was over, all defendants—Manson, Krenwinkle, Atkins, Leslie van Houten—were found guilty and sentenced to death; fortunately for them, the death penalty was repealed in California and they wound up with life imprisonment instead.

More trials would take place, however: for Bruce Davis, Bobby Beausoleil, Steven Grogan, Charles "Tex" Watson. All would be found guilty. Bruce Davis turned himself in to authorities on December 2, 1970, a few days after the disappearance of Manson Family trial lawyer Ronald Hughes (to be discussed below), after spending the anniversary of Crowley's death in the sewers beneath Los Angeles. Charles "Tex" Watson—who led the killers in sheer viciousness and rage—was found guilty on October 12, 1971: again, Crowley's birthday. Manson himself was held in a special jail cell on the thirteenth floor at the courthouse, the one that had been specially built the previous year for Sirhan Sirhan.

Manson's lawyer, Irving Kanarek, was a flamboyant attorney with a knack for constant objections, frivolous motions and generally wasting everyone's time. One of the best—possibly apocryphal—stories about him tells of his objection when a witness was asked to state his name. "Objection!" yelled Kanarek. "Hearsay! His mother told him his name." He was, however, an effective trial lawyer in spite of the opprobrium in which he was held by fellow attorneys and judges. Yet, in Manson's case, he had virtually nothing to work with. Manson at one point even attacked the judge, leaping up to the bench, and had to be dragged down and put in chains. Kanarek himself had an odd and suggestive background, for this lawyer of many years practice in the State of California had begun his career as a chemical engineer. A rocket engineer. Specializing in propulsion systems.

It was Kanarek who addressed the court one day during the Easter holiday and, after reading aloud from the New Testament, asked the court if they really knew for certain that Charles Manson was *not* Jesus Christ?

Kanarek eventually had some sort of nervous breakdown years later, and wound up in a mental institution for a short time even as he was being sued. And even though his opponents knew where he was at the time, they didn't inform the judge as to Kanarek's whereabouts. Even so, he was one of the lucky ones. Another Manson attorney was not so lucky.

Ronald Hughes became Leslie Van Houten's attorney, even though he had no trial experience.[32] Manson's approach to litigation was unusual, to say the least. He was not particularly interested in going free or in getting a vigorous—or even a barely effective—defense. He was more interested in making his message known, in converting the judge, the lawyers, the jury and the rest of the world to his way of thinking. He was also insistent on the "Family" staying together and providing a united front. To these ends, the lawyers he chose were more representative of his personal, mystical agenda than they were of an attempt to beat the system. The selection of Irving Kanarek and Ronald Hughes was reflective of this. Kanarek could be counted upon to say the most amazing things during the trial, even going so far as to openly wonder if perhaps Manson really was Jesus Christ. Ronald Hughes, as a man totally unprepared for a murder trial, was the perfect choice—to Manson's way of thinking—to defend Leslie Van Houten, who was on trial for the La Bianca murders only. Initially, there was an attempt to separate Van Houten's defense from the rest of the Manson Family, but that was shot down even though it may have given her a better chance. The important thing was to keep the Family together, both in the courtroom and outside. What they did not need was a savvy trial attorney pulling all sorts of tricks that would get some of them off and leave the rest behind. If Manson was going down, they were all going down.

Outside the courtroom, Lynette Fromme was doing her best to hold the Family together. She became the nucleus of what was left of the Manson cult, and ostensibly the one who transmitted Charlie's orders to the rest of the clan, orders that resulted in the deaths of several more people. Orders that resulted—according to Sandy Good—in the death of attorney Ronald Hughes, the "first of the retaliation murders."[33]

At a break in the trial on the weekend of November 27, 1970 Ronald Hughes decided to go camping at Sespe Hot Springs, something he did quite often. The springs are about two hours drive northwest of Los Angeles. Hughes would go up there on a Friday night and stay until Sunday. That weekend, the weekend before he was to begin his portion of the trial involving Leslie van Houten, he disappeared.

He was last seen alive on Saturday, apparently in good health and good spirits. There had been a flash flood that weekend, and speculation was that he was stranded. The people who had driven him up that weekend were found, and they claimed that they left early because of the rain but that Hughes wanted to stay longer. They themselves became stranded when their car got caught in the mud, and they had to hitchhike back to Los Angeles.

This was something of a problem for the trial, of course, with Miss Van Houten insisting she wanted no other attorney than Hughes. Eventually, the court appointed another attorney for her and the trial proceeded. The new lawyer was determined to do what he could to save Van Houten, which sent Manson into a rage. His plan was to have Van Houten testify against herself and in favor of Manson, to exonerate him, and her new lawyer was having none of it. The judge insisted that new counsel be found for Leslie Van Houten in spite of everyone's objections. That was on December 2, 1970. That same day, Bruce Davis and his current girlfriend and Manson Family member Brenda McCann (Nancy Pitman) surrendered to authorities. This raised a great deal of suspicion in the minds of defense and prosecution attorneys alike. Vincent Bugliosi, the lead prosecutor, felt sure that the events were related. Why would Bruce Davis—who was wanted for two murders (Hinman and Shea)—turn himself in when the police had no idea where he was? And surrender only a few days after the equally suspicious disappearance of Leslie Van Houten's defense attorney? Indeed, on the same day that the judge decided that she needed a new lawyer? It seemed obvious to many people that Manson was behind the strategy, possibly designed to create a mistrial.

Hughes had become increasingly independent over the course of the trial. It seemed certain that he would call Leslie Van Houten to the stand with the intent to crucify Manson, when Manson wanted the reverse to take place. In addition, Hughes feared Manson, and Manson knew this. Everyone knew it. Hughes made no secret of the fact that Manson scared him, but he was going to do what he had to do as an attorney to provide the best possible defense for his client. His client was not Charles Manson; it was Leslie Van Houten.

His body was reported discovered on the last day of the trial, badly decomposed and face down in a pool of water. The decomposition was so bad that an autopsy revealed very little. It was believed at first that he had simply been caught by the flash flood and drowned. Although many had their suspicions, they had no evidence and no eyewitnesses to work with.

Yet, when filmmaker Laurence Merrick was making his own documentary film on the Manson Family, Sandra Good told him—in front of a witness—that Ronald Hughes was murdered. The timing of the murder was, of course, highly suggestive of a motive: to keep him from doing his duty before the jury that coming Monday and defending Van Houten at the expense of Manson. This is essentially what Sandra Good confirmed.

Merrick's film, *Manson*, was nominated for an Academy Award in 1973. Merrick had been an acting coach for Sharon Tate, and had easy access to the Family members who were still at large. He was shot to death at his studio in Hollywood in 1977.

Family members were still involved in murder and attempted murder. Brenda McCann, aka Nancy Pitman, was arrested on November 11, 1972 in Stockton, California. Brenda had been Bruce Davis' girlfriend, with whom she had been on the lam in the Los Angeles sewers for months before they turned themselves in during December 1970. This time, she was found in a house which contained a body buried in the basement, that of Lauren Willett (19), who had been shot in the head. Along with McCann were two members of the Aryan Brotherhood, as well as another woman named Priscilla Cooper (21). Both women had X's carved into their foreheads, identifying them as Manson Family members. What alerted police to the house was the fact that a car parked outside belonged to a man who had been murdered a few days earlier in Northern California. James T. Willett was a former Marine, and had been found in his Marine uniform: killed with a shotgun and decapitated. As the police were busy arresting the four people in the house—which contained a small arsenal of weapons—Lynette "Squeaky" Fromme called and asked to be picked up, evidently in the slain Mr. Willett's car. The police were only too happy to oblige.

The motive for the murders remains unknown to this day. It is known that the Willetts had been associates of the Family for some time, at least a year if not longer according to Bugliosi[34]. Bugliosi also wondered if James and Lauren Willett were the same James and Lauren who had driven Ronald Hughes to his campsite; if so, their deaths would be in accord with the Family's tradition of murder-as-cover-up. Bugliosi was unable to find the original James and Lauren, who had long since moved from their last known address. Eventually, the two men of the Aryan Brotherhood confessed to the crimes and were sentenced, as were Nancy Pitman and Priscilla Cooper. There was nothing to hold Lynette Fromme, so she was set free.

And in September 1975, she attempted the assassination of President Gerald Ford in Sacramento, California. She was convicted and has spent all her life since then in prison, except for an escape attempt from the Federal Correctional Institute at Alderson, West Virginia during the Christmas holidays of 1987, when she heard a rumor that Manson had contracted cancer. She was found in the woods a few days later, and brought back to the prison. In 1989, Lynette Fromme was transferred to Marianna, Florida.

Ruth Ann Morehouse, a young native of Minot, North Dakota, whose father tried to rescue her from Manson but who later became a devotee was involved in a bizarre attempt to murder a witness, one Barbara Hoyt, in Hawaii.

Barbara Hoyt (17) had been with the Family since April of 1969. She was present at Spahn Ranch when Donny Shea was murdered, and heard his screams. She was told by Ruth Morehouse (known as "Ouisch") of ten additional murders they had committed besides the Tate and LaBianca killings. She had heard so much at the ranch—and also at other Manson hideouts such as the Barker Ranch in Death Valley—that she was an important material witness and could tie together names, dates and places.

Barbara Hoyt agreed to cooperate with the authorities and act as a witness in the trial against Manson and company, even though she was afraid for her life. However, before she could testify, Lynette "Squeaky" Fromme, Ruth Ann "Ouisch" Morehouse, Catherine "Gypsy" Share and Steve "Clem" Grogan convinced her to go to Hawaii instead. Barbara agreed to leave California jurisdiction and hide out in Hawaii until the trial was over. It seemed like the line of least resistance. That was on September 6, 1970.

She flew to Honolulu with Morehouse and stayed in the penthouse suite at the Hilton Hawaiin Village Hotel.[35] Like so many assassins who figure in American history over the past hundred years, they had first class travel accommodations and no indication exists of where the money came from. The same time every morning, Ouisch would leave the hotel and make a call to the Family from a pay phone. On the morning of September 9th, she was summoned back to California and given certain other instructions. She made arrangements to fly back that afternoon, but Barbara Hoyt was to remain behind in Hawaii.

They went to the airport together, and Ouisch suggested to Hoyt that she eat something, even though Ouisch herself wasn't hungry. Barbara ordered a hamburger, and Ouisch carried the tray to a table while Barbara stood in line at the cash register to pay for it.

By the time Barbara had returned to the table, Ouisch had laced the burger with a mega dose of LSD.

Ouisch—Ruth Ann Morehouse—then boarded her flight, leaving the now disoriented Barbara Hoyt alone in the airport. Hoyt began to feel very strange, and started wandering around and then began running in the street. She was found sprawled outside in traffic, and rushed to the emergency room where her life was saved. After that incident, she was eager to testify against the Family.

Catherine "Gypsy" Share was not to be outdone. Her parents had been members of the French resistance against the Nazis during the Second World War, and had been executed. She was raised by a foster father in the United States, and had become an accomplished violinist... as well as a dedicated Communist. When she finally met the Manson Family, her Communist beliefs became muted, as she adopted more and more of the Manson philosophy and actually found herself marrying one of the pro-Nazi Aryan Brotherhood. It was Catherine Share who appeared in the soft-porn film *Ramrodder* with fellow Mansonite Bobby Beausoleil, both appearing as Indians and Bobby as a murdering warrior with a knife.

As the trial against Manson progressed, Share and the other members of the Family began developing practical relationships with members of the Aryan Brotherhood, a racist prison gang that has been implicated in all sorts of violence both inside and outside prison walls. In this case, it was an attempt to spring Manson from jail by first robbing a store that sold weapons. On August 21, 1971, Catherine Share and Mary Brunner—along with four men who were also Family members and in at least one instance (Kenneth Como) a member of the Aryan Brotherhood—robbed the Western Surplus Store in the Hawthorne section of Los Angeles of roughly 140 guns, storing them in a van parked in the alley behind the shop. The LAPD had been called to the scene by a silent alarm, and a gunfight ensued in which seventy rounds were fired. No one was injured, and the six Manson Family members were arrested.

It was later discovered that the attempted theft of the surplus store was part of a larger plot to free Manson by hijacking a 747 and killing hostages until he was freed. During the trial, one of the accused—Kenneth Como—managed to escape by sawing through the bars on his cell on the thirteenth floor. He was picked up by Sandy Good, but Sandy smashed up the van and Como fled on foot. He was apprehended a few hours later.

Eventually, Catherine Share would get ten years to life, Mary Brunner would get twenty to life, Kenneth Como fifteen to life, and the others various sentences. Catherine Share would later marry Kenneth Como. Mary Brunner—the very first Family member and the father of Manson's son Valentine Michael—served six and half years, and is now living under an assumed name in the Midwest. Valentine Michael—named after a character in the famous Heinlein novel *Stranger in a Strange Land*—is alive and well and wants nothing to do with his father. (He was the subject of a series of articles and interviews in *Nerve* magazine.) Catherine Share eventually divorced Como, and has turned a new leaf, distancing herself completely from Manson and the rest of the Family. One of the other Hawthorne robbery culprits, Family member Dennis Rice, is now an ordained Christian minister, as are two of his sons, who were "Manson children" at Spahn Ranch.

THE MANSON-NIXON LINE (WITH COMPLIMENTS TO ROBIN WILLIAMS)

Readers may wonder why I took so much space to outline the history of the Manson Family. Readers of Book One know I have focused on it since the beginning of this study, which concerns, after all, the identification of the sinister forces that have influenced American life, culture and politics since the earliest days of our history. I trust that my purpose will become more clear as the chapters progress and my thesis becomes more compelling. This is difficult terrain. This is about evil. Standard appraisals and explanations of evil will not suffice if we are to truly confront it, and vanquish it. As Americans, we have trusted our leaders who have always pointed in another direction every time we were threatened. The American Revolution. The War of 1812. The Mexican War. The Spanish-American War. World War I. World War II. Korea. Vietnam. Grenada. Panama. The Persian Gulf. Afghanistan, Iraq.

The only war fought on our soil in nearly two hundred years was the Civil War, and the fight was over slavery and the right of states to secede from the Union. That war was costly, bloody, and hard fought; but, in a sense, it was too easily won, for when it was over, and the South defeated and the slaves emancipated, we thought we had solved our internal problems. We thought we had solved the problem of slavery. We thought we understood the rights of our citizenry. We thought we were all on the same page in our hymnals. We did not attack root causes. We had treated a symptom of evil, and thank God for it; but we did not banish the sickness from our shores.

Now, in the wake of a horrific attack on the United States—specifically on New York City and the Pentagon—we are faced with another threat, and once again our leaders are pointing abroad. Yet the technology of terror was designed, built, and delivered from the United States, and Charles Manson was—and still is—the epitome of this technology. We have not studied the phenomenon closely; like all good Americans, we have fought the war, captured the enemy, put him behind bars and forgotten all about him. But the demon in the smoke that crawled out of the God Struck Tower on September 11, 2001 bore the face of Charles Milles Manson, the bastard son of America and product of its institutions and—even more importantly—scion of its bartered Soul. This is not easy to understand now; it will become easier and more certain as we proceed a little further, for what we are dissecting are the limbs, organs and nervous system of the Manson Secret.

Two major strands of American history meet in 1969: Hollywood, with all that the idea of Hollywood implies, and another strand that is much more elusive, more difficult to define with a single word, but which represents the dark nightmare side of politics. We may think of it as Watergate, as long as we remember it includes everything from what Nixon termed "the whole Bay of Pigs thing" to political assassinations, support for Nazi war criminals, right wing military dictatorships, and bags of dirty money. We like to think of these two strands—Hollywood and Watergate—as opposing forces, as Us and Them, but in the strange non-Euclidean geometry of the American psyche, these parallel lines meet in a tight little knot in August 1969.

The technology that had been researched, developed and fine-tuned by our own intelligence services since the end of World War II found its apotheosis in murder and madness. Americans, more than any other people in the world, love their illusions, their dreams, their flowery phrases and idealistic declarations. They have created an entire industry based on illusion: Hollywood. The deep effect that film has had on the human psyche has yet to be analyzed or even sufficiently addressed. We err if we believe that film is only stagecraft made more brilliant, more accessible. Stagecraft itself is a form of occultism, as teachers such as Stanislavsky realized at once; cinema is occultism plus light. It is powerful, and it is one of the reasons why so many foreigners hate America with an abiding passion; hate America enough to kill it. The only nation that comes close to America in the intensity of its film industry is India, and India recognizes the power of cinema to the extent that certain types of film are *never* made in that country: x-rated pornography (even kissing is rare) and occult-oriented films. Sex and magic.

American intelligence, on the other hand, plumbed the depths of sex and magic (and drugs) to understand illusion, and to manipulate it and make it a weapon. They used the prisons as testing grounds, violent criminals and psychopaths as subjects. They broke through. The seal was broken. And demons were unleashed.

American filmmakers did the same thing. The manipulation of illusion, the challenge to reality that takes place in a movie theater, may only be momentary, an hour or two in a darkened temple before the icon screen of transmitted light; but its effects are long-lasting. Hence, the propaganda film.

Maybe all films are propaganda films. Our enemies certainly see it that way; and maybe we don't know our own strength. We never learned how to use this medium in the most efficient way. Like the mad scientists of MK-ULTRA, we play with the technology, test it, write it up in reports; people like Charles Manson take it and sharpen it.

Richard Nixon was born and raised within spitting distance of Hollywood and the back lots. He spoke in terms of theater, of acting. He met his wife on the stage. His policies paved the way for another actor to become President. He consulted psychics and preachers, and toyed with converting to Catholicism. He protected Nazis who pretended to be priests. He understood the power of illusion, and the manipulation of reality. He was open about it. He counseled others in the philosophy of deceit; because lies and truth are all relative when it comes to power.

Power, to people like Manson and Nixon, is the only reality, the only absolute. Nixon *had* to proclaim Manson guilty to the press; he had to address the one other man in the country who understood power, and truth, and evil, and murder the way he did. On the plane of the real world as understood by the media and the public at large, Manson was an insignificant crook compared to Nixon, the President of the United States, undeserving of the President's attention or comment; but on another plane, Manson and Nixon were warring black magicians, fighting over airtime and the fifteen-second sound bite. Manson was manipulating illusion, and that was supposed to be Nixon's forte.

Manson may be virtually illiterate, but no one doubts his intelligence. He was a natural at what he did; his followers are now more numerous—more than thirty years after the Tate and La Bianca killings—than they ever were before. He has attracted support from racist, right-wing, and neo-Nazi organizations all over the world. It is not the intention of this author to state unequivocally that Manson was created in prison labs by the G-scale engineers of MK-ULTRA; but he could be the Mind-Control Poster Boy of 1969.

The "Manson-Nixon line" is a term coined by Robin Williams, the actor and comedian, as a pun on the Mason-Dixon Line, which separated the Northern and Southern states in nineteenth century America, with the newer version separating two different states of mind. Yet I sense something more profound in Williams' turn of phrase: Manson and Nixon as the Alpha and Omega of a scarlet thread running through the American soul, a Great Divide separating Americans from each other, and from the rest of the world, and from what they know to be good, honest and virtuous. A thread of expediency, cynicism, pragmatic choices and *realpolitik* where the end justifies the means … and sometimes, not even that.

When, as detailed in *The Nine*, Frank Olsen was pushed out the window of the Statler Hotel in New York City in 1953 and fell ten stories to his death, he was the first of those who fell from the doomed World Trade Center almost fifty years later. The technology that destroyed him created the terrorists of Abu Nidal, Hamas, Hizbolleh, and Al-Qaida. He—and they and so many others—were victims of the Manson Secret.

Endnotes

[1] Kenneth D. Wald, *Religion and Politics in the United States*, Washington, DC 1992, p. 42
[2] George Plimpton, editor, *Beat Writers at Work*, Modern Library, NY, 1999, p. 225
[3] Norman Mailer, *An American Dream*, Flamingo, NY, 1965, p. 205
[4] R.T. Rundle Clark, *Myth and Symbol in Ancient Egypt*, Thames and Hudson, NY 1991, p. 115
[5] Ibid., p. 115
[6] John Marks, *The Search for the "Manchurian Candidate,"* Times Books, NY, 1979, p. 211
[7] Martin A. Lee & Bruce Shlain, *Acid Dreams*, Grove Weidenfeld, NY, 1992, p. 18
[8] Ed Sanders, *The Family*, EP Dutton, NY, 1971, p. 122
[9] Vincent Bugliosi with Curt Gentry, *Helter Skelter*, Bantam, NY, 1995, p. 647
[10] Ward Churchill & Jim Vander Wall, *The COINTELPRO Papers*, South End Press, Boston, 1990, p. 205
[11] Ibid., p. 207
[12] Frank J. Donner, *The Age of Surveillance*, Vintage, NY, 1981, p. 248
[13] John Gilmore & Ron Kenner, *Manson: The Unholy Trail of Charlie and the Family*, Amok, Los Angeles, 2000, p. 89
[14] Ed Sanders, op. cit., p. 262
[15] Ibid., p. 262

[16] Maury Terry, *The Ultimate Evil*, Bantam, NY 1989, p. 596

[17] Ibid., p. 594

[18] Roman Polanski, *Roman*, William Morrow, NY, 1984, p. 313, 314

[19] Ibid., p. 315

[20] Ibid., p. 315

[21] Ibid., p. 312

[22] Ibid., p. 323

[23] Maury Terry, *The Ultimate Evil* (Revised Edition), Barnes & Noble, NY, 1999, p. 533; Ed Sanders, *The Family*, (Revised Edition), Signet, NY, 1989, p. 57

[24] Terry, (revised edition) op. cit., p. 534

[25] Sanders, (revised edition) op. cit., p. 232

[26] Ibid., p. 242

[27] John Phillips with Jim Jerome, *Papa John: An Autobiography*, Dell, NY, 1986, p. 299

[28] Sanders, (revised edition), op. cit., p. 307

[29] Bugliosi, op. cit., p. 363

[30] Phillips, op. cit., p. 309

[31] Polanski, op. cit., p. 315

[32] Jess Bravin, *Squeaky: The Life and Times of Lynette Alice Fromme*, St Martin's Press, NY, 1997, p. 111

[33] Bugliosi, op. cit., p. 652

[34] Ibid., p. 650

[35] Ibid., p. 474

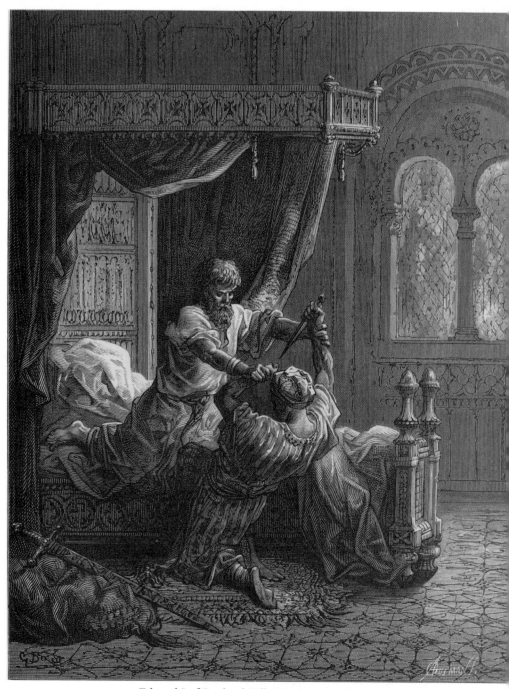

Edward I of England Kills His Attempted Assassin
Attacked in his bed, Edward I struggles to turn the weapon against his assailant,
and succeeds in killing the Muslim.

CHAPTER TWELVE

THE ROOTS OF TERRORISM

The Syrian Nizaris, who possessed a vulnerable and small principality in a hostile milieu, made an important impact, quite disproportionate to their numbers or political power, on the regional politics of the Latin East. This was particularly the case when they were led by Rashid al-Din Sinan, their most famous leader and the original 'Old Man of the Mountain.'
    —Farhad Daftary, *The Assassin Legends*[1]

Seest thou not that We have set the devils on the disbelievers to confound them with confusion?
    —Qu'ran, 19:83

Nothing is true; everything is permitted.
    —saying attributed to Rashid al-Din Sinan

In early 1947—the same year as Aleister Crowley's death in England, the infamous UFO sighting by Kenneth Arnold, the Roswell crash, and the creation of the CIA—some scrolls were found in the caves of Qumran in what is now Israel. The ramifications of this discovery have yet to be felt by the average man and woman living in the twenty-first century, two thousand years after the scrolls in question were written and hidden in the clay jars of Qumran. More discoveries took place over the intervening years, not only in Qumran but also in Nag Hammadi, a site in Egypt where the first of the "Gnostic Gospels" were discovered in 1945. Taken together, the finds represent the single most important challenge to the accepted belief and dogma of Christianity, and to the historical record of Judaism and even of Islam, which is largely based on Jewish and Christian scripture and tradition. Along another line, the find also represents the accidental revelation of the existence of one of the oldest secret societies in Europe, the Middle East and Central Asia: a society so old, and with secrets so well-kept, we don't even know what to call it. The pieces of those secrets—like a handful of pottery shards on an archaeologist's table—are slowly being assembled into something recognizable, but it may still be years before the whole story is understood, even by scholars. What has been discovered so far, however, has caused eminent historians of Christian, Jewish and Islamic origins to completely reevaluate their thinking.

Barbara Thiering, Elaine Pagels, Hugh Schonfield, J. M. Allegro and Robert Eisenman are some of the mainstream Biblical scholars whose books on the subject of the identity of Jesus, of his brother James, of Simon Magus, of Judas Iscariot, of all of the original apostles, of the gospels (of which there are somewhat more than the usual four), and of various sects, cults, heresies and traditions have formed a kind of "anti-history" that calls into question the last two thousand years of European belief systems, political affairs, and ecclesiastical developments. Allegro, one of the early Dead Sea Scrolls scholars along with Schonfield and Eisenman, also saw a drug connection which he popularized in *The Sacred Mushroom and the Cross* (Doubleday, 1970), a thesis considered scandalous in its time.

These discoveries have made it possible for other studies to be undertaken—usually by popular journalists—that question every facet of accepted knowledge and wisdom concerning the Bible, Church history, medieval history, the Crusades, the religious wars of Europe, and the blood-lines of kings and mystics alike. Books by authors like Michael Baigent, Richard Leigh, Henry Lincoln, Graham Hancock, Christopher Knight and Robert Lomas, Lynn Picknett, Clive Prince, and many others have all followed in the wake of these discoveries, popularizing some of the more arcane data, and sometimes imagining or speculating on the rest. The books by these other authors are usually strong on sources, regardless of how outlandish their conclusions may seem. Obviously serious about their research, they want their theories to be taken seriously. Though what results, quite often, is a great deal of infighting and criticism of each others' work, this does little to dampen the enthusiasm of the reading public for this type of scholarship. It cracks open a door to the inner sanctum of academia, and finally allows the rest of us a glimpse at what our own history may really be like. One such opening began in 1966, when the standard history of the last two thousand years of western civilization was seriously challenged by a renowned scholar—who would eventually be nominated for the Nobel Peace Prize—and the world has not been quite the same since.

I am referring, of course, to the publication of *The Passover Plot* by Dr. Hugh J. Schonfield.

In 1966, America was in the midst of the Johnson Administration and an escalating war in Vietnam. The hippie movement was in flower, and would reach its apotheosis in the Summer of Love in 1967. Martin Luther King and Robert F. Kennedy were still alive. In that year, Dr. Schonfield—an important Biblical scholar and one of the first to examine the Dead Sea Scrolls of Qumran—published a book designed for the general public on what the Dead Sea Scrolls (and other recent research) had to say about the life and death of Jesus. His conclusions were so controversial that even Dr. Schonfield himself characterizes his subject as "the strangest human enterprise in all recorded history."[2] Yet, his conclusions were perfectly in accord with what Middle Eastern and European secret societies have always insisted, even as long ago as the first century A.D., which is that Jesus never died on the cross, but was still alive when he was taken down a bare three hours after having been crucified; or, as some other scholars insist, that he survived the events narrated in the New Testament, and lived to a ripe old age. Naturally, if it could be proved that such was the case, then the entire Christian edifice comes tumbling down, for nothing is as central to Christianity as the item of faith that Christ died on the cross and was resurrected—came back to life, rose from the dead—forty hours later. Schonfield later expanded his findings in a number of other books and papers, including one— *The Essene Odyssey*—which addresses some of the issues concerning the relationship of this Biblical scholarship to later investigations of the Knights Templar and the Freemasons, as developed in *The Holy Blood and the Holy Grail* by Baigent, Leigh and Lincoln.

This latter work (published in the United States in 1982 as *Holy Blood, Holy Grail)* was as controversial in its time as *The Passover Plot* fifteen years earlier. Again, we are told that Jesus did not die on the cross, but that his bloodline survived, even though his descendants were often pursued and persecuted by a Church which could not allow this obvious challenge to orthodoxy to become public knowledge. We are told of Jesus' heirs manifesting as the Merovingian kings, and that the Knights Templar were repositories of the sacred secret of the Holy Blood, the "Sang Real," a secret that was passed down to the Rosicrucians, the Freemasons, etc.

Thus, according to this theory, a political and religious dynasty has existed in hiding for two thousand years and has had an inordinate amount of influence over the progression of world events, as certain select leaders—in politics, religion, science, culture—were brought in on the secret and made members of this intellectual elite, and given the key to understanding the codified mysteries of millenia. While Schonfield did not wholeheartedly support the conclusions of *Holy Blood, Holy Grail,* he did offer his own speculation that the Biblical Jesus wound up far from home. Schonfield tended towards the idea that Jesus wandered out of Palestine, across the Afghan frontier and into the heart of Kashmir, and was buried in a tomb built in accordance with Jewish tradition in the fabled city of Srinagar, where it can be seen today.

That the world—at the time of this writing, in the first decade of the twenty-first century—is on the verge of a horrible world war that could germinate either in Palestine or in Kashmir is satanic testament to the force of religious and political events that transpired in these two regions two thousand years ago, events that have been shrouded in mystery, in propaganda, in fantasy, but whose truths have been carefully preserved by a brotherhood of initiates, passed down in codified form for millenia.

All of the theories of the existence of a secret society of enlightened men, a society that has existed down through the ages, have as their origin either a band of geometers and architects based around the creation of the Egyptian pyramids or a similar guild of craftsmen who were involved in the erection of the Temple of Solomon in Jerusalem ... and sometimes both (as in the case of the Freemasons). The technology of architecture and construction was once believed to be sacred, and geometry was held to be a powerful art. The Freemasons still use the square and the compass as their universal symbol of God as the Great Geometer, a reference to their alleged involvement in the creation of some of the world's most enigmatic and compelling monuments including everything from the pyramids to the Temple of Solomon to Chartres Cathedral and the layout of Washington, D.C.

This combination of science and magic, of geometry and *goetia*—at the service of a lawful King—is what makes the idea of an ageless secret society of wise men timeless and still relevant today. In ancient times, this society was probably not secret, since it was in the employ of the State; but as illegitimate rulers became the crowned heads of Europe, the society that once supported the State went (or was driven) underground, and their arcane knowledge went with them. Such is the belief today held by many. When we consider how many American political leaders throughout the past two hundred years were Freemasons—and hence were exposed to these ideas, whether they embraced them or not—then we must ask ourselves if any of these ideas have received confirmation or corroboration from scientific and academic sectors, confirmation that was revealed only at the highest levels of government. One feature of this "lost science" was obviously an item on the agenda of the Central Intelligence Agency, that of occult control of the human mind, consciousness, memory and will.

The Egyptian Pharaohs were both religious and political leaders; the power they held over their people was absolute. King Solomon is also associated with *occult* power. The grimoires that falsely bear his name—*The Greater Key of Solomon, The Lesser Key of Solomon*—are evidence that the association of the name of Solomon with ceremonial magic and the control over demonic forces was taken for granted by centuries of magicians and sorcerers. Solomon was a Jewish king, and the surmise is that this occult power was passed down to generations of holy Jewish leaders, down to the time of Jesus. Some sources attribute the idea of a "genie in a bottle" to the time of Solomon and the building of the Temple: that the spirits he conjured to build the Temple were imprisoned in a jar that had Solomon's Seal upon it, and thus were unable to escape, until at one point the bottle washed up on shore and it was opened by a curious passerby, causing the demons to fly to the four corners of the world. The *Keys* of Solomon are said to be the means whereby these demons may be forced to obey the will of the magician, since they include Solomon's Seal, which is a reminder to them of their time in spiritual "durance vile."

It is further insisted by many that the Knights Templar discovered some of this power during their sojourn on the Temple Mount in the early days of the twelfth century. The precise nature of this discovery is not known. The Ark of the Covenant? The Rod of Aaron? The secret of the Passover Plot? But it seems they did discover *something.*

It would explain a great deal if they had.

THE HASHISH EATERS

Nearly a thousand years ago, the Western world was enthralled by tales of Islamic terrorism, espionage, sabotage and assassination. It was believed that religious fanatics, devotees of a mysterious Islamic leader who lived in an impregnable mountain fortress, had ordered his men to infiltrate enemy cities and assassinate their leaders, Christian and Muslim alike. There was no defense against this secret network of killers. They could show up at any time, anywhere, to carry out their murderous agenda. Even worse, they were not afraid to die, and would gladly undertake suicide missions where their chance of survival was nil. This organization came to be known as the *hashishiyya,* an Arabic word that means "hashish eaters." It was from this word that the European languages derived their word *assassin,* demonstrating a conscious equivalence between this obscure (to the West) religious sect, drugs, and the practice of political murder.

Much of what has been written about the Assassin cult was based on hearsay, rumor, propaganda and innuendo. In reality, the Assassins were an Ismaili sect of Shi'ite Islam, the Nizaris (named after their loyalty to Nizar, an Ismaili Imam they supported against the Fatimid Caliphs), and their penchant for secrecy and disinformation was due in large part to the fact that their faith was proscribed by the predominantly Sunni authorities, as well as by other Shi'ites. While much has been made of stories that the cult used hashish as a means of brainwashing their trained killers, there seems to be very little evidence that this was so. Farhad Daftary, quoted above, is scornful of Western attempts to paint the Nizaris as hashish-gobbling programmed assassins with secret rituals and a hierarchy of degrees. However, even Daftary has a problem explaining why they were specifically referred to as *hashishiyya* by fellow Muslims. He describes a world in the centuries after the death of the Prophet as one in which two main branches of Islam—the Sunni and the Shia—fought for hegemony in the region. The Sunni—as the more orthodox, conservative branch—found the Shia to be heretical in some matters of faith, and treasonous in matters of politics. The Shi'ites believe that Muslims should owe their spiritual allegiance to the blood descendants of the Prophet's family, through his cousin Ali; the Sunni followed the leadership of the Prophet's friend, Abu Bakr. The term "caliph" means "successor," and the Shi'ites believe that the descendants of Ali are the rightful Caliphs, successors to the Prophet, branding the Sunni Caliphates therefore illegitimate.

We may note here that when Grady McMurtry declared himself head of the OTO—as opposed to other contenders abroad in the land—he chose the term "Caliph." For a German-born quasi-Masonic secret society, this doesn't appear to make a great deal of sense, especially when one looks at a blasphemous reference to Mohammed in the *Book of the Law* that would certainly incite a thundering *fatwa* from the throats of the Ayatollahs, if not an outright *jihad*; however, a look at the rituals of the OTO will demonstrate how closely the Order believes itself to be the repository of Middle Eastern secrets. Sadly, the Francis King publication of those rituals has disappeared due to a concerted effort by the OTO to remove them from library and bookstore shelves; a bit like locking the barn door after the horse has been taken out and shot.

In addition to the rightful Caliphs, Shi'ites believe that there are secret teachers, or Imams, who guide the faithful in this world and are the representatives of the Prophet on earth. The mainstream Shi'ites await the return of the last—the twelfth or "hidden"—Imam, which they believe could be imminent, and the more fanatic (or devout, take your pick) will do whatever it takes to ensure that the Imam is incarnated into a world made clean of disbelievers. The Shi'ites of the Ismaili sect—to which belonged the Assassins—had a more complicated millenial belief, which will be discussed below.

Until the return of the Imam, however, the Shi'ite leadership of the day—and specifically the more mystically-inclined Ismailis, from which the Nizari were descended—understood the value of keeping a low profile. The theological differences between Shia and Sunni are not great, but as usual the slightest of differences makes for tremendous internecine violence and bloodshed. It was the arrival of the Crusaders in the eleventh century that exacerbated what was already a bloody conflict, and the Shi'ites (today a minority compared with the rest of Islam, representing about ten percent of the whole) lost no time in figuring out a way to capitalize on the problem and to set Christian and Sunni at each others' throats, playing one side against the other.

The Sunnis had already characterized the Nizaris as "hashish eaters" in their own writings. Daftary suggests that this was due to the use of the term as a pejorative against people of low class: the ignorant rabble. Princeton University Professor Emeritus Bernard Lewis—in a tightly-focused account entitled *The Assassins: A Radical Sect in Islam*—concurs on this important point.[3] Yet, the term seems to be used specifically in reference to the sect of the Nizaris and not in general use as a term to describe other sects or faiths.

Thus, while the jury is still out on the real history of the Assassins (there are very few historical documents available, even in Arabic or Farsi, on the development of the sect), we can view what has come down to us over the centuries as the West's perception of this cult and how it may have influenced not only Western intelligence agencies but also the popular imagination of the disaffected Muslim populations of the Middle East. We can also see how rumors of fraternization with the Shi'ites came to condemn those Christian Crusaders who did have secret rituals and a hierarchy of degrees: Crusader knights whose legacy—real or imagined—resulted in the creation of such occult lodges and secret societies as the Freemasons and the OTO.

And, as we shall see, we come full circle in the present day when we examine the case of an American intelligence officer who fell victim to the torture and interrogation practices of a new cult of *fedayeen*, who learned the hated science from the same sources as the West.

Muslims in general find the very concept of Crusader to be offensive. When President George W. Bush referred to the war on terrorism in the wake of the September 11, 2001 attacks on New York and Washington, he called it a "crusade," and immediately evoked the ire of Islamic groups who charged him with a lack of sensitivity on this issue; Islamic militants pointed to the expression as indicative of what they perceived to be Bush's real intention: a holy war against Islam. Thus can a single, simple word so quickly lead to horror.

In fact, the Islamic elements that complained the loudest about Bush's quite natural and unconscious use of the word "crusade"—a word in common English and American use that has referred to all sorts of projects, campaigns, and undertakings—should have known better. The word has been used in the English language for years without any religious connotation, and certainly not in the context of a holy war against anyone or anything. Be that as it may, Muslims themselves use the term *jihad* with reckless abandon, and insist to non-Muslims that it is a neutral term which refers to any type of "extreme effort," or struggle, including a moral or spiritual struggle within oneself. Thus, should the term "crusade" be similarly understood, as any type of all-out effort.

What is worse, however, is the sanctimonious position of Islamic apologists who castigate American political leaders for their use of the term, as if the actual Crusades happened only a few years ago—and not more than six hundred—and were a brutal attack on a peaceful people with no hostile intentions towards the West. Gleeful that Americans—and especially their elected officials—have so little knowledge of history and so little understanding of its importance (notably President Bush, who, as we have often seen, has little awareness of foreign geography or the niceties of foreign policy), they spin stories about supposed Western imperialism against the East and rely upon guilt and sympathy to promote the idea that Islam is a much-maligned and misunderstood faith.

In this day and age of mass communication, video cassette recorders and DVD players, home computers and the Internet, one wonders why Islam is still misunderstood? Is it because Muslim leaders still misunderstand the West? To be sure, it is quite likely that Buddhism, Daoism, Hinduism, Shintoism and other faiths are also misunderstood … but Islamic leaders themselves have done nothing to ameliorate the negative image of Islam in the "West," whereas Buddhist, Daoist, etc. leaders have been successful in attracting Westerners to their faiths, as well as in projecting a positive image to those who come across Eastern religions in the news or on their street corners. The Dalai Lama comes to mind. Yet, at the moment, the only coherent image the West has of Islam is as an intolerant, inflexible, anti-feminist, anti-Zionist, anti-American cult of fanatics, whether they are terrorists from the Middle East or followers of Louis Farrakhan in America.

That the first shot was fired against the West by Muslim armies marching on Europe in the eighth century A.D. has been conveniently forgotten. The Prophet was barely cold in his grave before his followers fought, first among themselves, and then against everyone else, as they cut a path through North Africa all the way to Gibraltar and across the Straits into what is now Portugal and Spain, and up to France before being blocked by the armies of Charles Martel in the eighth century A.D. But they did not leave Europe entirely, remaining behind in Iberia and taking Sicily for a while. There were Muslim kingdoms in Europe until 1492, when the Alhambra was liberated from Mohammed XI by the combined armies of Ferdinand and Isabella. Thus, Muslims held sway in Iberia for nearly seven hundred years. The glories of Cordoba and other Muslim cities on the Iberian Peninsula are a matter of historical record.

The progressive attitude towards science and art that contributed so greatly to the Renaissance is what the West *should* know of the flower of Islam. Yet, due to infighting and squabbling among the members of the *ummah*—the Muslim community—there has been no unified effort to promote Islam as a religion of progress, scientific curiosity, and peace. Various Arab nations compete with each other rather than cooperate. The plight of the Palestinians is used as a tool and a weapon to prop up first one Arab regime and then another. Arab intellectualism and Islamic theology is suborned to various national political agendas to the point that there is no unified voice of Islam, and the West only hears from those Muslim spin doctors they fear the most: the terrorists.

During the height of the Moorish kingdoms of Europe, at the very end of the eleventh century A.D., the first Crusades were mounted from France. Troops were sent overland to the Middle East, first to protect Constantinople and the Byzantine Empire from attack by the Seljuk Turks, and then to attack the city of Jerusalem and bring it into Christian hands. The invasion and sack of Jerusalem was brutal, and savage. Thousands of Muslims and Jews were needlessly slaughtered by Christian armies on July 15, 1099. Of this, there can be no doubt, as all records—Christian and Muslim—agree on the details. There followed a see-saw conflict that had the Christians in charge one day, the Muslims the next, for hundreds of years, until the Christians were finally ejected once and for all in the thirteenth century, and Muslim armies were on the march once again into the Balkans under the banner of the Ottoman Empire, an empire that would last until World War I reorganized everyone's priorities.

Thus, the history of Christian-Islamic hostilities is long and complex. Neither side has a monopoly on righteousness where the Crusades—and all they represent—are concerned. At the same time, however, historians agree that Islamic rulers were much more tolerant towards Jews than any Christian empire in Europe ever was, before or since. Christians and Jews were considered "people of the Book," i.e., they were mentioned in the Qu'ran as predecessors of Mohammed and were considered "protected" until they could come to their senses and convert to Islam. After all, Islam itself was a religion of conversion, beginning with the Prophet himself and extending to the rest of the Arabian Peninsula before going on the warpath everywhere else. It was not an indigenous faith, growing out of the paganism of Arabia, Mesopotamia and Egypt. It was a syncretist creation of the Prophet, who blended elements of Christianity, Judaism and native Arab practices and beliefs, taking what he liked and ignoring the rest.

The Ka'aba, for instance, is an example of this. This holy shrine in Mecca which all Muslims are required (if possible) to visit at least once in their lives on the special pilgrimage known as the Haj contains a lump of meteoric stone that was worshipped by the pagan Arab population for centuries before the birth of Mohammed. In fact, the annual pilgrimage to Mecca was a feature of Arab life long before the birth of the Prophet. When Mohammed captured Mecca and made it the holy city of Islam that it is today, he removed the 360 pagan idols from the stone's shrine and transformed it into the central icon of the faith. This act has not been studied extensively in the West, and it is hoped that scholarship one day will examine the importance of this artifact and what it really represented to the pagan Arabs and then to Mohammed, and what it means today to his followers.

The fighting between two factions of Islam began after the death of the Prophet on June 8, 632. The Shi'ites, as mentioned, owed their allegiance to the Prophet's cousin, Ali. The vast majority of Mohammed's followers, however, decided to follow his best friend and father-in-law, Abu Bakr. While both factions revere Mohammed and the Qu'ran and, to a large extent, the *shari'a* (Islamic law) equally, the differences between the two factions are such that open hostilities have never entirely disappeared in the nearly 1400 years since the Prophet's death. This has been exacerbated by nationalist and tribal fighting among members of the same factions. The conflict was subdued somewhat during the five hundred years of the Ottoman Empire when a large part of the Muslim world was under the political control of the Turks, but of course it didn't go away. With the end of Turkish hegemony in the region in 1918, the Balkanization of the Middle East began, made more problematic by the Balfour Declaration, which eventually led to the creation of the State of Israel in the middle of the newly-liberated Arab territories.

All of these difficulties have as their common origin the history of the ancient Middle East. To understand the Arabs, one must understand Islam. To understand Islam, one must understand the Arabs. Most people do not have sufficient time to undertake the kind of study necessary to bring the Middle East into a focus sharper than that of the cameras of CNN or the dispatches from various desert battlegrounds. They tend, instead, to interpret events through a Christian or Jewish filter, and this plays into the hands of those who would foment discord, hatred and bloodshed. By setting up a Christian–Muslim polarity (or a Jewish–Muslim polarity) they can expect to temporarily unite Muslims of differing backgrounds, culture and traditions against the common enemy. While Muslim leaders have been slow to exploit Western media in an attempt to clarify Islam and Arabism to the non-Muslims of the world, Western leaders have been equally slow to understand and exploit the differences—national, historical, cultural, traditional, sectarian—between the Arab countries and their neighbors, such as Iran, Pakistan, and Afghanistan. Most Americans, for instance, don't know where the Kurds come into the equation. They don't know who the Druze are, or what their relationship is to Islam. They don't realize that Iranians (for instance) are not Arabs. They don't understand what Muslims are doing in Bosnia. They don't know the difference between a Shi'ite and a Sunni.

When the Crusaders invaded Jerusalem in 1099, they wasted little time in expanding their base further inland and along the Mediterranean coast. Once Jerusalem had become "secured" by Christian forces, a curious band of brothers set off from France to take up residence in Solomon's stables, near the site of Solomon's Temple, urged by the famous Catholic cleric, St. Bernard of Clairvaux. These were the famous Knights Templar, the Knights of Solomon's Temple, spiritual progenitors of the Freemasons and the OTO, and thereby hangs a tale.

As noted above, the Shia split with the Sunnis over the question of legitimate successors to the Prophet. The Shia believed legitimacy lay with Ali and his blood descendants. Thereafter, the Shia split still again; in fact, many times. The Druze are a Shi'ite sect, for instance; in fact, they are very secretive, have an additional set of scriptures and are ostracized by other Muslims for their heretical views. The Ismaili sect of Shi'ism is our focus here, and they split off in their belief that Ismail, the eldest son of Jafar al-Sadiq (the sixth Imam) was the rightful heir of Ali and thus the seventh Imam, whereas the rival Twelvers believed that Ismail's younger brother was the seventh Imam. These Shi'ites—the Twelvers—are the dominant religion in Iran today, and are the largest Shi'ite sect in the world. The Ismailis, on the other hand, developed largely in secret and created a coherent system of faith and thought that was attractive to many social elements in the Middle East, especially the intellectuals on one hand and the disenfranchised on the other.

Ismaili Shi'ism is a kind of Islamic Qabalism. The belief that the Qu'ran has both an exoteric (*zahir*) and an esoteric (*batin*) meaning is fundamental to the sect, and this idea of hidden or secret knowledge appealed to many who could not understand why the world was so full of sorrow and misfortune when the Prophet had shown the world the right way of living and worship; certainly, there was some secret knowledge of the world, knowledge that was encrypted in the holiest of books, the Qu'ran, for those who were intelligent enough to see beyond the obvious meanings and could divine the hidden truths. (The parallels with the Jewish Qabalistic tradition are obvious.) As scholars such as Barbara Thiering and Hugh Schonfield have demonstrated, the Jewish sect of the Essenes also used code in their writings to disguise important events and the identity of important persons, thus similarly creating two levels of sacred literature: the exoteric and the esoteric. (In fact, it is entirely possible that Essenic beliefs contributed to the creation of the Ismaili doctrine, as the Essenes had spread throughout the region now known as Iran, Iraq, Afghanistan and Pakistan hundreds of years before the birth of Mohammed.)

This type of knowledge could empower the poor, whose only asset was their soul, their passion, and whose only weapon was their belief. It was a form of neo-Platonism believed to have derived from Muslim contact with the Greeks and their philosophical systems, as well as by encounters with Gnosticism, Zoroastrianism, and various Christian sects. It was a syncretist system which still relied on the Qu'ran as the final arbiter of spiritual Truth, but which used the various philosophies and sciences of the West as instruments to deepen understanding of the world.

Also, secrecy begets paranoia; the need to seek for hidden answers and conspiracies behind everyday events develops when a social group is suppressed, ostracized or in some other way shoved to the sidelines and no longer "in the loop" of the dominant party, religion, or culture. When one does not know what the other knows—or what the other is doing, or discussing—then speculation leads to suspicion, which can color an entire belief system. This hard-wired paranoia of the Ismailis—and especially of the Nizari sect which became known in the West as the Assassins—contributed to the creation of an intelligence organization unparalleled in the East, and which in turn led to the creation of what were probably the world's first "terrorists."[4]

Central to the Ismaili belief system is the Imam. Ismaili theologians proposed a world of cycles, in which hidden or silent Imams alternated with visible Imams. Regardless of whether the Imam was visible or not, he normally functioned through his representative, the Senior *D'ai*. The *d'ai*—which means "summoner"—was visible proof of the existence of the Imam. (It is interesting, and perhaps coincidental, to note the existence of a "summoner" in the annals of witchcraft; the "man in black" of the Salem trials was a summoner who called the faithful to the sabbat, and the term "summoner" is still used by some modern adherents of the Wicca movement.) The Senior *D'ai*—the *Hujja* or "Proof"—was also in direct contact with the Imam, even though others around him were not; thus we have an early example of the Secret Chief concept that would be so important to the Golden Dawn, a manifestation of the "Great White Brotherhood" of the Theosophists: hidden Masters who guide the world's spiritual development and who function through a handful of intermediaries. The Imam—like the Brotherhood—is human, but imbued with divine powers and abilities beyond the normal range of possibility.

The Ismaili sect divided yet again, into those who followed the Fatimid Caliphs—who were very powerful and influential in their day, and who created the oldest continuously-running university in the world, the Al–Azhar University in Cairo—and those who were loyal to Nizar, the eldest son of the previous Caliph, who was ousted from his appointed role by a scheming military dictator. Nizar fled to Alexandria, but was eventually captured and killed. Many Ismailis (especially those in the East, in Persia, Syria and what is now Iraq) felt that Nizar was the rightful heir to the throne, and decided not to recognize the authority of the new Caliph, a puppet of the dictator in Cairo. Thus were the Nizaris, later known as the Assassins, born.

At about this time, the Crusaders began their first invasion of the Middle East.

Responding to a call from Alexius I, the head of the Byzantine Empire which was ruled from Constantinople, that the Seljuk Turks were threatening his Christian kingdom, in 1095 A.D., Pope Urban II called for a crusade to help Alexius defend Christianity in the East and to take the Holy City of Jerusalem. The Seljuks had consolidated their power in what is now Turkey, virtually up to the walls of Constantinople. Armenian Christians, Greek Christians and Syrian Christians were in danger of having their cities and lands overrun by the new political, military and religious force that had its spiritual origins in the Saudi Arabia of the Prophet Mohammed, but its ethnic origins in the Asian steppes. Even the other Muslim territories of the Middle East were unhappy with the way the Turks were in ascendancy, and plotted how best to contain the Seljuk threat. As the bumbling Crusader armies finally secured the Byzantine capitol after several false starts, they went on a protracted campaign to capture the main cities along their route to Jerusalem, taking Edessa, Tarsus and finally Antioch before marching on Jerusalem in 1099.

Hasan i-Sabah was an educated Iranian and Twelver Shi'ite who eventually converted to the Ismaili form of Islam and spent some time in the court of the Caliph in Cairo. Becoming embroiled in the internecine warfare between the Fatimid and Nizari branches of the Ismailis, he cast his lot with the Nizari and wound up back in what is now Iran, secretly searching for a base of operations from which to wage unceasing warfare against the Seljuk Turks.[5] He chose the impregnable mountain fortress of Alamut, located in the Erbuz mountain range that hugs the southern coast of the Caspian Sea. At the same time, much of the territory of the Levant had come under control by the Seljuks. The Seljuks were new converts to Islam, and more Central Asian in nature than Arab. They were not part of the Arab feudal states with their complicated genealogies and tribal loyalties, and imposed a different sort of political reality on the Arab and Persian populations. Muslim or not, they were foreign invaders and Sunnis as well. The Fatimid Caliphate was disintegrating; it no longer held appeal for the masses who felt the moral bankruptcy of the regime and were turning more and more to the antinomian and millenarian "new preaching" of Hasan i-Sabah. Islam was in crisis, and so was the entire political infrastructure of the Middle East.

To a devout Muslim, the separation of Church and State that is familiar to the Western countries has no meaning. In Islamic countries, government and religion are one. This is one of the contributing factors to much political unrest in the Middle East, as religious differences automatically threaten government leadership. Religion and political administration must run together as one; if one deviates, then the spiritual structure of the country as well as its political nature is disrupted.

In a way, this is the other side of the coin from Communism, in which the *absence* of religion is by government decree. While in Islamic countries, church and state are one (as it were), in Communist countries the state is one; there is no church—no scripture, no ecclesiastical hierarchy, no liturgical requirements, no alternate power base—to worry about. However, as events have shown in the past fifty years of world history, that attitude was akin to whistling in the dark. Once religious bars in Communist countries were lifted, entire underground networks of religious and occult groups were revealed. This would be unthinkable in an Islamic state ... except for the existence of secret religious/political organizations, groups holding heretical religious beliefs and hence subversive political agendas as well.

Thus, in Sunni territories and in Twelver Shi'ite territories, to be a Nizari was to court danger: imprisonment and execution. The Nizaris were not stupid, and they did not embrace suicide as a group, even though they encouraged suicidal practices by their agents, as we shall see. Instead, they developed a strategy of "precautionary dissimulation of one's true religious belief in the face of danger"[6]—in Arabic, *taqiyya*—of pretending to be whatever the ruling government of a given territory wanted them to be, while maintaining themselves secretly steadfast in their Nizari faith. The Nizari thus became a kind of spy or "sleeper agent," going about one's business in the hostile environment and pretending to adhere to the hated precepts of the evil faith of one's neighbors, all the while waiting for the order to rise up and strike.

Hasan i-Sabah began his career in Persia as a secret *d'ai* of the Nizaris, and thus as a sleeper agent himself. Eventually, he became a minister of this "new preaching," the *hujja* or proof of the invisible Imam, charged with revitalizing Islam both as a spiritual and as a political force in the world. The other Muslims—Sunnis, and those Shi'ites who were not part of his Nizari sect—were heretics and enemies to be destroyed. He could not do this with a standing army; the vast cities of the Muslim world were stronger and richer than he and his band of followers in the mountain castle of Alamut and the other isolated fortresses they would come to conquer. But he had another weapon at his disposal, one that carried the Ismaili concepts of *taqiyya* (dissimulation) and *batin* (esotericism) to their logical conclusion: political murder.

Assassination.

More than any other Muslim sect or organization, the Nizaris embraced the concept of political murder as a strategy central to their survival and success. The records at Alamut show dozens of assassinations carried out by loyal followers of Hasan during his lifetime. He was able to control large geographical areas and make his decisions felt everywhere in the Islamic world without ever leaving his mountain fortress at Alamut. For thirty-five years, Hasan i-Sabah stayed at Alamut and only left his residence twice, and that was to go onto the roof.[7] Devout, abstemious, studious, and completely focused, he maintained iron control of Alamut and of all the territories under his command. He had his own son put to death for drinking wine (alcohol is prohibited to Muslims). As an intellectual leader, he mastered "geometery, arithmetic, astronomy, magic, and other things."[8] He obviously felt the weight of his responsibility as living proof of the existence of the hidden Imam, and sought to prove himself worthy of that mystical trust his entire life. This included ordering the assassinations of nearly fifty Muslim leaders.

There is controversy over whether or not the Assassin cult had a degree system of secret initiation. Iranian historian Farhad Daftary thinks not; he admits that there were different levels of understanding or learning within the sect, but these he believes were rather informal.[9] Bernard Lewis takes a different view, and maintains that the Nizaris under Hasan were a rigorous secret order with a degree system of initiation.[10] He ranks these (from lowest to highest) as respondents, licentiates, teachers, preachers, and the Proof, *Hujja*, or Senior *D'ai*, i.e., Hasan himself. There may be more ranks within these, as evidence is scant and confusing. Some authors have insisted the Assassins had seven degrees, others nine. Daftary dismisses this as ill-formed propagandizing by the enemies of the sect, whether Muslim or later, European, commentators. Clearly, not all the votes are in yet.

Hasan's assassins were carefully selected and, as the cult became more sophisticated, so did the selection and education process of the assassins, which may have involved disguise and language instruction. Regardless of the degree of preparation, the most important aspect of the assassin's readiness is that he be willing to strike in a public place for maximum effect, and thereby lose his life for the cause. Hasan's enemies were often stabbed to death in mosques while they were at prayer. At other times, while walking in the streets or being carried on litters. It didn't matter. And a few carefully selected victims, brought down in broad daylight by murderers who welcomed their own death as a passport to Paradise, caused many other leaders to offer tribute and toe the Assassin line without any further demonstration of ability.

That a small, devout, Muslim band of true believers based in an impregnable mountain fortress could strike at kings and princes whenever they choose, going to their own deaths in the process if need be without hesitation, all in the name of God and under control of a charismatic leader—who does not, himself, risk his own life—bears so many similarities to the events of the past fifty years in the Middle East that it beggars belief. Suicide bombers, terror attacks, plane hijackings … we have seen all of this before.

Hasan i-Sabah created his band of murderers nine hundred years ago, and in many ways they are still with us, and have been admired and emulated by successive incarnations of Shi'ite zealots down to the present day. Bernard Lewis accuses Hasan of having created terrorism as a political weapon.[11] The main difference from today's terrorist is that Hasan murdered leaders and used assassination with surgical precision, selectively and carefully, while his modern counterparts attack non-combatants, civilians, women and children: the innocent, who die in mass bombings and strafings. They have found—as the Assassins eventually discovered to their chagrin when dealing with the Templars and the Knights Hospitaller—that if you killed the leader of a Western army or government, another would come along to take his place. Assassination of Western leaders does not solve the political problems created by democratic governments; there is always a vice-president, a deputy minister, another general, another battalion, another air raid.

Furthermore, while Hasan and his followers did not attack civilian populations (it is, after all, against the Qu'ran to do so), their spiritual heirs do. It has become a war of children against children, women against women; the disenfranchised of the East against the rich, self-satisfied, decadent West: stereotypes fighting stereotypes. What began as a political war in Hasan's time has become a cultural war in ours. The West is evil to the Shi'ite fundamentalists; America is the Great Satan. The Devil. The King of Devils. Not only because it is Christian, not only because of its support for Israel, although these are substantial issues in their own right. No; it is because Western culture—aided and abetted by Western technology—threatens Eastern culture, threatens to overwhelm the Faith. The West has movie stars; the East has martyrs.

Everyone on the planet knows who Madonna and Arnold Schwarzenegger and Sylvester Stallone are. What American knows the names of the Palestinian martyrs of the hideous Israeli and Christian Phalange attack of September 15, 1982 on the Sabra and Chattila refugee camps in Lebanon, where even the sick were dragged from their hospital beds and shot? Or the names of the teenaged suicide bombers—school children—who vainly, futilely try to avenge those deaths with dynamite and C-4 taped to their bodies? Yet, their photographs are plastered all over the walls in Beirut, Ramallah, Baghdad, and other Arab cities and towns and are traded like baseball cards among the young, the same young who danced in the streets when the World Trade Center was bombed; the same young who smiled and laughed in the coffee shops of Kuala Lumpur when the image of the God Struck Towers was flashed on the TV screen courtesy of CNN. "Finally," one could almost hear them think, "we are in the movies, too."

When the Crusader armies marched into Jerusalem, the status was reversed. Islamic civilization was far advanced at that time, and the Europeans were the unbathed barbarians, raping and pillaging their way into the Holy Sepulcher. Their information concerning Islam was scant, and they did not go to any lengths to improve their knowledge. The Muslims were enemies of Christendom and that was all they had to know. To study Islam too deeply might have been seen as an unhealthy interest in a demonic practice, and was thus avoided by virtually every European who lived in the Middle East at that time.

Rumors abounded in later years that the Assassins and the Knights Templar had just such an unhealthy relationship. This was promulgated primarily by the famous Orientalist Joseph von Hammer (*The History of the Assassins*, London, 1835), who jumped to a lot of conclusions concerning both Assassin and Templar alike. He went so far as to assume that the Assassins were the inspiration for the organization of the Templars, pointing to a similarity in dress and hierarchical structure, and went on from there to insist that the secrets of the Templars were those learned at the feet of the Assassins. This theory has been exploded many times over the past two hundred years, but it is still a central idea in the present-day Ordo Templi Orientis, which views itself as a survival of the original Knights Templar and which, in its initiation rituals, demonstrates an affection for the idea that the Ismailis and the Templars were well acquainted and had exchanged occult knowledge and initiations. As mentioned previously, this is most openly seen in the title of the American OTO leader as "Caliph." The German secret society which gave birth to the OTO *did* believe it was the repository of occult knowledge from the Middle East, much of it sexual in nature, which formed the basic character of the Order. (This knowledge was, however, admittedly of recent acquisition and not the result of a thousand years of secret cultivation.) The confusion of Templar with Nizari, however, hearkens back to the errors of von

Hammer and his readers, errors which themselves were based on the charges brought against the Templars by the Church and by the French king who wished to see the Order destroyed, and could only do this by associating the Templars with the grossest forms of heresy and Satanism.

Most recently, Farhad Daftary has found evidence to support some of the speculation concerning the relationship between the Templars and the Assassins (specifically, the Syrian branch of the Nizari Assassins based in and around Damascus). There is ample documentation to show that the Assassins and the Templars had financial and other relationships. Daftary characterizes these as "complex," as well he might, as for the most part Templar records were destroyed in the fourteenth century at the time the Order was suppressed by King and Pope. While somewhat more is known about the Hospitallers and the Assassins (the relationship was political, to form an alliance against Saladin, the leader of the Sunni Muslims who threatened the Nizaris as well as the Crusaders), the relationship with the Templars is not so well understood or explicated. The Hospitallers, of course, were not suppressed and information about their operations is considerably better known. Both military orders were warned by the Church on several occasions about their unhealthy relationship with the Assassins, and with Muslims in general. The Church did not condone the tidy little arrangement in which the Nizaris paid a tribute to the Hospitallers for protection against Saladin, and in which the Nizaris agreed to assist the Hospitallers against their common enemy as well.

Daftary complains about the general ignorance of Western commentators on Islam and on the Assassins in general; however, the close working relationship between the Crusaders and the Assassins is a matter of record in both European and Islamic sources. Only the details are secret, and especially so in the case of the Templars. The Templars and Hospitallers were held in captivity by the Muslims for more than a year at one period, and it is said that they learned Arabic at that time (which, of course, makes sense). Templar Grand Masters are known to have had Arabic-speaking secretaries and to employ Muslim informers in the courts of the caliphs.

I submit that the Templars were more open to cross-cultural exchange than were their colleagues in *Outremer* (the Crusader States), and their brilliance at intelligence-gathering, banking, architecture and other accomplishments demonstrates intellectual abilities which require a certain amount of honest observation. The Templars and Nizaris were both secret, religious orders that were also military in nature, and they would have respected each other for that, if for nothing else. In addition, the Templars would have wanted to know as much as possible about the Assassins without necessarily understanding a great deal about Islam in general, and it would have been to the benefit of the Nizaris to ensure that their philosophy constituted the heart of the Templars' knowledge of Islam.

We know that there was a cultural and philosophical exchange between the Templars and other religious sects in Syria and the Middle East, sects of various denominations encompassing the spectrum from Jewish heretical groups to Gnostics, Christian heretics, and various Muslim splinter groups including what appear to be Muslims with quasi-Christian sensibilities, such as the Mandaeans who revered John the Baptist. Evidence of this is contained in one of the most bizarre charges against the Templars, made in 1307, that they worshipped an idol they called Baphomet. The significance of this will be discussed a little later in this chapter, but it constitutes a compelling piece of evidence that the Templars *were* involved in occult teaching and ritual that they learned during their mission in the Middle East. This would have been especially possible after a remarkable event known as the *qiyama*, what is perhaps the most scandalous event in Nizari history, an event that was known to the Templars and other Crusaders, as is evident from some of the histories that have come down to us from the twelfth century.

It was during the month of Ramadan, the month of fasting in which all Muslims are expected to refrain from eating and drinking of any kind between sunrise and sunset. It was on the seventeenth day of the month, the anniversary of the murder of Ali, a day that is marked by all Shi'ites, some of whom work themselves up into a frenzy of self-flagellation. It was the year of the Hegira 559; in the Julian Calendar, it was the 8th of August 1164.

What follows is not the idle fantasy of Christian commentators. The details are in general agreement from Christian to Muslim, from Sunni to Shi'ite, and they are as follows:

On that day, the head of the Nizaris—Hasan II—the grandson of the founder of the Assassins, Hasan-i Sabah, performed a strange ritual at Alamut in the presence of his followers, who had been summoned from the four corners of the Nizari empire. He erected a pulpit, facing west, with four banners at the corners. The banners were white, red, yellow and green. The people he had summoned arranged themselves around the pulpit on the right and left sides, and directly in front. They all had their backs to Mecca.

At noon, Hasan II—dressed completely in white—approached the pulpit and announced the millenium.

Addressing all the inhabitants of the world of men, of angels, and of the *jinn* (the spirits, from which we get the word "genie"), he proclaimed that the hidden Imam had spoken to him and told him that the old Law—the *Shariya*—was abrogated, and that the time of the Resurrection was at hand. He then invited everyone to a banquet, there, at noon, in the midst of the fasting month of Ramadan and on the anniversary of the murder of Ali, to emphasize his proclamation that the time of the *Shariya* was ended. Messengers went out to all the Nizari strongholds, carrying the same message. A shock wave went through the community, and news of it reached the ears of Muslim and Christian alike. Either Hasan was, as he proclaimed in his speech, in direct communication with the Hidden Imam who had released the faithful from their spiritual obligations, or he was insane, or he was deserving only of a blasphemer's death.

The Christians understood the complicated message to mean that Hasan had accepted Jesus Christ, since he had announced the Resurrection! The Resurrection, in this sense, meant nothing of the sort. As Daftary explains,

> Only the Nizaris were now capable of comprehending spiritual reality, the immutable truths hidden behind all the religious laws; and, as such, Paradise was made real for them in this world.[12]

Or, as the Persian chronicler Juvayni writes,

> ...the Resurrection is when men shall come to God and the mysteries and truths of all Creation be revealed, and acts of obedience abolished, for in this world all is action and there is no reckoning...[13]

In other words, as the popular journalists have written, "Nothing is true; everything is permitted."

As Lewis and other historians have noted, this new dispensation was embraced by most of Hasan's followers without question, including in the Syrian strongholds.[14] Thus, the Assassins abandoned all pretence of following the Islamic law, discontinued praying five times a day facing Mecca, and began drinking and eating whatever suited them, whenever it suited them. Although there is no documentation for this, it can be safely assumed that the consumption of hashish was then also—if not encouraged—easily tolerated. Perhaps this event in 1164 gave the greatest impetus to the derogatory nickname of the Nizaris: the *hashishim*—the eaters of hashish—the Assassins.

Hasan II did not live long to enjoy the new dispensation. On the 9th of January 1166 he was stabbed to death by one of his brothers-in-law, who could not abide the blasphemy of his leader.

However, Hasan II was succeeded by his son, Muhammad, who continued the doctrine of the Resurrection and even expanded upon it, reiterating it as the new Nizari doctrine. And so it was, until Muhammad's son abolished it after the elder's death (possibly by poisoning) in 1210 A.D. Thus, the era of the *qiyama* lasted less than fifty years; but the effect this philosophy had on the Nizaris and on the people who feared them was profound.

In 1152, the Syrian Nizaris had begun paying an annual tribute to the Knights Templar of 2000 gold pieces.[15] This arrangement lasted throughout the *qiyama* period, even when the Nizaris tried to have it removed by the Christian ruler, King Amalric I. The Templars had the Nizari envoy himself assassinated for even daring to suggest that the tribute be lifted.

Then, in 1187, the great Muslim ruler Saladin sacked Jerusalem and took the Grand Masters of both the Knights Hospitaller and the Knights Templar into captivity, where they languished for a year. This, however, did nothing to stop the Nizaris from paying tribute to the Templars. Even when they had signed a mutual assistance treaty with the Knights Hospitaller in 1228, they continued to pay their annual fee to the Templars as well. The Nizaris had no reason to cooperate with Saladin, especially after the announcement of the *qiyama* since during that time (1164-1210) the Nizaris were considered heretics and blasphemers, having more in common with the Christians than with their fellow Muslims. The Nizaris were even known to have assisted the knights in their own internal struggles with the Christian rulers, a situation which gave rise to thunderous missives from Europe commanding the knightly Orders to desist having anything to do with the Nizaris.[16]

While the contribution of Muslim historians such as Daftary are valuable and important to an understanding of the Assassin phenomenon, their conclusions sometimes suffer from the same narrow viewpoints as the western historians they criticize. For instance, Daftary seems upset that Christian Europe would view the rise of Islam with alarm. As he writes:

> ...Christian emperors were even more alarmed when the Muslims extended their hegemony from North Africa to Spain in the eighth century, and later, in the ninth century, to Sicily and other Mediterranean islands.
>
> Thus, the seeds of prolonged antagonism between the Christian and Muslim worlds were planted, and Islam, the 'Other' world, began to be perceived as a problem by western Christendom, a problem which in time acquired important religious and intellectual dimensions, in addition to its original political and military aspects.[17]

These paragraphs would be humorous if the subject matter were not so important. Presumably, when a continent is invaded by foreign armies with a foreign faith—what Daftary calls "extending their hegemony"—they may legitimately be "perceived as a problem"!

This is evidence of the clash of world-views between Muslims and Christians; and is one of the reasons why western historians and commentators have so little accurate information about the Assassins. Daftary admits in many places in his book that virtually all of the information about the Nizari Assassins available to the outside world was promulgated by their enemies. The Muslims themselves spread scathing, morbidly fantastic tales about the Assassins, and it is from the Muslims that they got their nickname, the *hashishim*. How, then, were the Crusaders or other European chroniclers to obtain more accurate information? Obviously, the only way that was possible would be from the Assassins themselves.

THE MYSTERIES OF THE CATHEDRALS

That the Crusaders—and specifically the Templars—brought back important knowledge from the East, however, is beyond doubt. The access of European scholars to the works of the Greeks, the Arabs, the Persians and others caused a sudden explosion of creativity in France, for instance. Ironically, the building of the great Gothic cathedrals owes much to the architectural knowledge of the Muslim Middle East, knowledge that was put to use to create some of the most magnificent European churches ever seen. Geometry, medicine, astronomy, and alchemy were only some of the prizes taken back to France by the Crusaders, including the mysterious Templars and their allies. (Indeed, *algebra* and *alchemy* are phonetic transliterations of Arabic words.) The knowledge of how these disparate disciplines hung together in a cosmic framework of esoteric correspondences was the master key to the secret of the Saracens (as the Arabs were wrongly called), a secret that is revealed in the apse, nave and flying buttresses of the Gothic cathedrals, no less than in the strange statuary and other ornamentation that has baffled commentators for nearly a thousand years.

Louis Charpentier was probably the first to call the intricate relationship of the Knights Templar and the gothic cathedrals to our attention. In his *Les Mysteres de la Cathédrale* de *Chartres* (1995), he put forward a startling theory that Chartres—like the other gothic cathedrals of France—was the repository of arcane knowledge from the East, and the evidence in stone of an explosive secret that would rock Christianity if it were known. At once a machine for expanding consciousness and a testament to "hidden history," Chartres Cathedral lies at a nexus of science, religion and mysticism. The dimensions of Chartres are shown to be equivalent to those of astronomy and music; the carved statues on the outer walls to tell a story of how a secret treasure was brought from the Temple of Solomon by the Knights, and how this treasure enriched both the Order and the Church. This story has gone on to create an entire industry based around early Church history, Jewish messianic lore, and sacred geometry, as represented in such blockbusters as *Holy Blood, Holy Grail, The Messianic Legacy*, and dozens of other studies in various languages, as well as television documentaries. Chartres Cathedral itself became a magnet for New Age seekers, and it now has its own website.

Basically, the idea is this:

The Order of the Knights Templar was founded in 1118 and formally chartered in 1128 by St. Bernard of Clairvaux. Nine impoverished French knights made their way to Jerusalem in order to provide protection for Christian pilgrims going overland through Turkey to visit the Holy Land. Obviously, there was very little nine knights were going to accomplish if their mission was to police a thousand miles of road through hostile territory. Instead, they were based at the Al-Aqsa Mosque (from where Muslims believe the Prophet once ascended to heaven), which is built over part of Solomon's Temple.

Solomon's Temple was the center of Jewish worship since ancient times. It had been built according to legend by King Solomon himself, with the help of demonic beings he summoned by magic. It was destroyed by invaders, rebuilt, and then destroyed again. By the time the Knights Templar had arrived on site, it was a ruin in sorry shape. According to the story now prevalent in New Age circles, the Knights spent their time in Jerusalem digging and looking for something in the vicinity of the Temple. It seems they found what they were looking for, and brought it back in a hurry to France.

The controversy is over whether this "treasure of the Templars" was a physical object or some kind of secret knowledge. Those of the Charpentier school feel it was both. Charpentier suggests that the Templars brought back with them the Ark of the Covenant, lost centuries before at the last destruction of the Temple. The Ark, of course, would be the single most important artifact of Judaism, because it would contain the original stone tablets on which the Ten Commandments were inscribed by the hand of God. It would also contain the mystical Rod of Aaron, a magic wand with divine powers. The Ark, according to the scant information given in the Bible concerning its use, was so powerful that if touched by the unworthy it would bring instant death. The Jewish tribes used it as a kind of weapon in battle, parading it around before their enemies who then fell before them in disarray. The Lucas–Spielberg film, *Raiders of the Lost Ark*, contains a fairly accurate rendition of some of the legends associated with the instrument, as well as Nazi interest in locating it.

To Charpentier, the Ark was something more than a weapon. A device for calculation, a kind of geomancer's compass, is one possibility; one that would have enabled the Templars to build the domes and buttresses of the cathedrals. It was also secret knowledge. As Charpentier tells us, there is no crucifix in Chartres Cathedral. He says that strange omission indicates that the Templars did not believe that Christ was crucified, i.e., believed that he lived, had children, and that his descendants also had survived, a theme developed at great length in *Holy Blood, Holy Grail* by the team of Baigent, Leigh and Lincoln. If Christ was not crucified (or, at least, did not die on the cross, as has been suggested by historians over the past two hundred years) it would explain the most potent charge against the Templars, that in their initiation ceremonies they were expected to trample upon a cross. This might have been a bowdlerized account of what was actually taking place, i.e., a renunciation of the basic, the most central, idea of Christianity: that Jesus was executed, buried, and rose from the dead.

If the Templars believed that Christ did not rise from the dead, then they shared this belief with their Muslim counterparts, and it is no wonder that they were violently suppressed by the Church. Indeed, recent research tends to support the idea that the Templars had Muslim aides, and that many spoke Arabic and took a keen interest in Islam as well as in the many heretical Christian sects abroad in the Middle East at the time, sects that owed much to Gnosticism and Zoroastrianism. As has been demonstrated by Lewis, Daftary and other historians of the period, the Templars had a close working relationship with the Syrian Nizaris, a relationship that spanned the period of the infamous *qiyama* instigated by Hasan II and continued by his son, Muhammad II. This would have exposed them to the apocalyptic and millennial cosmologies of the Ismailis, as well as to other "alternative" religious and historical beliefs.

They may have heard the legends current at the time indicating that someone—either an apostle, or possibly even Jesus himself—had traveled to Kashmir, a refugee from religious and political persecution, and died in Srinagar. They might have heard of the existence of alternative forms of the *Gospel of Mark*, an "unedited" version of the Gospel found in Egypt which refers to an occult initiation conducted by Jesus. They might have heard of the *Gospel of St. Thomas*, a mystical work considered an integral part of the Scriptures in what is now Ethiopia, where the Ark is said to have been taken after the fall of the Second Temple. They might have heard that the bloodline of Jesus survived and that there was—somewhere in the world—a current and living King of the Jews. This exposure to eastern mysticism and alternate history could explain the precise charges leveled against the Templars by King and Pope, charges that were not laid against their hated rivals, the Knights Hospitaller.

And if these stories *are* correct, then the House of David may have survived the last two thousand years of world history and—according to recent Biblical scholarship supported by discoveries in the Dead Sea Scrolls, among other texts—one of its current incarnations would be the King of the Jews, thus casting in doubt the legitimacy of the Catholic Church and, indeed, of all of Christianity. Over one billion believers would find themselves without a belief.

Charpentier—and others who have followed his thinking—feel that this may be the Great Secret of the Freemasons, Templars, and other secret societies of Europe, knowledge handed down quietly because of the danger to the bloodline should Church or State discover it. This, then, is the true meaning of the Holy Grail, for *San Greal* could be a pun on *Sang Real*, Holy Blood. The bloodline of Jesus.

What has all of this has to do with anything? If there is any truth at all to the above conjectures, then the careful edifice of the last two thousand years of Western civilization crumbles like a house of cards. The Muslims and the Jews would have no problem with the discovery that Jesus was never crucified, never rose from the dead, and had—instead—lived a long life and produced offspring who made their way to Europe or to India where they live to this day. They would only shake their heads and say, "I told you so." The Buddhists, Shintoists, animists, pagans and others in the Far East, Africa, and distant parts of the world would give the news only a passing glance. But it would shake the governments and institutions of the West like nothing before.

Christianity, *per se*, would cease to exist, and with it the cherished beliefs and ideals of almost a quarter of humanity. Political and religious leaders would struggle to fill the void with some kind of generalized humanism, a religion centered around an ambiguous God of no discernible personality or color, with a scripture cobbled together with the better parts of Thoreau, Thomas Paine, and perhaps Walt Whitman. Morality itself would be called into question, and one could imagine millions of people—robbed of even the shimmer of God's love and the shadow of God's wrath—going on a warpath of murder, rape and robbery. Crosses would be pulled down from steeples like busts of Lenin in Red Square.

Thus, if this were indeed the truth, the need to cover it up would be absolute. Cynical pragmatists in the Vatican as well as in the world's governments would do what they could to keep a lid on the secret, and perhaps do so in the belief that they were saving civilization. At the same time, it would be necessary to reveal a little of the truth, bit by bit, in selective doses to select individuals, knowing that eventually the truth would become known to everyone; by revealing the truth in degrees, one controls the fallout: a much safer approach than simply dumping the news on the front page of the *New York Times*.

Thus, we have the *raison d'etre* of the modern secret society.

THE NAME OF THE ROSE

The Freemasons believed themselves to be the inheritors of the architectural secrets of the Great Pyramid and the Temple of Solomon, as well as of the other secrets of the Knights Templar. In fact, in America their boys' auxiliary is named after the last Grand Master of the Templars, Jacques de Molay, who was arrested—along with the rest of his French knights—on Friday, the 13th of October, in the year 1307. De Molay was later executed, burned at the stake on March 18, 1314, professing his innocence to the last, after years of hideous torture at the hands of his coreligionists. His Order was scattered to the winds (those that survived) and wound up in Portugal as well as in Scotland. It is said that the sails of Christopher Columbus' caravelles bore the scarlet cross of the Templars, and that Templar knights rode to the assistance of the Scots at Bannockburn.

Romance aside, it is the strange combination of architecture, ritual and secret knowledge that concerns us here, for it is a combination that can be found in ancient Egypt among the pyramids as well as in Chartres Cathedral among the pews. It is an essential element of the Freemason mystique, and has become the focus of intense scrutiny by some modern intelligence agencies. It survives in the design of the temple of the Golden Dawn as well as in the various initiatory rites of Freemasonry, and the idea that the East has a secret technology of the mind, of occult power—an idea that has its origins with the controversy and scandals surrounding the Templars—bore fruit in the creation of the Rosicrucian Society in the early seventeenth century, a Society that had tremendous influence on the arts and sciences of the next two hundred years, and which was brought to America in several forms by English and German immigrants.

By delving back into time, into the deserts of Arabia and the Levant, the ruined temples of Jerusalem, the stone cathedrals of medieval France, the jar-buried scrolls of Qumran, the alchemical laboratories of Prague, and back even further to the mysteries of ancient Egypt and Sumer, we confront the origin of some of the issues that trouble us today. For the recurring idea of the existence of a science that bridges the gap between mind and body, and perhaps between body, mind and some other human faculty—the soul, the spirit, the *petit bon ange* or the *gros bon ange*, the *ka* or the *ba*, the *shen* or the *qing*—persists throughout history in both the West and the East. Furthermore, if it does exist, the organizations with the funding, the power, and the *necessity* of harnassing its technology today would be the intelligence agencies which are, after all, the spiritual descendants of the Nizari Assassins, the Templars, the Rosicrucians, the Illuminati, the Masons, even the votaries of Haitian *voudon*: secret organizations with secret membership, whose ideals may have been forged in religion, mysticism or simply pure idealism, but who owe their allegiance to political forces and will use covert methods to accomplish their goals.

Whether or not there was any basis in truth for the allegations that the Assassins used hashish as a mind-control substance, the important thing to remember is that the world—including many Muslims—*believed it to be so*, and believed that therein lies a key for unlocking the mindless killer in us all.

Premier among the secret societies believed—in the West—to be at once occult and political was (and in some cases remains) the Freemasons. (The East has its parallel in the Chinese secret societies that sprang up in response to the excesses of the Qing Dynasty, with much similarity to the Freemasons, except that the Chinese societies degenerated into criminal gangs, while this charge has never been laid against the Masons.) The Freemasons have been accused of every kind of blasphemy, treachery, and subversion by their critics; admirers and critics alike point to the organization's supposed origins in the shadow of Solomon's Temple, and some go even further and associate its teachings with the nameless cult that designed the Egyptian pyramids. Modern journalists—notably in the books of Lynn Picknett and Clive Prince—have gone so far as to demonstrate a historical continuum between the Egyptian pyramid builders, the Temple of Solomon, the heretical Christian cults of the first few centuries A.D., the Knights Templar and the Freemasons.[18]

It was the Masonic Society that gave birth to Professor Weishaupt's Illuminati in Bavaria on May 1, 1776: a group that was decidedly political as well as philosophical and which was eventually surpressed by the Bavarian authorities, as the Templars had been four hundred years earlier. It was a manifestation of a general air of revolutionary activity, established as it was on the eve of America's own Declaration of Independence from England. England at that time was a kingdom being run by George III, a man more at home with the German language than English. One of the leaders of the American revolutionary movement was Benjamin Franklin, a Mason and an intimate of French revolutionary and occult circles in Paris. Later in the century, of course, France would experience its own revolution after lending its support to the American template. A story current at the time has an unknown revolutionary running through the palace at Versailles shouting, "Jacques De Molay, thou art avenged!" The horror-stricken European nobles accused the revolutionary movement of France of having been masterminded by secret societies, and of course the Masons (and the Illuminati) were the first accused.

In the nineteenth century, America went through a paroxysm of anti-Masonry, and an Anti-Masonic Party was formed, out of which the Whigs and later the Republican Party would be created from its disparate limbs. One merely has to replace the word "Masonry" with the word "Communism" to appreciate the gist of the speeches and broadsides against this secret society with its "godless" agenda. America was going through a period of intense soul-searching in the early days of the nineteenth century, after the second defeat of the English during the War of 1812. Religious fanaticism and fundamentalism was on the rise, and the Masonic Society was identified as one of the sinister forces attempting to move America into worship of alien gods, while at the same time taking its orders from mysterious European masters. It was also a time of anti-Catholic feeling, for the Catholics were perceived as owing allegiance to the Pope before Country and God. Their religion was seen as idolatrous and superstitious, a kind of "outer court" of the Masons, who were seen as a bit more sophisticated but no less idolatrous. This was ironic, of course, in that Catholics were forbidden to join the Masonic Society; the Church saw Freemasonry as the survival of Templarism, which they had fought into the ground hundreds of years earlier. Secret societies with secret rituals were anathema to organized religion, which sought to remain the sole channel to Godhead.

Joseph Smith, an occultist at heart, embraced Freemasonry in the years before his murder, and Masonic ideas and ritual were incorporated into the Mormon liturgy, as was detailed in Book One. When Hitler came to power in the twentieth century, he banned all occult organizations and reserved his special ire for the Masons. Architect of the Final Solution Adolf Eichmann cut his eye teeth in the SS while working on the Masonic files, before he was finally diverted to another group that was considered as great a threat to the race as the Masons: the Jews. In the Freemasonry Section, he compiled lists of Masonic temples, libraries and other holdings as well as membership lists, and maintained a museum exhibit on Freemasonry that was visited regularly by Heinrich Himmler. Masonic property was seized everywhere in the Reich, and the artifacts sent directly to the SS for examination and storage, or eventual destruction.

Thus, Freemasonry has not had an easy time. Like any secret society, it is the target of those who believe that any group of persons meeting in secret must be up to no good; yet, today there is a Masonic temple in virtually every American town of any size, and the Masonic Society headquarters in Washington, D.C. is on Pennsylvania Avenue, but a stone's throw from the White House. George Washington was inaugurated as America's first president wearing Masonic regalia, and many future presidents would be Masons as well as an overwhelming number of senators and congressmen. Yet, few American non-Masons have a clear idea about the origins of the Society, or even its purpose (other than charity).

According to most established histories, the Masonic Society's official birth was in the year 1717,when the first Grand Lodge was announced, and allegations that the Order has a more ancient lineage was generally derided by academics until recently. As more documentation has become available, it seems clear that the Freemasons had existed for at least one hundred years prior to the formation of the Grand Lodge, and perhaps as much as two hundred years. This sounds dubious at first, since there are no published works on the Freemasons before the eighteenth century; or so it would seem.

Scotland boasts some of the earliest Freemasonic lore, and Masonic temples and lodges have been identified in Scotland as early as the sixteenth century. Further, when the Grand Lodge announced itself in London in 1717, the Freemasons of York protested and formed a rival lodge, saying that their organization was much older and had nothing to do with the lodges in London. Thus, there seems to have been a Masonic tradition in Scotland and northern England long before the heavily-publicized formation of the Grand Lodge. If this is so—and current academic research supports it—then where did the Masons come from?

The official Masonic line is that their brotherhood began in the shadow of the Temple of Solomon. The original Masons had been architects and builders in the employ of King Solomon, and the Master Mason—one Hiram Abiff—was later murdered by three assassins in an attempt to discover the "Master Word." This Word was assumed to be the password used by higher ranking Masons to enable them to receive a higher pay scale, one's position in the hierarchy of builders being determined by which password one held. If one could know the password of a Master Mason then one would be compensated at a higher rate. Such is the story. Unfortunately, Abiff refused to part with the information and was killed, his body buried in a shallow grave. Later, his body was dug up and searched to see if he had written the Word anywhere, but the Word was lost.

This odd story is the central myth of the Masons. While there are stories about the Egyptian pyramids, the orthodox origins of the Freemasons are said to belong to the days of Solomon's Temple. That would mean, of course, that the Masons are more than three thousand years old. While that chronology satisfies some, there are others who question the story with an eye to discovering its real secret.

This secret may have been discovered in the recent past by an amateur historian from Kentucky. Due to a fortuitous set of circumstances having nothing to do with the Freemasons, John J. Robinson stumbled upon compelling proof that the Freemasons had their origins with the Knights Templar, and that the Templar Order had survived in England and Scotland after the official destruction of the Knights by order of the Pope. The evidence begins with the famous Peasant Revolt of 1381, in which there was a general uprising in England against the Church and the King, which resulted in the destruction of property all over the kingdom and the murder of many high-ranking clerics and nobles.

Robinson demonstrates beyond reasonable doubt that the attack was directed specifically against the Knights Hospitaller, the Templars' hated rival since the days of their mutual origin in the desert sands of Palestine, and inheritors of the Templars' assets when the Templars were suppressed by Papal decree. Robinson's book—*Born in Blood*—is a worthwhile addition to Masonic studies, even though it contains no footnotes or other academic impedimenta that would have elevated it to more lofty status among scholars; its connecting the Peasant Revolt with a "Grand Society" operating in secret in the British Isles, a society convincingly identified with the Knights Templar, is alone worth the price of admission. Robinson also shows that Templar shrines were spared the attacks, which left thousands dead and many beheaded as the revolt wound its way directly to the Tower of London. The leader of the revolt was known only by the name Walter the Tyler, which is suggestive, since the "tyler" is a Masonic office in the rituals of the temple. All this indicates that the Masonic society has its origins in the Knights Templar, as many historians have always insisted (albeit without the benefit of documentation).

The investigative team of Baigent and Leigh—in *The Temple and The Lodge*—have gone further, showing how the Templars escaped Europe at the time of their suppression and wound up in Scotland, among other places. They discuss the disposition of the Templar fleet, a substantial armada of ships that mysteriously disappeared at the time of the Order's destruction, and suggest that the fleet enabled escaping Templars to make it as far as the coast of Scotland and even, in at least one case, as far as Greenland and possibly to Mexico.

In fact, one of the more startling discoveries in *The Temple and The Lodge* is the report of a Templar grave, in what is now Israel, adorned with the by-now famous compass and square insignia of the Freemasons. This grave dates to the thirteenth century, which again indicates that there existed an identity between the Templars and the Masons. While this had always been a fantasy or a supposition by conspiracy theorists of the Right and the Left, the combined weight of the various clues as given by Robinson, Baigent and Leigh, and other recent research (such as that by David Stevenson in his *The Origins of Freemasonry*), now clearly points to Templar survival in the form of the Freemasons.

The only missing link in the story now is whether (and how) the Templars and the Assassins shared information, including not only military and political intelligence but also information of a more esoteric nature. This has also been a belief of conspiracy theorists, who jumped to the conclusion that since the Templars and the Assassins shared some of the same real estate and had some of the same enemies, that they must have—of necessity—become friendly. Indeed, this was one of the accusations against the Templars by the Church when they finally clamped down on them in the fourteenth century. They were said to worship an idol called "Baphomet" (a suggestively Arabic sounding name) rather than Jesus, and to have engaged in other unlawful practices of a distinctly Islamic nature.

It is said that the Templars' aversion to putting a crucifix—a representation of the body of Christ impaled on the cross—in their Gothic cathedrals was an indication that they shared a horror of idolatry which they inherited from either the Jews, the Muslims, or both. (Iconography is forbidden in both religions, although abstract design is usually permitted; Catholicism, however, embraces statues and paintings of Christ and the Saints, and the Orthodox Christians permit paintings—the famous ikons—but not statues.) The insistence on representing divinity in the form of sacred geometry and number only is a main feature of Islam, and this may have been one of the major influences on Templar thinking in the design of the Gothic cathedrals as well as in the ritualized and sacralized geometry of Freemasonry.

The reference to Baphomet is actually quite important, and bears some digression here. For centuries, no one knew what that name meant, and many wondered if it was a corruption of "Mahomet," a common medieval spelling of Mohammed, the Prophet and founder of Islam. Aleister Crowley, on assuming the leadership of the English OTO used Baphomet as his Order name, since the Templars were said to worship Baphomet, and Crowley was never averse to a stiff drink, a good cigar, a warm woman, or a devoted follower. It was up to Dead Sea Scrolls scholar Dr. Hugo Schonfield to solve the mystery, however. Using a well-known and often-used Qabalistic cypher known as *Atbash*—in which the first letter of the Hebrew alphabet is equivalent to the last letter, and so on—he applied the technique to the name *Baphomet* and came up with *Sophia*, the goddess of Wisdom. Thus, the Templars may well have been worshipping Wisdom in their secret councils; even more, Wisdom in a cryptic, Qabalistic dress. Even more again, Wisdom as Sophia, the consort of Simon Magus, one of the legendary fathers of the esoteric cult known to posterity as Gnosticism. *Baphomet* comes to us down the centuries, then, from the Templar Inquisition records as a signal to the Bretheren: a secret word with its solution buried in its seemingly random combination of letters. A "lost Word." A "Mason word." In fact, a word that was hidden using an ancient Jewish cypher, the same cypher that was in use by the Essenes.

That is still not proof of a link between the Templars and the Assassins, however. If anything, it demonstrates that the Templars were in communication with Jewish and Gnostic groups in the Middle East. But the belief that there was an exchange of secrets between the two groups is persistent, in spite of scant evidence one way or the other. What did they have in common?

In the first place, what many do not realize is that the Knights Templar were first and foremost monks. They were a monastic order, with a monastic rule. They took vows of poverty, chastity and obedience like any other Catholic monks. They owed their allegiance to the Pope, and to no other man: neither king nor cleric. They were forbidden to bathe. They were forced to wear sheepskin and leather, even in the pounding heat of the desert lands they went to conquer. They were not allowed any privacy at all. They were forbidden even the most casual contact with women. They were forbidden alcohol, and were allowed two meals a day. They were also expected to fight to the death, regardless of the circumstances, if their superior so ordered it. They were not allowed to retreat in battle unless the odds were greater than three to one, and then only if their superior allowed them to retreat. The regulations against wine and women would have made the Muslims feel at home. Their willingness to die for their religion would have made the Nizaris feel at home.

They were initiated in secret. Even the monastic rule of the Order was not revealed in its entirety until a Knight had achieved the highest rank. This secrecy was an unusual factor in the composition of the Order, not something normally practiced by other monastic orders. And Templars could not divulge anything of these initiation rites, or of the monastic rule, under penalty of death.

Obviously, the Templars and the Assassins shared much of the same mindset. The passion for secrecy, and the willingness to die if ordered to do so, were two very important things the two groups had in common. In addition, they were both religious orders, devoted to God, and they were both military organizations devoted to conquest. The main difference between them—aside from religion—was the fact that the Assassins operated in secret, in disguise, with lethal precision, whereas the Knights Templar were everywhere obvious by their mode of dress, and they struck as soldiers, in the open field, *en masse*. While the Assassins would take a castle by murdering its ruler, the Templars took a castle by overwhelming its forces in the heat of bloody conflict. But that would all change on October 13, 1307, when the Templars were arrested throughout France and the order went out to crush them in every part of the Catholic empire. At that point, the Templars went underground like their Nizari counterparts, and they suddenly had much more in common than ever before, for they suddenly had a common enemy in the Catholic Church and the Catholic kings of Europe.

The story of why the Order was suppressed, its leaders arrested, tortured and executed and its holdings seized and, in many cases, handed over to the hated Knights Hospitaller is a matter of historical record, and we will not dwell on it too deeply here. Basically, the Crusades had been lost. There were only a few Europeans left in the Middle East, tenaciously holding on to scraps of land along the coast of what is now Lebanon and Israel. The various principalities of Italy were at each other's throats, with the Venetians at war with the Genoese and everybody at war with France. Jacques de Molay, the Grand Master of the Order, was called to France for what he thought was going to be new marching orders and a budget for a new Crusade to take back the Holy Land. Instead, he was arrested, along with all of his lieutenants throughout France, on that fateful Friday the Thirteenth and charged with heresy. The instigator of this "night of the long knives" was the new King Philippe le Bel of France, in tandem with Pope Clement V. The reason was a desire to take over the vast holdings of the Templars throughout Europe, and wherever else they could be found, and to eliminate the Templars as a political threat.

At this point in European history, the Templars were not only the richest religious order but the richest organization of any kind. Philippe le Bel owed the Templars money, as did most of the crowned heads of Europe. Many have credited the Templars with the creation of the modern banking system. Although elements of this had already been in place in various parts of the world, the Templars turned banking into an art form. With their monastic vows of poverty and obedience, they were a logical choice to be entrusted with money; with their international network of Temples and multilingual scribes throughout Europe and the Middle East, they were an obvious channel for transmission of funds through the various ports to enable and facilitate trade between nations. In short, the Templars became rich. And wealth means power.

But the King could not simply round them all up and have them killed. He needed a legitimate reason, and this he found through informants and spies: the Templars were heretics. They practiced strange rites in secret. They trampled on the cross. They worshipped an idol they called "Baphomet." They engaged in homosexual intercourse. They hired Muslim aides, and had learned Arabic and the ways of the mysterious East. They did not believe in the Crucifixion of Jesus or His Resurrection. They owed their loyalty to foreign masters and alien gods.

There may have been some elements of truth in the accusations, but the Templars had always prided themselves on being answerable to no one but the Pope himself. This loyalty to the Church, and their willingness to undergo tremendous privations in both war and peace, was ignored during the *auto da-fe* that took place in that time. Many Templars—far from France—managed to escape and to take some of their wealth and records with them. Iberia was still a mixed bag of Christian and Muslim states, and it is known that some Templars found asylum there. Others made for England and Scotland.

But the damage had been done: the very Church to which the Templars had given their lives and devoted their souls had turned on them, and turned on them with a vengeance. Their Grand Master, Jacques de Molay, was finally burned at the stake. This was an intolerable state of affairs, and if the Templars had indeed learned heretical secrets in the East then this *contre-temps* seemed to prove them right. The men on the thrones of Catholic Europe and on the throne of St. Peter were evil men, unworthy of the faith of the Templars and of the trust of the people. God had forsaken his Church and abrogated the divine right of kings. The Templars were no longer bound by their previous oaths, but they were still trained as military monks, still had their weapons in some cases, still had their secret networks throughout the civilized world, and were still in contact with the Church's enemies, should they be needed.

As they burrowed deep within the towns and villages and cities of Christendom, they established safe houses where they could meet and exchange information. These were known as lodges, and eventually developed into the Masonic Lodge we know today. Sixty years after the execution of Grand Master De Molay, these lodges formed the backbone of the Peasant Revolt which attacked Hospitaller knights and temples with rapacity throughout England. They fought alongside the Scots against the English and, it is said, metamorphosed into the clandestine organizations that fomented rebellion against the evil kings of France and England in the French and American revolutions, and against the royal houses of Prussia and Bavaria. Eventually, even the Russian Revolution was blamed on the Freemasons, the Illuminati and their illustrious forebear, the Order of the Knights Templar. It got to the point where even Winston Churchill noted the power and influence of these covert organizations over European history.

Given the weight of the supporting academic scholarship, there can be little doubt today that the Freemasons owe their existence to the clandestine network of Knights Templar that was established in the beginning of the fourteenth century. Thus, the organization—in general terms, without reference to a specific lodge—is over six hundred years old; more, if we consider its birth to date from the first expedition by Hugh de Payens, the first Templar Grand Master, to Jerusalem in 1118. In that case, the Freemasons are a nearly nine-hundred-year-old organization, and their origin in blood and religion, in the Journey to the East of the Crusades, makes them a template for future cults awash in secret rituals, privileged information of an occult nature, and political aspirations.

The beliefs allegedly adopted by the Templars, however, including the worship of Baphomet/Sophia and the rejection of the crucifixion, owe their origins to an even earlier date, and for that we have to go back two thousand years to the first Christian century and the Gnostic and Essene forces that surrounded the earliest days of the Church.

THE GNOSTIC GOSPELS

In 1945, a series of discoveries was made of a cache of Gnostic texts in a village in Egypt. This find, known collectively as the Nag Hammadi Library, was buried for safekeeping in the third century A.D. The Gnostics were well-established in Alexandria by this time, where the Ptolomies had first saturated this area of the Middle East with Greek philosophy and culture. It was this mixture of Platonic, Pythagorean, and pagan philosophy, science, art and religion that had such a profound influence on both the Jews and the local pagan population, and which, in a way, allowed the spread of a new Jewish cult outside of Israel and into the world—the Gentile, pagan world—at large.

For if it should survive at all, the new cult of Christianity, based on the teachings of the mysterious leader known as Jesus, would have to survive outside Judaism. The political environment of Israel at the time of Christ has been described at length by Robert Eisenman and Barbara Thiering, among others, so I will not go into detail here. It is enough to say that tremendous infighting in the Jewish population had made it possible for Greeks and Romans to keep Israel enslaved for centuries, and the most critical element of this internecine conflict was the struggle over foreign cultural influences.

In the second century B.C., educated and sophisticated Jews wanted their sons to study abroad, to learn Greek, and to dress in the Greek manner. The Seleucid Empire—the Syrian parallel to the Ptolomaic kingdom of Egypt, i.e., successor to the conquests of Alexander the Great—was in control in much of the Levant, including Palestine. In some cases, Seleucid rulers actively opposed Jewish religion and customs. This was known as the "Time of Wrath," and it was during this time that the Chasidim or "the Pious" were born, and when the mysterious "True Teacher" or "Teacher of Righteousness" made his appearance, an event that was heralded by the Jewish cult of the Essenes.

The Essenes were a purist sect of Jews who were renowned as healers, and who many thought had the gift—or the science—of prediction, a capability believed to have derived from their exceptionally holy lives and the devout attention they paid to the study of the sacred books. The Essenes were millennialist in a sense: they expected the arrival of the Messiah at any time, particularly in the Time of Wrath, which was believed to be the End of Days. Their scriptural writings speak of a lineage of priestly kings going back to the time of King Solomon and his confidant Asaph. Asaph was a master of the occult arts and possessor of the "Ineffable Word of God," which enabled him to perform miracles.

This Word—like the lost Word of Hiram Abiff, also of Solomon's Temple—is a recurring theme in Masonic ritual and literature as well as in ancient Jewish lore, and has a special place in the Qabala, which concentrates on words and letters and the power certain combinations and pronunciations can give to the initiated practitioner. This idea of the power of language is reflected in the Gospel according to John, the most mystical of the four Evangelists, which begins, "In the beginning was the Word, and the Word was with God, and the Word was God." In the Gnostic writings found at Nag Hammadi and in other places, a great emphasis is placed on words of no identifiable meaning, what archaeologists call "abracadabra," or meaningless sounds.

Obviously, since it seemed that no words from the everyday vocabulary of a language possessed any special power (else we would have all witnessed it many times in our lives), the magic words must be those that have no usage in common speech, words that are otherwise unrecognizable. Gibberish. And since these magic words could be phoneticized and written down anyway—and possibly seen by the unworthy—the secret of their power must lie in their method of pronunciation, a method that would be passed down to the initiate during the course of special ritual. In the later occult lodges of the nineteenth and twentieth centuries, this method was known as "vibration" rather than pronunciation, for it was acknowledged that speech (and, indeed, all sound) is vibration or sound waves. Therefore, magical pronunciation must consist of a special way of creating those very sound waves, a method of speaking or chanting or singing that would convey the power of the word in its very sound, its particular vocalization.

The constant repetition of select words or phrases over and over again—like the mantra of Hinduism and Buddhism, designed to lead a practitioner to exalted states of awareness, into contact with God—was the technique Dr. Ewen Cameron used in the depatterning experiments at his infamous clinic in Montreal on behalf of the CIA. The difference was that his patients were bombarded with these words for hours on end over electronic speakers placed under their pillows until they were quite insane. This same technique was used (with no success whatsoever) in the bombardment of David Koresh's compound in Waco, Texas, and in the sonic attack on Panamanian president Manuel Noriega, who was in hiding in a compound controlled by the Vatican, except that in Noriega's case the selection was pure rock 'n' roll.

If the good Doctor Cameron, or the ATF and the FBI, or the Marines had followed the procedures as originally developed by the Hindus and the Essenes and the Qabalists, they might have tried using some of the "meaningless gibberish" or "abracadabra" of their sacred books rather than specific words and phrases, some of which would have unknown connections with their victims' belief systems, especially in the case of Waco. Had they relied upon the seemingly meaningless mantras of the Gnostics, for instance, the results might have been interesting, and even more spectacular than the failures of Cameron, Waco and Panama City.

The "Ineffable Word" was only one aspect of the Essene occult teaching, however; their main interest, outside of the purely religious and apocalyptic, was medical. In Egypt, they were known as *Therapeuts*, which implies a general acknowledgment of their healing capabilities. They were said to have a good knowledge of herbs and "therapeutic stones" and their application in a variety of diseases. When we consider the Essene lifestyle, belief system, and reputation for healing and prediction, we can see how they could have survived in one of the most famous eruptions of spiritual passion since the Cathars and Albigenses of the thirteenth century: the sudden appearance of the Rosicrucians.

Even the respected Biblical scholar Dr. Schonfield agrees:

> The influence of the Essenes of Egypt, known in the first century A.D. as Therapeuts, was particularly strong. Philo of Alexandria learned much from them. The Rosicrucians could look back to an Essene impetus from Egypt relating to arcane matters associated with the Sun-King and Master of Wisdom King Solomon, who had created the Temple in conjunction with the Master Asaph ben Berechiah. And these things were the foundations of Freemasonry.[19]

Thus what we have before us is a continuum of belief and practice—religious, historical, medical, architectural, occult and astronomical—that stretches for thousands of years backwards in time, much as the popular legends of Freemasonry would have it. And the continuum includes everything from the Temple of Solomon to the Essenes, the story of Jesus, the Knights Templar, the Rosicrucians and the Masons, as well as heretical sects such as the Cathars, the Bogomils and the Albigenses. It is an anti-history, a history below the surface of what is generally and popularly accepted as the truth, comprising elements from Judaism and Christianity and their offshoots, such as the Gnostics, as well as elements of Zoroastrianism and Islam. What is more, associated with this anti-history is a remarkably coherent and internally consistent set of psychological and spiritual practices that involves what we know as ritual magic, alchemy, astrology and sacred geometry: an anti-science whose secrets were the targets of some of the most advanced (and certainly most serious) governments in the world, from the time of the philosopher-kings of Europe down to the present day's CIAs and KGBs and terrorist organizations, an anti-science that was put to the use of interrogation, psychological warfare, "brainwashing" and mind control.

But it was not intended that way.

While the truth about the life of Jesus, the dispositon of the Ark of the Covenant, the architecture of the Gothic cathedrals, etc. presumably could be known through archaeological research and examination of ancient documents and histories, the operational secrets of the Essenes and other groups which share a common heritage were considered so powerful that they were protected by cyphers, passwords, ritual gestures of identification, and other arcane impedimenta: not through jealousy or greed, but because the same secrets that could be used to heal could also be used to kill. Thus the medical doctor could also become the poisoner; both disciplines derive from the same basic secret, the knowledge of the properties of plants and minerals. That is why a very high level of spiritual devotion and attainment was required of those who desired to share in this information, as a safeguard against the secrets being misused. In fact, the rules of the occult Orders were very specific on this point: the sacred knowledge—when used in society—could *only* be used to heal. The rest of the knowledge was to be kept secret and never used for personal power in the world, only for deeper spiritual understanding. This attitude is quite apparent in one of the most famous and influential documents printed in seventeenth century Europe, the *Fama Fraternitatis*.

Published in 1614—but with manuscript copies in evidence as early as 1611—the *Fama Fraternitatis* was the announcement of the existence of a secret body of pious and learned men, the Bretheren of the Rosy Cross, who were dedicated to humanist principles and who were somewhat in support of the religious reform movement taking place in Europe at the time. Thus, they wedded secrecy to wisdom to politics, all in a few short pages which begin with the discussion of their founder, one C.R. (identified in later documents as Christian Rosenkreutz), who was born in Germany but who traveled to the Middle East at a very young age and learned all he could of the occult arts before returning to Germany via North Africa and Spain.

Much of the document is taken with the discovery of C.R.'s tomb, and of the sketchy history of the Bretheren after C.R.'s death. The combination of the mystical with the scientific (the Bretheren were pledged to offer their services to the public only as healers, and to keep their membership in the Order and the rest of their arcane knowledge secret) with a bit of the political captured the imaginations of readers all over Europe, in what has been called "the Rosicrucian Furore." Many were desperate to sign up with the Order, if it could be found; others went into print either supporting it or castigating it.

Shortly thereafter, another document—the *Confessio Fraternitatis*—appeared, which offered more information on the Order as well as being more shrill politically, especially where the Pope was concerned. This hatred of the papacy would have been a hallmark of the Templars after they were suppressed, when they felt they had been betrayed and abandoned; but many in Europe had reason to despise the corruption of the Vatican at that time. The importance of the *Confessio* is perhaps in its giving of actual dates. Here we learn that Christian Rosenkreutz was born in 1378, and lived to be 106 years old, which means he died about 1484. As mentioned in the *Fama*, his tomb—when discovered—bore the inscription "*Post 120 Annos Patebo*," which means, "After 120 years I will open." Thus, we can conclude that the Tomb of Christian Rosenkreutz was opened in the year 1604.

Taking the story to be allegorical, we may wonder if the birth of Christian Rosenkreutz shortly before the Peasant Revolt in England has any significance, especially if we can accept that the Revolt was the work of the Knights Templar, in hiding since 1307. It may be that the Masonic Society was born at that time in 1378, went underground again in 1484 during the period when Islamic kingdoms in Iberia were being lost (at the "death" of Christian Rosenkreutz, possibly indicating Islamic support for the society in the intervening years), and then made made its way back to the light in 1604. But that is all conjecture; the dating seems quite specific, and may refer to events other than what we know of the Masonic Society.

There is, however, one very important clue common to both the *Fama* and the *Confessio*, and which is emphasized in both texts, and that is the strange odyssey of Christian Rosenkreutz to Damascus. We are told that he made his way to Damascus, where he learned Arabic and studied at the feet of the Eastern masters there. We may assume that Christian prelates were not the masters being cited. The area around Damascus at the time was rife with Syrian Nizaris who, although they had lost their stronghold in Damascus much earlier, were still active in the region and would remain so for centuries, tolerated by the Ottomans. In addition, it was to the "Land of Damascus" that the Essenes and other religious refugees had often fled in order to find sanctuary and a place where they could practice their beliefs in relative security. Both these Rosicrucian documents mention this sojourn in Damascus as the central event in the religious and occult education of Christian Rosenkreutz, for when he leaves Damascus and travels to other regions—Fez in North Africa, and Salamanca in Spain—he views the quality of arcane teaching there as somewhat inferior to what he had learned in Damascus.

Further, in the *Confessio*, we read,

> ...as those which dwell in the city of Damascus in Arabia, who have a far different politick order from the other Arabians. For there do govern only wise and understanding men, who by the king's permission make particular laws; according unto which example also the government shall be instituted in Europe (whereof we have a description set down by our Christianly Father) when first is done and come to pass that which is to precede.... Even in such manner as heretofore, many godly people have secretly and altogether desperately pushed at the Pope's tyranny, which afterwards, with great, earnest, and especial zeal in Germany, was thrown from his seat, and trodden underfoot...

Thus, we have in one paragraph a fascinating clue as to the Rosicrucian lineage and philosophy. For what Damascenes would have a "different politick order from the other Arabians"? And how does this fit with the impulse to resist the Papacy and actually to destroy it? What Arab philosophy would the Rosicrucians emulate? Obviously, it had nothing to do with mainstream Islamic government. Is this entire paragraph an allusion to the Syrian Nizari sect, the cult of the Assassins? And its anti-Papal stance a revival of the revenge of the Templars? Or is it even deeper than that, referring to a survival of Essenism, which did have a different government, a "different politick order" from Jewish, Christian and Muslim groups alike?

Like the Church and like Islam, the Masonic Society and the ephemeral Rosicrucian Order have had their share of renagade branches, formed by members who long for more initiations, different initiations, greater exclusivity, or who feel that the personal character of the lodges is not conducive to spiritual illumination or occult power. It is from these offshoots of Masonry and Rosicrucianism that organizations like the Golden Dawn and the OTO had their origins, groups that eventually led to Aleister Crowley, Jack Parsons, and L. Ron Hubbard. The fact that Freemasonry and Rosicrucianism had their spiritual origins in Syria, either through association with the Knights Templar or through some other collaboration with Islamic, Christian or Jewish heretical sects there, is important to a complete understanding of western secret societies, for it was from Syria that the Templars would have learned of the legends surrounding the crucifixion of Jesus, of the existence of Gnosticism and the War of Light versus Darkness, of Baphomet/Sophia, and of sacred geometry and Qabalistic numerology. It would have been from the Syrian Nizaris that the Templars would have learned of the infamous *qiyama* of Hasan II at Alamut and the doctrine that the old law was abrogated for the faithful....

...That, in contemporary terms made popular by Western journalists and amateur historians, "Nothing is true; everything is permitted."

Endnotes

[1] Farhad Daftary, *The Assassin Legends*, I.B. Tauris, London, 1995, p. 94
[2] Hugh J. Schonfield, *The Passover Plot*, Bantam, NY, 1969, p. 7
[3] Bernard Lewis, *The Assassins: A Radical Sect in Islam*, Oxford University Press, NY, 1967, p.12
[4] Ibid., p. 130
[5] Daftary, op. cit., p. 31
[6] Ibid., p. 6
[7] Lewis, op. cit., p. 44
[8] Ibid., p. 62
[9] Daftary, op. cit., p. 21
[10] Lewis, op. cit., p. 48
[11] Ibid., p. 130
[12] Daftary, op. cit., p. 41
[13] Lewis, op. cit., p. 73
[14] Ibid., p. 73
[15] Daftary, op. cit., p. 67
[16] Ibid., p. 76

[17] Ibid., p. 49

[18] Lynn Picknett & Clive Prince, *The Templar Revelation*, Corgi Books, London, 1998

[19] Hugh Schonfield, *The Essene Odyssey*, Element, Shaftesbury, 1998, p. 166

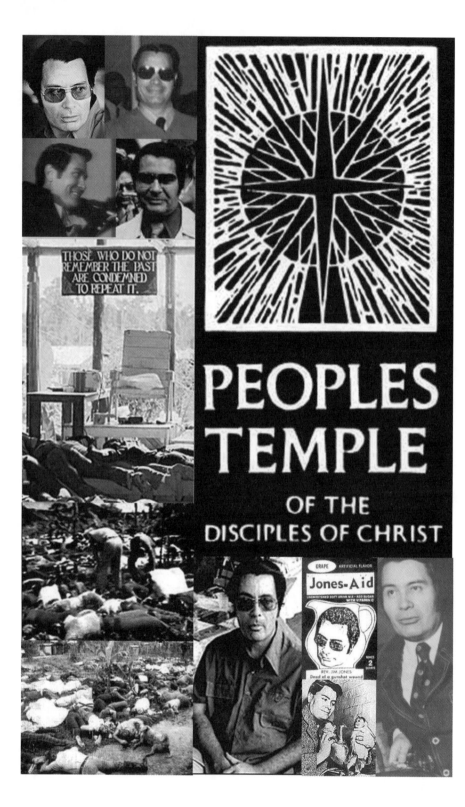

THOSE WHO DO NOT REMEMBER THE PAST ARE CONDEMNED TO REPEAT IT.

PEOPLES TEMPLE
OF THE
DISCIPLES OF CHRIST

Jones-Aid

GRAPE ARTIFICIAL FLAVOR

UNSWEETENED SOFT DRINK MIX • ADD SUGAR
WITH VITAMIN C

MAKES
2
QUARTS

REV. JIM JONES

Dead of a gunshot wound

CHAPTER THIRTEEN

HEART OF DARKNESS

I take it, no fool ever made a bargain for his soul with the devil: the fool is too much of a fool, or the devil too much of a devil—I don't know which.
  —Joseph Conrad, *Heart of Darkness*

To corner him for the Agency, it was recognized at Langley that the Devil must be made respectable. Working through conduits, the Scientific Engineering Institute helped fund a course in sorcery at the University of South Carolina. Two hundred and fifty students enrolled. The scientists of Operation Often studied carefully the results of classes devoted to fertility and initiation rites and raising the dead.
  —Gordon Thomas, *Journey Into Madness*[1]

I stared at the clumps of bodies in front of the communications center. I couldn't bring myself to leave them. I noticed that many of them had died with their arms around each other, men and women, white and black, young and old. Little babies were lying on the ground, too. Near their mothers and fathers. Dead.
  Finally, I turned back towards the main pavilion and noticed the dogs that lay dead on the sidewalk. The dogs, I thought. What had they done?
  Then I realized that Jones had meant to leave nothing, not even the animals, to bear witness to the final horror.
  —Charles A. Krause, *Guyana Massacre: the Eyewitness Account*[2]

"The horror! The horror!"
  —Conrad, Heart of Darkness

In November 1969 Charles Manson was in jail, but had not been charged yet with the murders at the Tate and LaBianca residences. He was arrested on October 12, 1969 on other charges, along with a number of his followers, who were scattered throughout the prison system awaiting trial. The Manson Family culpability in the Tate and LaBianca homicides would not be suggested until December. Until then, he was cooling his heels on what was a simple credit card fraud beef, and calmly expecting to be released at any time.

Steve Brandt, though, had committed suicide in New York City that month in terror over the killings and the possible existence of a hit list that would have included his name as a close friend and confidante of Sharon Tate.

At the same time, a couple—Al and Deanna Mertle—were experiencing some marital troubles. They had been married exactly a year before, in November of 1968, and each had children by a previous marriage; but they were finding it increasingly difficult to communicate with their kids and with themselves, and felt they were growing apart.

They decided to visit the minister who had married them, and one night they had dinner with him and his wife and the subject of a new church in Redwood City, a town some three and half hours from their home in Hayward, California, came up in conversation. They agreed to go to the church the following Sunday, and as it happened the event truly changed their lives.

And quite possibly ended them.

They joined the church in 1970 and stayed with it through thick and thin for the next six years. When they left in 1976, they were afraid for their lives. They campaigned vociferously against it, and did what they could to inform government and civic leaders of the threat it posed to society. They spoke of beatings, sexual abuse including the rape of men, women and children, public humiliation, torture, brainwashing, and the mind control of children, including sleep deprivation and being made to witness terrible punishments meted out for the slightest of offences and, sometimes, for no discernible offence at all. The leader considered himself a God, said he was the reincarnation of Jesus and Lenin, and demanded absolute obedience from his followers, who numbered in the thousands. It was Charles Manson and his Family writ large and fine-tuned.

In November of 1979 the Mertles published a book about their experiences. In February 1980, they were murdered in their home along with their teenaged daughter, each shot in the head execution-style by person or persons unknown. Their triple homicide has remained unsolved to this day.

The Mertles had published their book under a pseudonym: Jeannie Mills. It was entitled *Six Years With God* and was subtitled *Life Inside Rev. Jim Jones's Peoples Temple*.

The Jonestown massacre took place on November 18, 1978. In spite of tremendous media coverage, the case has never been satisfactorily explained, or the murders of over nine hundred persons ever really solved. The first police officials to be summoned to the crime scene described evidence that is at wide variance to that found in the official American reports. Bodies were missing, and then found. Numbers were juggled with reckless abandon. Cover stories were tried out, and then dropped in favor of more credible ones. Money was missing. Guns were missing. Documents were missing. And, as usual, witnesses started dying of unnatural causes.

Even the biography of the man at the center of the holocaust, Jim Jones, was sketchy and open to interpretation. His presumed close association with Dan Mitrione was never investigated by the US government or, if it was, the results were never made public. Mitrione was the man taken hostage and then killed by the leftist guerrilla Tupamaros in Uruguay in 1970, revolutionaries who knew that he was a CIA agent with AID agency cover. Jones and Mitrione had known each other in Indiana, where Mitrione was a cop specializing in juveniles and Jones a fifteen-year-old sidewalk preacher, and they *were* both in Brazil at the same time in the early 1960s: Mitrione with a police training unit that was under Agency for International Development (AID) cover, and Jones in some murky capacity that involved the US consulate.

Mitrione, it is now known, was involved with the training of Latin American police forces in the use of torture and drugs in interrogations, under the auspices of the now-defunct and cynically-entitled Office of Public Safety (OPS), an Orwellian organization that was formed during the Eisenhower administration. Mitrione was an avid practitioner of the methods he taught and, according to one of his trainees in Uruguay in the late 1960s, he would pick up homeless people on the streets to be used as guinea pigs in his training sessions, bloody interrogations which were always conducted in a soundproof room. In Montevideo, this room was in the basement of his home. When the derelicts died during the course of the "training," their bodies would be dumped back in the streets as a warning to Communist insurgents.

The drugs and techniques, of course, were the direct and unequivocal legacy of ongoing MK-ULTRA research. According to John Marks,

> In 1966 CIA staffers, including [John] Gittinger himself, took part in selecting members of an equally controversial police unit in Uruguay—the anti-terrorist section that fought the Tupamaro urban guerrillas.... Agency operators worked to set up this special force together with the Agency for International Development's Public Safety Mission (whose members included Dan Mitrione, later kidnapped and killed by the Tupamaros). The CIA-assisted police claimed they were in a life-and-death struggle against the guerrillas, and they used incredibly brutal methods, including torture, to stamp out most of the Uruguayan left along with the guerrillas.[3]

John Gittinger was the "MKULTRA program's resident genius."[4] He developed something called the Personality Assessment System (PAS). An incredibly complex system, it resisted computerization due to all the variables, and at one point Gittinger had something like 29,000 separate test results on computer printout in his office that he mined for data on the personalities of drug addicts, prostitutes, homosexuals, criminals, the easily hypnotizable, etc. His specialty was uncovering the "underlying personality structure—discrepancies that produce tension, conflict, and anxiety."[5] Gittinger had left his mark on virtually every aspect of MK-ULTRA, from the San Francisco "safe house" where prostitutes were observed with their johns behind two-way mirrors, to the attempt to develop an aerosol can that sprayed LSD, to the selection of secret police in Uruguay to assist Dan Mitrione in his endeavors.

During the same period, Andrija Puharich (of Arthur Young, MK-ULTRA and "Council of the Nine" fame) was also in Brazil investigating the famous "psychic surgeon," Arigo, while Arthur Hochberg (of Robert Mullen and E. Howard Hunt fame) was also in Brazil working for the CIA station there. Guy Lyon Playfair, an English-born biographer of Uri Geller and the author of several books on paranormal phenomena, was living in Brazil researching macumba and other Brazilian occult practices at the same time (working occasionally for *Time* magazine among other sources of income) and from 1967-71 was working for the *same* CIA front—AID, the Agency for International Development—that Dan Mitrione used as a cover! (As an aside, even the infamous medical doctor and war criminal, the "Angel of Death" at Auschwitz, Josef Mengele—one of the most wanted men in the world at the time—was living in hiding at a farm ninety-three miles north of Sao Paulo in 1962, and thus only a few hours' drive from both Sao Paulo and Belo Horizonte.) So, it was one big happy, psychotic, dysfunctional family: Jim Jones, Dan Mitrione, Andrija Puharich, Arthur Hochberg, Guy Lyon Playfair, Josef Mengele, even Arigo the psychic surgeon. But we are getting way ahead of the story.

We must spend some time with the Jonestown episode because it pulls together several disparate scarlet threads in this tapestry of politics, drugs, intelligence agencies, religion, mind control, and murder. Some commentators and journalists have gone overboard with accusations of Nazi involvement, and have claimed that Jonestown was "a CIA medical experiment." As outlandish as these claims seem *prima facie*, with Jonestown we are on the very threshold of the unbelievable. The documentation that does exist makes it virtually impossible to accept the official story of Jonestown as it has been handed down since that day in mid-November 1978 when Congressman Ryan was shot and over nine hundred others murdered. While the mainstream media has been content to cluck and shake their heads over the Jonestown massacre as an example of "what happens when people follow a religious leader blindly" and leave it at that, there was in reality so much more to the story of Jim Jones, the Peoples Temple, and the 913 murdered men, women and children that, if nothing else, the story needs to be told for their sake, most of whom never had a decent burial and many of whose bodies were never even identified.

LORD JIM

Cornelius, who had made himself at home in the camp, talked at his elbow, pointing out the localities, imparting advice, giving his own version of Jim's character, and commenting in his own fashion upon the events of the last three years. Brown, who, apparently indifferent and gazing away, listened with attention to every word, could not make out clearly what sort of man this Jim could be. "What's his name? Jim! Jim! That's not enough for a man's name." "They call him," said Cornelius, scornfully, "Tuan Jim here. As you may say Lord Jim.... He is a fool. All you have to do is kill him and then you are king here. Everything belongs to him ..."

    -- Joseph Conrad, *Lord Jim*

The basic facts of the life of Jim Jones are a matter of public record. He was born James Warren Jones in the small village of Crete, Indiana on May 13, 1931. Crete doesn't appear on most roadmaps today, although its larger neighbor, Lynn, can be found about twenty miles north of Richmond, Indiana on the Ohio border, due east of Indianapolis. Jim Jones' father was a World War I veteran who had been gassed in the trenches and was considered disabled, living on a pension. A Quaker by birth, he was now a proud member of the Ku Klux Klan and a night watchman for the town, licensed to carry a handgun on his rounds. Jones' mother, according to one account, had been an anthropologist doing field work in Africa and had returned to Indiana soon after going there; the reasons are not clear. Thus, the marriage between these two people, widely separated in age, background and belief, is fairly incredible but nonetheless a fact.

Jim Jones and Charles Manson were contemporaries; Manson was born in 1934, only three years after Jones, and had a similar upbringing. Where Jones' father was a former soldier in the trenches of the Great War, Manson's father—at least in the eyes of the Ashland courts—was one Colonel Scott, of unknown background and unspecified military service (where did the "Colonel" come from?). They both were raised by very religious Christians who were not members of the immediate family. In Manson's case, we are talking about his West Virginia relations with whom he was housed when his mother was in prison. In the case of Jim Jones, the religious influence was a Mrs. Kennedy, who was his babysitter in Lynn after school while his mother worked at an aircraft plant in Richmond. Mrs. Kennedy was a devout Methodist, and it was from her that he got his first taste of the Bible and then wound up holding mock church services for other children at his home.

Then, at about the age of fifteen, he began preaching on the sidewalks in Richmond. This was certainly odd behavior for a high school student, and is an indication of how much he was attracted to religion: going from make-believe Sunday services at his home to actually preaching on street corners in town. It was at that time that he met Dan Mitrione, who was a police officer in Richmond, although the exact nature of their relationship remains mysterious and unexplored. It was in Richmond nonetheless that the seeds of Jonestown would be planted.

By the time he was ready for his senior year in high school, the Second World War was already over and his parents had separated. Jim Jones moved with his mother to Richmond, and he enrolled in Richmond High School while at the same time finding work as an orderly in Reid Memorial Mental Hospital. It was at Reid that he met his wife, a nurse four years his senior. He married Marceline Baldwin in the Methodist Church in Richmond on June 12, 1949 and the newlyweds moved to Bloomington, where Jim Jones would attend Indiana University.

Jones took a part-time job as a night watchman, which was what his father had been doing to supplement his army pension, and what a generation of other sinister gunmen have been known to do, such as David Berkowitz (the "Son of Sam") and Mark David Chapman, the killer of John Lennon. He began to drift away from the degrees he had been working towards, first the business degree and then the law degree, and then eventually even the degree in education. But by 1952 Jim Jones had finally found his true calling: as an assistant minister for the Somerset Methodist Church in Indianapolis. It was at Somerset that the phenomenon we know as Jim Jones was spawned.

Somerset was located in a poor white neighborhood in Indianapolis, a town as racist as any other in the United States in 1952. Jones, however, preached a gospel of racial tolerance, which was not accepted by the white community but which did attract black worshippers. By all accounts he was a charismatic speaker, but he supplemented his preaching with a fair amount of legerdemain: healing the sick in the manner of fraudulent faith healers the world over who remove cancerous growths from their patients with mesmeric passes, the shouting of Biblical phrases, and the generous use of concealed chicken livers as "tumors," which are revealed at just the right moment to effect the "cure." Eventually, Jones was kicked out of Somerset, but by then the damage had been done. He was not formally ordained into the ministry until much later, but he had developed a following throughout southern Indiana and Ohio nonetheless, aided by his frantic schedule of prayer services and radio programs, a campaign that wooed black people into a church organization that would include only whites in leadership positions.

At that time, the early 1950s, Jones' politics were by all accounts as virulently anti-Communist as those of his fellow clergymen, and his radio programs and preaching carried a clear anti-Communist message. This was, after all, the McCarthy Era and anti-Communism was fashionable in some circles (just as socialism was in others), and for a Christian minister in the Midwest who traveled the circuit between Cincinatti, Dayton, Richmond, Indianapolis and Fort Wayne, it was to be expected that he would preach against the godless Russians and the atheist Chinese. Politically then, before his trip to South America, his politics would have been considered sound by US government officials.

As the operation became more sophisticated, though, after his mysterious sojourn in Brazil, Jones gradually abandoned any pretense at standard Biblical terminology or theology. Jones began to speak of revolution, and of Jesus as a socialist. He began to gradually mock and villify the God of the Jews, the "Sky God" as he called him, and to identify Jehovah with satanic forces bent on the destruction of humanity. It was pure neo-Nazism, except it was so convoluted that most of his followers would never have recognized it for what it was. As detailed at some length in my previous work, *Unholy Alliance*, the Nazi ideologists of the Third Reich had reinterpreted the Bible in such a way that the God of the Israelites was Satan. This has become standard theology in such racist organizations in America as the Christian Identity movement.

Lucifer was the "light-bringer," and intent on delivering humanity from the clutches of the evil Jehovah. This is also a Gnostic belief, as demonstrated in the scriptures uncovered at Nag Hammadi in Egypt in 1945. In this system, the Serpent in the Garden of Eden was the true God, who wanted to deliver the human race from the blind Creator God, the Demiurge who wanted Adam and Eve as his personal slaves. This deity is equivalent to the H.P. Lovecraft creature, the "blind idiot god of chaos," for it was he who created material forms with reckless abandon and who—in his blindness—believed he was the Superior Being and demanded that Adam and Eve worship only him. According to Gnostic legend, this being—Samael—was then chastised by the other gods for his vanity in assuming the mantle of Supreme God. That other gods existed is plain to see by the Biblical injunction, "I am the Lord thy God, thou shalt have no other gods before me," implying that there were other gods to be dealt with.

This multiplicity of gods with Biblical geneaology is what gave rise to the theology of the Process Church of the Final Judgment, as discussed in Book One. This form of Gnosticism also influenced Charles Manson, and he began to identify himself with Abraxas, a famous Gnostic deity whose numerological equivalent is 365, the same as the number of days in the year and thus representative of time itself. With the Nazis, the neo-Nazis, and the Christian Identity movement in the United States, Europe, and Latin America, we are experiencing a strange resurrection of first and second century Gnosticism: Gnosticism with a vengeance.

Some of this is evident in the sermons and speeches of Jim Jones as well, except that in his case he was obviously abandoning all pretense at religion of any kind and was trying to develop a popular political movement using all the creaking machinery of old-time religious revivalism. Imagine, if you will, all the ritual, pomp and ceremony of religion but without any mention of God. Imagine people signing over everything they own to a "Temple" that preaches neither Jehovah nor Jesus, but Lenin and Mao. In addition, Jones also preached reincarnation—not exactly a mainstream Christian belief, but one familiar to the early Gnostics—and claimed he was the reincarnation of

Buddha, Jesus, Lenin, and the progenitor of the Bahai religion, the Bab. In other words, like his contemporary Charles Manson, Jim Jones was God; and by demanding total obedience and unstinting worship from his followers, he was unconsciously identifying himself with Samael, the "blind idiot god of chaos."

As Kenneth D. Wald points out in his *Religion and Politics in the United States*, the early American political campaigns were based on Christian tent revivalism:

> Candidates rallied supporters with torchlight parades, tent meetings, door-to-door canvassing, and public declarations of faith, the same methods pioneered by evangelists seeking religious converts.[6]

Jones merely took this one step further and mixed radical politics with Christian revival *sturm und drang* to the point where people thought they were in a church on Sunday—from all the singing and preaching, the handsome Reverend in his robes and aviator sunglasses, shouting and waving his arms in the pulpit (with no Bible in sight)—but were really at a political rally. An ersatz *socialist* political rally.

There is evidence to show that Jim Jones and his wife, Marceline, visited Cuba in 1960, for reasons unknown. It is here that the story takes on all the hallmarks of an intelligence operation, for there appear not one but two Jim Joneses, two different passports, and mutually contradictory itineraries throughout the period 1960-63.

Probably the best source of information on this period of Jones' life is contained in the parapolitical journal *Lobster*, a British publication that has long been a favorite of conspiracy theorists and investigative journalists. It is here, in issue number 37, that some of the most frightening information about Jim Jones was presented by veteran journalist and television documentary producer Jim Hougan (of *Spooks* and *Secret Agenda* fame). Entitled *Jonestown, The Secret Life of Jim Jones: A parapolitical fugue*, it gently debunks some of the wilder theories about Jonestown, while giving evidence for a scenario that is, if anything, even more unsettling. As I began to write this chapter, I was ignorant of some of the very firm connections that existed to support my own thesis, and I am thankful to Jim Hougan for the benefit of his two years of research on Jim Jones and Jonestown undertaken in the United States and South America.

Hougan has shown that Dan Mitrione and Jim Jones did know each other, and that Jones actually referred to his friendship with Mitrione several times during the course of his taped speeches at Jonestown. This is important, for it brings us one step closer to a true understanding of the events of 1978. More importantly, Hougan demonstrates that Jones was known to the CIA and the FBI before the massacre, and that the CIA maintained a file on Jones that coincided quite precisely with Dan Mitrione's career as an overseas "trainer" of foreign police forces. That is, the file on Jones was opened when Mitrione began to work for the AID-sponsored OPS program and was closed when Mitrione was killed in Uruguay in 1970, a period of roughly ten years spanning the Castro revolution in Cuba, the socialist victory at the polls in Guyana, the Bay of Pigs invasion, the assassination of President Kennedy, the socialist victories in Brazil, the military coup in Brazil, and even the assassinations of Bobby Kennedy and Martin Luther King. This coincidental opening and closing of Jones' file in tandem with Mitrione's career leads Hougan to believe that this was an indication of a Jones–Mitrione working relationship. If so, it has implications far worse than even the Jonestown massacre provides, for it means that Jones was infiltrating religious organizations, and specifically *black* religious organizations, on behalf of the United States government.

Jones visited Cuba in February of 1960. Certainly an awkward time for an American clergyman to be in Havana! Castro had just taken power the previous year, in January of 1959, and the Bay of Pigs plotting was already underway. The American presidential election of 1960 was months away. Yet, Jim Jones chose this time to visit what was practically a war zone.

According to a Cuban whom he met in Havana during that trip, Jones was involved in trying to arrange for Cubans to emigrate to the United States. This was part of a larger American policy of encouraging Cubans to defect from Castro, in order to weaken the Cuban economy as well as win some propaganda points. Jones was specifically trying to recruit black Cubans to come to Indianapolis where his Peoples Temple was still located. It seems that nothing much came of this plan, but Jones was evidently working on behalf of American political interests when he was there. He brought back with him photographs of himself in Cuba and most curiously a photo taken of him standing next to a downed aircraft that had been flown by anti-Castro Cubans—not exactly on the main tourist circuit, even in revolutionary Cuba. The anti-Castro Cubans were bombing the sugar cane fields in a further attempt to destabilize Castro's regime, and one of these photos shows a pilot's dead and mangled corpse. As Hougan points out, this type of photo would have been of extreme interest to American intelligence.

Did Dan Mitrione recruit Jim Jones one day on the streets of Richmond, Indiana? Did he note that Jones seemed to have a rapport with black people, something quite unusual for a white teenager in 1950s middle America? Was there a larger agenda, especially at a time when the FBI and the CIA were worried that a black revolution could threaten the existing American institutions and disrupt the status quo? Was Jones supposed to provide both an intelligence source within the black community, as well as a safety valve for the anger and resentment felt by a race that had been enslaved and even then were struggling for basic human rights?

If Jones did have an intelligence agenda, and was working for Dan Mitrione in some capacity, then it might go a long way towards explaining the two passports and, incredibly, the two different versions of Jim Jones.

Like the strange appearance of one, two, many Oswalds in New Orleans, Mexico City, and Dallas, which has plagued Kennedy assassination researchers for years, there were at least two men traveling to South America at that time named Jim Jones.

As pointed out in Hougan's research, Jones had two passports issued to him at two different times. One, issued in Chicago on June 28, 1960 and another issued in Indianapolis on January 30, 1962. The problem is twofold. First, as there is strong evidence (on the basis of an eyewitness account, an affidavit signed by Jones during that period in Cuba, etc.) that Jones was in Cuba in the first few months of 1960, how did he travel there if his passport was not issued until June 28? Secondly, why the two passports, as the first one issued in 1960 certainly would still be valid?

It is certain that Jones was in Cuba in February of 1960. It is also certain that he visited Cuba again a year later. And there is further evidence—also incontrovertible, and verified by newspaper accounts printed at the time—that Jones had visited Guyana (when it was still called "British Guiana") years before he ever set up the commune known to the world as Jonestown. In fact, according to an eyewitness—a Cuban he eventually brought to the United States in August 1960 to stay with the Temple in Indianapolis—Jones appeared to have been well-traveled by that time and "knew Latin America well. He had already been to Guyana, and wanted to start a collective there."[7] The assumption is that Jones also spoke Spanish, since the witness—Carlos Foster—did not speak English at that time, and they spent entire days for a week discussing plans for bringing Cubans to the United States. (Why, Jimmy, we never knew ye!)

Then, in 1961, the Jim Jones phenomenon becomes positively …otherworldly.

He was named as the Director of the Indianapolis Human Rights Commission when he was thirty years old, by most accounts, which would mean sometime in 1961. One wonders what the duties of a Human Rights Commission director would have been in Indianapolis in 1961, but whatever they were, by October he was resigning the post after having spent a week in a hospital due to stress. He had been hearing "extra-terrestrial voices"—shades of Aleister Crowley and Aiwaz, or of Barney and Betty Hill, whose celebrated abduction by a UFO had taken place the previous month in New Hampshire—and having seizures.[8] These symptoms sound quite serious, and would be evidence of a psychotic episode, perhaps a schizophrenic or schizophreniform disorder, but alas we have insufficient information about Jones' particular illness, rendering further speculation futile.

At the end of October, Jones left Indianapolis for a few weeks of rest and recuperation, in Hawaii according to most accounts. Unfortunately, as Jim Hougan points out, this story is patently false, for the Guyanese newspapers have Jones in their country in late October 1961. He could not have been in both Hawaii and Guyana the same week of October. Not in 1961. Further, he is supposed to have stopped in Mexico City during that time as well, which renders the impossibility of being in three different countries spread that far apart in the same week. For those who have not attempted to visit Guyana, it is a difficult place to reach today, and was even more so in 1961. There were no direct flights from Honolulu to Georgetown. The airfare—in 1976 when the author was contemplating a trip, two years before the Jonestown massacre—was also prohibitively expensive, as Guyana is off the main tourist routes. One typically flew via Trinidad or Jamaica or one of the other Caribbean islands.

All of this simply goes to say that Jim Jones could not have been in both Hawaii and Guyana the same week. Further, there is evidence that Jones had been under psychiatric care in San Francisco and—as Hougan points out—some have offered the opinion that Jones went to Hawaii in order to "receive psychiatric care without publicity."[9]

The idea that Jones might have spent time in a mental hospital in Hawaii is rich with further implications, for one of history's most infamous assassins—Mark David Chapman—also spent time in a mental hospital in Hawaii, and Hawaiian hospitals also came under investigation for their possible role in a network of drug trafficking that involved the organization now believed to have been responsible for the Son of Sam murders in New York City. Also, and for reasons that are really not very clear, several of the Manson Family women, to keep one of their own out of the witness chair during the trial of Charles Manson, fled to Hawaii, where they fed her a hamburger laced with an overdose of LSD. The unfortunate victim—Barbara Hoyt—wound up wandering in the busy streets of Honolulu and was taken to a hospital for observation and treatment. This betrayal by her fellow Family members led to her becoming a *very* cooperative witness against them once she recovered. Why the Manson Family chose Hawaii is open to speculation. It would have been just as easy—and far less expensive—to have moved the witness to one of the other states or even to Canada or Mexico. The selection of Hawaii seems either serendipitous or evidence of a deeper agenda.

Nonetheless, what *is* known about Jones beyond any doubt is that he was under psychiatric care at the Langley-Porter Neuropsychiatric Institute in San Francisco, a hospital that conducts experiments on behalf of ARPA, the Advanced Research Projects Agency of the Defense Department, and where "virtually every survivor of the Jonestown massacre was eventually treated."[10] Jones' medical files have been withheld from scrutiny, even though Jones has been dead since 1978.

So, we have two passports, two distinct destinations, and many motives. Jones in Guyana was preaching against Communism. Jones in Cuba (during one trip) was attempting to lure Cubans into the States, and during another was meeting with Fidel Castro. Jones in Mexico was up to God knows what. And finally Jones was in Brazil. But the usual reasons given for his trip there also defy the chronological record.

The usual impetus described is an article published in the January 1962 edition of *Esquire* magazine entitled "Nine Places to Hide." In the event of a nuclear war, according to the article, there were nine safe places on the planet that would be immune from both bombs and radioactive fallout. One of these was Eureka, California and another was Belo Horizonte, Brazil. Jones is described as extremely paranoid about nuclear war, and desperate to find somewhere to sit out a holocaust. Although he was based in Indiana at the time, and therefore much closer to Eureka, California, for some reason Jones decided that Brazil was the place to be, and he moved himself, his wife, a personal friend and his wife, and their four children to Belo Horizonte that year.

The problem with this scenario is that Jones was already in Guyana in October of 1961. The article on Jones was published in the *Guyana Graphic* on October 27, 1961, so the story that he stopped off in Guyana on his way to Brazil doesn't wash. And the story that the *Esquire* article prompted his trip also doesn't wash. It wasn't in print in October of 1961.

The months between October of 1961 and April of 1962 are a black hole in his biography. It seems evident that he was not in Indianapolis, but aside from that there is no way to know where he was or what he was doing. All that is certain is that he arrived in Sao Paulo, Brazil on April 11, 1962. According to a friend who knew Jones in Brazil at this time, he had arrived in Sao Paulo from Cuba.[11] The problem with this account should be obvious to anyone who remembers the period, because it is only a year after the Bay of Pigs invasion, and only six months before the Cuban Missile Crisis. How many Americans were touring Havana at that time? In addition, the same eyewitness claims that Jones showed her a photograph he had taken with Fidel Castro. This was the same American minister who made anti-Communist speeches in Guyana the year before.

Will the real Jim Jones please stand up?

Jones may have admired Castro's style of public speaking, for it so mirrored his own: lengthy speeches lasting hours, filled with revolutionary rhetoric, paranoia and *ad hominem* appeals to the better angels of our nature. But this foreign travel of the Joneses is mysterious and hard to understand on the basis of the existing documentation. So much of it is not explained. So much of the information that is available is contradictory. Witnesses describe Jones' lifestyle in Brazil as lavish; others as meager at best. Witnesses say that Jones was setting up an orphanage in Brazil, but for whom and with what funding is not described; others say that Jones did no missionary work at all in Brazil, but left the house each morning with a briefcase and returned each evening with few comments on where he had been or what he had done. He would make passing references to Naval Intelligence (à la Ron Hubbard) or to other government work; people who knew him in Brazil thought of him as a spy: no Brazilians who knew Jones during his stay there and can attest to his Christian missionary work have been discovered.

Whatever took place in Brazil, by the time he returned to the United States he had undergone a conversion to socialism, a conversion that would eventually lead him to espouse Communism as the only way. He dropped his pretense of being a Christian minister in the 1960s and began openly supporting revolutionary activity, particularly an end to racism. This could have been an honest conversion, based on witnessing firsthand some of the very poor conditions in South America and understanding that the United States was at least partially to blame for the suffering. On the other hand, the conversion—as so many have charged—might have been false, a cover story being developed for a far more sinister purpose. After all, most of the people who were murdered at Jonestown were black. Most of the people doing the killing were white.

As mentioned previously, Jim Jones was in Brazil at the same time as Dan Mitrione, whom he had known from their common sojourn in and around Richmond, Indiana. Mitrione had since left Richmond to join the FBI, and eventually became an instructor of foreign police departments on behalf of the Office of Public Safety, which worked hand-in-hand with AID, the Agency for International Development. Mitrione's work involved training police investigators in the finer techniques of interrogation. This work was eventually heavily criticized by the US Congress when word of its excesses began to be known publicly in the 1970s, and the unit was disbanded and reorganized under other supervision. But it was in the 1960s that the damage had been done.

State Department, military and CIA operations in Latin America were notorious for their rapacity during that time. It is a matter of public record that the CIA managed to orchestrate a military coup in Guatemala in the 1950s, the Bay of Pigs invasion of Cuba in 1961, the election of a supposedly pro-US Forbes Burnham as Prime Minister in Guyana over his socialist opponent Jagan (who later expressed himself as satisfied with the results of the rigged election, when it was learned that Burnham himself was even more of a socialist than Jagan!), and, of course, the US-sponsored overthrow of the Allende regime in Chile on September 11, 1973. The police forces of Latin America have all received training of one kind or another from US specialists working for AID, OPS, or the US military directly; and this training has taken place either in the United States or, during the 1960s, more likely in the foreign country itself, far from the watchful eye of congressional oversight committees.

Indeed, the US government does not know what training programs were in place during that time or how much they cost, as they were often buried under other appropriations and other budgetary columns in the annual reports. But it was millions upon millions of dollars for dozens of programs spread throughout the various Departments and Agencies. In the unlikely event that it is ever shown that Jonestown *was* a "CIA medical experiment," there will be no documentation to support the contention. The personnel, equipment, contingency plans and budgets will all be buried in just the way government accountants and bookkeepers know so well: just as they had done for the international police training programs of the 1960s; just as they had for the mind-control experiments of the CIA, until a blunder revealed four boxes of financial papers sitting in a basement at Langley long after the rest of the documentation had been thoroughly shredded by Richard Helms and his Dr. Strangelove, Sidney Gottlieb.

During the same era, the author himself was employed by a large government contractor and Fortune 100 company, the Bendix Corporation, where I was privileged to work in their International Marketing Operation, located on Broadway in mid-town Manhattan. At Bendix—from 1973-79—I witnessed several occasions where my employer was used as a cover for intelligence activities and police and military support operations all over the world. Indeed, in the wake of the Watergate revelations, several newspapers carried stories about the involvement of Bendix "field engineering personnel" in the training of Saudi Arabian troops, as one example. We read these reports avidly in the office, looking for the names of people we knew. In Argentina, local Bendix employees and their expatriate manager were kidnapped by left-wing revolutionaries and held hostage. Our sales rep from Caracas, Venezuela—from the swashbuckling firm Representaciones Godoy—would fly to New York in his private plane and walk into our offices wearing a sidearm, much to the consternation of our security staff. I remember watching the telex machine one day as our man in Lebanon sent his sales report and purchase orders; in the middle of transmission, the machine died and we held our collective breath. Civil war had just begun, and our office was in the middle of the war zone in Beirut. Finally, after an agonizing wait of about twenty minutes, the transmission resumed. It was the last we would receive from Beirut, and our man transferred to another Middle Eastern location where the sound of small arms fire did not punctuate the night.

Considering that our clientele involved everyone from the Shah of Iran to the military procurement departments of countries all over the globe, it was no wonder that we would be used as a cover for intelligence operations. Financial arrangements at Bendix for international accounts were also so byzantine and complex, involving the payouts of huge "commissions" and the awarding of bizarre orders for seemingly useless equipment, that we began to understand that US intelligence agencies could have easily financed many of their operations simply by using Bendix sales people and sales agents in the target countries as conduits for funds, funds that would go both ways. For instance, we once sold to the Government of Pakistan *six* early-warning type radar systems. Six! The United States itself only had one of the same type at the time. It was understood that the contract for the six systems was, in reality, a contract for something else altogether; that the Pakistani government was paying for other services or equipment that it was considered best to conceal from the watchful eyes of journalists and congressmen. And so it goes.

Thus, when the author heard some of the stories about Dan Mitrione, as well as about Operation Condor in Latin America, Operation Phoenix in Vietnam, etc., he could well imagine how easily the finer details had been arranged. Had Jim Jones been in Brazil on some sort of assignment—either for the CIA, or for some other agency such as Mitrione's OPS—his funding would have been easy to source and to hide. As a contract agent, he might even have been paid in cash, with a paper receipt signed either in his name or in a mutually-agreed upon pseudonym.

It is known that Jones returned to the United States with money, not an easy miracle if one's whole time in Brazil was spent in missionary work, living close to the bone and building an orphanage, as he claimed in his speeches.[12] In an emotional confession before his assembled followers, in fact, he said that they were so broke in Brazil that he had to become a gigolo and sell his body to the rich and eager wives of local Brazilian businessmen in order to raise money for the impoverished children under his care, and all with his wife Marcelline's approval. One must pause for a moment and brush a tear from the eye in sympathy with the tremendous sacrifice Jim made—over and over again—in order to put food on the table for the starving orphans of Belo Horizonte!

And, if such really is the case ... where is the Reverend Jim Jones Memorial Orphanage?

THE BOYS FROM BRAZIL

"The precise pain, in the precise place, in the precise amount, for the desired effect."
-- Dan Mitrione (in *Killing Hope*, by William Blum)

Brazil in 1962 was in virtual chaos. Janio Qaudros had been elected in 1960 on an anti-corruption platform. His vice president was the Brazilian Workers Party candidate, Joao Goulart. (In Brazil, presidents and vice presidents are elected separately.) Seven months later, however, for reasons that have never been revealed, Quadros resigned the presidency and threw the country into a constitutional crisis. By rights, Goulart should have taken the oath as president, but due to his socialist politics, the army resisted his inauguration. Finally, he was allowed to take office, but only with reduced responsibilities. The job was to be shared with a newly-created position of prime minister, someone who was acceptable to the military and could keep the socialist president in line.

Finally, in 1962, a national referendum held by Goulart reversed the 1961 decision, and Goulart was allowed to take full powers and remove the prime minister. This did not, however, happen with the full cooperation of the Brazilian military authorities. Brazil was as much in the midst of the Cold War as the United States and the other powers. Brazil, alone of all countries in South America, had sent troops to Europe to fight in World War II, specifically in Italy, and the Brazilian army considered itself a close working ally of the United States. Goulart, on the other hand, was seen as a Communist, and Brazilian and American military and intelligence forces began to cooperate to find a way to have him overthrown. Mitrione was in the middle of that plotting, and his training of the Brazilian police forces involved not only the usual third-degree and torture techniques but also "political" training. Both the United States and the Brazilian right-wing viewed Goulart as a revolutionary in the pocket of the Soviets and the Cubans, and this message was brought across by American advisors like Dan Mitrione.

This was the political environment in which Jim Jones and his entourage found themselves. Goulart's presidency had just been assured by the national referendum, and the Brazilian Army was in the grip of fear of a Communist takeover of their country. Of course, Christian fundamentalist churches could be counted upon to support the Army and the right-wing against Communist "evangelism" in the countryside. Godless Communism was the common enemy of all Christian churches, so a successful American preacher like Jim Jones could be expected to add his support to American and Brazilian efforts to counter the attraction that Goulart and other Communist sympathizers had for some of the electorate. There is no doubt in my mind, based on long experience in South America and Asia, that the presence of Jim Jones in Brazil in 1962 had political overtones, whether or not he was actually in the employ of an intelligence agency or simply cooperating with an old friend like Dan Mitrione. Religious groups in South America have long been politically affiliated or politically active; World Vision is only one example of an organization that is widely reported to have cooperated extensively with American intelligence services in South America.

During Jones' time in Brazil, the economy began to deteriorate. Goulart struggled to keep the country afloat as foreign loans were called in, loans that had been made to Brazil during the previous administration. By 1964, when Jones was leaving Brazil, inflation had reached 100 percent, and there was no foreign money coming into the country to help it stave off the creditors. In January and February of 1964, desperate to hold on to power and to keep the military at bay, Goulart organized political rallies in major cities throughout

Brazil. He nationalized the oil refineries and put a cap on the expatriation of profits by foreign investors. Finally, he made a speech to the Brazilian Army, asking the noncoms to refuse to carry out any order by their officers if the order was not in Brazil's best interest. This speech was carried on national television. It was all the excuse the Army needed.

On March 31, 1964 the Army seized power in Brazil, and Goulart went into exile. Forever. A few months earlier, Jim Jones went home.

While Jim Jones was ostensibly setting up an orphanage or missionary operation (and it is perhaps relevant to note here that Jones had not yet been actually ordained as a minister by any church; that would not happen until after his return to the United States in 1964), Andrija Puharich was in Brazil to investigate the claims of "psychic surgeon" Arigo. Also at the same time, Guy Lyon Playfair was living and writing in Brazil about a variety of topics, but concentrating on his main interest: the paranormal. Both Puharich and Playfair would later become involved with Uri Geller, the Israeli psychic who dazzled the world with his apparent ability to bend spoons with his mind. As for Playfair, he was working for *Time* magazine and eventually for the AID office in Rio.

Brazil is a greenhouse for occult societies and alternative religious practices. When the author was there in the 1990s, it hadn't changed much from the 1960s. Native practices such as *macumba, umbanda* and *candomble* are very popular, and with every level of society. More surprisingly, the works of Alan Kardec are also popular. Kardec was a nineteenth-century spiritualist who wrote on a wide variety of occult themes, mostly having to do with contacting spiritual forces. In addition, basic grimoires of European ceremonial magic—such as the *Greater* and *Lesser Keys of Solomon*—are widely available and treated with reverence. All this operates in close proximity to the Catholic Church and to many different Christian sects, from Pentecostals to Evangelicals to standard Presbyterian and Methodist churches. Add to this the largest Japanese community outside Japan, located in Sao Paulo, and you have quite a mixture of spiritual beliefs and practices, which of course include Buddhism and Shintoism. Faith healers and spiritists abound, and new occult techniques and teachers are embraced with fervor. The sacrifice of animals occurs on a regular basis, in the deep jungles of the Amazon River basin as well as in the high-rises of Sao Paulo and the *favelas* of Rio de Janeiro.

According to Hougan's sources, Jones was there to study the phenomenon of David Miranda, a Pentecostalist minister who started his own congregation—the Church of God is Love—in Brazil in 1960-61, shortly before Jones' arrival. Miranda's mix of Christian fundamentalist Pentecostalism with faith healing and (as accused in 1999) money laundering would have attracted the like-minded Jones. Hougan believes, however, that there might have been another element to Jones' fascination with Miranda, and that would have been the CIA's interest in "mass conversion techniques" as part of its

MK-ULTRA program. Certainly, Jones' visit to Brazil coincides with a major effort on behalf of the CIA to study primitive religions worldwide, from the psilocybin-eating Indians of Mexico to the Yoruba faith healers of Nigeria. This was not only a CIA interest, for the military had also actively pursued these studies in the name of psychological warfare. The manipulation of the masses—whether by drugs, hypnosis, or other means—would have been of extreme interest to the CIA and the military, and people like David Miranda would have become a focus of this interest. Today, Miranda's operation spans the globe, particularly in developing countries, and is worth many millions of dollars; it was probably a model for Pat Robertson's Christian Broadcasting Network and the Christian Coalition, which has also been involved in supporting right-wing military dictators from Mobutu of Zaire to Taylor of Liberia to Rios Montt of Guatemala and the Contras of Nicaragua (as we shall see later on).

Brazil is a multi-racial society, built by the Portuguese with imported slaves from Africa and indentured servants from Asia. (Guyana, its next door neighbor, is populated almost completely by Africans and East Indians; the native American population is a distinct minority.) In the Brazilian bush can be found a wide variety of Native American tribes, their numbers dwindling as the rain forest is cut down and their cultures lost forever. The Brazilian capitol of Brasilia—located not on the coast like Sao Paulo and Rio de Janeiro, but in the interior—is surrounded by animists and spiritualists of every stripe, and government officials are known to frequent these practitioners to ensure the success of their respective careers. It is a country steeped in respect for the paranormal, and therefore no wonder that the psychic surgeon Arigo should have known such acceptance there.

Andrija Puharich had gone to Brazil in August of 1963 with businessman Henry Belk,[13] a former agent with the Office of Naval Intelligence (ONI), heir to the largest chain of department stores in the southeast United States (the Belk Stores which are headquartered in Charlotte, South Carolina), and founder of the Belk Research Institute, of which Puharich was president, an institute created for the study of paranormal phenomena. Belk had also been acquainted with Dutch psychic Peter Hurkos but, according to one account, became disillusioned with Hurkos when Belk's ten year old daughter and only child went missing shortly after Hurkos had done a psychic reading for Belk and predicted nothing of the sort. His daughter was found dead by drowning and, according to the same source, it was Hurkos who saw the site where she would be found. That was not enough for Belk, of course, who felt that if Hurkos had any real powers he would have warned Belk of the tragedy so that he could have averted it. The Belk family is famous in South Carolina; they have endowed various educational institutions and have been major contributors to charities. William Henry Belk, the founder of the department store chain, began in 1888 with a small store in Charlotte which he named

The New York Racket. (Cynics will claim the name was a case of psychic premonition by the energetic Presbyterian businessman!)

According to one source, the two had gone to Brazil to investigate Arigo at the suggestion of John Laurence, an RCA engineer who worked with NASA and who was actually on the committee that formed NASA in 1958. In Puharich's book, *URI*, Laurence is described as "one of our researchers" in a group of medical specialists put together by Puharich in 1968 to return to Brazil to study Arigo,[14] and the one who spotted a UFO at the same time. Laurence's specialty with NASA and RCA was satellites, and it is possible that his role in Brazil was linked with the development of communications satellite technology. Laurence's other interests obviously involved the paranormal, and it is not clear what his relationship was to Puharich and why he would have invited Puharich specifically to come to Brazil at a time when that country was on the verge of a military coup to counter what was believed to be a nascent Communist insurgency. Further, as Puharich admits that Laurence was a specialist in satellite technology and worked for the Astroelectronics Division of RCA in New Jersey,[15] and thus would not seem to have had medical training, one wonders why he was present at all. Yet, there we have it. An unusual grouping of individuals in Brazil during the precise timeframe when both Brazilian and American intelligence agencies were pondering what to do about Goulart and the Communist menace: former agent and CBW specialist Puharich, police trainer and torture specialist Mitrione, local specialist in Brazilian occultism Playfair (who would later find work with AID), wealthy businessman and paranormal aficionado Belk, and NASA and RCA engineer Laurence. If we really want to stir ourselves up into a paranoid frenzy, we can add Josef Mengele to the mix.

Mengele had escaped justice after World War II and eventually found himself in Brazil in late October 1960, staying first in Sao Paulo before winding up, in the 1962-64 time period, at a farm about ninety-three miles north of Sao Paulo, which puts him within an easy distance of both Sao Paulo and Belo Horizonte.[16] Mengele, of course, was a notorious medical practitioner at Auschwitz, responsible for experiments on live subjects and with special interest in twins. It was Mengele—the Angel of Death—who would stand at the train station when the boxcars of Jewish prisoners were unloaded, telling the bewildered, starving victims "Right" or "Left," to live or to die. Of course, Mengele was in hiding after the war, desperate to avoid Israeli commandos, and would not have been hobnobbing with the likes of Jim Jones or Dan Mitrione or Andrija Puharich. It is only another example of the action of a sinister synchronicity at work in history.

However, it can be stated with some degree of certainty that the political events in 1964 that returned Brazil to the control of the military were welcome news to Mengele. A socialist or Communist in power meant worse conditions for Nazis on the run, particularly if the regime was pro-Soviet. The Russians have no sense of humor when it comes to Nazi war criminals; witness their intransigence in the case of Rudolf Hess, who was the only prisoner left at Spandau by the time he died in 1987, more than forty years after the end of World War II. Considering how deeply American intelligence agencies were protecting Nazis after the war, and how closely Brazilian and American military and intelligence agencies were cooperating, we can be sure that the local authorities would not have been looking too hard for Josef Mengele.

We can, however, posit a relationship between Jones and Mitrione due to their common origins in and around Richmond, Indiana and Jones' statements to that effect in his Jonestown speeches. Puharich and Playfair certainly knew each other, and both knew Geller. In fact, Geller would refer to Puharich as his "CIA case officer." Did the investigation of Arigo have an intelligence aspect? And, considering that Jim Jones made a very public spectacle of "psychic surgery" in the United States, by palming rotten chicken livers and holding them up as evidence of cancerous tumors extracted from his adoring congregants by nothing more than blind faith and mesmeric passes, was there any contact at this time between Arigo and Jones or Jones and Puharich? Unfortunately, we shall never know. Arigo, Puharich, Mitrione and Jones are all dead.

However, one connection can be made, to be filed perhaps under the "six degrees of separation" rule. In February of 1953, Andrija Puharich had been redrafted into the US Army, and posted to the Army Chemical Center in Edgewood, Maryland, where he would remain until April of 1955. His duties are not described anywhere in any detail, although evidence examined in Book One demonstrates that at least some of his responsibilities involved experiments under the CIA mind-control effort. Before Puharich's posting, one Dr. Laurence J. Layton was posted to Dugway Proving Grounds in Utah, a test center for the Chemical Warfare Division of the US Army; this was in November of 1951. In March of 1952, Layton had been named Chief of the US Army's Chemical Warfare Division, a position he held until 1954. In other words, Dr. Layton was—at least on paper—Dr. Puharich's boss.

The relevance of this will become clear shortly. Suffice it to say for now that Dr. Layton—and especially his children, Larry Jr. and Deborah—would play a major role in the events that led up to the Jonestown massacre and that Larry Jr. is still in prison, the only man ever convicted of murder in that hideous event, while it was his sister, Deborah, who had been an important influence on Congressman Leo Ryan's decision to go to Jonestown in the first place.

And, in one more bizarre twist to this story, another associate of Puharich and the busy occult circle around Arthur Young, Jack Sarfatti, Ira Einhorn and the rest was physicist Russell Targ, who by his own admission was involved with the Al and Jeannie Mertle group of Jonestown survivors. In fact, he was the Director of Counseling at the Mertles' Human Freedom Center in Berkeley, California in 1979, and worked for them for "almost a year" until he left to join the Stanford Research Institute (SRI) to study psychic phenomena. It was the Mertles who, under a pseudonym (Mills) wrote an exposé of the Peoples Temple entitled *Six Years With God*. A few weeks after Targ left their employ, the Mertles were found dead, murdered execution style in their home.[17]

DISCIPLES OF THE MILLENIUM

Upon Jones' return to the United States he quickly found himself formally ordained as a minister, and began setting up shop as the Peoples Temple, first in Indiana and then relocating to Ukiah, California. According to Jones, the relocation to Ukiah was of a piece with the *Esquire* magazine article that said the nine safest places in the world included Eureka, California. Now, Eureka and Ukiah are quite distant from each other and, to make matters worse, Ukiah is quite close to several military installations around San Francisco which would be targets in the event of a nuclear strike. No matter; somehow Jim rationalized his choice in his own mind.

By 1968, things at the Peoples Temple had become quite spooky. The Bible was being replaced by Jones' political oratory. The good citizens of Ukiah were getting worried about this strange preacher in the aviator sunglasses who peppered his "sermons" with obscenities and his theology with Marx. In addition, the white community of Ukiah was nervous at the growing numbers of blacks who were joining the Peoples Temple and causing cultural distortion in their little town. Jones began casting about for another home, and this would eventually become San Francisco.

In the meantime, he managed to attract some of his most important members (and defectors). He would also become heavily involved in the health-care industry, and in California politics. What does not compute in reviewing his career is how Jim Jones—if he was truly the psychopath as painted by the press and government reports—was able to garner such support from bureaucrat and politician alike. We can understand the influence of a charismatic preacher over the multitudes; that is, after all, the basic premise of broadcast television: to be able to communicate effectively with the largest mass of viewers one must tailor one's programming and vocabulary to the level of a sixth grade public school education. That is basically what Jones did, as is evident from the tape transcriptions of some of his speeches, including the last one made during the massacre at Jonestown. What we cannot understand is how this same individual was able to function effectively with governors, mayors, and businessmen who—at least theoretically—should be able to spot a con artist at thirty paces; some of the power of these men (and they were mostly men) resides in the ability to spot the same power in others. Jones had the admiration and support of his flock, which numbered in the thousands, and he made substantial donations to the religious organization that eventually adopted the Peoples Temple and insured its legitimacy: the Disciples of Christ.

Garry Wills, in *Under God: Religion and American Politics*, notes that the Disciples of Christ have given the United States three presidents: James Garfield, Lyndon Johnson, and Ronald Reagan.[18] (Oddly enough, the first was assassinated and the third would be the target of an assassination attempt. Only Johnson, it would seem, escaped the attentions of an assassin, although he became president due to the assassination of his predecessor.) The Disciples of Christ is a millennialist sect, and this is probably why—again, according to Wills—Reagan "felt so comfortable with biblical language about the end time whenever he met with fundamentalists."[19] Indeed, not only Reagan, but other members of his administration held deeply apocalyptic beliefs, men such as Defense Secretary Caspar Weinberger and Interior Secretary James Watt.

These high government officials held a Biblical, fatalistic acceptance of the idea that the End Times had come and were upon us; that the Second Coming of Christ was imminent and that the events of the world were pointing towards the meltdown of civilization and the ensuing Rapture. America was, therefore, and however briefly, in the hands of an administration that believed in the literal truth of the Book of Revelation, the Apocalypse (however one interprets the phrase "literal truth" when it comes to the hallucinatory prose of that work). Most Americans were blissfully unaware of this fact, and the implication that their government was on a collision course with the Evil Empire based on Biblical prophecy and Christian Fundamentalism, as if we were living in the twelfth century instead of the twentieth. How dangerous was the world in the 1980s! One wonders what Soviet intelligence made of all of this, ignoring for the moment that their celebrated revolutionary, Bakunin, was an avowed Satanist and that Stalin's daughter was a follower of the Russian mystic Gurdjieff....

Oddly, Wills does not mention Peoples Temple or Jonestown in this study of American religion and politics, although he does agree that in America, religion and politics can never be truly separated. The Disciples of Christ were born in that same mad religious fervor of the early nineteenth century's religious revivalism that brought us the Awakenings ... and the sight of an impoverished farm boy with a book of medieval spells summoning an angel on a mound on the night of the autumnal equinox in upstate New York: the Angel Moroni and the boy Joseph Smith.

Lest we believe that millennial and apocalyptic beliefs are a legacy of America's purely European and purely Christian ancestors, there is the parallel case of the Native American Ghost Dance phenomenon which culminated—in 1890—with the massacre of the Lakota Sioux at Wounded Knee. Without going overmuch into historical and ethnographic detail, suffice it to say that the Ghost Dance was originally designed to bring the Native Americans close to nature and to heal the wound they perceived had been made by the arrival of the white man and his profligate ways. It was believed that if the tribe performed this sacred dance daily then the breach between heaven and earth would be mended and the earth renewed, and all the buffalo that the white men had killed would be reborn and would wander the earth as in the Golden Age, and the white people themselves would be destroyed by a flood.

The Ghost Dance as such was instigated by a Native American prophet, Wovoka, who had a vision of God telling him to teach the Ghost Dance to the people. This occurred years after the famous Battle of Little Big Horn, in which Chief Sitting Bull destroyed the forces of General Custer. Sitting Bull had been exiled, then imprisoned in the United States, then freed to live on a reservation. The Lakota tribe was moved onto a reservation, and forced to become farmers rather than the hunters and gatherers they always had been. They had no idea about farming and began to starve to death, prohibited from carrying weapons and hunting for their food. In secret, they revived the Ghost Dance and met in the hills to pray for deliverance.

It was believed by the American forces that Sitting Bull was somehow behind the Ghost Dance movement and was using it to foment discord and hatred against the whites (as if they needed any instigation). They arrested and killed Chief Sitting Bull on December 15, 1890 and then pursued his followers into the hills. The massacre of Wounded Knee took place on December 29, 1890 and was the last major battle between Native Americans and whites. The exact number of slain Lakota Sioux is not known, but was estimated to be between 200 and 300, mostly non-combatants: women and children, including infants. A number of American troops were also killed, mostly from "friendly fire." The Sioux were wearing "ghost shirts" that had been specially prepared and blessed by their medicine men, and they believed the shirts would render them invulnerable to bullets. They were mistaken.

The Lakota were looking for the millennium, but instead they found Apocalypse Now. The parallels to Montsegur, to Masada, and even to Waco are too numerous to mention, and any interested reader can find sober histories detailing the sad fates of the Lakota, as well as of the Cathars, the Branch Davidians and other "cults" that were deemed too dangerous to exist. The story of the Peoples Temple, however, differs from these examples in several important ways, as we shall see; but we should note that Jim Jones was a close friend and supporter of American Indian Movement (AIM) leader Dennis Banks, who himself led a ten-week protest and occupation of the original Wounded Knee site in 1973.

As more and more congregants signed over their life savings, their social security checks, and their tax refunds to the Peoples Temple, the church became, if not wealthy, at least well to do. Jones, fearing racial backlash in Ukiah, moved his congregation first to Orlando and then to San Francisco in 1972, to an old synagogue on Geary Street in 1972. By that time, he was already something of a political power in the state. He was the foreman of the grand jury of Mendocino County, and one of his top aides—Timothy Stoen—was an assistant district attorney for Mendocino County. That meant, essentially, that Peoples Temple represented the power of both the grand jury and the DA's office: a powerful combination, but it is not clear whether this power was put to actual use.

It is clear, however, that for whatever reason (genuine revolutionary charisma and sincere love of his fellow humans or a secret intelligence agenda) he became popular and powerful in the State of California after his return from Brazil and his move from Indiana. It was during this transitional period that he met the pseudonymous Al and Jeannie Mills—who would be murdered a few months after the publication of their book on Jonestown—and the Laytons. Two of the Laytons—Thomas N. Layton and his sister Deborah Layton—have also published books on the subject. Their brother, Larry Layton, Jr., is the one still in prison for his role in the Jonestown massacre: the murder of Congressman Leo J. Ryan.

As the Laytons are at the very heart of the story, we need to take a closer look at the family in order to ascertain the shift and shadow of the sinister forces that brought them together in fissionable combination with Jim Jones; for it is clear that the major players in this story all had prior professional experience in secret military and intelligence projects, and that Congressman Ryan was on the trail of CIA medical experimentation in his home state of California at the time he was murdered by the son of a man who was in charge of all US Army Chemical Warfare, a brilliant scientist who was deeply conflicted over his role as master of chemical weapons and their delivery systems.

Once again, as we have so often in this study, we must return to Germany in the war years.

Many people that like to accept tradition as it is, without even questioning it, are religious in this superficial, conventional way ... They merely accept a picture they have in their imagination, colored with the strange and sweet feeling of memory from childhood and early youth.... It is living somewhere back in our unconscious mind and shows up in everything we 'feel' toward other people, situations and ourselves.

This picture memory plays the most important part in the religious concept of most people as they are nowadays. And it is a dangerous one....
-- Lisa Philip, in a letter to Laurence Layton dated Sept. 15, 1941[20]

The Layton family is, of course, two families: the Laytons of Boomer, West Virginia and the Philip family of Hamburg, Germany. There is some mild controversy over the ancestral lineage of the Philip family, and one commentator (Meiers) has attempted to prove that they were Nazis. This does not seem likely, as the same commentator does admit that they were related to the Nobel-Prize winning physicist, James Franck, who was—like the Philip family—a non-practicing Jew. According to Dr. Laurence Layton, the Philips also claimed to be related to a sixteenth-century Spanish cardinal, which is an unusual pedigree for Jews,[21] particularly in the sixteenth century, although possible. As for the Laytons, Laurence Layton's ancestors in Pennsylvania had been Quakers (although Laurence himself was now a Methodist, raised by a Methodist grandfather), and Lisa Philip had become a Quaker shortly after emigrating to the United States, and was a member of the State College Friends Meeting at Pennsylvania State College where she was studying,[22] thus sharing a strange link with Ruth and Michael Paine, who were also Pennsylvania Quakers, albeit a generation later.

Dr. Laurence Layton was born in Boomer, West Virginia—a small town about fifty miles southeast of Charleston along the Kanawha River, in an area of burial mounds and prehistoric mystery—on March 8, 1914. His maternal grandfather, Sheldon Nutter, was "a circuit-riding preacher, Baptist and Methodist on alternate Sundays, in the hills of Virginia, West Virginia and Kentucky"[23] and was general manager for the Mark A. Hanna Coal Company in Boomer. His father, John Wister Layton, was an electrical engineer credited with the design of the circuit breaker, among other devices.[24] John Wister Layton married Eva Nutter on January 18, 1913. Laurence Layton was their first child.

At the age of nineteen, Laurence Layton fell in love with the sixteen-year-old Mildred Arthur, a girl from Kentucky who had come to Boomer to visit relatives. Unfortunately, Mildred had a friend back in Pikeville, Kentucky: one of the Hatfield clan. He came to visit one week and Laurence—thinking he was Mildred's boyfriend—became depressed and quit college two days later, fleeing to Scranton, Pennsylvania where his mother and her new husband lived. (His father, John Wister Layton, had died at the age of thirty-one from a staph infection.)

It was in Scranton that Laurence Layton first made the acquaintance of the Young People's Socialist League, which was meeting in a YWCA in town. (Oddly enough, future CIA mind-control czar Sidney Gottlieb would also be active in the Young People's Socialist League, in his case at the University of Wisconsin, and during the same timeframe.) Layton stayed involved with the Socialists for about a year, and then returned to West Virginia, where he eventually garnered some local fame as a youthful inventor and scientist and went on to earn a master's degree, leaving shortly thereafter for Pennsylvania State to get his doctorate in chemistry. These were the late 1930s, the years just before America's entry into World War II. Six thousand miles away, in Europe, the Nazi menace was building strength after strength, and millions of lives were in terrible jeopardy.

Lisa Philip was born on July 14, 1915 in Hamburg, Germany, to Hugo and Anita Philip. The Philip family was descended, it is claimed, from Sephardic Jews—the "Asiatic" Jews rather than the more Slavic Ashkenazi Jews of Eastern Europe—and had been in Europe for a thousand years, arriving in Spain during the Moorish conquests and leaving during the subsequent

Inquisition in the fifteenth century, which forced the Philips out of Spain and eventually into Germany. Lisa Philip was raised as a German, and had never visited a temple or celebrated any Jewish holidays. They observed Christmas and Easter, and had never identified themselves as Jewish at all. This gave rise to some suspicion among later commentators that the Philip family was Nazi, particularly considering the fact that Lisa's father, Hugo, was a banker and stockbroker whose accounts included I.G. Farben and Siemens, companies later identified as integral parts of the German war machine.[25]

The Philip family was cultured and sophisticated. Their home was done in the Bauhaus style, and they cultivated music and the arts. When the political situation became untenable, the Philip family began to make arrangements to leave Germany forever.

Lisa Philip was the first to leave, on May 6, 1938 aboard the SS *Manhattan*, bound for New York. Her passport, according to Thomas Layton, was stamped *Juden* or "Jewish." Her sponsors in the United States, the Berlin family, met her at the dock and took her to live with them in Philadelphia. Her parents were not so fortunate, finding it very difficult to leave Germany and emigrate to the United States along official channels. Things looked very bleak when they were turned back at the Italian border and sent on a return train to Germany. Rather than face a horrible fate in the camps, Hugo and Anita Philip took an overdose of Veronal.

They were saved, however, when a conductor found them unconscious and took them off the train in Austria, putting them in a hospital. For the time being, they were under Austrian supervision, even though Nazi officials were visiting the hospital daily to inquire after their condition. They managed to convince friends in Vienna to sponsor them until they received their American visas and, with the help of these friends and the American Society of Friends (the Quakers) spent four months there under heavy Nazi observation, before finally being allowed to leave for America on March 20, 1940.

In the meantime, Lisa Philip had moved to Chappaqua, New York (at the time of this writing, the new home of former President Bill Clinton) and found employment with a Congregationalist minister, Reverend Galen Russell. Attending church every Sunday with the Russells, Lisa Philip had become not only Americanized but Christianized. By the fall of 1940, she found another position, this time at Pennsylvania State College as a physical therapist (in the college's hospital). It was there that she met Laurence Layton.

They were introduced by a mutual friend, Franz Werner, in early 1941, and on October 18, 1941 they were married.

On December 7, 1941 the Japanese bombed Pearl Harbor, and the United States entered World War II.

Laurence Layton could have been drafted, but his wife wrote to her relative Dr. James Franck to get him an appointment with the University of Chicago so that he could avoid the draft. Franck did manage to arrange a posting for Layton, but he instead received a student deferment through regular channels and decided to stay on at the University of Pennsylvania. Had he accepted Franck's offer, he would have been involved with the Manhattan Project, which is what Franck was working on in Chicago.[26] Instead, he finished his doctorate and wound up working for Eastman Kodak at their headquarters in Rochester, New York. That job did not last very long, but the Laytons' first child—Thomas—was born there. In November of 1943, Laurence Layton decided to take a job as an assistant professor at the University of Maryland, a position he held for three years, during which their next two children—Annalisa and Laurence John, Jr.—were born. After the war, Dr. Layton found employment at Johns Hopkins University and eventually published important work in the field of cortisone treatments for arthritis.[27] This led to a higher profile for Layton, and he came to the attention of the US Army.

On November 5, 1951 he arrived at Dugway Proving Grounds in Utah, where he was named chief of biochemistry of the Army's Chemical Warfare Division. In the spring of 1952, he was named chief of the entire Chemical Warfare Division.

During the preceding years spent in Maryland, the Laytons had regularly attended Sunday meetings with the Quakers and considered themselves sincere Friends. Quakers are pacifists and have a very negative attitude towards warfare, finding the idea of armed conflict repugnant. (During the Vietnam War, it was common for Quakers to declare themselves conscientious objectors and to find themselves assigned to non-combatant duties in hospitals and other public services. The fact that Richard Nixon was a Quaker is one of history's ironies ... or dirty jokes.) However, chemical warfare must seem even worse: especially as countries were busy writing laws against both chemical and biological warfare without actually banning warfare altogether.

There is a common denominator among people of different racial and ethnic origins that such weapons are inhuman and should be forbidden. Yet, this devout Quaker and man of high morals—so high, in fact, that he could never accept the fact that his devoted wife and the mother of their three children, Lisa Philip, was not a virgin on their first night together—accepted the job with the Army, even though his work was being recognized on an international level and he had been lecturing on it in Europe. No one, not even his eldest son Thomas Layton—who is now a well-known and respected archaeologist with many awards and honors to his name—can explain this strange about face. Yet, there is no denying that it happened, and that Dr. Laurence Layton was "responsible for the publication of ten classified reports on research aspects of chemical warfare and more than 100 reports on chemical weapons systems."[28] All that in only the two years he was employed by the Army. Dr. Layton was therefore quite an enthusiastic sponsor of chemical weapons, averaging one report on chemical weapons systems per week and five classified reports on chemical warfare per year. It was during his tenure as head of the Army's Chemical Warfare Division that some of the military's most controversial experiments on unwitting human subjects were taking place, such as the spraying of *aspergillus fumigatus* over populated areas. *Aspergillus fumigatus* is an infectious organism that affects the "lungs, bronchi, external ear, paranasal sinuses, orbit, bones, and meninges."[29] The organism can, in fact, cause death.

During the first three months of 1953, for another instance, the city of Minneapolis was subjected to a total of eighty-one hours of an aerosol spraying of zinc cadmium sulfide (to simulate a bacteriological attack) during the hours of 8:00 P.M. to midnight, and 1:30 P.M. to 5:00 P.M.[30] No one was warned about these events, of course, and everyone was exposed: men, women and children. The same type of simulation was undertaken in St. Louis during the following three months, from April to June of 1953. No testing was done of the humans who had breathed the chemical, and no follow-up was ever reported to determine what effect, if any, the testing had on the health of the general population.

Other tests, involving the aforementioned *aspergillus fumigatus* as well as *serratia marcescens* and *bacillus subtilis*, were undertaken in the 1950s, and some of these projects were undertaken during Layton's tenure. The Army has insisted that these organisms—used to simulate such toxic substances as anthrax—are harmless to human beings, even though the medical literature available at the time shows clearly that they are, indeed, dangerous and—in some cases—fatal to human beings.

The most famous germ warfare test, though, was undertaken a little before Dr. Layton's tenure as CW chief, and that was the test over San Francisco in 1950, in which several people were taken ill and one died. Thus, Dr. Layton was both heir to a tradition of experimentation on unwitting populations and for two years the man in charge of the entire program. Perhaps coincidentally, and as described in John G. Fuller's memorably-entitled *The Day We Bombed Utah*, both Utah and neighboring Nevada were the scene of a controversial series of tests of atomic weapons during the time that Dr. Layton was living there. Specifically, a test with the code name "Dirty Harry" took place on May 19, 1953, and the fallout from the blast affected both human beings and livestock in both states.

That test had been preceded by many others over the years since 1951, and although Dugway was considered as a site for these tests, it was passed over due to its proximity to large population centers. Everyone in Nevada and Utah was aware of these tests, however, and the Army began to realize that large amounts of radiation were affecting citizens as far away as Troy, New York in the form of radioactive rain. Dr. Layton would have known all about these tests, of course, even though they were taking place outside of his area of responsibility. His tests—also involving unwitting citizen populations—were of weapons systems, but of a chemical and biological nature rather than atomic or nuclear.

It is important to remember that this was the Cold War, and that drastic measures were not only considered but often employed in the struggle to defend the country against every sort of attack from the Soviet Union and China; that does not justify using human beings as unwitting guinea pigs, of course, but it puts these operations in some sort of context. That Dr. Layton was dismayed by the uses to which the science was put is evident from his reluctance to stay with the program; that he performed excellent service for that program is also in evidence, to wit his one hundred reports on chemical warfare systems and the ten still-classified reports published during his short tenure with the Army's Chemical Warfare Division. Such, perhaps, is the structure of the human mind, able to support two such contrary natures simultaneously, each as strong as the other, both vying for dominance at the expense of the soul.

Later, in 1954, Dr. Layton transferred to the Naval Powder Factory at Indian Head, Maryland, where he would work with ICBMs and missile systems; but in the midst of this vigorous military research and development there was a tragic note. On May 10, 1952 Dr. Layton's mother-in-law, Anita Philip, committed suicide in New York City.

Hugo and Anita Philip had emigrated to the United States in 1940 and thus escaped the hideous fate of many of their friends and fellow Jews. But Anita Philip had never quite escaped the Nazis in her mind. Her suicide is one of the strangest episodes of this story, and there have been several attempts to explain it. The generally-accepted theory is that—due to the classified nature of her son-in-law's work for the Army—a routine background check was in progress on her family, and that it is the heavy-handed approach of the FBI that contributed to her paranoia that the secret police were after her once again. An expanded version of this theory has it that Anita Philip was so distraught over her son-in-law's work for the Army that she was moved to shame and despair.

She left a note, and there is in it a hint of guilt over an undisclosed indiscretion:

> My friends, know that I, free and proper, am a good American. But I was a gossip and have been entangled in a network of intrigue.[31]

The letter was written in German, so perhaps something of its nuance was lost in the translation. It is strange that it would be addressed to "my friends," as if to a wider audience than her children and family, whom she mentions later on in the brief note. Does the word "friends" perhaps refer to her fellow

Quakers? Alas, we shall never know. Nor shall we know what she meant by "I was a gossip and have been entangled in a network of intrigue," which is certainly suggestive of something other than paranoia over an FBI investigation. To whom was she gossiping? What was she saying? What was the network of intrigue? The family brushes it off as a symptom of her failing mental state. But after writing the note, and signing it with a simple initial, "A," she leaped to her death from her apartment window.

A year later, and another person connected with the Army's Chemical Warfare Division would fall from yet another window in New York City. That person, of course, was Frank Olson and there is every indication that he was murdered by the CIA.

With Dr. Layton in Utah and Dr. Olson in Maryland, there was also Dr. Puharich, also in Maryland and also at Camp Detrick where Olson was stationed. All three men worked for the Army in chemical and biological weapons research, and all at the same time. The fact that the CIA was running its own operation in conjunction with the Army at Camp Detrick at the time Dr. Layton was chief of the Army's Chemical Warfare Division indicates that these men were all known to each other, if not on a personal basis then surely by name and function. Olson fell to his death in New York in November of 1953, and it is perhaps more than a coincidence that Dr. Layton decided to leave the Army's CWD soon thereafter to start work for the Navy in Indian Head, Maryland.

Other men connected with the CIA found themselves dying under mysterious circumstances at the same time. While much of the focus has been on Dr. Frank Olson—thanks to the brave and tireless efforts of his son, Eric—the other deaths have been ignored until recently. With the new developments in the Olson case, reporters and investigators have begun to look at other suspicious deaths and the tally is surprising.

A former State Department employee and suspected Soviet agent, Laurence Duggan, fell to his death from his 16th floor office window in Manhattan on December 20, 1948.

Former Secretary of Defense James Forrestal fell from the 13th floor of the US Naval Hospital at Bethesda, Maryland on May 22, 1949: a case that has all the earmarks of an "assisted suicide," and which many family members believe was homicide.

On January 24, 1953, State Department official and suspected CIA agent James C. Montgomery was found dead with a cord around his neck, his body completely nude. The death was ruled a suicide, but then-Congressman Fred E. Busbey of Illinois didn't believe it and called for a full investigation in the House.

Lifelong intelligence agent Speyer Kronthal was found dead on April 1, 1953. The cause of death was believed to have been a self-administered drug overdose. A high-ranking CIA official, Kronthal was revealed in 1975 to have actually been a Soviet double agent.

Duggan and Kronthal have been revealed to be Soviet agents—well, revealed by the CIA—and perhaps we can consider their executions appropriate, if not justified. We have no such reassurances on the case of Montgomery, none at all on Olson, and especially not on James Forrestal. Could it be that a government agency which finds it expedient to execute suspected Soviet spies without due process of law could also find it expedient to execute other men with whom they have "issues"?

At any rate, by July of 1957 Dr. Layton had accepted a (relatively benign?) position as a research scientist for the US Department of Agriculture, at a laboratory near Berkeley, California. The family up and moved to the Bay Area and looked forward to a healthier environment, free from talk of payloads and weapons systems and lethal chemical agents. A new addition to their family, Deborah Layton, had been born in February 1953 (she was conceived the week of Anita Philip's death).

As the 1950s moved into the 1960s, the Layton children were as affected by the growing youth culture as any other youngsters. Deborah Layton became very problematic, getting involved with drugs and teenaged depression and alienation. Thomas Layton had become cerebral and intellectual and was already moving in his own circles, as was big sister Annalisa. Laurence Jr. was consciously avoiding the draft for the Vietnam War, and was working in hospitals and waiting for confirmation of his conscientious objector status.

Deborah Layton—after a stint in the United Kingdom at a strict Quaker school—was finally drawn into the Peoples Temple experience by her brother Larry. This was when the Temple was located in Ukiah, California. Gradually she became very involved with the group and was entrusted with greater and greater responsibilities by Jim Jones. She found herself becoming part of an inner circle that handled the money, and was involved in moving funds out of the United States and into bank accounts in Latin America and Europe. Just as Rev. David Miranda of Brazil would be accused of doing some twenty years later, Jim Jones moved millions of dollars out of the country using church members as "mules," carrying the cash with them and depositing it in various accounts spread over the globe.

In addition, Deborah's mother—Lisa Philip Layton—also became involved with the Peoples Temple. Things were never that close between Lisa and her husband Laurence, and she saw the Peoples Temple as an adventure to be shared with her children. Lisa Layton, the German-born Jewish refugee from the Nazis, would emigrate to Guyana with Deborah, and would die at Jonestown months before the massacre itself.

Larry Layton, the youngest son of Dr. Laurence Layton, had had his share of emotional turmoil growing up and found himself involved with drugs and all the other alternative experiences available to the youth of the sixties. But in the Summer of 1968, he and his new wife—Carolyn Moore, the daughter of Rev. John Moore, a Methodist minister—moved to Ukiah, where Larry got a position as an aide at the Mendocino State Mental Hospital and was working on obtaining his conscientious objector status. His wife visited the Peoples Temple and came back impressed with Jim Jones and the Temple experience.

The "Peoples Temple of the Disciples of Christ of Redwood Valley" had been incorporated in the State of California since November 26, 1965. In 1967, Jones had been named the foreman of the Mendocino County Grand Jury and was also the Director of the Mendocino and Lake Counties Legal Services Foundation. His wife, Marceline Jones, had become a state nursing home inspector and, in the process, the Peoples Temple had opened three convalescent homes and a home for boys, and even a pet shelter. Thus, suddenly the Peoples Temple was in the health-care field, and its leader was heavily involved in local politics. His assistant pastor, Tim Stoen, was also an assistant district attorney for Mendocino County. The church was acquiring a power base.

At the time Carolyn Moore Layton decided she wanted to join the Peoples Temple, she was considered perhaps the most attractive woman in the church and this came to the notice of its priapic minister. He decided that he wanted Carolyn as his mistress, so he orchestrated the divorce of Carolyn and Larry in 1969 by first having Carolyn publicly humiliate Larry in front of the congregation. The influence of Jones was so great that Larry meekly accepted Jones' suggestion that he should divorce Carolyn since they were so incompatible. Jones then offered another one of his flock as a substitute on the spot, and the bewildered Larry—pressed to choose someone—selected a blonde, blue-eyed former hippie chick, Karen Tow. Done. Larry and Karen were married, and Carolyn became Jones' paramour, eventually becoming pregnant by him and bearing their child, a boy they named Kimo (the Hawaiian equivalent of "James"). In order to provide a legal father for the birth, Jones had Carolyn marry another Temple member.

Then, in 1970, Deborah Layton met Jim Jones for the first time. (That same summer, Jones' associate—case officer?—Dan Mitrione had been killed by the Tupamaros in Uruguay, leaving Jones high and dry but not without resources in the government.) By the mid-1970s she had become one of his most trusted followers, an essential partner in setting up the Jonestown facility and managing the administrative and financial matters of the church both in the States and, eventually, in Guyana. Her brother, Larry, was just as deeply involved and was part of the security force that guarded the Jonestown complex, a security force that was more like a troop of prison guards than a defensive army to protect the members from outside hostilities.

By that time, it was hard to tell the difference between Jonestown as beleagured commune and Jonestown as *stalag*. Jones had become increasingly paranoid about government intervention. His socialist rants from the pulpit of the Peoples Temple church in Ukiah and, later, in San Francisco became increasingly full of dire warnings about the doom facing America and the coming race war that would target groups like the Peoples Temple and its followers. Like any good member of the Disciples of Christ, Jones' view of the late twentieth century was apocalyptic.

There would be a conflagration, perhaps a nuclear war, and only those he managed to save would survive the holocaust. Jones' vision of an imminent race war was eerily similar to Manson's. One could say they were on either side of the same argument: Jones (ostensibly) wanted to preserve the black people of America and Manson wanted them destroyed. Both, however, saw race war as inevitable. When the dust cleared, however, Manson had killed only white people (with an attempted murder on one black drug dealer); Jones had killed hundreds of black people in Jonestown.

In March of 1976, Jones was appointed to the San Francisco Human Rights Commission, a reprise of his role with the Indiana Human Rights Commission in the early 1960s. In September of that year, there was a testimonial dinner in his honor that was attended by San Francisco Mayor George Moscone, Lt. Governor of California Mervyn Dymally, Angela Davis, Eldridge Cleaver, and many other luminaries.

His popularity and importance were such that by March of 1977 he was sharing a table with First Lady Rosalyn Carter at the Democratic Convention Dinner, after having met in previous months with President-elect Jimmy Carter's transition team and Vice President-elect Walter Mondale. Suddenly, Jim Jones was a force to be reckoned with in California state politics, and therefore at the national level as well.

And this publicity attracted some unwelcome attention from the media.

THE POLITICS OF THE FAMILY

In October 1976, a month before the US presidential election that would put Jimmy Carter in the White House, a man named Bob Houston decided he would leave the Peoples Temple. He wrote a letter of resignation to Jim Jones on October 3rd. On October 5th, he was dead.

He was not the first victim, and certainly would not be the last. Jim Jones exceeded even Charles Manson in sheer brutality and convoluted, complex mind-control games. Like Manson, he retreated from society with a band of followers. In Manson's case, it was to the desert; in Jones' case, it was to the jungle. Both had millennial expectations. Both could not countenance defection from the "Family"; such disloyalty was punishable by death.

The 'family' becomes a medium to link its members, whose links with one another may otherwise be very attenuated. A crisis will occur if any member of the family wishes to leave by getting the 'family' out of his system, or dissolving

the 'family' in himself. Within the family, the 'family' may be felt as the whole world. To destroy the 'family' may be experienced as worse than murder or more selfish than suicide.
—R. D. Laing, *The Politics of the Family*, 1969

In the 1960s, the writings of Scottish psychiatrist R. D. Laing became very popular with alternative mental-health-care professionals, people who felt—like Laing—that perhaps schizophrenia was more a spiritual state than an actual illness or disease, and could be treated with metaphysics rather than electroshock and lobotomies. His seminal work, *The Politics of Experience*, could be found on many a bookshelf in college dorms and hippie communes. His more clinical work, such as *The Divided Self, Self and Others* and *The Politics of the Family*, reinforced the message of political liberation through spiritual liberation, of mental health through spiritual health. Laing focused on the family as the origin of most mental problems as well as most social problems, and in this he was not much different from Freud and generations of social workers. Laing, however, took the argument to a different level and used his findings in clinical psychiatry to extrapolate a larger vision. To Laing, schizophrenia was not necessarily a break-down, it could also be a "break-through."

Laing's work was attacked, predictably, by other psychiatrists who felt that schizophrenia was not a metaphysical playground but a serious and debilitating mental illness whose only hope of a cure was through surgery—the dread lobotomy—or electroshock, or drugs. When chemical imbalances were found to be at the heart of schizophrenia and thus the disease could be treated with chemicals that would redress the imbalances, Laing's theories were abandoned as so much quaint hippie furniture from the sixties.

However, Laing's basic premise was not necessarily invalidated by the discovery that there exists a link between chemicals and mental states. After all, the CIA had spent millions in an effort to clearly define the relationship between hallucinogens and consciousness. Science, however, preferred to believe that there was a direct cause and effect relationship between chemical imbalance and mental illness: the technological approach was to use chemicals to create an artificial balance wherein the illness would disappear. For Laing, this was just another form of lobotomy. It did not speak to the spiritual imbalance that had caused the illness in the first place—it treated the symptom and not the cause—and by using drugs to create the illusion of psychic integration, one merely swept the core problem under the rug. But the mechanistic approach to psychiatry and psychotherapy—demanded by a mental health profession which felt that psychology should be as "scientific" as possible—meant that more holistic theories would be abandoned in favor of chemical, surgical and electroconvulsive therapies.

The methodology of Jim Jones—both at the Peoples Temple in Ukiah and San Francisco and especially at Jonestown—was a combination of both approaches. Religion is, after all, a close cousin to psychotherapy and psychology in general. Like Manson, Jones had his "family." The followers were to call him "Father," not like the Catholic custom of referring to all priests as "Father," but in a more intimate way. Only Jones could be called "Father" at the Peoples Temple. All the members were his virtual children, and they demonstrated this in their submissive and dependent attitude towards him. And whenever any of them wished to "defect"—that is, simply leave the church—it was considered tantamount to an act of betrayal against Father and against the entire Family.

Jones used psychodrama extensively in his dealings with subordinates and the members of his congregation, a psychodrama composed of equal measures of fire-and-brimstone sermonizing, sexual politics, public humiliation, and—it is believed—drugs. The pharmacy at Jonestown was heavily weighted in favor of narcotics and psychoactive compounds, and it is not clear to what extent these drugs were used in the everyday life of the commune. As for sex, Jones constantly complained of his continuous need for sex, and would enlist as many women as he could in his sexual stable. He would then ridicule the sexual lives of his male followers, and insist that all men but him were basically homosexual.

He would control the sex lives of the members of the Peoples Temple, and arranged marriages between couples who were then not allowed to have sex. He would demand that wives complain publicly about the lack of sexual performance or prowess of their husbands, while demanding as well that they praise Jim Jones in that department. In other words, it was Mansonism writ large and, if possible, even uglier. Ostensibly, the rationale behind all of this was the spiritual liberation of his followers. In fact, the clever use of these techniques ensured not the liberation of his awe-struck congregation but their near-total enslavement.

Ed Sanders, in his book about Charles Manson and the Family, stated that if the Pentagon ever formulated the Manson Secret, the world would be in trouble. One wonders if Jonestown was an example of such a formula: a white man, with murky intelligence connections and political activity in Latin America and the Caribbean during the sixties, becomes the leader of a large black congregation and orders them all to their deaths. If this had been in a novel, it would have been dismissed as unbelievable.

Soon, the press began to get wind of the weird circumstances surrounding the Peoples Temple. Any organization that powerful in state politics would certainly come under scrutiny, and it was only a matter of time before the newspapers and magazines began to do exposés of life at the church. This situation was exacerbated by the defection of several church members and their open discussions with the media. This, coupled with the FBI raid on Scientology offices when it was discovered that the Scientologists were infiltrating the government and spying on government agents, made Jim Jones increasingly paranoid about a government raid on the Peoples Temple, which he painted in terms of the fascists attacking the socialists.

In the 1970s, this was a distinct possibility. On January 22, 1974 Governor Ronald Reagan of California, in his State of the State message, announced plans for the creation of a "violence center" to study the causes and cure of violence among youth, minorities, etc. The plan was to use an abandoned nuclear weapons test site in the Santa Monica mountains; although it was conveniently close to Los Angeles, it was also remote from populated areas, hard to reach, guarded by barbed wire fences and secure buildings, and considered an excellent site for the type of research Reagan was intending to carry out. This did not materialize, mostly due to public outcry over the very idea of a secret government center to study violence as divorced from the social conditions that contribute to violence, such as poverty, lack of education, etc. Many people feared—rightly or wrongly—that the center would be used to develop a more efficient and more oppressive security apparatus in the state where the Los Angeles Police Department already had a reputation for a harsh and swift response to crime, particularly minority crime. This was coming at a time when the Watergate hearings were reinforcing a negative view of government interference in domestic life, interference that would be escalated once Reagan became President in 1981.

At the same time, California Congressman Leo J. Ryan was making a name for himself as a government watchdog. He had co-authored the Hughes-Ryan Amendment, which required the CIA to get prior approval from Congress before undertaking any covert activity. In addition, he was asking questions about the CIA's mind-control projects in the State of California, as he wondered whether or not the notorious members of the Symbionese Liberation Army (SLA) had been the willing or unwilling beneficiaries of the MK-ULTRA program while serving time at Vacaville.

The SLA was a bizarre revolutionary militant group, whose claim to fame was the kidnapping of publishing heiress Patty Hearst on February 4, 1974 only a few weeks after Reagan's controversial "violence center" announcement, and it has been a favorite subject of conspiracy theorists for decades, who believe that the SLA was a front for a domestic CIA operation. The mere fact of the kidnapping itself, with Patty Hearst being subjected to brainwashing by the SLA cadres and then sent out to help them rob a bank, was headline-grabbing news for weeks, even though many people could not understand what it all represented.

She had been blindfolded and subject to sensory deprivation, held in a closet, and raped by her captors: circumstances familiar to political prisoners all over the globe and particularly in the Latin American nations where men like Dan Mitrione trained the security forces. When Patty Hearst was finally freed she was put on trial for armed robbery as if she were legally culpable, a subject on which many psychiatrists disagreed passionately. It brought many of the old CIA mind-control experts out of the woodwork, although they were not necessarily advertised as such. Dr. William Sargant, who was a friend of Dr. Frank Olson and who advised the British intelligence agencies on interrogation and brainwashing techniques, was one of those who examined Patty Hearst, as was Dr. Martin Orne and Dr. Robert Jay Lifton, the latter an expert on Chinese mind-control techniques.

Much was happening between 1973 and 1975. Donald DeFreeze, the commander of the SLA, had earlier been a prisoner at the Vacaville facility that was used by the CIA as part of their mind-control experimentation program. At Vacaville, an organization was set up to raise black consciousness—the Black Cultural Association, or BCA—which was under the direction of Professor Colston Westbrook. Westbrook has since been identified as a former intelligence officer who served in the Far East during the 1960s and, in fact, worked for AID—the same agency that provided cover for Dan Mitrione and, perhaps, Jim Jones in Brazil—during the same years that Mitrione was with them. It is tantalizing to speculate about a handoff of Jones from Mitrione to Westbrook; or perhaps after the murder of Mitrione, Westbrook simply picked up where he had left off. We know now that Jones spent time at the Langley-Porter Neuropsychiatric Institute during the 1960s and 1970s; Westbrook had been a psychological warfare officer in Vietnam, Japan and Korea. At Vacaville, he may have been involved in the MK-ULTRA testing and manipulation of violent inmates. Therefore there may be connections between these men, but Jones is dead and Westbrook isn't talking.

What is more stimulating in terms of bizarre synchronicities is the fact that four members of the SLA had come to Berkeley from Bloomington, Indiana. (The SLA never had more than a few dozen members at its height.) Emily and Bill Harris and Angela and Gary Atwood had been students at the University of Indiana, just as Jim Jones had been almost twenty years earlier. And they wound up in Berkeley—a suburb of San Francisco—at about the same time that Jones was shifting his attention away from Ukiah and towards San Francisco, where he had a large and enthusiastic congregation. (He bought an old synagogue on Geary Street in late 1972, and moved his operational headquarters there in 1975.) Jones was heavily involved in black liberation politics (witness his relationship with Angela Davis and Eldridge Cleaver), and the SLA was allegedly a black liberation army. There is no way that they would have been unaware of each other in San Francisco in 1973. Jones was too prominent, for one thing. He was active in state and local politics. His church was a magnet for black people, and he preached a boisterous revolutionary, socialist and anti-racist platform. In addition, his members were actively involved in mental hospitals and other health-care institutions in California, working as volunteers or as paid employees.

After the nineteen-year-old Patty Hearst was kidnapped on February 4, 1974, by April 15 she had become "Tania" (named after Che Guevara's lover) and had joined the SLA. She is photographed in a beret and holding a rifle during the robbery of a bank in San Francisco by the SLA. The public's confusion over this bizarre change in Hearst's status could find only one possible solution: Patty Hearst had been brainwashed. Pundits appeared on television talking about "Stockholm Syndrome," the identification of a victim with his or her captors after a prolonged period in their custody. The young, conservative heiress must have been programmed to participate in these acts; there could be no other explanation.

The police were mobilized in an intensive manhunt to find the SLA and bring them to justice. No one who was in front of a television will ever forget the day in May when SWAT teams destroyed a house in such an intensive storm of gunfire that the building collapsed in flames. Six members of the SLA—including Donald DeFreeze, their leader known as "Cinque"—were killed in the conflagration. Patty Hearst and Bill and Emily Harris were not in the building at the time. The May 17, 1974 attack was criticized by some members of the press, especially when it became obvious that the inhabitants of the house—and of surrounding buildings, some of which were damaged in the fire—were given little opportunity to evacuate or surrender. If Patty Hearst had been in the building at the time—something which the SWAT team presumably did not know—she would have been killed with all the rest, and the story of her captivity and "brainwashing" would have been lost forever.

However, on September 18, 1975—more than a year after the SWAT attack and more than eighteen months after her kidnapping—Patty Hearst was found and captured by the FBI in San Francisco. She would be convicted of the armed bank robbery, even though specialists insisted on the obvious: that she was mentally conditioned by her captors and forced to adopt an alternate identity. She had even fallen in love with one of her captors, Willie Wolfe, also known as "Cujo." Wolfe had died in the SWAT attack.

In January 1979, President Jimmy Carter commuted Patty Hearst's sentence and she was released from prison. She served twenty-one months of a seven-year sentence. In January 2001 she was pardoned by President Clinton as one of his last official acts as President.

The existence and actions of the SLA are so strange, and so illogical, and so out of context that the organization has been subject to the full-court press of the conspiracy theorists. The leader of the SLA—Donald DeFreeze, or "Cinque"—was black. Virtually everyone else in the SLA was white. (This is a mirror-image of the Peoples Temple, where the leader was white and the congregation black.) The group was believed to be Maoist, but the evidence for this was flimsy. Further, they claimed responsibility for the murder of Dr. Marcus Foster—Superintendent of the Oakland school system—in 1973 … by two white men who had used makeup during the commission of the crime, making themselves look black. This attempt to incite a race riot had been prefigured, of course, by the Manson Family attacks on the Tate and LaBianca households in 1969.

DeFreeze himself was a police informant who spent very little time in prison, even though he had a record of arms-dealing, among other felonies. When he left prison, he simply walked out, leading many to assume that his escape was an inside job. This was after prolonged contact with known intelligence officer Colston Westbrook. Although the SLA was painted in the worst possible colors as a violent revolutionary group, their record as violent revolutionaries is rather weak. They make so many mistakes, and reveal themselves to so many people during the course of their life "in hiding," losing large quantities of arms and ammunition at various poorly-disguised safe houses, that it is possible to view their actions as those of *agents provocateurs* and not as genuine revolutionaries. At one point they even hijack a car and driver, drive around for a few hours introducing themselves, and then let the driver free: actions reminiscent of the life of Lee Harvey Oswald prior to the Kennedy assassination, where he was seen in used-car lots talking about killing Kennedy, and then at a rifle range doing the same.

Congressman Ryan may have been getting a little too close to the truth when he demanded that the CIA inform him of any relationship between Donald DeFreeze and MK-ULTRA. They responded in writing to his office on October of 1978, stating that there had been no connection that they could find (remember, most of the documents had been shredded long before). The wording is a perfect example of a typical CIA response and is worth quoting at length:

Dear Mr. Ryan:
Thank you for your letter of 27 September to Admiral Turner requesting confirmation or denial of the fact of CIA experiments using prisoners at the California medical facility at Vacaville.
It is true that CIA sponsored testing, using volunteer inmates, was conducted at that facility. The project was completed in 1968....
Your letter referred to Donald DeFreese [*sic*], known as CINQUE, and Clifford Jefferson, both of whom were inmates at Vacaville. In so far as our records reflect the names of the participants, there is nothing to indicate that either was in any way involved in the project.

The letter was date-stamped "18 Oct 1978," and bore the signature stamp of Frank C. Carlucci.[32]
There are several points worth mentioning about this "non-denial denial" (as they used to say at the Washington *Post* during the Watergate investigation). The first is the misspelling of Donald DeFreeze's name, which—as any lawyer knows—is a way to cover one's ass in the event that the denial is

proved false. It means that there was no one at the facility being tested who bore the name "Donald DeFreese." The CIA has used this tactic before. Yet, let us allow that it was an honest mistake, a typographical error by a typist. Then there is the question of "our records."

In the first place, the key MK-ULTRA records, of which the Vacaville experiments would have been a part, were all destroyed in 1973 (except for four boxes of accounting and bookkeeping records). So, the CIA had no records of it at all. In the second place, the letter is very careful to hedge even further: "In so far as our records reflect the names of the participants," Very clever, considering that in all likelihood no records existed and, anyway, the name of DeFreeze was misspelled.

Then there is the statement by future-CIA Director Carlucci that the project which had drawn Congressman Ryan's scrutiny "was completed in 1968." DeFreeze did not become an inmate at Vacaville until 1969. Thus, we are left with the distinct impression that the CIA had nothing to do with DeFreeze. But, from 1970 on, DeFreeze was in twice-weekly contact with Colston Westbrook, former intelligence officer under AID cover, psychological warfare officer, and Vietnam veteran, who created and ran the Black Cultural Association at the facility. By running an operation at the prison at arm's length, the CIA had what is known as "plausible deniability." When DeFreeze was being sought by police during the SLA fiasco, he repeatedly warned that Westbrook was a CIA officer, but his warnings were taken as the ramblings of a deranged Communist and black revolutionary, and few paid his charges any attention.

A month to the day after he received his non-denial denial from the CIA, Congressman Ryan was dead on the ground at Port Kaituma, Guyana.

It wasn't only a suspicion about CIA activity in California that bothered Ryan, however. The son of an old friend of his had died under mysterious circumstances, and his friend had pleaded with him to look into it. His friend was a well-known press photographer, Robert "Sammy" Houston. His son, Bob Houston, Jr. had died two days after resigning from the Peoples Temple.

Here is another case of Jim Jones deciding that his married followers should divorce. He "assigned" Joyce Shaw to marry Bob after the Jones-initiated breakup of his first marriage. Bob married her at Jones' urging, and they set up one of several foster homes run by the Peoples Temple, which took care of twenty children in addition to Bob's own two kids. But, according to Thomas Layton's book about Jonestown, Bob Houston asked too many "probing questions" and was subject to brutal beatings in the famous Peoples Temple boxing matches.[33]

The boxing matches were one way Jones controlled his flock through physical punishment and fear. An accused person had to stand passively in the ring as one of Jones' lieutenants beat them. The accused was not permitted to defend himself. Bob Houston evidently suffered through more than one of these in order to show his loyalty to the Temple and specifically to Jim Jones, but it wasn't enough. Houston worked two jobs to support his family and to send two thousand dollars every month to the Peoples Temple. Two thousand dollars a month in 1976 wasn't a bad donation; on the contrary, it was serious money. The questions Bob Houston was raising, however, were putting them all in jeopardy.

The press had already been critical of the Peoples Temple in 1972. Lester Kinsolving was a reporter (as well as a minister) who investigated the Peoples Temple, and although the worst thing about his article was probably the observation that a number of Temple employees carried firearms, his newspaper was picketed by Temple members and a mail-in campaign was organized by Temple staff to smear Kinsolving and have him run out of town.[34]

In another case, journalist George Klineman was meeting with Temple defectors, and the Temple decided to spy on him to the extent of tunneling under his house and listening to his conversations.[35]

Thus, the last thing the Temple needed was Bob Houston free and at large and talking to the press. His own father worked for Associated Press, and that one fact was probably enough to incite the Temple leaders when they received his letter formally announcing his resignation. He worked a second job as a switchman on the railroad, and his mangled body was found the next day on the tracks.[36] Then his father went to his friend Congressman Ryan and asked for his help in getting to the bottom of the case. It was another episode in the growing chorus of voices complaining about the conditions at the Peoples Temple.

Deborah Layton was initiated into some of the worst excesses, including having been raped by Jim Jones three times in 1976 during the course of her employment at the Temple, even at one point acquiring a sexually transmitted disease. To complete the humiliation, she was singled out by Jones in one public meeting as one of those who had had sex with him. In addition, Jones revealed that he had also had sex with Karen Layton, the woman Larry Layton, Jr.—Deborah's brother—had taken to wife at Jones' urging. He had done so, he said, because Larry Layton (like all other men) was really homosexual and could not satisfy his wife the way Jim Jones could. Further, part of this public humiliation ritual was the insistence that all of the women who had had sex with Jim Jones had approached him, not the other way around, and that Jones was simply being kind and generous to them by relenting to their sexual desires.[37]

It was in that same year of 1976 that Jones began to expatriate the Temple funds to banks in Panama and Switzerland, using Deborah Layton as one of the administrators of these funds and as a courier. He had simply been amassing too much wealth—he had one hundred thousand dollars in cash in a safe at the Temple to cover "incidental expenses"[38]– and he was getting thousands of dollars of cash donations every week, in addition to members' Social Security checks and real estate that was signed over to the Temple.

Deborah Layton made several trips over the course of a year or so to these foreign banks, setting up accounts and depositing cash. Thus, when the dust had cleared after the Jonestown massacre, one of her tasks was helping government officials locate and seize the millions of dollars in those accounts.

Jones had made another trip to Guyana in 1973,[39] and was seriously considering moving his congregation there, where he would be free from both press and legal scrutiny. By 1976, he had already leased nearly four thousand acres of land from the Guyanese government, and Temple members were down there clearing the land and getting ready for a major influx of Americans.

No one knows exactly why Jones chose that particular site. Its location close to the Venezuelan border—a hotly contested area by both countries, by the way—is suggestive of a hidden agenda. Some commentators believe that having more than one thousand Americans living so close to the border would blunt Venezuelan military action to take that land for itself. Others, including the present author, believe that he was simply being smart: having his settlement close to another international boundary meant that, in the event of a problem with the Guyanese government, he could quickly be safely inside Venezuelan territory.

This was the same strategy employed by fugitive Nazi Paul Schaefer, who set up his notorious Colonia Dignidad on the Chilean border with Argentina, and may have used his colony's proximity to Argentina to make his escape when the Chilean authorities finally raided the estate in the 1990s. Colonia Dignidad was another "religious" community with a political agenda (it had been used as a torture and interrogation center by the Chilean secret police during the overthrow of President Salvador Allende in 1973), was completely populated by German citizens (as Jonestown was by American citizens), was run by a minister of religion who was also a sexual sadist, etc. In both cases, orphaned children and foster children were exported to the colonies, and financial subsidies derived from their respective governments. In both cases, the colonies had shortwave radio communications with their offices in the country's capitols. Those offices were used by members to influence government officials, and, in the case of Jonestown, one Temple member was ordered to become the paramour of a Guyanese government official. And on and on. The parallels are almost too numerous to mention.

Yet another disturbing coincidence lies in the fact that the site chosen by Jones was in the Northwest District of Guyana, the same place where—in 1845—a Reverend Smith called together the local Native American population (including the Arawaks, Tituba's countrymen), and told them the Millennium was at hand. When it did not materialize, Smith's four hundred followers committed mass suicide on the spot, believing they would be resurrected as "white people."[40] The parallels to the Jonestown event are too strong to be ignored.

We can, of course, choose to categorize this uncanny synchronicity as "mere coincidence," as if the mass suicide of four hundred in 1845 and the mass murder of nine hundred in 1978 should be reduced to a scientific curiosity at best, or a scientific absurdity at worst. However, as we have noted before, in history there are documents ... and there is blood. And as the fictitious detective Sherlock Holmes remarked in his very first appearance—in a story about Mormonism, no less, and secret societies and cult homicide—there is a scarlet thread of murder running through the tapestry of life. It runs among the Indian mounds of Charles Manson's hometown, Ashland, Kentucky, and the mounds of Chillicothe, Ohio and Moundsville, West Virginia, familiar to the inmates of the prisons built on those sites, people like serial killer Henry Lee Lucas, as well as Manson himself and Lynette Fromme. It runs to the doomed jungles of Guyana, where the Arawak faithful went willingly to their deaths a century before nine hundred Americans did likewise. Blood cries out to blood, and history repeats itself.

America had first learned in some detail of the CIA's domestic spying program as well as its mind-control projects in 1975. The information was provided by the Rockefeller Commission Report, published in June of that year, and evidence presented in that report rang alarm bells in the home of the Olson family, as they recognized the facts surrounding the death of Frank Olson and learned, for the first time, of his unwitting participation in an LSD experiment being run by Sidney Gottlieb. This was also the year that Lynette "Squeaky" Fromme attempted the assassination of President Gerald Ford, leading everyone to agree that the Manson Family was still armed and dangerous, and abroad in the land.

By June 1977, things were getting too hot for Jim Jones and the Peoples Temple. *New West* magazine was preparing an exposé of the Temple, and Jones began to panic. Complaints started to trickle in to government offices in California about the church and its bizarre practices. Important Temple members—such as Assistant District Attorney Tim Stoen—began to "defect," and to tell their stories to the media and to the authorities. The word "cult" was being used, and "brainwashing," and people became suspicious and fearful. Jones finally fled to Guyana himself on July 13, 1977, leaving trusted members like Deborah Layton in charge of things (especially the money) in the States.

THE RETURN OF THE NATIVE

Deborah's mother, Lisa Philip Layton, had decided to join the Peoples Temple sometime in 1973 after attending one late-night meeting there at the San Francisco Temple with her daughter Deborah. This veteran of Nazi Germany found something comforting and uplifting about Jim Jones and the raucous Temple services, and soon began making the long trip to the Los Angeles congregation three times a week.[41] This developed into a kind of devotion or even fanaticism, and by November 1974 she had moved out of her home with her husband, Dr. Layton, and asked him for a divorce.[42]

As her involvement with the Peoples Temple grew, so did her paranoia. The Temple was fearful of secret government action against it, or so Jones liked to claim. The postulation of a hostile outside force—whether one exists or not—is a useful tool for binding the members of any group together, and as the Temple grew in power in the seventies, so did its paranoia. Lisa Philip Layton had reason to fear this type of intervention, however, because she had witnessed it in Nazi Germany; and then there had been the suicide of her mother in New York City, a death attributed to Anita Philip's fear of what she felt was some sort of secret police investigation. By working with the predominantly black congregations of the Peoples Temple, Lisa Layton felt herself identifying with their oppression as well as becoming accepted and even loved. She began to adopt Jones' beliefs and fears as her own. She thought she could identify who was a CIA "plant" at the Temple.[43] And she put her money where her mouth was. When her divorce had become final, she donated something like three hundred thousand dollars to the Peoples Temple, a very large sum in those days.[44]

Thus, when the opportunity arose for her to travel to Guyana and live in the workers' paradise that was Jonestown, she was eager to do so and traveled there with her daughter Deborah in late 1977, arriving in Georgetown on December 7 and in Jonestown itself on December 14. It was then that both women began to experience the dreadful living conditions and draconian "security" measures that dominated Temple life.

Deborah was sent to work in the fields for six weeks, a grueling and impossible regimen in the jungle, subject to insects, venomous snakes, sunstroke, dehydration and overwork. The Temple members lived on rice and beans, and a little water (depending on the rainfall). It was, essentially, concentration-camp living, with the ever-present security forces alert to any deviation from the fixed routine, any complaint, no matter how reasonable or how minor. For infractions, one could be imprisoned in "the box" for extended periods of time, fed on a liquid diet—with vital signs monitored daily to ensure that the inmate was still alive—and subjected to interrogation by the security team until they were satisfied that the inmate was giving the correct answers. Children were subject to even worse treatment, taken to a well at the bottom of which two adults would be hiding in the water, waiting to grab the unfortunate child's legs and drag him or her under the surface of the brackish water. After a long session of that, the child would be allowed to return to the surface, and then would have to walk all the way back to the compound through the jungle, repeating over and over, "I'm sorry, Father."

Eventually, once the medical center had been built and enlarged, troublesome members would be imprisoned there and drugged heavily until their anti-revolutionary attitudes had been adjusted. The pharmacy at Jonestown contained Thorazine, as well as "Quaaludes, Demerol, Seconal, Valium, Nembutal, morphine—enough to fill the ordinary needs of a city of sixty-five thousand people."[45] Another source records that large quantities of Haldol and Mellaril in liquid form were being shipped to Jonestown.[46] Normally, these would be taken in pill form. The liquid form could be used for injections, which is a rare way to administer these drugs, or, more significantly, as a means to give the drug to people without their knowledge. All this pharmacopoeia was for a commune that never numbered more than twelve hundred souls.

The question of whether or not there were other drugs present at Jonestown—hallucinogens and other psychoactive substances useful in mind-control experiments—has never been satisfactorily answered. However, the drugs of which we *are* aware could readily be used in behavior modification treatments, which they obviously were.

By 1977, Jones had yet another problem on his hands. His former assistant pastor, Timothy Stoen, the Assistant District Attorney, had defected. First to go was his wife, who left the Temple, separated from her husband, and claimed custody of their four-year-old son. Eventually, Tim Stoen also left the Temple, but by that time their son was in Jonestown. The Stoens fought Jones for custody of their child, and this was another legal nightmare for Jones, who claimed that he had fathered the child himself.

When the Supreme Court ruled in the Stoens' favor, demanding the extradition of the boy, Jones went ballistic and threatened—not for the first time—that his entire community would commit mass suicide if the Guyanese government acceded to the extradition demand. In a panic, Temple lawyers and other spokespeople in the States began phoning everyone they thought could help in this situation, and Temple attorney Charles Garry arranged a phone call to Jones from Angela Davis, Huey Newton and American Indian activist Dennis Banks to beg him to reconsider. At the same time, the wife of the Guyanese ambassador to the United States was reached—oddly enough, in Indiana where she was visiting a friend—and when the dust had cleared, the Guyanese government had bowed to the pressure from Jones, and the extradition proceedings were delayed.

Perhaps not surprisingly, the example of Jim Jones' news reports to Jonestown provides one of the strongest arguments against government management of the press. Loudspeakers were set up all over the settlement, like something out of M*A*S*H. They would go on at any time, day or night, and Jones would regale his captive audience with the details of the latest book he was reading, or news reports from journals and magazines he supposedly had in his cabin. No one was allowed to see these publications, of course. During these readings, he would inform his people that—for instance—Los

Angeles was being evacuated due to drought and famine, or that the Klan was on the rampage, killing black people or enslaving them in camps. The people of Jonestown—having absolutely no access to the outside world in any way, shape or form—were reduced to either believing Jones' accounts and thanking God they were safe in the jungles of Guyana, or in disbelieving them and keeping that dangerous secret to themselves.

Suicide practice runs became frequent in the last years. At that point, with so few calories in their diet, a heavy workload of clearing jungle and raising some pitiful crops, and the constant loudspeaker harangues and forced marches—and worse—of the security staff, some people actually became indifferent to whether they lived or died. While romantic relationships were frowned upon unless encouraged or approved by Jones and sex was considered "counterrevolutionary," suicide itself was considered a revolutionary act by Jones, and he told his followers that they would be reincarnated in a better world. This was essentially the same rationale given to me by an American Nazi, who defended the genocide of the Jews and the Gypsies by claiming that—since there would be no more Jewish or Gypsy bodies after they were all killed—they would have to be reincarnated as Aryans. And of course Reverend Smith, more than a hundred years earlier, had told his Amerindian followers in Guyana that if they committed suicide, they would be reincarnated as white people. And so it goes.

A US State Department officer, Frank Tumminia, visited Guyana in 1978 and made a report, saying that the communards appeared "drugged and robot-like in their reactions to questions and, generally, in their behavior towards us visitors."[47] Officials visiting as late as November 1978, however, had no such observations and came away thinking everything there was just fine.

But back in December 1977, after a week in Jonestown, Deborah Layton had made plans to escape. She took the opportunity of a planned cultural program in Georgetown in March 1978, and she managed to stay in Guyana's capitol until she could arrange her return back to the United States. In the meantime, the Temple staff in Georgetown was told to approach the Soviet Embassy and try to get permission for the entire Jonestown population to emigrate to Russia. Deborah Layton was involved with this maneuver, which did not result in anyone actually going to Russia, but was part of an ongoing set of negotiations opened by Jones with both Russia and, to some extent, Cuba. The Russians, naturally, were a little leery of accepting the twelve hundred or so Americans, about seventy-five percent of whom were black—not a common racial group in Russia.

By the middle of May, Deborah—in a series of cloak-and-dagger moves to evade Temple members, and one false start due to documentation problems—managed to get into an Embassy car and get taken to the airport for her trip back to the States. Her brother, Larry Layton, was still in the US, and Deborah tried to warn him not to go down to Guyana if called. His sister,

Annalisa, made a warning phone call, and Larry replied he was not planning to go anywhere; but his mood was cool.

He then went to his father's house, dressed in his hospital uniform, and mowed the lawn. He appeared to be in a drugged state, although these would not have been recreational drugs at this time, since Larry had become a devoted member of the Peoples Temple, even if he had slacked off considerably during Jones' absence. Then, still dressed in his hospital uniform, he dove into the swimming pool.

His father, Dr. Layton, was just about to take some action, fearing that his son had gone over the edge, when the phone rang. It was for Larry. Larry got out of the pool and answered the phone. He listened. He hung up. He left immediately. And was on a plane bound for Guyana that night.

A WATERGATE OF THE CULTS

Tim Stoen encouraged her to make her information public; he felt that her story would be the beginning of a "Watergate of the cults."
  —Min S. Yee & Thomas N. Layton, *In My Father's House*[48]

Religion, like Watergate, is a scandal that will not go away.
  —Victor Turner[49]

Deborah Layton began working very hard to raise some awareness of what was happening in Jonestown. She knew that Jones' constant threats of mass suicide were not merely empty attempts to win sympathy or support for his plight, but could very possibly turn deadly in a heartbeat. She became the focal point for defectors and for people who had family living in Jonestown. She appeared in the press, wrote letters to government officials, and lobbied everyone who could have any impact at all on the escalating tensions in Guyana. Her mother was still down there, very sick, and she feared for her life and for the lives of her friends. Even her estranged husband, Phil Blakey—a man she met when she was at the Quaker school in England, and with whom she was never able to have a genuine married relationship, due to the Temple—was still there, working in the fields.

When she spoke with ADA Tim Stoen, he urged her to go public with everything she knew. She was, after all, one of the trusted members of the Peoples Temple (or had been) and knew about the money laundering, the psychodramas, the phony cancer cures, the raising from the dead, the revolutionary speeches, the attempts to flee to Russia … her story would open a can of worms that would reach back into other cults. It would be the beginning, said Stoen, of a "Watergate of the cults."

Not much was made of that statement at the time; it was probably considered a bit of hyperbole on Stoen's part. The nation, after all, was still "wallowing in Watergate," and there were congressional and senate committees every year on some aspect of government corruption or secret government operations. The revelations were coming fast and furious. Tim Stoen—a district attorney, after all, and an intimate of the Peoples Temple—evidently felt that the information Deborah Layton had in her possession would start an important enquiry into the operation of cults, an enquiry that would reveal much more about them than had been ever suspected.

Unfortunately, the "Watergate of the cults" that Stoen hypothesized never took place, because the events in Jonestown in November of 1978 were so hideous, and the cover-up so complete, that no such "Templegate" ever transpired. Jonestown entered history as one of the western world's great icons, a mystical portrait that means different things to different people, painted by trained political mystics who knew the right amount of spin to employ (the same way Russian ikon painters know how to apply gold leaf on the haloes of the saints), a hoodwink that would be used later to explain the ferocity of the attack on the Branch Davidian compound in Waco, Texas. What the western world learned in the aftermath of Jonestown was what it was intended to learn. A moral for the story was ready and waiting in the wings.

As Deborah Layton agitated for a full-scale investigation of Jonestown, Jim Jones was on the attack. He had invited veteran conspiracy theorist and attorney Mark Lane to Guyana, ostensibly to lecture on the life (and the assassination?) of Dr. Martin Luther King, Jr. But when he arrived back in the States after his visit to Jonestown, Lane immediately embarked on a legal campaign against the US government over its alleged persecution of Jonestown, the Peoples Temple, and Jim Jones. Jones' paranoia about the CIA, FBI, IRS and other government agencies found a receptive ear in Mark Lane, whose work on the assassination of President Kennedy was well-known. It seems incredible that Lane would have visited Jonestown and not come away with serious misgivings about what was going on there, but his visit was short—only a few days—and Jones typically rehearsed his congregation beforehand and created a festive atmosphere for guests, as he would with the visit of Congressman Ryan in 1978. In addition, Mark Lane was first an attorney, and one specializing in unpopular causes it would seem. The Peoples Temple had deep pockets, and Lane could have been looking at this as any other legal gig. Who was he to argue with State Department officials who found nothing sinister in the Jonestown commune?

And there might have been another element to the relationship. We know now, for instance, of Jones' involvement with people like Dan Mitrione, and of Jones' trips to Cuba and Guyana in the early 1960s, as well as of his mysterious psychiatric treatment at Langley-Porter. How much of this did he tell to Mark Lane? How much of this did he spin in just the right way to indicate to Lane that he was dealing with a very serious nexus of government mind control, political action and torture? How many hints did Jones drop of his prior experience with intelligence operations? How much more did he promise Lane if only Lane could get the US government off his back long enough? There were bits and pieces of an autobiography by Jones found among the wreckage of the Jonestown settlement after the massacre. Was this a manuscript being prepared for Mark Lane?

This author finds it difficult to believe that Mark Lane would have gone so far out on a limb for Jim Jones after only one visit of a few days in Jonestown unless he had found something very valuable there. Lane must have been the victim of dozens of people laying their paranoid trips on him over the years—especially after the publication in 1966 of his book on the Kennedy assassination, *Rush to Judgment* and of his subsequent work, *A Citizen's Dissent*, published in 1975—people claiming to have inside information on the assassination of President Kennedy, or that of his brother, Bobby, or that of Martin Luther King, or of any of a host of other scenarios. Why would he choose to cast his lot, as it were, with Jim Jones, a paranoid fanatic in the middle of the jungle, as close to Joseph Conrad's crazed character Kurtz in the *Heart of Darkness* as any man alive?

In the first place, money. We know, from the Thomas Layton book that Lane was paid ten thousand dollars up front for his legal assistance in suing the US government. The Peoples Temple had deep pockets; they were getting—in Social Security payments alone—sixty-five thousand dollars a month mailed to Guyana. Very little of this money was actually spent in Guyana for the residents of Jonestown, who had to make do with the most primitive living conditions imaginable, a near-starvation diet, and a heavy workload. The ten thousand dollars paid to Lane was probably only a down payment. The Peoples Temple could turn into a cash cow.

In the second place, revelations about CIA involvement in Latin American politics, secret police, and training in brutal interrogation techniques. The latter had already been the subject of several government investigations by that time, however. Jones would have had to have had something more worthwhile than that, something juicier. If there was anything there, though, it never surfaced. Mark Lane has not published anything remotely explosive on the subject of Jonestown. It may be a case of attorney-client privilege ... except that in this case his client is dead. So, what's the story, Mark?

Congressman Leo Ryan (D-CA) had also begun his own investigation of the Peoples Temple. His friend's son—Robert Houston—had been killed just at the time he was trying to leave the church. That, coupled with new charges surfacing in the press and in the form of petitions and letters being circulated by relatives of the Jonestown community, pushed the Peoples Temple to the forefront of Ryan's consciousness. He arranged a clandestine meeting with Deborah Layton and taped her two-hour statement about the conditions at the Jonestown compound as well as her own involvement over the prior seven years. Former Temple members Al and Deanna Mertle were also busy organizing and petitioning. Stories of children suffering at the Jonestown settlement and being held against their will—or against the will of their parents—were surfacing, and the heat was on the government to do something before the situation got completely out of hand. Deborah Layton pressed her case on Congressman Ryan, insisting that there was a very real possibility of mass suicide in the jungle.

Ryan was convinced that there was at least the possibility of disaster. A hands-on type of politician—who had worked undercover for two weeks in an inner-city school district as a teacher, and had spent a week as an inmate in the State's prison system so he could understand the conditions first-hand—Ryan was no stranger to dangerous situations. He made the arrangements to go to Jonestown himself, and his secretary—filled with ominous presentiments of death—urged the Congressman to make out his will before he left, as she was doing. A reporter who had interviewed Deborah Layton was convinced she was lying, making the whole thing up, and did not file a report on his interview with her concerning the situation in Jonestown.

He took a bullet in the wrist and another in the arm at the Port Kaituma airstrip.

Ryan notified the Peoples Temple officially of his upcoming visit, which prompted a response not from Jim Jones but from Mark Lane, now operating as the Temple's attorney. Lane tried to get Ryan to change his schedule. At the time of the proposed visit, Mark Lane was in Washington, D.C., where he was working on the Dr. Martin Luther King, Jr. assassination investigation. An important witness to the events leading up to the assassination was a woman—Grace Walden—who had been institutionalized for mental illness after she insisted that James Earl Ray was not the gunman. She was the landlady of the apartment complex that was used as the sniper's nest, and she identified someone else entirely as the shooter. Mark Lane was trying to get her story out in front of the House Assassinations Investigation Committee, but when he heard that Ryan had ignored Lane's plea for rescheduling and was on his way to Jonestown, he dropped everything—although he had worked on the King case for years, and had even taken the steps to obtain legal custody of Ms. Walden from the mental hospital where he found her—and instead flew immediately to Guyana to intercept the Congressman's party.

What happened next is so well-known, and has been covered in so many books, articles and documentaries, that I will not waste the reader's time with a detailed examination of the timeline leading up to the Jonestown massacre. There are a few salient points which should be viewed in context, however, and to these we turn our attention.

Congressman Ryan was held up in Georgetown for a few days, as Jim Jones had refused him and his party—which by now included newsmen and representatives of the "Concerned Relatives" group—until his attorneys Mark Lane and Charles Garry could get to Guyana. Ryan had met with

State Department officials in Washington a few days before his visit, and had asked Deborah Layton to address them as well. The State Department people professed to have no knowledge of Jonestown at all, and had nothing to contribute to the meeting.

When Ryan arrived in Guyana, he met with the local US Embassy staff as well as with the local office of the Peoples Temple. His patience wearing thin, he informed the two Temple attorneys that he was chartering a plane and flying out to Port Kaituma whether or not Jim Jones approved. The lawyers made a hurried radio call to Jonestown and convinced Jones to let the party come.

An eighteen-seat chartered plane took the group to Port Kaituma, but they were met by Temple members, who took only a handful of persons back with them, leaving the rest behind at the Port Kaituma airstrip. One of the members accompanying Ryan to Jonestown was Richard Dwyer.

Dwyer's involvement in this—and subsequent discoveries about his background in intelligence—is one of the more suggestive elements of the whole saga. Dwyer was a career intelligence officer, working under State Department cover at the US Embassy in Georgetown. He was, according to several sources, the CIA Chief of Station for Guyana. As such, he could be expected to have very good information on Jonestown; unfortunately, he did not choose to share this information with Ryan or his party. It was well-known in Georgetown that the Peoples Temple had strong influence with the Guyanese government; Temple women were expected to develop personal relationships with Guyanese officials, and one such woman was the mistress of the Guyanese ambassador to the United States. Dwyer would have had to have known all of this, as Georgetown is small as capitals go, a place where gossip is about the only entertainment there is. Further, as CIA station chief, it would have been his business to know all about the Peoples Temple political involvements, not only with the Guyanese government but also with the Soviet Union and Cuba, as the Temple had approached both of these countries—through their embassies in Georgetown—as possible relocation sites. Yet, Dwyer—and the State Department in general—remained strangely silent on the subject of the Peoples Temple and offered very little assistance to Congressman Ryan before and during his trip.

Ryan managed to visit Jonestown, and during the course of his two days there was approached by several Temple families who asked him to take them with him back to the States. At one point, Ryan was attacked and held at knife point by one of Jones' followers, who had to be restrained by Mark Lane and Charles Garry; it made for a dismal end to the Congressman's visit, and although Ryan had intended to stay longer, the atmosphere had changed and discretion seemed the better part of valor.

A truck was organized to take the Congressman's party—plus anyone else who wanted to leave—back to the Port Kaituma airstrip. The truck began filling up. One of the "defectors" was Larry Layton. It was November 18, 1978.

Remember that Larry was called back suddenly to Guyana after the defection of his sister, Deborah. He had been sinking in his father's swimming pool, dressed in his hospital X-Ray technician's uniform when the phone call came. He left his father's home at once and flew to Georgetown that evening.

It is Larry Layton's presence at Port Kaituma that is one of the more troubling aspects of the entire case. Larry had had problems growing up in the Layton household, but then many children of the sixties had problems with the generation gap: drugs, sex, and rock 'n' roll were the pathways to a different, altered state of consciousness and political and social awareness. He married the daughter of a minister, Carolyn Moore, and they both joined the Peoples Temple and became intimately involved in the church hierarchy including the dread PC, or Planning Commission, which was really the "inner court" of the Temple, the place where Jones could rant and rave for hours on end about politics, metaphysics, and especially about sex. It was during those PC sessions—to which only the most devoted (or important) were invited—that Larry lost Carolyn to Jim Jones, and was instead "assigned" to Karen Tow. Carolyn became a vociferous supporter of Jones and even bore him a son, Kimo. Larry and Karen, however, were not to have sex at all unless approved in advance by Jones. Instead, Larry was forced to make humiliating "confessions" of his homosexuality and of his homosexual attraction for Jones before the assembled throng of PC regulars.

Larry Layton's psychological and spiritual disintegration—begun years before with hallucinogens and religious yearnings—was exacerbated by the type of psychological mind games that Jones was playing. Jones after all was a religious leader and a political leader of sorts; he held a captive audience in the Planning Commission, whose meetings were usually held only at night and through to the early hours of the morning, exhausting the participants, including at times Jones himself, who was the only one allowed to eat and drink during the marathon sessions. Layton, like all the other PC attendants, had been worked on in a highly-charged, emotionally-draining controlled atmosphere. Jones was quite aware of the effect that the isolation and insularity of the scene would have on the psyches of his flock. He demonstrated this during a session in which a young boy was accused of stealing. Jones lightly drugged the boy, telling him he could strike him dead. By the time the drug began to take effect, the boy was quaking in fear. He was revived briefly, in the darkened church and to the sound of the other members of the congregation making terrifying sounds, as if the boy had descended to the very pit of hell. The boy was then "brought back from the dead" by Jones, and the traumatized child promised he would never commit another crime in his life. This is the environment in which Larry Layton found himself.

He became, in the terminology of Erich Fromm, a "true believer."

So, when the time came for the defectors to go back to the airstrip with Congressman Ryan, and Larry Layton hopped aboard the truck, the other defectors tried to warn the Congressman's party that Layton was not a genuine defector and that there would be problems. But, in the chaos of the leave-taking, Larry was brought along to the airstrip with the others.

Back in Jonestown, Jones knew that the end had come. He began to tell his flock that the plane would explode in the sky; that the pilot would be killed by one of the people who had gone to the airstrip. Thus, the plan was revealed, and the words captured on tape. The transcript of that tape has since been made available, and besides the oblique reference to the assassins on their way to kill Congressman Ryan there is also one other disturbing clue that has bothered researchers and commentators for years: the references to Dwyer.

Jones several times insists that Dwyer be allowed to leave; in fact, he doesn't want Dwyer in Jonestown at all when the curtain comes down and calls over the loudspeaker to have him taken away. As we have seen, Dwyer was likely the local CIA Chief of Station. Why, suddenly, is Jones worried for his safety? If the whole congregation is going to commit mass suicide (as the cover story would have it), then why would Jones care one way or another about Dwyer?

According to the press reports by eyewitnesses, Dwyer was on the truck with Layton and the Congressman's party. Dwyer was ostensibly going to return to Georgetown with them. However, Dwyer was wounded in the attack on the Port Kaituma airstrip: not seriously, it seems to have been a flesh wound in his thigh. Witnesses saw blood on his pants leg, but did not see a wound. Whatever the details of the wound, it did not prevent Dwyer from running into the jungle to hide with a few other survivors, and then organizing the events of the next twenty-four hours and shuttling back and forth between the airstrip and the town of Port Kaituma.

Why did Jones think that Dwyer was still at Jonestown? And why did he care?

The truck arrived at the airstrip, and shortly thereafter another vehicle arrived with three members of the Jonestown security force. There were two planes on the airstrip, one a small, single-engine craft and the other a larger plane to accommodate the growing party of defectors. Dwyer had just arrived from another part of the airstrip with a policeman holding a shotgun. The Jonestown security people marched up to the policeman and seized his shotgun. Neither the policeman nor Dwyer seems to have made any attempt to resist. A tractor pulled up to the airstrip, carrying more Jonestown security people, parking a trailer between one plane and the next and trying to determine who was going on each plane. Those defectors still on the tarmac, and fearing the worst, began to run to the jungle. The Temple security forces opened fire on the Congressman's party, killing the NBC news crew first as they were filming the murders. They then walked up to Leo Ryan, already wounded on the ground, and shot him in cold blood, leaving his body lying on the tarmac next to the plane.

Larry Layton had boarded the single-engine Cessna first—shoving himself forward ahead of everyone—and was armed; he either picked up a pistol earlier at Jonestown or it had been planted in the plane. Since all the Temple defectors had been checked for weapons before boarding, it seems more likely that the gun had been planted in the plane, which is why Layton insisted to Ryan that he have a seat on that particular aircraft.

He began shooting in the plane as it was trying to take off during the attack, wounding defectors Monica Bagby and Vernon Gosney before his revolver misfired and it was taken from him by defector Dale Parks.

There were others at the airstrip at the time, local Guyanese troops in fact, guarding a military plane that was being repaired, who made themselves scarce when the shooting started. The congressman's party did not have any weapons—thanks to the surrendering of the policeman's shotgun to the Temple security forces—and were sitting ducks. Bob Flick, an NBC producer, ran to the troops and begged them for help. They refused. They said it was a conflict between Americans and had nothing to do with them. He asked them for a weapon in order to defend himself. They refused again. They sat and watched five people being murdered in cold blood, and when the murderers took off in their tractor for Jonestown after the killing, they made no move to pursue them but instead let them pass.[50]

Back in Jonestown, the word reached Jim Jones that the Congressman was dead. No one knows how the information reached him so quickly. There had to have been a radio at the airstrip that was used to transmit the information, either from one of the planes or from somewhere else nearby. Once the information was relayed, however, the White Night was begun. Jones went on the loudspeaker and called everyone's attention, and began talking about the need for them to kill themselves.

Dwyer then went into action. Larry Layton was standing casually on the tarmac and talking to two Guyanese policemen. The defectors raised the alarm, pointing to Layton, and finally Dwyer walked over to the policemen and demanded that Layton be placed under arrest. They refused initially but then agreed, and took Layton back to Georgetown. He would be the only person charged and the only person ever convicted of the Port Kaituma attack and of conspiracy to murder Congressman Ryan.[51] Dwyer had his scapegoat; there was no need to look any further for the other gunmen.

What was Larry Layton doing, standing around the airstrip and chatting with Guyanese policemen just after shooting two people and attempting to shoot a third?

The events of the day became even more horrible. Attorneys Mark Lane and Charles Garry were permitted to escape into the jungle. The rest of the Jonestown compound was subjected to a lengthy harangue from Jim Jones as he attempted to convince them all to commit suicide. He asked mothers to kill their children first, and then to take their own lives. What actually transpired, however, has never been clear, and the crime scene investigation—such as it was—was one of the worst travesties of justice in the history of any country.

Many of the victims bore gunshot wounds, which argues strongly against the suicide-by-Kool-Aid story that was disseminated shortly after the massacre. Those who did survive recall the sounds of gunshots in such abundance it sounded like a war. The security forces had armed themselves with heavy automatic weapons at the start of Jones' plea for suicide and were ensuring that none would escape the compound. Jones had allowed Lane and Garry to leave, and had demanded that Dwyer also leave. It is possible that Dwyer was in Jonestown at the time of the massacre, since there are hours during that afternoon and night after the airstrip attack when it seems he was not present at Port Kaituma. In any event, Jones believed that Dwyer was there, and repeatedly asked that someone take him away.

Aerial photographs of the site days later would show the famous scene of bodies all over the compound; millions saw those photographs in the news magazines, but few came to the obvious conclusion: the bodies were all lying facedown and in many cases neatly arranged, indicating that the story of mass suicide might have been in error. It beggars belief that everyone in Jonestown would have fallen forward onto their faces after taking the cyanide-laced grape drink. It is entirely possible that the bodies were arranged that way to make their identification more difficult when photographed from above. It is also entirely possible that the bodies were arranged that way by persons unknown after the massacre. For it was a massacre.

Initially, the body count—performed by the first contingent of Guyanese troops that arrived the morning after the massacre—was only about two hundred. Later, as the days went on and more investigators (and curiosity-seekers) arrived, the body count was corrected upwards. At first, it was believed that the grand total would come in at three hundred sixty-three, of which eighty-two were identified as children. Yet, as the body count increased, the incredulous wanted to know how it was possible that it could go from 363 to 913; how was such a wide variation possible?

The explanation given was that some of the bodies were those of children, and that the adult bodies had fallen on top of them, rendering immediate location and identification difficult. In other words, there were more than five hundred bodies hidden under the first 363. That did not seem possible, particularly as the initial counts showed that of the 363, more than 80 were children. It simply did not make sense, and it seemed as if someone, somewhere was lying about the body count on behalf of some hidden agenda.

What made matters worse was the discovery of some 789 American passports at the scene. If there were only 363 bodies discovered, then 426 other souls were unaccounted for and possibly on the run through the Guyanese jungles. One had to put a stop to *that* rumor at once, and the body count was adjusted upwards to the point where 913 became the official number. But, to be perfectly honest, there was no verifiable, official record of the number of corpses, and only about three hundred had ever been positively identified.[52] Photos of some of the bodies show that they were wearing identification bracelets on their wrists, the type commonly used in hospitals to identify patients. No one knows why this was done, and particularly why those bracelets mysteriously disappeared somewhere between Jonestown and the American air base where the bodies were eventually shipped, thus rendering further identification even more difficult. (Three bodies were actually *lost*, and turned up in storage lockers in southern California years after the fact![53]) The bodies were left in the open jungle air for days, and had reached a particularly loathsome state of putrescence, rendering hellish the task of coroners and medical examiners. In fact, there were virtually no autopsies performed on the bodies recovered.

Only seven autopsies were ever performed on the more than nine hundred bodies found at Jonestown, and only one of those showed any sign of cyanide poisoning. In fact, the autopsies were not performed until a month after the bodies had been embalmed! The first forensic specialist on the scene was a Guyanese doctor, and his initial report on the massacre is widely at variance with the story that was later given so much publicity in the foreign press.

Dr. Mootoo, Guyana's chief medical examiner, noted that many of the victims had puncture wounds from syringes on their shoulders, where they could not have possibly injected themselves. In addition, cyanide was present in bottles labeled Valium, and Mootoo assumed that the victims had been given the fictitious Valium and discovered the switch too late, as they lay dying. To summarize his findings, he believed that the evidence strongly supported a charge of homicide in at least seven hundred cases. The tissue samples that he collected at the site—representing tests of more than twenty bodies—were handed over to an official of the American embassy for onward transmission to forensic specialists in the United States. They never arrived, and to this day no one knows what happened to them.

As if anyone needed additional mysteries to solve, Jim Hougan points out one more incredible anomaly: the CIA knew that there were mass suicides in Jonestown at 4:44 A.M. on Sunday morning, Guyana time. But the site had not been visited until mid-morning that same day by Guyanese troops. How did the CIA know that there had been mass suicides in Jonestown at least six hours before anyone else did?

One of the planes involved in the attack at Port Kaituma had managed to leave and make its way to Georgetown the night of the 18th, but the only news they had was of the attack on the Congressman's party at the airstrip and the murder of five people whose bodies still lay on the tarmac. No one knew about the massive death toll at Jonestown until the next day. Yet, somehow, the

CIA knew all about it and was already spinning the story as a "mass suicide." Hougan believes the probable source to be Richard Dwyer; in addition, a CIA memorandum concerning Guyana refers to a CIA "field station" in Guyana, giving rise to speculation that there was another CIA operation in Guyana beyond that of Dwyer's embassy posting.

AFTERMATH

The deaths did not end with the massacre at Jonestown. As in the case of the Manson Family murders, people connected with the case continued to die from gunshot wounds for quite some time after the discovery of all those bodies in the jungle. At the beginning of this chapter, we noted that Al and Deanna Mertle—who had published a book about their Jonestown experience, replete with the sexual escapades and physical and mental torture of followers—were murdered in their home in February of 1980, only a few months after their book was published, in a case that has not been solved. They were not the first, and not the last.

Only nine days after the Jonestown massacre, San Francisco Mayor Moscone—whom Jones had helped to elect in the 1976 campaign—was shot dead, as was Harvey Milk, the famous defender of gay rights in government. There are numerous photos of Moscone and Jones, and even at the height of the Peoples Temple scandals in the press, Moscone stood behind Jones and was vocal in his support of the church. There is some circumstantial evidence to suggest Peoples Temple involvement in these deaths, but nothing substantial enough to warrant a full discussion at this point. The presence of a longtime Peoples Temple member—Bonnie Thielmann—however is suggestive. Ms. Thielmann lived with Jim and Marceline Jones in Brazil in the 1960s, and continued her involvement with the Peoples Temple right up to and after the Jonestown massacre. She was on the plane with Congressman Ryan that flew into Georgetown as one of the Concerned Relatives—even though she was not related to anyone in Jonestown—but she did not go to Jonestown with the group, staying behind in the capital instead, and then flying back to the States with Tim Stoen.

She attended (uninvited) Leo Ryan's funeral in California, latching onto Mayor Moscone and using him as her entrée into the private funeral service. She is said to have whispered something to the Mayor which left him visibly shaken. He had been receiving anonymous phone calls from people claiming to be members of the Temple or relatives of members, warning him to be very careful and insinuating that the Peoples Temple wanted him dead. Clearly, he felt that the massacre in Jonestown was somehow connected to him personally, and not only because of his support for Jones. He urged that survivors of the holocaust be treated by a psychiatrist, unfortunately a psychiatrist associated with the Langley-Porter clinic, the same institution that had been treating Jim Jones for his mysterious ailment, an institution that also specialized in classified Defense Department research, including the effects of ELF (extremely low frequency) waves on humans.

Mayor Moscone began to fear for his life, and on November 27, 1978 he lost it to a bullet.

Dan White had resigned his position as City Supervisor earlier that month, and then tried to retract the resignation but failed. There was some conservative support to have White (a former police officer) reinstated, but it seems that Moscone was just as happy to have White out of the way. At 9 A.M. on the 27th of November, White drove to City Hall with his aide, Denise Apcar. Ms. Apcar went into City Hall through the front doors and metal detectors, but White decided to find another way into the building. The loaded, five-shot revolver he was carrying would not pass the metal detectors.

He went in through a basement window, assisted by some workmen. He used the story that he did not want to go through the front doors because there were demonstrators outside supporting his reinstatement (which was true), and that the side doors were locked and he had forgotten his keys (not exactly true, he had surrendered his keys earlier, at the time of his resignation).

He went upstairs to the Mayor's Office, waited patiently in the outer office until Moscone was ready for him, and then went in and had a heated discussion with the Mayor. He then fired four rounds into him, and left by another door.

He went down the hallway, reloading as he walked, and stepped into Harvey Milk's office, asking him for a private word. Milk joined White in another room, where he was shot five times.

White left City Hall and phoned his wife, meeting her away from home. Eventually, he surrendered himself to the police and confessed to the crimes, even though he told the investigators that he walked through the murders in a kind of stupor, having blacked out on the way to City Hall and having no memory of the actual killings.

What happened next became a landmark in the history of jurisprudence. Dan White's lawyers came up with the infamous "Twinkie Defense," based on their allegation that Dan White committed the murders while in diminished mental capacity due to an over indulgence in junk food. He was convicted of the lesser charges of voluntary manslaughter and sentenced to seven years, eight months in Soledad, in segregation from the main prison population. He was freed on parole in January 1984 after serving only five years.

On October 21, 1985, White was found dead in his garage, a victim of probable suicide from carbon monoxide poisoning.

The motives for the Moscone and Milk murders were never very clear. White had no particular agenda against Moscone. He had resigned his city position for the simple reason that it would not pay enough to support him and his family. He then decided to retract his resignation, but there was no legal precedent for it. All in all, it did not seem enough to warrant his insane plan to murder the Mayor. As a political and moral conservative, he probably despised gay activist Harvey Milk; it's possible that he considered killing Milk at the same time as Moscone on general principle. But we will never know; White had confessed to the crimes, and it only wanted a decision by the courts as to whether the homicides were murder or manslaughter. The question of motive was not explored because, quite simply, White insisted he didn't even remember committing the crimes. His death raises more questions than answers, since it occurred at a time when White was planning to move his family to Ireland permanently.

On July 31, 1980 the surviving children of Congressman Leo Ryan's family brought a lawsuit against the United States of America in the matter of Ryan's assassination. They charged that the State Department knew in advance of the dangers inherent in a trip to Jonestown, but failed to warn the Congressman in advance. They further charged that Jonestown was a CIA mind-control experiment, and that the community was heavily armed, and was infiltrated by CIA agents, among whom they named Richard Dwyer and Deborah Layton's estranged English husband (and former Quaker) Philip Blakey. It was Blakey who had gone to Guyana years before the rest of the Peoples Temple, in order to clear the land and prepare the site for habitation. His role has always been open to speculation, as he seemed to be Jones' right-hand man. The suit was dropped, for reasons that have never been revealed, although many still persist in their belief that Jonestown was a CIA operation of some kind and, if it was, the only type of operation that makes any kind of sense would be something along the lines of MK-ULTRA or some other, related, mind control experiment, since we are told by CIA that MK-ULTRA had been discontinued in the 1960s.

One of the Ryan family children eventually went on to become involved with the Cult Awareness Network (CAN) after the lawsuit against the CIA was dropped. Other influential members of CAN at one time included Dr. Margaret Singer, long associated with the Langley-Porter clinic, as well as notorious CIA mind-control psychiatrist Dr. Louis Jolyon West. These doctors had also been involved in the defense of Patty Hearst, asserting she had been brainwashed.

Larry Layton was acquitted of all charges in Guyanese courts, but had to stand trial again in the United States. His first trial ended in a mistrial; he was tried again a few years later and convicted, and is still in prison as of this writing. He is the only person to have been tried and convicted in the Jonestown case, and the only crimes he is actually known to have committed are the shootings of the two Peoples Temple defectors in the Cessna, both of whom were wounded but not killed. The actual murderers of Congressman Ryan and the four other individuals at Port Kaituma have never been identified, apprehended, or charged in any way by anyone. It is almost certain that they were still alive at the time of Larry Layton's numerous trials.

Deborah Layton went on to retrieve the money that Jim Jones had salted away in Switzerland and Panama, but it is not known whether she found all the money Jones had hidden or just a portion. Jones' affairs were heavily compartmentalized, and several of his higher-ranking PC staff had access to overseas accounts and funds. There are also persistent rumors that some of the security staff escaped into the jungles with a suitcase full of cash. The Temple owned three sailing vessels in Guyana, which were all at sea at the time of the massacre. One of these was named *Cudjoe*, ironically enough, since it was also the *nom de guerre* of Patty Hearst's SLA lover, William Wolfe. Another vessel was the *Marceline*, the name of Jim Jones' wife. Evidence of conspiracy, or of sinister forces at work behind the flimsy façade of reality? Who were on these vessels? How many were they? Where were they dropped off? No one seems to care.

Bonnie Thielmann, Terri Buford, the Mertles/Mills, Thomas Layton, and Deborah Layton have all written or co-written books on Jonestown, each providing their own particular spin and adding to the general information—or disinformation—on the case. Tim Reiterman has written a book, as has Charles Krause, both newsmen present at Port Kaituma when the shooting started. Mark Lane has also written a book about Jonestown. So have other survivors.

"MISTAH KURTZ – HE DEAD."

As for Jim Jones himself, his fate is also open to question. His death was ruled a suicide, by a self-inflicted gunshot wound. The pistol he is alleged to have used, however, was found far away from his body. At least one researcher—Michael Meiers—insists that the body that was identified as Jim Jones at the scene could not have been Jones, because the body does not match some essential physical characteristics, thus giving rise to the "Jim Jones double" theory; that Jones may have had a double is supported by some circumstantial evidence, as shown in the Jim Hougan article. In Meiers' view,[53a] the real Jim Jones is sipping banana daiquiris on a tropical beach somewhere, enjoying his millions in relative peace. Hard to believe? Sure. But, as so often in this study, we are confronted with more questions than answers. One wonders, for instance, where Dwyer was at the moment Jones was killed? Jones wanted him gone; thus he seemed to have been there at the time of the massacre. Was he Jim Jones' executioner, playing the Marlow to his Kurtz? Or was it a bit more like the Martin Sheen and Marlon Brando characters in *Apocalypse Now*, with Brando's crazed but successful renegade Colonel—surrounded by his Montagnard Army who revere him "as a god"—who must be assassinated by Sheen's Captain Willard.

In the original theatrical release of the film, we are shown an image that is frighteningly reminiscent of what might have happened at Jonestown. In this scene, which is nowhere to be found on the videotapes and DVDs that have since been produced, the end credits roll up over the sight of Colonel Kurtz' jungle encampment being razed by napalm, killing all the inhabitants. Although this finale is suggested by other events in the film—such as the discovery of Kurtz' manuscript with the words "Drop the bomb! Kill them all!" scribbled across one page—the actual firebombing of the site is not shown on later releases.

I like to think that Jim Jones *was* Colonel Kurtz; that he had been recruited by the CIA in his early days, and then become increasingly psychotic as his personal and spiritual isolation grew. I like to think that the CIA used him and his Guyana operation for a variety of experiments *in situ* because it was outside the United States, in the middle of nowhere, far beyond any possibility of congressional interlopers (until events forced Congressman Ryan's hand), and anyway the victims were poor, black, and socialist; by openly accepting Jones' rabid form of "apostolic socialism" and parroting his fear of an attack by the fascists, the Nazis, the KKK, the CIA, the FBI, etc., they had placed themselves beyond the pale. They could not be repatriated. Bringing a thousand paranoid black people who had been through the fires of hell together back into the United States could only have been seen as a terrible liability. Furthermore, who knew what some of them had witnessed at Jonestown? What tales would they tell?

As the tropical night deepens, the loudspeaker blaring the last, crazed harangue of Jim Jones, like the Brando character reciting poetry and broken, bitter prose over the radio deep within the jungles of Cambodia, and with the Jonestown population falling to the effects of cyanide, or to bullets in the back of their skulls, Richard Dwyer creeps along the wooden planks of the pavilion and fires the coup de grâce *into the brain of a madman.*

I hope I may be forgiven if it seems that I have gone off the deep end with this theory, but stranger things have happened. We have left other people behind, in dangerous territory, in the hands of torturers and psychopaths. Why should the Peoples Temple be any different? And by spinning the story so that it looks like mass suicide, we can assuage any guilt we may have over the exact manner of their fate. After all, they killed *themselves*. It's sad, and tragic, and a warning to us all ... but *we* had nothing to do with it.

The Peoples Temple settlers in Guyana had come in search of God, in search of paradise, in search of spiritual liberation. Religion, after all, was their primary motive. Jones had abandoned religion very early on, ridiculing the Bible, but at the same time claiming that he was the reincarnation of Jesus and Lenin, among other heroes. He was merging religion and politics, in a way that has become all too familiar now, promising a workers' paradise "on earth as it is in heaven." In robbing his believers of an afterlife, of a blissful existence on the other side of death, and giving them only horror in this life,

Jim Jones worked the ultimate blasphemy. God became, for the hopeful, idealistic parents, and innocent, wide-eyed children of Jonestown, a hungry tiger lurking in the jungle darkness, its eyes shining in the reflected light of their souls. These were people who wanted what everyone wants: peace, security, happiness, a bright future for their children, and the knowledge that they are doing good in the world and furthering the spiritual liberation of the planet at the same time. This is what Jim Jones promised them. Instead, he gave them despair.

As they stand in the compound the jungle night darkened, the sound of gun fire chilling them like some satanic orchestra as their friends are being shot, the rounds marching closer and closer to the center of the mass as the men march up and down the columns of the helpless. The helpless who suddenly realize that they are breathing their last moments on earth, an unspeakable fear mingling with the tears and the screams of mothers poisoning their children, husbands embracing their wives for the last time in horror and in desperate love, surrounded by evil men and a hostile landscape, all hope dying within their hearts in a dreadful plummet as, one by one, their friends and family fall to the vermin-infested earth, never to hope or pray or dream or laugh again.

They were so very far from home.

Robert Graves once wrote, in reference to the Gordian Knot,

> Alexander's brutal cutting of the knot, when he marshalled his army at Gordium for the invasion of Greater Asia, ended an ancient dispensation by placing the power of the sword above that of religious mysteries.[54]

Perhaps so. Perhaps the modern world is still in the grip of that conceit, that military conceit of absolute power. The CIA recognized that there was military value in those religious mysteries, however, and strove to make those mysteries serve the State. They picked up the two pieces of whatever knot they had severed, savagely and without concern for the souls of the men and women destroyed in the process, and tried to find out how it was tied.

"God," said Nik Aziz, a powerful Malaysian politician and dangerous Islamic fundamentalist, "is a gangster."[55]

Amen. But as I once wrote in another time, another place, and as the Jonestown victims learned too late to save their lives, "God is the only safe thing to be."

Endnotes
[1] Gordon Thomas, *Journey Into Madness*, Bantam, NY, 1990, p. 276
[2] Charles A. Krause, *Guyana Massacre: The Eyewitness Account*, Pan Books, London, 1979, p. 132

[3] John Marks, *The Search for "The Manchurian Candidate,"* Times, NY, 1979, p. 178-9

[4] Ibid., p. 164

[5] Ibid., p. 166

[6] Kenneth D. Wald, *Religion and Politics in the United States,* Washington, DC, 1992, p. 44

[7] Jim Hougan, "Jonestown, The Secret Life of Jim Jones: A parapolitical fugue," *Lobster,* vol. 37, Summer 1999, p. 10

[8] Ibid., p. 12

[9] Ibid., p. 13

[10] Ibid., p. 13

[11] Ibid., p. 14

[12] Jeannie Mills, *Six Years With God: Life Inside Rev. Jim Jones's Peoples Temple,* A&W Publishers, NY, 1979, p. 243

[13] Andrija Puharich, *Uri,* Anchor Press, NY, 1974, p. 26

[14] Ibid., p. 30

[15] Ibid., p. 31

[16] Gerald L. Posner & John Ware, *Mengele: The Complete Story,* Dell, NY, 1987, p. 167-192

[17] Russell Targ & Keith Harary, *The Mind Race: Understanding and Using Psychic Powers,* New English Library, London, 1986, p. 103-106

[18] Garry Wills, *Under God: Religion and American Politics,* Simon & Schuster, NY, 1990, p. 144

[19] Ibid., p. 144

[20] Min S. Yee & Thomas N. Layton, *In My Father's House,* Holt, Rinehart & Winston, NY, 1981, p. 45

[21] Ibid., p. 42

[22] Ibid., p. 44

[23] Ibid., p. 4

[24] Ibid., p. 6

[25] Ibid., p. 19

[26] Ibid., p. 49

[27] Ibid., p. 58

[28] Ibid., p. 64

[29] Leonard A. Cole, *Clouds of Secrecy: The Army's Germ Warfare Tests Over Populated Areas,* Rowman & Littlefield, Totowa, 1988, p. 45

[30] Ibid., p. 61

[31] Yee & Layton, op. cit., p. 66

[32] Can be found in various places, including the recently-released BLUEBIRD CIA files, and in *Bluebird* by Colin Ross, Manitou Communications, Richardson TX, 2000,. p. 385

[33] Yee & Layton, op. cit., p. 172

[34] Ibid., p. 168

[35] Ibid., p. 168

[36] Ibid., p. 172
[37] Ibid., p. 177
[38] Ibid., p. 180
[39] Ibid., p. 185
[40] Hougan, op. cit., p. 12
[41] Yee & Layton, op. cit., p. 158
[42] Ibid., p. 161
[43] Ibid., p. 161
[44] Ibid., p. 161
[45] Ibid., p. 219
[46] Mills, op. cit., p. 83
[47] Yee & Layton, op. cit., p. 232
[48] Ibid., p. 274
[49] Victor Turner, *Revelation and Divination in Ndembu Ritual*, Cornell University Press, Ithaca, 1975, p.32
[50] Krause, op. cit., p. 96
[51] Ibid., p. 97
[52] Hougan, op. cit., p. 4
[53] Ibid., p. 5
[53a] Michael Meiers, *Was Jonestown a CIA Medical Experiment?*, Edwin Mellen Press, Studies in American Religion, Number 35, Lewiston NY, 1988, ISBN 0-88946-013-2
[54] Robert Graves, *The Greek Myths*
[55] *The Star*, Kuala Lumpur, Sept 2, 2002, p. 2

THE NEW STANDARD

Smiling gunman fires five
bullets into ex-Beatle

JOHN
LENNON
SHOT DEAD

CHAPTER FOURTEEN

HAPPINESS IS A WARM GUN

I made a decision to be crazy, or schizophrenic; a psychopath or a sociopath, whatever it is you have to be to do the things that I did. It's a choice anybody can make.
   —Mark David Chapman[1]

MARKS: Is there any psychiatric significance to his mental condition that's attributable to religious beliefs?
SCHWARTZ: I cannot call them, in and of themselves, delusional, since they are not unique to him.
   His concept of religion, of God, is an extremely fundamentalistic one. As he himself says, he doesn't just believe in Satan, he knows that Satan is here on earth.... Right or wrong to a great extent is decided in his life by a struggle between God or God's angels, and Satan, or Satan's demons, who struggle for possession of his will.
   —Testimony of Dr. Daniel Schwartz in sentencing hearing of Mark David Chapman on August 24, 1981[2]

But the struggle between freedom and Communism is, in its essence, not an economic conflict but a spiritual one.
   —Ronald Reagan, August 31, 1984 letter to World Anti-Communist League[3]

So it was not a well-planned intrigue, it was the Devil himself.
   —August Strindberg[4]

The Jonestown hearings took place in 1979. A lawsuit was brought against the CIA in July 1980 by relatives of Congressman Leo Ryan, who believed that the CIA knew much more about Jonestown than they told the Congressman. On October 18, 1978—and thus exactly a month before the massacre—CIA Deputy Director Frank Carlucci had written the Congressman to tell him that although the CIA *had* conducted mind-control experiments at Vacaville, they had not involved with Donald DeFreeze (Cinque) of the Patty Hearst kidnapping "insofar as our records reflect the names of the participants."

Lisa Philip, the mother of Larry Layton and Deborah Layton, had died in Jonestown of cancer three months before the massacre. Although this survivor of Nazi Germany lived to see serious problems in the Peoples Temple "paradise," she did not live to see the horrible devastation of the White Night, and perhaps one should be grateful for that if for nothing else.

Carolyn Moore—Larry Layton's first wife and mistress of Jim Jones, mother of his son Kimo—was dead at Jonestown. Karen Tow Layton, Larry's second wife and sometime sexual partner of Jim Jones, also died during the White Night. It is not known when Jones died: did he wait for all of the others to die and then take his own life? Was he shot by one of the security guards at some point during the proceedings? Was he "terminated with extreme prejudice" by a CIA officer present at the scene? We may never know. We can assume, however, that Jones died with the screams of his followers in his ears and the sight of bodies falling all around him as far as his eyes could see.

Larry Layton was the only person ever charged with murder and conspiracy to commit murder in relation to the events of Jonestown and Port Kaituma. He had been seized at the Port Kaituma airstrip on the urgings of Richard Dwyer, even though the Guyanese police were reluctant to do so, and, indeed, Dwyer had no authority in Guyana to order anyone's arrest. It was necessary to charge someone with the murder of the Congressman, and Larry Layton was the only one who remained behind at the scene to be charged. No one else was ever arrested, tried or convicted, even though Peoples Temple defectors who survived the rampage would have recognized exactly who had done the shooting. There is no evidence that the shooters died at Jonestown with the rest of the commune. Once Larry Layton was in custody, there was no need to look any further, and thus he could bear the responsibility for all of it. Once someone was in custody—reminiscent of the events at Dallas in 1963 and Los Angeles in 1968—the police stopped looking anywhere else. Although Layton was convicted of conspiracy, no other conspirators were apprehended or charged. Layton was a conspiracy of one.

To put this in some kind of perspective, we have to remember that it was in 1977 that the Senate hearings took place on the CIA's mind-control operations, which involved everything from BLUEBIRD to ARTICHOKE to MK-ULTRA and MK-NAOMI to OFTEN. The revelations came as a stunning surprise to many Americans, and the CIA's efforts to downplay the projects as basically worthless and non-productive were met with incredulity. In July of 1977, *New West* magazine published (in their August 1 issue) an investigative report on the Peoples Temple which was anything but congratulatory. Only a few days later, on August 3, 1977 the Senate hearings on MK-ULTRA took place. Simultaneously, a public outcry against the Peoples Temple began, and there were demands that it be officially investigated by the government. Jim Jones, in that hostile climate, began making plans to get out of Dodge and to move to the presumably more welcoming and benign climate of Guyana.

On October 31, 1977 (Halloween), President Carter's Director of the CIA—Admiral Stansfield Turner—summarily fired over eight hundred of the Agency's covert operations personnel, reducing the CIA's operational staff from 1,200 to less than 400, virtually overnight.[5a] Known as the "Halloween Massacre," Turner's move created an unofficial network of eight hundred "disgruntled former employees." It is a miracle that these men, with their specialized training picked up at The Farm and other Agency locations, did not "go postal"! (Arthur Hochberg was one of those fired that day who subsequently disappeared from public view.) However, many did find themselves working for the Reagan–Bush presidential campaign, actively supporting a former CIA Director (George Bush), whom they felt might get the Agency back on track. Campaign posters began to appear at CIA headquarters at Langley, with the "Reagan" half of the poster torn away, leaving only "Bush." On the other hand, radical protesters at the Republican National Convention in Detroit on July 14-17, 1980 wore buttons that said, "Shoot Bush First."

Shortly after the "Massacre," Leo Ryan, the Congressman who co-authored the Hughes-Ryan amendment forcing CIA to advise Congress in advance of covert activities, proceeds to Guyana and is slain on November 18, 1978, as we have seen. The people of Jonestown are killed in a massacre of horrific proportions. Large quantities of drugs are found at the scene, drugs that are later described as "mind-control" substances, but which include everything from Valium to cyanide. The amount of drugs found is far in excess of what the thousand inmates of Jonestown would or could use in the normal course of living. That, and the involvement of the son of Dr. Laurence Layton (formerly of the Army's Chemical Warfare Division) and others with suspicious backgrounds in government, the military and medicine, gives rise to speculation—so soon after the MK-ULTRA hearings—that Jonestown itself was some kind of mind control experiment gone awry.

Then, on November 4, 1979 a mob of Iranian students attacked the US Embassy in Teheran, Iran and took fifty-two Americans hostage.

Americans will not soon forget the searing image of our people being rounded up, blindfolded and bound, in the midst of thousands of screaming Shi'ite students. Americans will not forget the sight of these same students trying to tape together the millions of strips of shredded documents that the staffers had tried to destroy when the students were leaping over the embassy walls. Whereas two years previously Admiral Turner had fired most of the CIA's covert operations officers, he must have thought he could have used them now.

There was no way to get into Teheran and free the hostages. There would have to be a negotiation for their release. But first, there was tremendous propaganda value in having these once-proud Americans so helpless, as the television cameras of the world trained their lenses on Teheran—helpless and terrified the way the Shah's dreaded secret police, the SAVAK, had kept Iranian citizens in a constant state of fear and anxiety for decades. Beginning in 1960, and thus during the same period that Dan Mitrione was training secret police in Brazil and Uruguay, the CIA was training SAVAK (as were the Israelis who had long maintained a "de facto" relationship with Iran due to the fact that Iran is a nation of non-Semites who feel they have nothing in common with their Arab neighbors except Islam, and even then their version—Shi'ism—is considered heretical by most other Muslims). The Shah himself, after all, had been put in power in Iran by the American CIA in an operation of which the Agency is still quite proud. So turnabout was fair play in the eyes of revolutionaries, and there was thus no real hurry on the Iranian side to negotiate a return of the hostages.

This was the Carter presidency. Jimmy Carter had been elected largely as a kind of backlash against what was perceived as the excesses, corruption and constitutional violations of the Nixon years. He was the first Democrat in the White House since 1968, and Carter's homely, simple Southern Christian personality seemed like the perfect antidote to nearly eight years of Vietnam, Watergate, student rebellions, race riots, and assassinations. It looked as if it was going to be an administration of healing from the "long national nightmare" that was Watergate and the Nixon presidency.

Carter was elected in 1976, at the time of the nation's bicentennial. It had been two hundred years since a group of Freemasons and freethinkers had declared their independence from England and "fired the shot heard round the world." It was an appropriate time for America to rethink and re-invent itself. Saigon had fallen in 1975. Vietnam was the first war America had lost. Gerald Ford had been president for a short time in the wake of Nixon's resignation over Watergate. The Freemason and former male model and partner of Harry Conover—Candy Jones' first mentor and first husband—and member of the Warren Commission had not exactly covered himself in glory. He had been physically attacked twice, most famously by Manson Family member Lynette "Squeaky" Fromme, who is still in prison because of the attempted assassination, and totally unrepentant. It was time for America to take some spiritual inventory.

The Senate hearings into the CIA's abuse of its charter were one prominent feature of the Carter administration, as was his selection of Admiral Turner as CIA Director. In the wake of the Watergate revelations—which were almost too sordid for most Americans to believe—a house-cleaning of Howard Hunt's old employer seemed very much in order. As the CIA was being dragged through the mud and hoisted on its own petard publicly, particularly with respect to its domestic spying activities under Nixon, Turner found he had the mandate he needed to fire all the odd birds in the Agency that still reveled in clandestine, cloak-and-dagger espionage. It was going to be a new era, one in which less importance would be placed on HUMINT (human intelligence-gathering) and more on fancy technology and spy-in-the-sky strategies. The Admiral obviously felt that agents with decades of experience in the field could be replaced by computer keyboards and exotic cameras.

But then the Iran hostage situation changed all that.

The CIA was blamed for not knowing about the Ayatollahs' threat to the Shah's regime in advance, and for not knowing what to do about it. The CIA was blamed for the raid on the US Embassy in Teheran and the fifty-two Americans now being held by fanatic Shi'ite students in various scattered and undisclosed locations all over the city. And Carter was being blamed for not solving the problem at once.

And then, there was the oil.

The Middle Eastern situation was precarious. The creation of Israel in 1948 and the subsequent wars with its Arab neighbors had threatened not only the delicate balance of power between Capitalist and Communist, between Zionist and Arab, between America and Russia, but had also threatened the world's supply of oil. America had helped Saudi Arabia develop its enormous oil reserves since the earliest days and had wisely remained on the country's good side, supplying it with arms, the latest in aviation technology, and training for its fighter pilots, its troops, its weapons specialists. It had thus ensured a ready supply of oil regardless of what happened between Israel and Egypt—neither of whom have any oil—and watched the developing situation between Iraq and Iran carefully; it was not enough to simply control the oil reserves in Saudi Arabia and Kuwait, we had to control the reserves of Iraq (second in size only to that of Saudi Arabia) as well as the transportation of that oil from the Middle East to Europe and America. That meant control-ling the Persian Gulf, which is bordered by both Iraq and Iran, with the rich oilfields of Kuwait especially vulnerable to Iraqi attack. If these two fought each other, the US could side with either one, or both, and thus be assured of access to the Gulf for its giant tankers. If they banded together, however, they could decide to make life miserable for oil exports, just as OPEC did for a short time during the famous "Energy Crisis" of the Carter administra-tion, until the unity between the oil producing nations fell apart and the oil embargo failed.

Many a book could be written—and many have—on Middle Eastern oil politics, and we will not go into all of that now. The taking of the American hostages was but another chapter in the ongoing saga of oil, race, religion, and history in a region that has been called everything from a tinderbox to a dynamite keg ... to the cradle of civilization. (And, oh, how that cradle will rock!) What we will examine here instead, and in brief, is the famous incident known to historians and conspiracy theorists as the "October Surprise."

LIVES IN THE BALANCE

In a replay of the Nixon–Chenault–Thieu secret arrangement to torpedo the peace talks and thereby prolong the Vietnam War in 1968—to assure that Humphrey and the Democrats would not taste victory at the polls—there is evidence that the Reagan–Bush campaign pulled the same stunt in 1980, to keep the hostages in Iran until after the November election, thus ensuring the defeat of the Democrats once again. In addition, just as the Nixon strategy in 1968 ultimately led to five more years of American involvement and American and Vietnamese deaths in Vietnam, the Reagan–Bush strategy in 1980 culminated in the Iran-Contra Affair, as advisors answerable to the President decided to ignore Congress and do what they could to aid the Contras in Nicaragua while at the same time providing weapons to Iran in exchange for the hostages. Once again, a sitting President's policy—being effected at the highest levels of international diplomacy, with many lives at stake not to mention the nation's foreign policy direction—was subverted by a political challenger to gain advantage in an election. In other countries, going behind the president's back and cutting a secret, separate deal with a foreign power would be called treason; in the America of the 1960s and '70s, it was business as usual.

The basic story of the October Surprise is as follows:

As Carter tried desperately to resolve the hostage crisis, his efforts were being undermined by a coalition of Republicans, Iranians and Israelis. When the Shah was deposed on January 16, 1979, ending thirty-seven years of rule, the Ayatollah Khomeini was back in Teheran two weeks later on February 1 (Candlemas). On November 4, students took over the US Embassy in Teheran. On April 7, 1980, President Carter froze Iranian assets and enforced an arms and trade embargo against Iran. This made Iran vulnerable to an Iraqi attack. Furthermore, much Iranian military equipment was of US origin and needed US-made spare parts. Israel had a large inventory of exactly the spare parts Iran needed, and they urgently wanted to sell those parts to the Iranians. Carter's embargo against Iran made that impossible … or, at least, very difficult.

And then, on September 22, 1980—the autumnal equinox—Iraq went to war against Iran.

Iran's backdoor contacts with Israel, coupled with Reagan's rising popularity in the polls, coalesced to form a cabal that would destroy Carter's chances for re-election. There is a controversy about who first contacted whom to set the covert operation going, but it was a *menage* made in heaven. The Israelis were able to sell arms to Iran, Iran got the arms they needed, and the Republicans were able to ensure that the hostages would remain hostages until after the election. Initial meetings were undertaken between Iran and the Republican Party in Madrid in late July of 1980, at the Hotel Ritz. William Casey—soon to be head of the CIA under Reagan—was present, as well as two other Americans using aliases, and a delegation from Iran. Interestingly, an Iranian delegate had met a only few weeks previously with a representative of the Carter White House, also in Madrid, on the 2nd of July. This developed into what appeared to be improving relations between Carter and Iran that September, which could have led to the release of the hostages before the election. However, Casey's machinations insured the failure of that.

Much ink has been spilled over the question of an October Surprise. The journalism that has appeared supporting either side of the issue has been flawed, or has not presented enough unequivocal evidence one way or another to close the case. It would seem virtually impossible to get this kind of closure, considering the people and organizations involved. Naturally, had the Republicans been actively involved in an attempt to cut a secret deal with a foreign government to win an election, they would not have left a lot of paperwork around as evidence; conversely, they would have covered their tracks very well with considerable planning before any meetings or telephone contacts, etc. Similarly, the Iranians would have no interest in proving or disproving any allegations and neither would the Israelis. The CIA isn't talking, and the US government has not been able to prove a case against the very people who claim that the October Surprise *did* happen.

Its attempts to convict Richard Brenneke and Ari Ben-Menashe of perjury—accusing them of lying about their testimony in connection with the events of the October Surprise—ended in acquittal for both men. Thus, in the eyes of the American legal system, Brenneke and Ben-Menashe were either telling the truth ... or, at least, they were not lying! In Brenneke's case, during a trial for his friend Heinrich Rupp in 1988, he "declared under oath that he had attended one of a series of meetings in Paris in late October 1980 where William Casey, Donald Gregg, and other American, Iranian and French individuals had convened to discuss the release of the US hostages in Iran. He said that Rupp had told him that George Bush was also present in Paris."[5] These were important allegations, being made at the time George Bush was running for president against Michael Dukakis. The US government decided to strike back—after the election—and in May 1989 brought an indictment against Brenneke for perjury.

In order to prove its case, all the government had to do was present witnesses and documentation to show that Brenneke was lying. Incredibly, the government provided no conclusive evidence to show that any of the individuals mentioned by Brenneke were actually where they said they had been. Incredibly, because the October Surprise took place at the height of a presidential campaign in which all or most of these individuals should have been very easy to reach and to locate. Phone records alone should have been available to prove (or at least substantiate) the claims of Bush, Casey, Gregg and others that they were where they said they had been, but there was no substantiation. Eyewitnesses contradicted each other and their own stories. The prosecution was a mess.

Facing five counts of perjury, Brenneke was acquitted on each one. That does not mean that he was telling the truth, of course; but it does mean that, for some reason, the government could not prove he was lying, and that is by far the most important conclusion to be drawn from the case. At the time of the October Surprise, neither Casey nor Bush were government employees or members of the intelligence services; the records of their whereabouts would not be considered matters of national security, but subject to the normal privacy regulations covering any American citizen and capable of being examined during the course of a jury trial. But they were not. This can only lead one to surmise that these individuals were acting in some official or semi-official capacity at the time in question, and were being protected by the government.

Ari Ben-Menashe was an arms dealer specializing in the sale of Israeli-made arms to Iran at the time. He was arrested in California on charges of smuggling C-130 transport planes to Iran, was held without bond for a year, and then acquitted of all charges. At that time, bitter and angry over his treatment by the government, he began to spill all he knew—or claimed to know—about the October Surprise affair and about Iran-Contra.

One's opinion of the truth or falsehood of the October Surprise allegations depends largely on whether or not one believes the witnesses who have come forward, and that is a tricky business. Gary Sick, a former US Navy career officer and staffer on the National Security Council during three presidential administrations, wrote a book about the affair in which he concluded that the October Surprise did happen, that the Reagan–Bush administration did conspire against incumbent president Jimmy Carter, and that the hostages were held by Iran until Reagan was safely elected and inaugurated. The hostages were released within minutes of Reagan taking the oath as President of the United States. And the arms sales to Iran began in earnest in the months that followed.

As if reprising his old role during the Vietnam War, former President Nixon had traveled to London a week after Reagan's 1980 nomination at the Republican National Convention to talk to the chairman of Bristow Helicopters, Alan Bristow, who had experience in Iran as a chopper pilot, and who had once planned a commando raid in Iran to retrieve the company's helicopter fleet.[6] Nixon met with Bristow at the US Embassy in London, and asked how feasible it would be to plan a second attempt at rescuing the Iranian hostages. Carter's first attempt, on April 25, 1980, had ended in disaster, with Delta Force commandos stranded in the desert as their helicopters crashed and burned during a sandstorm. It was generally believed that Carter would not make a second attempt, and instead was pursuing diplomatic means to resolve the crisis. Nixon was in London to arrange a non-governmental rescue attempt, presumably on behalf of the Republican Party. The plan was eventually dropped, because it would have required access to up-to-the-minute military intelligence on the hostage situation which even the Republican Party did not have, revealing that this was a private attempt to rescue the hostages and not an official one. Why, for instance, would Nixon have gone to a firm outside the United States to contract this mission if it had the blessing of the US president? Why abort the mission when Reagan would have had all the access he would need to military intelligence come January? There can be no other conclusion than that this was a separate initiative, undertaken by Nixon at the behest of the Reagan–Bush campaign and without the knowledge or consent of the Carter administration. It was a fallback option, a contingency plan should the negotiations with Iran in Madrid and Paris fall through for any reason. And Nixon would have been the perfect person for it, experienced as he was with the Thieu–Chennault arrangement of 1968, and his given general attitude towards Constitutional niceties during his years as President.

The rest, as they say, is history. Carter was roundly defeated at the polls, Reagan was elected, the hostages were immediately released, and Iran-Contra began to get up a nice head of steam.

What interests us about the October Surprise and the development of the plan into what eventually became known as Iran-Contra is the involvement of some of the strangest people ever to become associated with American politics—which, as the attentive reader may agree, is quite an accomplishment. In this case, we are talking about the woman who first blew the whistle on October Surprise with a book of the same title, a woman who worked for the Reagan Administration and who resigned her staff position, charging sexual harassment: Barbara Honegger.

Incredibly, Barbara Honegger brings us back again full circle to the weird, post-war group that first attracted our attention in Book One: the Round Table of Andrija Puharich, the same Round Table whose members were inexplicably linked to the assassination of President Kennedy. For it was Puharich, Honegger, accused murderer Ira Einhorn, and nuclear physicists Saul Paul Sirag and Jack Sarfatti who formed a nucleus of another sort in the 1970s, and who brought The Nine back to life—and back in operation—in the person of Israeli psychic and sometime intelligence agent Uri Geller. And, as we shall also see in Book Three, it is Sarfatti and his confreres in the community of quantum physicists who provide us a working model of the sinister forces we have been chasing so assiduously thus far.

RETURN OF THE NINE

In 1968, when the political situation in the United States was in turmoil, visionaries assassinated, students rioting, and Nixon cutting secret deals to win the election, Andrija Puharich met Ira Einhorn. Puharich at this time was heavily involved in paranormal research, but—due to his academic credentials as well as his status as something of an inventor (his specialty was electronic hearing-aid devices and, some say, electronic implants)—he was respected by those scientists whose broadmindedness encompassed the possibility of paranormal abilities such as ESP and psychokinesis. At the time he met Einhorn, he was "doing research in connection with the Atomic Energy Commission, working with the head of biophysics"[7]: Puharich, as usual, working with the paranormal but always under the aegis of a classified project of some kind, either for the military, the intelligence agencies, or other—equally secretive—government organizations, such as the AEC. Einhorn, who would later be indicted and eventually (in 2002) convicted for the murder of his girlfriend Holly Maddux, was something of a New Age entrepreneur at the time. He had read Puharich's *Beyond Telepathy,* a book that posited a connection between energy and information, and felt that it was one of the most important books of the decade. It was out of print by 1968, and Einhorn wanted to help Puharich find another publisher and get it back in print. The two then developed a close working relationship for a while, which was further energized by Puharich's discovery of Uri Geller in Israel in 1971.

Jack Sarfatti, on the other hand, had been a gifted child who won a scholarship to Cornell to study physics in 1956, when he was only seventeen years old. In 1953, however, and during the same year as Puharich and the Round Table were in contact with The Nine, Sarfatti had been getting strange phone calls at home. Much later, Puharich's book, *URI,* brought it all back. Sarfatti's mother began reading the book—which contains a description of the Round Table séances with the Dr. Vinod who channeled The Nine—and suddenly recognized the symptoms. She brought the circumstances to her son's attention and the memory of the strange phone calls came back in full force.

Sarfatti had been getting calls from someone speaking in a strange, metallic voice stating that it was the voice of a computer aboard a spacecraft hovering over the earth. These calls went on for a while, and would cause the young Sarfatti to wander around dazed. Evidently, the memory of the calls receded into his unconscious as he pursued his career in nuclear physics, and only the book by Puharich about Uri Geller brought it all back. The Nine claimed to be aboard a spacecraft, hovering over the earth, called Spectra. Sarfatti himself seemed selected at a very early age for something of importance. He was being tutored in a separate program for gifted children by a founder of American MENSA, Walter Breen, in a program that was funded (at least in part) by the Sandia Corporation. Some of this extracurricular training included lectures on patriotism and anti-Communism: heady stuff for a bunch of thirteen-year-olds. It would be Breen who would recommend Sarfatti for the Cornell scholarship.

There is a lot of Sarfatti email correspondence available on the Internet, much of which is concerned with quantum mechanics and nuclear physics in general, but some of which has to do with the events surrounding Spectra and The Nine. There are times when Sarfatti is obviously doubtful about the communications, wondering if they were the product of some bizarre sort of intelligence agency mind-control program. As Puharich was obviously involved in the series of séances which invoked The Nine at the same time as Sarfatti was getting the phone calls (which mirrored the information the Round Table was getting), there is at least the possibility that the calls were made by Puharich or by one of his associates (possibly Breen himself) as part of some wider program.

The fact that Puharich would also arrange long-term psychic experiments involving children at his farm in upstate New York in the 1970s gives one pause, considering the long military and intelligence background of Puharich. Were the 1970s experiments an outgrowth of whatever was happening to Sarfatti in the 1950s? Sarfatti does not seem convinced one way or another that the calls he received were extraterrestrial in origin (The Nine, or Spectra), or the result of a man-made intelligence trick; he is only certain (as is his mother) that he received them. One of the predictions made in the calls was that in twenty years he would become involved with a group of people whose mission was the acceleration of human evolution through contact with these otherworldly agencies. This is exactly what happened, for in 1973 he began to develop contacts with other, like-minded, scientists through the Stanford Research Institute (SRI) and eventually with Puharich himself. These contacts would eventually culminate in a business venture in the 1980s with Harold Chipman, a CIA Chief of Station in San Francisco, who was involved with SRI and the paranormal testing that went on there with Puharich and Geller, as well as with Russell Targ, Harold Puthoff, Ingo Swann, and the whole murder of crows that formed the most strictly controlled investigation of psychic phenomena that the United States had ever known.

The documentation concerning Sarfatti's relationship with Chipman (including Chipman's resume, which tantalizingly speaks of his language capabilities in Spanish, Mandarin Chinese, and … Tibetan) is available on Sarfatti's own website, as are huge strings of email exchanges on everything from Puharich and Geller and The Nine to discussions of quantum physics that are so arcane that amateurs are advised to keep their dignity intact by simply reading and not responding, as anyone who claims to add to the discussion is likely to be attacked if one can't back up one's statements with solid physics. There is no index to these exchanges, and many are very hard to decipher, as there are quotes within quotes within quotes from the correspondence that would require a Houdini to unravel; but the effort is usually well rewarded with some interesting bits of history.

In the 1970s, however, when Sarfatti was still developing the theories that would later make him famous in the world of physics, he was hanging out with Puharich, Uri Geller, and other notables in a hothouse atmosphere of radical thinking about science, communication, information, and psychic phenomena. Sarfatti claims to have introduced Geller to Jacques Vallee—the French UFO researcher of *Passport to Magonia* fame—and both to Steven Spielberg. Spielberg would later produce *Close Encounters of the Third Kind*, using Vallee as a technical adviser: Vallee the Anton LaVey to Spielberg's Roman Polanski. The character played by Francois Truffaut in the film is said to be based on Jacques Vallee himself. This same nexus of Puharich and Sarfatti is said to have influenced Gene Roddenberry in his development of the *Star Trek* television series. And behind all of this is the hugely influential figure of Ira Einhorn, usually referred to as "the Unicorn" after the translation of his surname into English.

For a while, Einhorn served as Sarfatti's literary agent (as he did with Puharich to get *Beyond Telepathy* reprinted). Einhorn was active in New Age pursuits, a kind of showman or P.T. Barnum of hippiedom, making connections and networking, bringing together people he felt should be brought together to create a kind of explosion of new thinking that cut across traditional disciplinary lines. So you had filmmakers talking to physicists, psychics talking to soldiers, and spies talking to everybody. Seminars were held, books and papers published. People like science-fiction author Philip K. Dick (who was discovered by Hollywood in the 1990s, unfortunately *after* his death) and Robert Anton Wilson could be found in *kaffeklatsch* with Timothy Leary, John Lilly, Saul Paul Sirag, and assorted G-men. There was a sense among these people that an event of momentous importance to the planet was imminent, and that they were in the forefront of whatever it was going to be.

Many of them had already had paranormal contacts of some sort (a list that includes Sarfatti, Wilson, Dick, Geller, Puharich, and many, many others) and were certain that these contacts signalled the beginning of a more overt presence by these beings. These were people with government grants and contacts at the highest levels of the US military ... and not only the US military. The Soviets were also involved, if only peripherally. And much of this was going on relatively un-noticed by the American people at large. Although they had seen Uri Geller bend spoons on national television, and had read the stories and novels by Dick and Robert Anton Wilson, for instance, they had no idea that all this activity was being produced by a loosely-organized group of intellectuals operating half-in, half-out of the mainstream ... and half-in, half-out of the US government. And it was not until 1974, with the publication of Puharich's book about Uri Geller, that anyone outside a small circle of friends and associates had ever heard anything about The Nine.

Now, one of the members of this loose association of physicists, psychics and spies was Barbara Honegger. Honegger's entry pass was a master's degree in the paranormal that she obtained from John F. Kennedy University. A somewhat peripheral figure in the Einhorn/Puharich/Sarfatti circle, she was for a time the girlfriend of physicist Saul Paul Sirag, who was a frequent contributor to the group. From there, she went on to greater glory as a Reagan staffer who had quit his administration over charges of sexual misconduct. She then published a book on the October Surprise, which earned her a great degree of vitriol from Republican congressmen who characterized her as someone who dressed as a "bunny rabbit" at staff meetings and who listened to voices in her head: clearly sexual abuse of a different kind. It was Honegger's book that triggered NSC staffer Gary Sick to write his own account of the October Surprise, and the groundswell of paranoia began to grow anew.

As if this story needed to get any stranger, Honegger then—according to accounts published on the Internet—befriended the wife of one of the Iran-Contra pilots, Gunther Russbacher; and now we are well and truly in over our heads.

Gunther Russbacher is not mentioned in many books on Iran-Contra for the simple reason that he was not an active participant in the arms-for-hostages negotiations with McFarlane, Secord, North and the others. He was, however, on the flight crew of the aircraft that took 400 TOW missiles to Iran in September 1985, and then was on deck again for the famous flight of Robert McFarlane, Oliver North and their staff to Teheran in May of 1986. He is identified as ONI (Office of Naval Intelligence) in Iran-Contra related correspondence, as was his colleague on these flights, Robert Hunt.

A letter to Robert Hunt from Moshe Ben-Manash, Special Envoy to the Israeli Ambassador to Washington, dated November 11, 1993, confirms the presence of Robert McFarlane, Oliver North, Robert Hunt, George Cave, Howard Teicher, Gunther Russbacher and John R. Segal on a flight that left Israel loaded with one pallet of spare parts for the Hawk missile system. Russbacher and Segal (the latter identified as CIA) are mentioned as the pilots of the aircraft.

Other documentation shows that Russbacher was the pilot for the initial shipments of TOW missiles to Iran in August and September 1985, and that Poindexter advised Bill Casey, the Director of the CIA, that a confidential account had been set up for Russbacher, Segal and the other staffers of the May 1986 Teheran flight, with the implication that these funds would be used to compensate their families in event that the mission ended in disaster.

Several years later, Gunther Russbacher married a woman who believes herself to be descended from royalty, a woman who also believes that she and her brother were experimented upon by the government when they were children, who believes that her eggs were taken from her when she was eleven years old, etc. Her stories—available on the Internet through various sites—are a bizarre trip through a very disturbed psyche. She recounts events whose participants are all high-ranking US government personalities—engaged in weird, uncharacteristic behavior involving Templar chapels, underground submarine bases, and the like—and an individual introduced to her as the "King of the World." The events resemble those of an early Bond film, but without John Barry's score. The unsettling thing about her reminiscences is that she often mentions people and events from the covert world in a perfectly nonchalant and matter-of-fact way. Even though her tales are outrageous, the little details are quite unnerving.

As an example, consider a posting on the Internet dated 9 Nov 1998:

> Gunther and I drove directly to Offutt Air Force base in Omaha. We stayed in VIP quarters. William Webster, the DCI was on one side of us. Brent Scowcroft, the NSA, was on the other side. George Bush was across the hall, and Dick Cheney was at the end of the hall.
>
> William Webster wore red shorts and a red Hawaiian shirt.
>
> The meeting was to upgrade Gunther on his SR 71 flying so he could fly a mission to Moscow. On the mission with Gunther were Brent Scowcroft, William Webster, Gunther's boss, the DCO (Director of Covert Operations) an Admiral named Wilhelm Johann. There was a fourth passenger, but Gunther would never tell me who he was.

Thank goodness.

The events described above were said to have taken place in July of 1990. It is a little strange to see George Bush (*pere?*) and Dick Cheney mentioned in the same sentence about an event said to take place a decade before Bush's son and Cheney would wind up in the White House. Bush Sr., of course, was President of the United States in July of 1990. To be sure, the email is dated November 9, 1998 but that is still long before Bush (*fils*) and Cheney campaigned together in the 2000 election.

If you're going to invent wild stories, then this is the way to go, I guess. Drop names like mad. Add the little details that give the reader a sense of reality: I can't get that image of William Webster out of my mind. It has poisoned me on red shorts forever.

In case there are readers who feel that the story may perfectly well be true, allow me to point out that according to this same posting, Gunther Russbacher had been in prison in St. Louis for a year: he had been arrested two days after he and Rayelan were married. Gunther was released in July 1990, and the couple "drove directly to Offutt Air Base in Omaha," where Gunther was evidently immediately being trained to fly a Stealth spyplane full of the intelligence elite to Moscow. Does any of this make any sense at all? Yet, there are copies of documentation available on the Internet—including a military record of some sort from Offutt Air Base—that would seem to support this story. At least in part. At least if we can believe that the documentation itself is real.

What we do have is Rayelan Russbacher (a/k/a Rayelan Allan) performing something called the "Avalon Mystery Mass" at the Church of Antioch in Santa Clara, California; perhaps I should say "concelebrating" the said Mass, along with Matriarch Mary Spruitt, and with that we are back at the ranch, for with Mary Spruitt and the Church of Antioch we are at home and hospitality with the wandering bishops of Book One

Mary Spruitt was ordained and consecrated by her husband, Herman Adrian Spruitt, who in turn held the Vilatte succession and a number of others. He was co-consecrated by a bishop of the Liberal Catholic Church (the ecclesiastical arm of the Theosophical Society) and by a bunch of other notables, some of whom share lines of succession with the Gnostic Catholic Church of the OTO, the American Orthodox Catholic Church (of David Ferrie fame), and so on, and so forth, and so it goes. In addition to the Avalon Mystery Mass, Rayelan Allan—at least, as of 1998—was also offering something called the *Dance Enchants*, a meditation method based on "temple dancing" which also forms a part of the Avalon Mystery Mass. (According to personal correspondence with the present-day leader of the church, Rayelan Allan was indeed a *priest* of the Church of Antioch and had worked with Matriarch Spruitt, but not after 1993.) To quote from her promotional material on the Web:

DANCE ENCHANTS is a simple and easy way to experience the bliss of meditation and the beneficial spiritual and mental changes found on a disciplined spiritual path. Whoever said that enlightenment couldn't be fun?

Indeed.

Yet, here we have the intrepid Rayelan Allan Russbacher feeding information to Barbara Honegger on Iran-Contra... the same Barbara Honegger who was Saul Paul Sirag's main squeeze... who has a master's degree in parapsychology... who was an intimate of the circle around Puharich and Sarfatti and Einhorn...

...and who today is a military affairs journalist for the Naval Postgraduate School, Department of the Navy. A journalist who warned Washington a week after the September 11 attack on the Pentagon and the World Trade Center that a fifth column within the American military and justice systems—including a judge, military officers, pilots, and even Israeli intelligence—had advance warning of the attacks and did nothing to stop them, and may, indeed, have had a hand in planning and carrying out the horrendous events of that day.

It... it... boggles the mind.

UNDER GOD

Reagan's apocalyptic view of history, and his near-Manichean view of the world, was never deeply dissected by the journalists of the time of his presidency. A member of the Disciples of Christ (which was, oddly enough, the religious background of the family of his would-be assassin John Hinckley, as well as of Jim Jones of the Peoples Temple) and a profound believer in the prophecies of the Bible, particularly the Book of Revelations, Reagan saw the world in black and white terms. The Soviet Union—we all remember—was characterized as the "Evil Empire." The missile defense shield—the Strategic Defense Initiative, or SDI—he proposed to protect the United States was referred to as "Star Wars." He saw the fight against Communism as a spiritual one, one which ran the risk of demonizing those living in Communist countries. Oddly enough, however, his administration was also characterized by the intense astrological interests of his wife, Nancy, leading some of us to wonder if the Reagan administration was a hotbed of Gnosticism.

What we had in the White House at that time—and probably what attracted many Americans to the Reagans—was a First Family representative of the strangest qualities of American life (Christian fundamentalism and chiliastic panic, astrology, xenophobia masquerading as anti-Communism, and the Hollywood-movie-star heritage of both the President and his wife) packaged in a non-threatening, homely manner by a grandfatherly authority figure. Many Americans could not understand the contempt others felt for Reagan and, perhaps rightly in a way, interpreted any anti-Reagan sentiments as anti-American. His popularity would only be increased by the failed assassination attempt by John Hinckley, Jr., an attempt that promoted Reagan into a kind of Jack Kennedy manqué, thus perfecting the icon.

But to many, the Reagan presidency was an assault on all that the Kennedy administration had represented. Many remembered Reagan's cooperation with the House UnAmerican Activities Committee during the McCarthy era. Many viewed his career as Governor of California with alarm, particularly his support for a proposed center to study violence that had all the earmarks of a concentration camp for undesirables. Critics of the far left, in a bit of self-conscious humor, began to equate Reagan with Regan, the demon-possessed character in *The Exorcist*. When it was discovered that Reagan's assailant—John Hinckley, Jr.—was the son of the *same* John Hinckley who had a meeting scheduled with Neil Bush (one of the Vice President's sons) the *same day* that Reagan was assaulted, conspiracy theories began to blossom once more in the land. That cynical 1980 campaign button—"Shoot Bush First"—suddenly took on a cautionary and prophetic meaning.

Before the Hinckley assassination attempt, however, another murder was being planned. We know the victim; we know the man who pled "guilty," and thus avoided a murder trial where evidence could have been presented in the glare of public scrutiny. What we don't understand is the motive; or, we suspect the motive and it is monstrous.

LET ME TAKE YOU DOWN

"You're not a saint. I'm not a saint. Yoko's not a saint. Nobody's a saint."
—John Lennon[8]

"I'm the Devil, and I'm here to do the Devil's business."
—Charles Watson

"...would you kindly inform [Charles Manson] that it was Paul McCartney who wrote 'Helter Skelter', not me."
—John Lennon[9]

It was a few weeks after the election. Reagan had just been elected President, and former CIA Director George Bush was elected Vice President. If we believe the conspiriologists, the Reagan plan to subvert the election process and deal directly with the Iranians on the subject of the hostages had worked. The hostages, however, had not yet been released. That would not happen until the day of the inauguration, a month away.

The mother of all conspiracy theorists—Mae Brussell—believed that the deaths of rock stars Jimi Hendrix, Janis Joplin, and Jim Morrison were in reality political assassinations, carried out in an attempt to defuse the counter-culture revolution, which was the only movement actively challenging the establishment on issues such as racism, the environment, sexual morality, the war in Vietnam, etc. She associated the premature deaths of the rock-and-roll icons of the Sixties with the Manson killings, believing they were all of a piece: an attempt to destroy the youth movement and pull America into line by a gray flannel assembly line of right thinkers and right believers, feeding the war machine.

However, I have found it difficult to subscribe to this theory, as attractive as the sentiment behind it may be. The history of rock-n-rollers is littered with the "exquisite corpses" of men and women who lived life at the very edge of human experience and who took tremendous chances—with their bodies, their minds, and their souls—and courted death by the very manner of their lives. Buddy Holly, the Big Bopper, and Ritchie Valens in that terrible airplane crash seemed to set the standard for the mayhem that would follow: Elvis Presley's demise from the inevitable complications due to his larger-than-life lifestyle, and on and on, from the senseless deaths from overdose and suicide of the sixties through to Kurt Cobain and the other tragedies of the nineties. It is too easy to hold a dark government plot responsible for these deaths, especially without a shred of evidence when, in fact, the evidence that exists all points in a different direction.

Yet it is when we begin to examine the slaughter of the rock stars that we come close—not to a specific conspiracy, but—to those sinister forces we have been tracking, forces that lurk behind the events in question. This is a study that goes deeper than the "deep politics" of Peter Dale Scott. It is, perhaps, closer to what the Italians mean when they speak of *dietrologia* or the "science of the left hand"; for that is what "sinister" means, anyway.

Before, however, we jump from our cautiously established platform of conspiracy and coincidence, built so carefully, throughout *The Nine* and herein, decade by decade and century by century, we must stop once more to pick at another thread in our study of scarlet. For of all the dead rock stars, there was one whose premature death was most clearly a murder and an assassination. This was not a rock star embarked on a hazardous journey of drink, drugs and exhaustion, but a man clearly comfortable with himself and his surroundings, a husband and father, a calm and rational human being who was at the brink of a comeback after a decade of silence. A man whose killer prayed to Satan hours before the trigger was pulled and who—Larry Layton-like, Sirhan Sirhan-like, Dan White-like—walked robotically through the motions of murder, in a trance-like daze, and found himself in police custody, staring bewilderedly out at the world from within a tiny closet of darkened dreams.

We are discussing, of course, John Lennon and the events of December 1980.

I never met John Lennon or his wife, Yoko Ono, although as a New Yorker I was frequently privileged to see them both around town. Eerily, a few years after John's death, I would find myself constantly running into Yoko on the street with an array of bodyguards in tow (Yoko, not me); but, as a typical New Yorker, I never approached either of them for an autograph or attempted to speak with them. We New Yorkers, you see, feel we are much too cool to approach celebrities; such behavior is reserved for tourists.

Or for assassins like Mark David Chapman.

Many people are aware that the Beatles had had a fling with mysticism back in the 1960s, and that with George Harrison it "took," and he became a lifelong Buddhist until his death, a passing that included the chanting of prayers by Buddhist monks. The gallery of photographs on the cover of the Sergeant Pepper album of "people we like" included Aleister Crowley. Yet of all the Beatles, probably John Lennon was the most cynical, the most skeptical. It was he, after all, who uttered the immortal line, "The Beatles are more popular than Jesus." It was a simple observation rather than a declaration of faith, but one which resulted in Beatles albums being burned across America's Bible Belt. His signature song, "Imagine," asks us to imagine that there is no heaven and no hell. In his conversation with Paul Krassner, quoted above, he immediately rejected any reference to anyone as a "saint." The conversation in this case concerned Mae Brussell. In a bizarre twist of fate, it was John Lennon who financed conspiracy queen Brussell's first published article, when Paul Krassner found that his printer, alarmed by the contents of the article, insisted on being paid up-front.

What many do not know about John and Yoko, however, is that they were fascinated with the occult.

John's approach seems much more in line with a no-nonsense attitude towards spirituality: he accepted that spiritual realities existed, but denied the authority of organized religions and cults to determine who should believe what. Occultism is a mechanical approach to spirituality; faith is not as large a component in western magical practice as it is in western religion. A religious person drives a car without knowing anything about its engine; an occultist is a mechanic who is not satisfied until he or she understands the machine and can, perhaps, build a better one.

Which may explain the visits of John and Yoko to the Magickal Childe Bookstore in Manhattan in the 1970s.

At that time, I was friendly with Herman Slater, the proprietor of the store, and had known him since the days when he ran the Warlock Shop in Brooklyn Heights where I lived. As the fame and notoriety of his establishment grew—being covered extensively in the overseas press as well as by local newspapers and television shows—he began to attract an equally notorious clientele. The Process would hang out at the Warlock Shop, as well as the odd Satanist and witches of various denominations. The Shop is alluded to several times in Maury Terry's *The Ultimate Evil* as a hangout for people who knew more about the Son of Sam murders than they were telling. And, amidst all of that publicity, would occasionally arrive John and Yoko Lennon.

Their tastes ran more to Egyptology in those days, and they would typically spend hundreds of dollars on books in a single visit. They didn't ask any questions; they knew what they wanted. They would show up during the middle of a weekday afternoon, a time when there were few other shoppers, and take their time going up and down the aisles in relative peace and quiet. We later learned that Yoko was very fond of fortune tellers, and had one or two that she relied upon extensively. In the years directly following the murder of her husband, she seemed to rely upon them even more.

I even invoked the "forces of darkness." I don't mean a demon with a tail and horns, but as a religious person I believe there are spiritual powers in the world and an evil side of the spirit. The point is I did the invoking, so the responsibility is mine.
—Mark David Chapman[10]

John Lennon is dead. The world is over. Forget it. It's just gonna be insanity…
—John W. Hinckley, Jr., taped on Dec. 31, 1980.

Mark David Chapman is something of an enigma. The back story to his assassination of Lennon does not really compute: the trip around the world, the work for the YMCA that is missing from their files, the visit to war-torn Beirut, the trips back and forth between New York City and Honolulu, the story about the "Little People" in his head, his abrupt decision to plead guilty and avoid a trial … all of these things put together make him look uncomfortably like your standard political assassin or serial killer. Like Lee Harvey Oswald and James Earl Ray. Chapman seemed to have had access to funds for overseas travel that are not accounted for by a salary. (Hinckley also traveled extensively throughout the United States in the weeks leading up to his attempt on Reagan's life, flying from New Haven—where Jodie Foster was going to school at Yale—to Nashville, Denver, Washington, etc.) Oswald lived in Russia. Chapman attempted to visit Russia… but opted for Beirut, instead. He spent time in Korea—as did Oswald, of course, and David Berkowitz (the "Son of Sam")—but not in the military; his employer was the YMCA. Chapman worked among Vietnamese refugee children at Fort Chaffee in 1975, as the Vietnam War came to a close. He used a Charter Arms .38 revolver when he shot Lennon: the same weapon favored by Arthur Bremer. He was hospitalized for mental illness in Hawaii after a suicide attempt; Oswald was briefly hospitalized for mental illness (after *his* suicide attempt) in Moscow. And, like Oswald, Berkowitz, and so many others, he never stood trial, thus cheating history of a public debate over the evidence.

There seems to be no doubt that Chapman did indeed pull the trigger of the gun that killed John Lennon. In fact, he stood around and waited for the police to arrive, calmly reading *The Catcher In The Rye*, that coming-of-age novel by former US Army intelligence officer J. D. Salinger. What is missing is a coherent motive. Of course, one does not need a motive in order to convict a killer if one has all the other evidence available including, in this case, eyewitnesses, the murder weapon, and a confession. What is under scrutiny here is not whether or not Chapman fired the weapon that killed Lennon. (Thankfully, since the ballistics evidence in the case of Lee Harvey Oswald, James Earl Ray and even Sirhan Bishara Sirhan has been attacked repeatedly by critics, and the ballistics evidence linking David Berkowitz to all of the Son of Sam killings is likewise very weak.) What *is* being questioned is the phenomenon of Mark David Chapman himself, and the strange coincidence in the timing of a murder of someone who could have been a very big fly in the ointment of a Reagan administration that was just coming into power.

John Lennon had been out of the mainstream for five years. Content to be a house-husband and father to young Sean Lennon, John did not record or even write many songs in the period 1975-79. He was not politically active. He had fought a hard battle with the American Immigration and Naturalization Service in order to remain in the United States—specifically New York City, a place he loved more than any other—and won … during the Carter administration, when heavy FBI and CIA surveillance on Lennon as a "dangerous extremist" was switched off. He and Yoko moved into the Dakota Apartments on Manhattan's Upper West Side, and therein the murky correspondences begin to merge.

The Dakota Apartments, of course, is where Roman Polanski filmed *Rosemary's Baby*. It is a beautiful, pre-War building with large rooms, high ceilings, and outrageous rents. The Lennons would eventually wind up owning four apartments at the Dakota, taking over the entire seventh floor.

The Dakota was so named because when it was built it was considered so far away from the city center that it might as well be in Dakota. At that time, the late nineteenth century, Dakota was still a territory of the United States and had not yet split into two states. Oddly, the very word "Dakota" will re-emerge in our investigation, linked to the Son of Sam cult, which links us to the Manson Family and thus right back to Roman Polanski and *Rosemary's Baby*. Another cult, this time including some well-known European fashion designers, was known to be operating in Manhattan out of another building, similar to the Dakota and called it's "sister building." This cult was linked to at least one death, that of a young woman who plummeted out of an apartment window à la the character in *Rosemary's Baby*. For now, however, let us look more closely at the sinister forces swirling around John and Yoko Lennon, forces that would work very hard indeed to ensure that Mark David Chapman and his Charter Arms .38 revolver were in the right place at the right time.

The problem inherent in most histories is not that they merely accumulate facts and details and stretch them into a narrative that purports to tell the truth of what actually happened; the problem is in what is kept in and what is left out. Histories must be essentially synopses of what transpired, with focus on the high points: when a certain battle was fought, or how many votes were cast, etc. We are then reassured that in this pile of data we are seeing what actually happened; it is a bit like summing up a marriage by reciting the date and venue of the ceremony, how many years the union survived, and how many offspring it produced. Documents are necessary, of course. They represent the skeletal matter of the corpse being examined. But there are documents, and there is blood.

The American attitude towards the concept of blood sacrifice is one of mixed incredulity and horror. Incredulity that such a thing as blood sacrifice actually exists anywhere in a civilized society, and especially in America; horror at the very concept of slaughter in the name of religion. The reaction of America during the "satanic cult survivor scare" of the 1980s is very revealing; some Americans firmly believed that an organized network of Satanists was stealing children—or breeding them deliberately—for use in ritual sacrifice. Other Americans immediately rejected the idea as absurd. Both, of course, were ill-informed.

Those who believed in the stories simply confabulated movie plots with reality and didn't bother to ask some of the obvious questions: where did the babies come from? Where are the bodies? Why is there no record of such widespread child snatching? Etc. Those who did not believe in the stories rejected evidence showing that many Americans are, indeed, involved in religious systems which prescribe blood sacrifices and that blood sacrifice is carried out on a daily basis in the country; although, of course, not of human infants. The Caribbean and South American religions of santeria, macumba, candomble, palo mayombe, voudoun and many others regularly sacrifice animals during the course of their rituals. In Haiti, human sacrifice did take place—euphemistically referred to as "the hornless goat" sacrifice—right through the nineteenth century, at least. Muslims practice animal sacrifice at specific times of the year, most notably during the Hajj: the pilgrimmage to Mecca, when hundreds of thousands of lambs are slaughtered. Hindu worshippers also incorporate animal sacrifice into their rites, and the altars dedicated to Kali are often awash in the blood of victims. As late as the nineteenth century (and, some say, the twentieth) the Hindu cult of the Thuggee also prescribed human sacrifice to honor their goddess, Kali; and also until very recently it was common for women to throw themselves on the funeral pyres of their husbands in a rite known as *suttee*, now officially banned but which still occurs with some frequency in the countryside.

In Malaysia, the newspapers often carry stories about human sacrifice taking place today. Some small cults have used human sacrifice as a means of ensuring lottery wins, and the bodies of several Caucasians murdered for that purpose were discovered in one village in 2001, their skulls used as ritual implements of power.

In South America and in the South Pacific, special laws were enacted—and enforced—to stop aboriginals from practicing head hunting and some related cannibalistic practices. There are men still alive today in Borneo (for instance) who regularly tasted human flesh.

And, of course, the Christian Eucharist is a celebration of sacrifice in which the congregants eat the flesh and drink the blood of Jesus Christ. There are today roughly one billion such God-eaters on the face of the earth.

David Ferrie, the American Orthodox Catholic bishop and anti-Castro gunrunner, practiced a form of voudoun in his apartment in New Orleans (North America's capitol of voudoun), killing chickens and calling on African gods while at the same time plotting to murder a President. Was Papa Doc Duvalier correct in stating that *he* had engineered the Kennedy assassination? Did voudoun call to voudoun, like blood calling to blood? Ferrie, with his white rats in cages, looking for a cure for cancer, not realizing that the cancer in America's soul was deeper than rat and syringe could cure.

Thus, the American attitude towards blood sacrifice is complex. The American tradition of political assassination is perhaps an eruption of this atavistic impulse, refined in the alembic of the Industrial Age to produce sacrificial rites where the feudal-era knife has been discarded. The machinery of the gun takes its place as the ritual implement of choice, not quite as emotionally satisfying, perhaps, as the visceral stabbing of the victim, but nonetheless effective and emblematic of the Western colonization of an entire continent where the firearm dominated over the bow and arrow and the tomahawk; and emblematic of the way America has developed since then, a nation of watchers-from-afar.

These grizzly scenes of political murder were recorded on video cameras and played out on television newscasts, just as Aztec rites were performed in public high on the pyramids of Teotihuacan along the Avenue of the Dead. The Eucharistic Mass had already prepared millions of worshippers for an "anemic" bloody sacrifice, one that takes place off-stage, behind the icon screen, on the other side of the altar rail, but whose elements are shared with the worshippers in the form of bread and wine; yet nothing is as emotionally satisfying, perhaps, as being a witness to the actual ritual death itself. Witness the public execution of Charles I, and the frenzied dipping of handkerchiefs in his blood by the mob.

That political assassination may be sacerdotal in nature, a spiritual or mystical act with all the attendant symbolism, mythology and invocation of dark forces that it implies, is not really a new notion to the American public, but perhaps it has not been described quite this way before. After all, we expect our serial killers to have mystical—if twisted—motives. Witness the murderers in the Thomas Harris novels based on his fictional "Dr. Hannibal Lecter," where our serial killer is in search of some type of personal transformation. In *Silence of the Lambs*, the killer wishes to change his sex by killing women and stripping them of their flesh and making, essentially, a "woman suit" out of their skin. He is acutely aware of the transformative aspect of his killings, for he inserts the larva of a special moth into the mouths of his victims after he is through with them.

The moth, of course, like the butterfly is an ancient symbol of transformation and regeneration through transformation. This degree of sophisticated reasoning is something the American public has come to expect from their fictional serial murderers. What is more, the villain in *Silence of the Lambs* is based loosely on the actual case of Ed Gein, who did kill women and preserve their flesh in a similar fashion. Gein was also the inspiration for the archetypal Hitchcock film, *Psycho*, in which the killer assumes the personality of his dead mother in order to perpetrate the killings, dressing in her clothes and speaking with her voice. Transgender transformation also hints darkly at the sexual nature of these crimes; the mystical element is elaborated upon by novelists, but nonetheless exists in the sexual fantasies of the actual killers themselves. Witness also Jeffrey Dahmer, perhaps the most emblematic of the ritualized serial killer with extreme sexual fantasies, cannibalism, rape, and blood lust, who designed an altar as a power center on which would be displayed the skulls of his victims … a throwback to the Borneo head hunters and the Malaysian cultists.

Why not, then, a mystical motivation for political assassins?

It seems obvious, somehow, in the choice of victims: John F. Kennedy; Robert F. Kennedy; Dr. Martin Luther King, Jr.; John Lennon. No one shoots a Jesse Helms or a Strom Thurmond. Or an Arlan Specter. Or Frank Sinatra, Dean Martin, or Donny and Marie. The victims selected are always icons of the best and the brightest, regardless of the reality of the personalities involved; or they are chosen because they threaten the politico-economic establishment. They are not trivial victims. Abraham Lincoln. Dag Hammarskjold. Olaf Pahlme. Che Guevara. No one successfully assassinated Hitler, although there were attempts. No one assassinted Mussolini; not really. He was brought down by an angry mob once the war was lost. No one assassinated Chairman Mao. Fidel Castro himself still lives, despite everyone's best attempts at the contrary.

It's the dreamers who die by an assassin's hand. Quite often, they are killed by men who are dreamers themselves.

Mark David Chapman was born on May 10, 1955 in a suburb of Fort Worth, Texas. His father was in the Air Force, a staff sergeant, while his mother was a nurse. Conspiracy theorists love that combination, of course, and believe it hints at other, stranger, connections. Whitley Strieber's father was also in the Air Force in Texas at the time of his birth, ten years previously, but in Strieber's case the Air Force base involved was Randolph, outside of San Antonio, and was the locus for the Nazi scientists who were brought over during Operation Paperclip, scientists who specialized in "aviation medicine." However, in Mark Chapman's case, the father was discharged soon after he was born and got a degree in engineering at Purdue University in Indiana before moving on to Decatur, Georgia, then Roanoke, Virginia and eventually back to Decatur, where he had been transferred by his job with the American Oil Company in Atlanta.

It's Chapman's interior life that interests us most, however. He described his private childhood fantasies to Jack Jones, who recorded them in his biography of Chapman, *Let Me Take You Down*. Instead of an imaginary playmate, Chapman had an entire kingdom full of imaginary playmates. He called them the Little People, and he was their king. If they dissatisfied him in any way, he would blow them up "and a lot of them would die," but they would forgive him later and everything would be okay. It's possible he got this concept the "Little People" from his fascination with the film *The Wizard of Oz*. He was so enthralled with this movie that when he went to New York City to kill John Lennon, he bought a still of the film that he left propped up in his hotel room.

Many commentators on Chapman and the Lennon killing focus on his identification with Holden Caulfield in *The Catcher in the Rye* since he was reading it when he was arrested in front of the Dakota, and because he flogged the book everywhere he went and to everyone he met, even "autographing" copies of the book, sometimes as Holden Caulfield. This element was picked up in the film *Conspiracy Theory*, where it is pointed out that Chapman was not the only killer to walk around with a copy of the book, and the film's plot talks of the book as a kind of mind-control trigger for selected political assassins of the MK-ULTRA variety. Before we look at that any deeper, however, we should first examine the role that *The Wizard of Oz* plays in Chapman's psyche, for we will uncover some startling clues.

With *Catcher*, Chapman can identify safely with the character of Holden Caulfield, a young man disgusted by the "phoniness" in the world, who leaves school and wanders around Central Park, eventually having a nervous breakdown and winding up in a mental hospital. With *Oz*, however, we are on shaky ground. For here Chapman identifies with Dorothy, the character played by Judy Garland. The plot of the film—based on the L. Frank Baum story of the same name about a young girl from Kansas who winds up "over the rainbow"—is similar to that of Maeterlinck's *The Blue Bird* which was, as we have suggested in Book One, the likely inspiration for the CIA mind-control project BLUEBIRD.

Dorothy is knocked unconscious during a tornado at her home in Kansas. This part of the film is in black and white. She then awakens in a different land, discovering that her house—which was picked up in the tornado—has landed on an evil witch, killing her. She finds herself surrounded by the Munchkins, a society of Little People who are grateful to her for having killed the evil witch. It is in this film that we first hear the song "Ding Dong, The Witch Is Dead," the same song that was sung at the gates of the White House when Nixon announced his resignation. Barbara Honegger was also once referred to disparagingly as a "munchkin" after her attack on the Reagan administration over the October Surprise. Thus, politically, the battle lines are drawn: Munchkins to the Left, Wicked Witch to the Right.

This, and the rest of the film until the ending, is in color.

In order to get back home, she must find the Wizard, who lives in the Emerald City. Along the way, she is befriended by a Good Witch, is targeted by another Evil Witch, and picks up a Cowardly Lion, a Scarecrow, and a Tin Man. And, as always, she is accompanied by her little dog, Toto. They must go through a haunted forest, and undertake other adventures in a very similar fashion to Maeterlinck's story, until they finally find the Wizard, who tells them he can't help them until the Wicked Witch is dead. So, off they go to destroy the witch, who has an army of flying monkeys. This done, they return to the Emerald City, and the dog, Toto, accidentally reveals the true identity of the Wizard: just a normal man hiding behind a curtain at a set of electronic controls that make him appear as a monstrous and all-powerful genie. That immortal line, "Pay no attention to the man behind the curtain," is uttered by this man, desperate to preserve his secret to the last.

The Wizard, however, proves to be wiser than even he believes he is, and the Cowardly Lion gets courage, the Tin Man a heart, and the Scarecrow a brain. Finally, Dorothy can return home by using a mantra and clicking the heels of her ruby slippers together … slippers taken from the corpse of the witch slain by her falling house … and she awakens back in Kansas. The mantra she repeats as she clicks her heels together, SS officer style: "There's no place like home. There's no place like home." A xenophobe's slogan if ever there was one. She awakens in her home (in black and white again) to her adoring family, who have all appeared in her "dream" as different individuals. There's no place like home, and there isn't a dry eye in the house.

The movie is a musical, of course, and the highlight is the most famous song from the film, "Over The Rainbow." It is a melancholy ballad about a yearning for home, but for an ideal home "over the rainbow," a kind of heaven on earth. Dorothy seeks that, but finds it instead in her own home, among her family. This is how Maeterlinck's story also ends. Although each series of adventures seems to take days and days, both hero (Tyltyl) and heroine (Dorothy) wake up in their own homes the following morning. Both hero and heroine discover that what they were seeking was always in front of them, in their own home. In Tyltyl's case, the quest was for a Blue Bird. In Dorothy's case, her ticket home was a pair of Ruby Slippers. The alchemists and tantrists among my audience will recognize the sexual symbolism immediately: blue for boys, and red for girls! More importantly, the device Tyltyl uses to "see" with enlightened vision is a diamond on his hat that he must twist in a certain direction. A diamond in the center of his head, then, is a famous Buddhist symbol, the adamantine substance; Dorothy's slippers are made from rubies. They are both precious stones and both have deeper meanings to adherents of Eastern religions as well as to practitioners of Western occultism.

Of course, there is an enchanted forest in *The Blue Bird* also, and it is as hostile to Tyltyl as the forest is to Dorothy and her friends. There are evil witches in each story. Both Tyltyl and Dorothy are accompanied by a dog. Both Tyltyl and Dorothy eventually pick up other companions along the way who are looking for their own salvation.

The message of *The Wizard of Oz*, however, can be seen in a more danger-ous light to someone like Chapman. The Wizard is obviously a "phony," not a real wizard at all but a charlatan who has been deceiving people with his showman's tricks, for his own personal gain. In the film, Dorothy unmasks the charlatan and forces him to do good deeds for the people of the city.

On the streets of New York, however, Mark David Chapman shot him with a Charter Arms thirty-eight.

We're not in Kansas anymore.

Chapman also walked the yellow brick road, just like Dorothy. He traveled around the world before meeting Lennon, and made the trip to New York City from Hawaii twice before actually pulling the trigger.

He also had his Munchkins, the "Little People" who were his subjects. In fact, the Little People had argued against his killing of Lennon and walked out on him when he told them he was going to do it. Thus, once again, the Munchkins prove themselves to be Leftists, at worst, or Democrats at best! Might it have been his affinity with the Little People in his mind that made Chapman so successful with Vietnamese refugee children during the summer of 1975 at Fort Chaffee, Arkansas?

Remember, these were days when drugs were rampant in high school halls. Lot of hippiedom. Lot of confusion. The war in Vietnam was going strong. We were lost in the forest.
—Mark David Chapman[11]

Mark was a loner in school, a type that was picked on and bullied. His mother was abused by her husband, Mark's father, and sought comfort in a close relationship with her son, whom she idolized, telling him he would be a great man some day. Mark found himself taking sides in the war between his parents, defending his mother against a remote but overbearing father. His mother would come into his room at times after being slapped around by her husband, and sleep in Mark's bed until the storm had passed.

Mark, ostracized at school and generally friendless, woke up one morning and found that there were Little People living in houses and apartments and going to work in skyscrapers … in the walls of his bedroom. He summoned them before him and ordered their assistance in protecting his mother against his father. To encourage them, he played Beatles music for them: in his head, beamed out along invisible wires to invisible speakers.

He would rock back and forth in front of the stereo and listen to the Beatles endlessly, applauding after every song as if he were at a rock concert. He had only one Beatles album, *Meet the Beatles*, and he inspected the album cover minutely, memorizing its details.

He was nine years old.

By the time he entered high school, he was undergoing substantial changes in his personality. From a clean-cut and awkward boy from a good family, he turned into a doper who cut classes and hung out with similar individuals. For once, he was part of a group and accepted. He grew his hair long, wore dirty bellbottoms that he never changed, and dropped acid and smoked grass at every chance he got. At the age of fourteen, he ran away from home and went to Florida, and lived on the beach for two weeks until his money ran out.

This episode is rather strange in its details. Mark had called a taxi service to take him to buy the airline ticket two weeks before his trip. The car that met him had two men in it. They dropped him off at a ticket office, and waited until he bought his ticket and then they drove him back, agreeing to show up in two weeks time, at five o'clock in the morning, in front of a diner, to drive him to the airport.

Strangely enough, the taxi arrived at the appointed hour with the same two men in the car. This is certainly a very odd circumstance. The boy was fourteen years old. There were two men in the taxi each time, not simply a driver. Who were these men? What were their roles? And why did they agree to meet him again at 5 A.M. two weeks in the future … and show up? The story does not make a lot of sense. Indeed, it is troubling. There is obviously more to the tale than Mark Chapman has told, and it is possible that he does not remember the incident very well; thus, it is one more strange mystery waiting to be solved.

Mark flew to Miami and took a taxi to the beach, where he hung out for some time and had a moderate series of adventures, including a walk of twenty miles to a rock concert in the Everglades under a broiling Florida sun. Eventually, a Cuban family in Coral Gables took pity on him and let him live with them for a few days before finally putting him on a bus back to Georgia.

It was the summer of 1969. Charles Manson was ordering the Tate and La Bianca killings. Jim Jones was ranting and ramping up in Ukiah, California. Everything was going to hell. And we were lost in the forest.

On October 25, 1970 Mark David Chapman had a satori of sorts. He had gone to a weekend religious retreat at the urging of a friend, the motivation being the presence of a lot of girls. It was a "charismatic fundamentalist congregation"[12] sponsored by the South Dekalb Presbyterian Church, and during the retreat they showed a film about the life of Jesus which seems to have made an impression on Mark, for he wrote down the date as if it were something significant, a "spiritual turning point."[13] On that same day, in California, Mary Bennallack was slain, the fifteenth victim of the Zodiac killer. That same month, Joel Rostau, a business associate of slain Tate-victim Jay Sebring, was murdered in New York City. The Manson Family was suspected of the crime, as they were of the death of Charlene Cafritz in Washington, D.C. the month before. Cafritz—a friend of Sharon Tate, Charles Manson, Terry Melcher and Alan Warnecke—claimed to have secret videotapes of the Manson Family, tapes that were never found. She died of a Nembutal overdose.

Cult killings went on that year, from the Zodiac killer to "Maxwell's Silver Hammer": according to Manson Family member Gypsy Share, they were responsible for the savage murder in July 1970 of two people on the beach near Santa Barbara. There was one survivor of that attack, who spoke of the killers wearing robes and chanting. And on September 18, 1970, Jimi Hendrix was found dead of a drug overdose in the London apartment of his German girlfriend, Monika Danneman. The Scotland Yard investigation documents were sealed.

Mark David Chapman had not yet become a born-again Christian. Although the date of October 25, 1970 was firmly etched in his mind as a day of spiritual importance, he returned to school and lapsed into his familiar drugged-out hippie routine. But one connection he made that weekend was to influence the rest of his life, for he met Michael MacFarland, the boy who would insist that he read *The Catcher in the Rye*.

In the summer of 1971, during the school vacation, Mark went to visit his grandmother in Ormond Beach, Florida. Still a hippie by his own standards, and still doing drugs—even though he felt a strong attraction to his new Christian friends and the comfort of religious community—he sought out other like-minded people and hung out doing drugs along the Florida coastline. It was when he returned home one day to discover that his wallet had been cleaned out by his newfound "friends" that he had a religious conversion.

"...I remember, when I realized that my buddies had gone through my wallet, feeling the lowest I had ever felt. I felt like nobody. Like nothing. Nothing at all."[14]

In the midst of his profound depression, he reached out to Jesus. He lifted his hands and asked Jesus to come to him. He described the moment to a psychiatrist at Riker's Island as a physical sensation of God entering his room, feeling a "tingling from the tip of the toe to the top of my head"[15] on his left side, for God was sitting on his left knee. Mark David Chapman had become born-again.

When he showed up for classes in the fall of 1971, he was a changed man. Gone were the hippie clothes, the dirt, the long hair, the rock-and-roll lyrics, the drugs. And gone was any fascination for the Beatles, particularly for John Lennon. He told his friends that *Imagine* was a Communist song,[16] a not unreasonable assumption for a high school junior to make. He was also incensed by Lennon's comment that the Beatles were more popular than Jesus. Like most devout Christians, he assumed that Lennon was boasting, when in fact he made the comment cynically, as his own worst critic.

The period of devout Christianity didn't last, however. Chapman was always wired a little too tight. During a typical prayer service replete with witnessing, praying, and singing, Chapman—who had written a Christian song and brought his guitar—found that there was no time or opportunity for him to play it after the three-hour-long session. The frustration grew in his heart and turned him off where the Christian prayer groups were concerned. Like discovering his "buddies" had ripped him off in Florida the summer before, Chapman felt again like nobody because the group had failed him.[17] He cast about, looking for another cause or another group, something else to join, somewhere he would be embraced.

And he found it, this Holden Caulfield manqué, as a counselor to children at the YMCA.

As he cleaned up his act, he volunteered as a counselor at the South Dekalb County YMCA and later became an assistant program director. He was, in fact, recognized as an important asset to the YMCA program. His rapport with children was tremendous. They hung around his neck, sat in a circle around him as he played his guitar, and generally just followed him around. In addition, Chapman found that he was a great fundraiser as well, and was honored by having his name "engraved on a tile above the Olympic size indoor pool that he helped build" for the YMCA.[18] Well, it wasn't his birth name, actually. It was "Nemo."

Those who remember the stories of visionary author Jules Verne will recall the figure of Captain Nemo. According to friends of Chapman at the time, he wanted the kids to call him Captain Nemo or just Nemo, and somehow the name stuck. There does not seem to be any clear explanation of why Chapman liked that particular name, except perhaps that he identified with the Jules Verne character who is an enigmatic and powerful commander living *20,000 Leagues Under the Sea*. At one point, during an awards ceremony when Chapman was being honored by the YMCA, the kids began to chant "Ne-mo! Ne-mo!" as he walked on stage to receive his award. Those were, according to Chapman, the greatest days of his life.[19]

What is astounding to a person looking, Umberto Eco-like, at the semiotics of history is the actual meaning of the name "Nemo," for it is Latin for "No one." That is, in fact, why the Verne character chooses that name rather than use his own birth name: he wanted to disguise his real identity and be known only as "Captain No One." Chapman, who all his life feared being a "nobody" a "nothing" was now universally acknowledged as such by the children, and praised for it. But sadly he never made the connection.

Indeed, as novelist Patricia Cornwell has documented in *Portrait of a Killer: Jack the Ripper—Case Closed*, even Jack the Ripper suspect Walter Sickert signed some of his famous letters to the press as "Nemo" and used "Mr. Nemo" as a stage name.[20]

Those who remember the book and the movie *The Exorcist* will recall the scene in which Father Karras attempts to decipher the strange language that the possessed child, Regan, has been screaming. He is playing a tape recording of the guttural voice over and over, until another priest tells him that the child is screaming English, backwards. When Karras plays the tape backward he hears the Devil, in response to Karras' question "Who are you?" reply, "No one. I am no one."

Chapman turned his academic career around, as well, and graduated from high school six months early. He went to live with his friend Michael MacFarland (who introduced him to *The Catcher in the Rye*) in Chicago, where the two of them entertained church groups with music and comedy routines. When this was not going anywhere, Chapman returned to Georgia and worked at the YMCA at a series of jobs, and even worked for a time at a mental hospital in Atlanta, on a floor specializing in children suffering from autism and other mental illnesses. "Little People." Then, in 1975, the YMCA sent him to Beirut.

Chapman had filled out an application to something called ICCP/Abroad, a non-profit program being run by the YMCA which placed American YMCA volunteers with foreign affiliates, as a kind of Peace Corps for YMCA camp counselors. This was in February 1975. As British researcher Fenton Bresler reveals, however, one got to choose where one was stationed. Chapman did not list Lebanon as his first choice, but rather, oddly, the Soviet Union.

He even went so far as to sign up for a Russian language course in anticipation of this trip, but was turned down at ICCP/Abroad because he did not already speak Russian. Instead, he got his second choice: Beirut.

There is no guidance available as to why this deeply committed Christian would have picked Beirut when Jerusalem was also available. No one seems to be able to give an answer to this perplexing question. Beirut was already in the throes of political upheaval and instability, and was only weeks away from full-blown civil war. Mark was one of only two people sent to Beirut by ICCP/Abroad, and he spent very little time there once the shooting started. He made a tape-recording of the small-arms fire going on outside his hotel room window, which he brought back with him and played for friends. He was obviously very shaken and paradoxically excited by this experience. From Fenton Bresler's point of view, he was sent to Beirut to be "blooded."[21]

To understand this reference, one has to remember that in 1975 Beirut was probably the CIA's largest Middle Eastern station, one responsible for intelligence activities throughout the region. One must also remember that the CIA had a history of engineering coups in the region, such as the one that placed the Shah of Iran back on the Peacock Throne. Although some researchers insist that the CIA maintained a school for the training of assassins in Lebanon, there is no proof of this available, of course. However, virtually every other Middle Eastern group with an axe to grind has had training camps in the region, and in addition the author knows of IRA and other European revolutionary and terrorist groups that trained in Lebanon during the same period.

Further, it is also known that the CIA used students studying abroad as a source of intelligence. As Bresler notes—and as anyone who was of the author's generation may remember—*Ramparts* magazine did a report on just that subject in 1967, which caused quite a furor at the time. Bresler's thesis is that Mark David Chapman was a CIA-trained assassin, and that the murder of John Lennon was political. Certainly, the timing is suggestive, as we shall see. Bresler has gone further, suggesting that a "split personality" was induced in Mark David Chapman, and that the alternate personality had only some tangential points in common with the original Mark David Chapman, such as—for instance—*The Catcher in the Rye*. Bresler's case is persuasive, and is consistent with what we already know of MK-ULTRA and other intelligence- and military-sponsored mind-control programs. Further, the target was both a cultural icon and a political figure in his own right, and someone who could have rallied American sentiments against what would become the Reagan and Bush administrations, Iran-Contra, arms-for-hostages, and the stepped-up war against the Soviet Union, a Cold War which would eventually result in the destruction-by-bankruptcy of its Communist government.

Upon his return to the States after the aborted Beirut mission, Chapman found himself at the newly-created Fort Chaffee, Arkansas, which was a kind of way station for Vietnamese refugees who had fled the fall of Saigon in April of that year. With him at Fort Chaffee was the former head of the YMCA station in Saigon, David C. Moore, who had only been in-country for about a week before Saigon fell, and who was now at Fort Chaffee helping the Vietnamese in their American orientation. This episode is ripe with significance.

Why would the YMCA have sent *anyone* to Saigon in April 1975? It was clear to even the most optimistic that the country was falling. Da Nang had fallen by March, long before Moore's arrival in Saigon. The North Vietnamese Army was advancing rapidly towards Saigon; the entire country north of the capital had already fallen. What was there to be gained by sending a brand-new administrator there at the time? It seems, in retrospect, insane. Unless there was a hidden intelligence agenda.

This same David Moore then appears at Fort Chaffee with some of these refugees, and rooms with Mark David Chapman who has just returned from … Beirut. Another falling city, resounding with sound of explosions and machine-gun fire. Together, the two were involved in some fashion with these unfortunate victims of what the Vietnamese call the "American War," ostensibly helping them in their relocation to American communities and in some cases adoption by American families.

These are only suggestive facts which, taken separately, perhaps mean little, but when taken together show the lineaments of a darker purpose. Once again, we are forced to decide whether there was a controlling governmental agency behind these events, with an agenda of its own, or whether instead these strange events are representative of a mystical nexus of deeper, unconscious spiritual forces that underlie conscious, visible phenomena. Either way, the conclusions are disturbing.

By the end of 1975, the Fort Chaffee refugee-placement program had completed its mission, and nearly 30,000 refugees had been placed in American communities throughout the United States. It was during his tenure at Fort Chaffee that Mark happened to shake the hand of President Ford, who had come to visit the resettlement camp. Thus, President Ford came into contact with some of the most notorious individuals of the late twentieth century: Mark David Chapman and would-be presidential assassin and Manson Family member Lynette "Squeaky" Fromme. Not bad for a president whose administration did not even last a single term. If we include his partnership with Harry Conover, the future husband of alleged mind-control victim Candy Jones, and his inclusion in the Warren Commission panel which effectively covered up certain aspects of the Kennedy assassination, we have a man whose history bears a bit more scrutiny

At that time, Mark had developed another, very odd, relationship with a man whose name is only given as the pseudonym "Gene Scott" in Bresler's book, but was later identified as "Dana Reeves" in the Jack Jones biography of Chapman.[22] This gentleman was an officer with a Georgia sheriff's department at the time Bresler's book was being written (1989), and it is not known where he is today, but his influence over Mark was powerful and bizarre. Chapman, who was said to despise guns and violence, became a gun enthusiast around this man and seemed to be under the control of his personality in some way. And as it turns out, it was this same mysterious individual who supplied Mark David Chapman with the hollow-point bullets he used to murder John Lennon.[23]

We don't know much more about him beyond the enigmatic references in Bresler's book, and the fact that he was with the Henry County sheriff's department as mentioned in the Jones biography,[24] but this strange mentoring of Chapman by a man from a police department resonates with the pairing of Dan Mitrione and Jim Jones: one, a police officer from a small town with an ulterior motive, and the other a young, religious man—a boy, really—who comes under his influence and then morphs from devout Christian into murderer. Both young men spent time abroad, financed by unknown sources of income, in politically unstable regimes. Both came home with palpable personality changes. Both men abandoned the Christianity of their youth, yet committed their heinous crimes in the name of a higher ideal. Jim Jones ridiculed the Bible and the concept of a "Sky God"; Mark Chapman invoked Satan in the hours before he killed John Lennon.

The implosion of Jim Jones in the jungles of Guyana was very public, very messy, and left a lot of loose ends, red herrings, and smoking guns. I think Mark David Chapman was a refinement of the same system. If Jim Jones was the "alpha" version of an experimental program, then Chapman was the "beta" release: a carefully constructed multiple personality with a tightly focused purpose, a single target, and ultimate deniability. There is evidence of the same type of sexual dysfunction in both Jones and Chapman: Jones was obviously bisexual, and had sexual relations with both the male and female members of his congregation, something of which he boasted openly and frequently—as well as constantly referring to the size of his penis—indicating in Jones some confusion over his sexual identity; documentation on Chapman's sexual relationships are somewhat murkier, but offhand references by someone who knew him during the Beirut episode seem to indicate that he was suspected of having an unhealthy interest in his young charges.[25]

His Georgia police officer friend got him a brief job as a security officer at DeKalb General Hospital,[26] and they shared an apartment in Atlanta during this time. Bresler intimates that possibly there was more to the relationship than simple friendship; the police officer was never married, but is described as handsome and Rambo-like in appearance. Others who knew the two of them during this period also indicated "complex undertones" to the relationship, which evidently continued through the Lennon assassination and well into Chapman's incarceration.[27]

Chapman's sexuality is frequently invoked as some kind of touchstone to the rest of his story, and it is worth looking at briefly. He did not have sexual intercourse until he was twenty years old, and this with a female roommate who was somewhat more worldly than he was. The fact that he was engaged to another woman at the time is said to have given Chapman an incredible feeling of guilt over this single sexual episode. He is also said to have been sexually attracted to older women, and fantasized about them being chained, naked, in a dungeon—in the basement of his high school—where they were forced to do what he wanted, which did not include intercourse but did include fellatio.[28] (This seems to be another version of the "Little People" fantasy, with Chapman in complete control over helpless victims who are forced to worship him under penalty of death. Was this then a repressed sexual fantasy, which threatened to erupt into his relations with children?)

As devout Christians, he and his fiancée struggled with the question of sexuality and prayed over it. He eventually told her about his one-night-stand with the roommate and she evidently felt betrayed by the revelation.

He tried to attend college with her at her university, but failed at that after a while, broke up with his fiancée, and wound up booking a ticket to Honolulu.

GOD'S LONELY MAN

Some commentators have written that Chapman's trip to Hawaii was for the purpose of committing suicide. Others have said that Chapman went to Hawaii for further training and indoctrination by any one of several classified military operations that were based on the islands. What we do know is that Chapman did, indeed, attempt suicide in Hawaii by means of a hose running from the exhaust pipe into the closed window of his car, but it was a pathetic and failed attempt and Chapman wound up in a mental hospital.

This juxtaposition of Hawaii and mental hospital is one that we encountered already in the case of Jim Jones. In Jones' case, the belief is that he committed himself to a hospital or clinic in Hawaii in order to avoid adverse publicity back on the mainland. Chapman would have had no such qualms. Yet, the nexus of Hawaii and hospitals comes up again in the Son of Sam case, where it was revealed that drugs were making their way onto the mainland from Hawaii by being secreted in bags of plasma. The plasma would arrive in a hospital in New York City and the drugs removed there by hospital workers who were one link in the supply chain. This trafficking in narcotics is said to be one of the main sources of income for the Son of Sam cult.

Chapman was in Hawaii at the time of the Son of Sam killings, and it is worthwhile to note that he did have access to unexplained sources of income during that time, income that helped finance his trip around the world and his subsequent flights to New York City leading up to the assassination of Lennon in 1980. In fact, one of the strangest episodes of Chapman's visits to New York was his taking a cab through the city and stopping for a few minutes at various apartment buildings where he seemed to be making pick-ups or deliveries, which makes no sense since Chapman supposedly knew no one in New York. At one point, he offered the cab driver some cocaine, which is also totally out of character for Chapman at that time (this was long after his "drugged out hippie" days in Columbia High School in Georgia) and has never been explained; but if Chapman *was* making drug deliveries in Manhattan it all begins to make much more sense: everything from the Hawaiian hospital connection to the multiple air fares to New York to the unexplained source of income to the strange cab ride and the offering of cocaine.[29] As I used to tell people in New York in the 1970s and '80s, if you overheard a conversation between two people and it didn't make any sense, it was probably about drugs.

While Chapman's murder of Lennon in New York—where the Son of Sam killings had been taking place—does not seem to be linked in any way to the Sam cult, and on the face of it appears to be a wholly-independent act, the parallels between David Berkowitz (the convicted "Son of Sam" killer) and Chapman are compelling, as we shall see.

Whatever the reason for his trip, Chapman quit his job in Atlanta, sold everything he owned, and flew to Honolulu in January 1977. After a short time there, loneliness building up inside him, he phoned his former fiancée in Georgia, and she convinced him to return, which he did ... believing it was because she wanted him back. As it turned out, she did not; she only thought she was helping him by urging him to return. Disgusted, he turned around and flew back to Hawaii.

At that point, he began to realize that he had a problem, and he phoned a suicide hotline and was eventually referred to the Waikiki Mental Health Clinic. That seemed to help somewhat, but still did not keep him from the suicide attempt with his car's exhaust on June 20, 1977, an attempt that failed when his plastic hose melted from the heat. He was eventually accepted into Castle Memorial Hospital, a private hospital run by the Seventh Day Adventist Church, where his fees were paid by the state's welfare system. He was diagnosed as being severely depressed, but not psychotic. He was released in two weeks.

Castle Memorial is located in a small town on the other side of the island from Honolulu. Mark Chapman decided to stay there and find an apartment, and was eventually hired by Castle Memorial, first as a maintenance man and then promoted to customer relations. Now we are back in the twilight zone, because—as with Jim Jones, Lee Harvey Oswald, and so many others we have come across—there seem to have been *two* Mark Chapmans.

Bresler has noted[30] that all the documentation possessed by Chapman at the time of his arrest checks out. His Hawaiian driver's license was issued in July of 1977, which is about right. The owner of the apartment where he stayed says that he did, indeed, live at the address on Puwa Place in Kailua where he said he was. Everything seems fine. Except that the owner says that Chapman was living with "a woman and three young children,"[31] and that they left owing a month's rent, had no electricity in their final month at the complex, and left the apartment in such a mess that it cost two thousand dollars to clean it up. A search of records at the post office and other agencies in Kailua failed to turn up any identification of the mysterious woman and her three children. The records of the apartment complex do not show Chapman as having lived there, even though it is the precise address on his driver's license.

This has led some researchers to believe there was a confusion, and there must have been another man named Mark Chapman involved. But how could that be? How could one Mark Chapman (in custody) show that address on his driver's license ... but not actually live there? How could the other Mark Chapman (mistaken by the landlord to be the man in custody) live there anonymously at the home of a mystery woman and her three young children, whom the apartment owner believes might have been her sisters?

Was Mark Chapman being "sheep-dipped"? Was a false story being planted, his traces obscured by conflicting records ... or no records at all? Chapman had been undergoing treatment at Castle Memorial; he told his therapist all sorts of things about his past, about Beirut, about his girlfriend in Georgia. No one seems to have known anything about him living in an apartment with four females.

Yet, at the time Bresler's book was being researched—more than five years after Chapman's arrest for the Lennon assassination—Chapman was still getting mail delivered to the apartment on Puwa Place.[32]

At any rate, on Oahu Chapman began dating again. One of his girlfriends was a woman twenty years older than he, a psychiatric nurse at Castle who was said to be an illegitimate daughter of comedian Oliver Hardy of Laurel and Hardy fame (as if this story could get any weirder). That relationship lasted for some months, until a local Presbyterian pastor convinced Mark that his relationship was immoral. Chapman would eventually move in with the pastor and his family and become reconverted to the fundamentalist form of Christianity the pastor preached. Then, in December of 1977, his parents came to Hawaii to visit. It was evidently a pleasant time for everyone, and Chapman was eager to demonstrate his newfound stability—both financial and emotional. Everything seemed to be going his way.

Then, six months later, Mark David Chapman went on a trip around the world.

According to Chapman's account, he had arranged for a loan from the hospital's credit union. The hospital has refused to confirm or deny this aspect of the case, citing confidentiality. Yet, Chapman had only been employed at Castle Memorial since August 1977. It seems unlikely that the credit union would have advanced him the money necessary for a world tour after less than one year of service. He had no other collateral that anyone has been able to discover, nothing to secure a loan that must have been a minimum of three thousand dollars by my estimation, allowing for the cheapest possible airfare and budget accommodations. Nonetheless, he was able to take leave from the hospital on July 6, 1978, for over six weeks after only ten months of employment, and, armed with his credit union loan and a thousand dollars he received from his father on Christmas, he visited Japan, Korea, Hong Kong, China, Singapore, Thailand, India, Nepal, Israel, Iran, Switzerland, the United Kingdom, France, Ireland and Atlanta, Georgia before returning to Hawaii. He stayed in YMCA youth hostels throughout the trip, armed with a letter of introduction from his old friend from Fort Chaffee days, David Moore, who was by now working for the YMCA in Geneva.

In Bangkok, he found himself spending the night with a prostitute, but otherwise his trip seemed uneventful from a sexual perspective. He did, however, see some very sobering sights in India and Nepal, and was in Iran only six months before the Shah was deposed and fled into exile. In Hong Kong, he was one of the first American tourists allowed to cross over into China, as the border had been opened the same week as his arrival.

In India, he arrived in Delhi and was able to visit the Taj Mahal and take a trip to Nepal. This meant some difficult traveling for a lone, young American: from Delhi to Agra (which is not too bad) where the Taj Mahal is located, and then up to the Nepali border across the province of Uttar Pradesh. There are trains from Delhi to Agra that accommodate the heavy tourist traffic to the Taj Mahal, and they take roughly two to three hours to make the trip. Getting to Nepal from Delhi, however, is somewhat more problematic depending on where one enters Nepal. Buses from Delhi to some of the closest border towns can take twelve hours. It is possible that he flew to Kathmandu from Delhi, but I have been unable to find any more detail about this part of his itinerary. One assumes that the local YMCA was able to arrange safe passage for Chapman. Nevertheless, he did see a cremation as well as overwhelming scenes of extreme poverty and desperation. During this world tour, he took something like 1,200 slides.

In Geneva, he met with his friend from Fort Chaffee, David Moore, and they discussed everything, including Chapman's failed suicide attempt. Moore tried to reassure his young friend, who was disappointed over his failure to finish college and get a degree, which would have enabled him to have a real career with the YMCA.

Mark Chapman arrived back in Hawaii on August 20, 1978, where he was met by his travel agent, Gloria Abe. He had been sending her postcards and letters constantly during his trip, and soon the two people found themselves in love.

Gloria Abe is the daughter of Japanese immigrants to Hawaii—her mother a Buddhist and her father a follower of the Japanese national religion, Shinto—and although she is a few years older than Chapman, she is younger in appearance. A thoughtful, patient woman with an interest in reincarnation and astrology, she was able to stand up under Chapman's constant self-doubt and erratic behavior, and even more she was moved by his religious fervor and Christian spirituality. In an eerie reminder of Jim Jones' youth, he told her that he used to preach on the streets when he was young, passing out religious tracts.[33] She found herself converting to Christianity at the same time she was falling love with him.

They were married on June 2, 1979.

Their minister was the same pastor who had re-converted Chapman to fundamentalist Christianity. At their wedding, for instance, there was no alcohol served to the one hundred or so guests. The wedding itself was not held at the pastor's church since, in fact, he did not have one. His congregation of less than thirty souls met in a room loaned to them by a local school on Sundays. As someone who worked for the Presbyterian Church in 1969 and 1970, I can attest that this was a somewhat unusual pastor and congregation. Chapman's pastor was on a mission, and his influence over Chapman seems suspect to me. Chapman's involvement with a fringe Christian operation—when surrounded by every sort of mainstream Christian denomination and observance—is of a piece with the rest of his life. Even when he became involved with the YMCA—certainly a venerable American institution, the Village People notwithstanding—it would be in a manner fraught with extreme expression and experience.

One learns to swim at the "Y," or goes on summer camp or day trips; but Mark David Chapman goes to Beirut for the YMCA as civil war is breaking out, then to Fort Chaffee to help with Vietnamese refugees in the months after the fall of Saigon. He then travels around the world, staying at various YMCA hostels and meeting his old friend from Fort Chaffee days—David Moore—in Switzerland. And, as we shall see, on his way to kill John Lennon he will spend a mysterious three days in Chicago: the same city where David Moore has by that time been reassigned, although Moore claims that he was not contacted by Chapman during that trip. Clearly, Mark David Chapman cannot do anything in an average, low-key fashion, even though most of the people who knew him describe him precisely that way: friendly, normal, responsible. Yet he pushes the envelope of his own personality, taking extreme positions on spiritual subjects, moving to Hawaii, marrying an older Asian woman, traveling throughout Asia and then to Europe on his own, dodging bullets in Beirut, working with Vietnamese refugees in Arkansas ... and still feels constantly alone, depressed, unfulfilled. Then, just when things seem to be working out okay, he swings in another direction entirely, ruining any chance he might have had for a "normal" life.

Two months into the marriage, and Chapman had prevailed upon his wife to quit her job as a travel agent and to get a job instead at Castle Memorial, where he was working. He did not like her long hours at the travel agency, and clearly seemed to want to dominate her time and to control her social interactions as much as possible. He then decided that they had to move to the other side of the island and commute to work by bus, selling off their car in the process. None of this made any sense, of course. Chapman was going out of his way to complicate his life, and that of his wife. Most people would try to move closer to their place of employment: Chapman chose the opposite strategy. Most people would, in that case, have held on to their means of transportation: Chapman sold the car, making them both rely upon public transportation.

And then, he suddenly decided he had an interest in art.

He began haunting art galleries and educating himself on art; he wound up buying some lithographs and then reselling them, borrowing money from his father-in-law, from his mother, from his credit union. It was a strange interlude. People who work in intelligence circles know that art is one way to disguise income: art is a very volatile commodity, and a painting can appreciate or depreciate in value quickly over time, or may simply become attractive to a collector who will pay more than the market price. That it was this series of transactions in art that supposedly financed Chapman's trips to New York makes one wonder, especially as the passion for art did not last long ... and especially as it seems Chapman paid back the credit union loan and the loan from his mother before his trips, while for some reason not paying back the $2,500 he borrowed from his wife's father, using that money to finance his New York travels. It is all very strange.

Then, towards the end of the art episode, he quit his job at Castle Memorial—days after the hostages had been taken in Iran—in an uncharacteristic quarrel with the human resources people over a promotion he claimed he deserved and did not get, and wound up instead getting a low-paying job once again as a security guard: on December 19, 1979, at an apartment complex across the street from what was then Scientology headquarters in Honolulu.

Chapman is known to have harassed the Scientologists. He is one of four individuals known to be doing so at the time. One of these four men was in the habit of making phone calls to Scientology offices and threatening members with death. It might have been a case of a security guard with too much time on his hands, but again Chapman may have had another agenda. He is said to have blasted Beatles music across the street in an effort to harass the Scientologists, but there is no indication that he was particularly fond of the Beatles at this time. He had objected to Lennon's "more popular than Jesus" statement while still living in Georgia, as we have seen; he had undergone a born-again Christian conversion in Georgia before this animosity towards the Beatles began, and then had undergone another conversion to the Presbyterian group before his marriage to Gloria Abe. It thus seems unlikely that he would be blasting Beatles music, if he was, indeed, blasting music at all. How does a security guard whose responsibility is the protection of an apartment complex manage to set up such a blatant operation without attracting the ire of his own employers? This is yet another part of the story that does not compute.

In addition, according to Chapman in his interviews with Jack Jones, he also harassed Hare Krishnas. He objected to the way they coaxed money out of passers-by.[34] He only stopped, afraid for his safety, when told by one person that the Krishnas could find a way to hurt him, that they were dangerous.

Then, in August 1980, he rediscovered *The Catcher in the Rye*.

As we have seen, this novel about a young man's coming of age was written by a former US Army intelligence officer, who served in Europe with the troops that landed at Utah Beach during the Normandy invasion of June 1944. The circumstances of J. D. Salinger's military career are—like virtually everything else in his life—shrouded in mystery. We know that his job involved the interrogation of captured German civilians who were believed to be spies, saboteurs or simply Nazis-in-hiding. We also know that he suffered some form of nervous breakdown during his career in Europe. And we know that, shortly after the publication of *Catcher*, he retired in complete anonymity to a small town in New Hampshire, a few miles from where this author once lived in the early 1960s. We also know that Salinger was—and possibly still is—a believer in Eastern mysticism as well as in psychic phenomena.

He claimed to be in telepathic communication with his first wife, whom he married in Europe during his military posting there (yet another mystery that has not been adequately described), and that they could go into trances and meet each other in the ether.[35] Virtually nothing is known of this woman, save that she was French and her given name was Sylvia.[36] She was also described as possibly being a psychologist, or an osteopath! Whatever the case, we know very little about her; what we do know is that Salinger signed on for a further six months of civilian work for the Defense Department in Europe after his official discharge in November 1945.[37] The nature of this work is not revealed. One of his biographers, Ian Hamilton, believes it had to do with denazification, which is entirely possible since that is what Salinger was involved with when he was wearing a uniform. It is believed that his interest in the occult began with his relationship to the mysterious Sylvia.

> It was suggested to us by an ex-army acquaintance that perhaps Salinger is still a spy, or that somewhere in his spying past there is a secret so secret that he now has no choice but to dwell perpetually in shadows, in daily fear, no doubt, of some terrible exposure.[38]

It is fascinating to contemplate the number of former intelligence officers who went on to write bestselling novels. Salinger is one; William Peter Blatty is another. Ian Fleming, of course, and E. Howard Hunt and Dennis Wheatley. In the non-fiction area we have such luminaries as Peter Tompkins and his "secrets of the pyramids" and T. E. Lawrence of Arabia and *The Seven Pillars of Wisdom*. Salinger, Blatty and Fleming, however, have had enormous impact on our culture, giving us unforgettable characters in Holden Caulfield, Regan and Fr. Damien Karras, and James Bond: an alienated teenager who has a nervous breakdown, a pre-pubescent girl possessed by demons and saved by a conflicted priest, and an invincible, not-so-secret secret agent. Fears and fantasies, courtesy of the American and British intelligence services.

In reality, perhaps, these characters have been transformed into ... teenagers who express their alienation by shooting each other, and the rest of us, with automatic weapons; Catholic priests who are suspected more of pedophilia than of saving the souls of small children like Regan (how many mothers these days would leave their little Regans alone with a Catholic priest?); and an intelligence service that overthrows regimes it doesn't like, assassinates the heads of sovereign nations, spies on its own citizens, and through all this still manages to shoot itself in the foot more often than not.

But, meanwhile, back at the ranch, Chapman latches on to *Catcher* again, perhaps seeing in it something of his old self, his true self before Hawaii and marriage, before Beirut and Fort Chaffee ... or perhaps, as Fenton Bresler suggests, it was handed to him by his controller. Regardless of how the book showed up in Chapman's environment, however, it began to once again exert a strong influence over his consciousness. He was becoming Holden Caulfield.

DOUBLE FANTASY

Hear me, Satan ... Accept these pearls of my evil and my rage. Accept these things from deep within me. In return I ask only that you ... give me the power ... The power to kill John Lennon. Give me the power of darkness. Give me the power of death.
—Mark David Chapman[39]

Now I say to you: I don't believe that Mark did it. It was terrible. It was the Devil!
—Mrs. June Blankinship[40]

Holden Caulfield, and Dorothy from the *Wizard of Oz*. It was all coming back to him now. Dorothy the savior of the Munchkins; Holden the Catcher in the Rye. There was no place like home, and the Little People had returned.

In 1980, Chapman is either unemployed or sporadically employed. He begins hanging out at the library; his physical appearance begins to deteriorate; he tries selling blood to raise money. His wife is still working; so they are surviving, but not much more than that. Incredibly, he has paid off all their debts—which had been mounting, including credit-card debt and various loans—and is at loose ends. He suddenly develops a renewed fascination for *The Catcher in the Rye* and buys two copies, one for his wife and one for himself. He signs them both as Holden Caulfield.

He reads a recently-published biography of Lennon, and finds himself apalled at Lennon's repudiation of his earlier life, the Beatles, his revolutionary ideals. He claims he is disgusted at Lennon's obvious wealth, since his signature tune *Imagine* contains the phrase "imagine no possession." Chapman is coming to the conclusion that Lennon is a phony.

Then, he is sitting in his apartment going through his record albums and comes across the Beatles' *Sergeant Pepper* album, sees the picture of Lennon in the small mustache and granny-classes, and decides then and there that he has to kill him.

We're one world, one people whether we like it or not.... Leaders is what we don't need.
—John Lennon[41]

It is October 1980. The *Double Fantasy* album is almost ready for release, containing seven cuts from Lennon and seven from Yoko Ono. John Lennon is making a comeback. A single from the album—*(Just Like) Starting Over*—is climbing the charts. There are photos of Lennon in the weekly and daily newspapers, interviews, and hints of a matured political consciousness.

Reagan is running against incumbent Jimmy Carter for the presidency. He is ahead in the polls, but not by much. It is this month that the alleged "October Surprise" conspiracy is taking place, with involvement by former-CIA Director and current-vice presidential nominee George Bush: an arrangement with the Iranian government not to release the hostages until after the election. This arrangement will grow into the Iran-Contra scandal, with arms-for-hostages deals involving the US, Israel and Iran, while Ollie North arranges illegal support for the anti-Sandinista Contra rebels in Nicaragua. Guns, drugs, money, logistical support. It will be a nightmare of *realpolitik* and dirty tricks, surpassing Watergate in abuse of the Constitution and contempt for the American people by those in power. But the stakes are very high, at least in the viewpoint of the conservative faction within the Republican Party. It is nothing less than a battle for the human soul, the destruction of the Evil Empire, and the fulfillment of what Ronald Reagan sees as the Biblical prophecies in the Book of Revelation.

The last thing they needed was an activist Beatle, one who would become a naturalized American citizen in 1981, and then be able to vote and rail against the administration, reawakening old sentiments of peace, love and rock'n'roll. Particularly not *this* Beatle, the one who said they were more popular than Jesus. A Beatle worth something in excess of $150 million in 1980 dollars. A Beatle who could, conceivably, run for an American political office one day, and do so without having to raise a dime for his campaign treasury.

Chapman is sitting in his living room, listening to Beatles records and bob-bing back and forth, *davvening*, rousing himself to a state of trance-like rage. He summons his Little People, for the first time in years. He needs to organize himself to go to New York City and murder John Lennon. If he does that, he knows, then the terrible pressure in his soul will be relieved. Maybe he will wind up in prison, or executed (New York did not have the death penalty at that time). Either way is okay with Mark David Chapman.

He signs himself out of his job for the last time, as "John Lennon." He then crosses out that name and signs his own. It is October 24, 1980.

Chapman buys a Charter Arms .38 revolver from a gun shop in Honolulu, but for some reason does not buy ammunition. It is October 27, 1980.

On October 29, he flies to New York City, and checks into the Waldorf Astoria, stays a few days, then changes to the YMCA, then the Sheraton Cen-ter, then the Olcott, which is down the block from the Dakota. He stakes out the Dakota, visiting every day, but also doing tourist things like Broadway plays, the Statue of Liberty, etc.

He tries to buy ammunition at a gun shop there. But one cannot buy am-munition in New York City, which has tough gun control laws, unless one has a New York City permit. Thwarted at this juncture, he decides to call on his old friend, the Georgia sheriff's officer, and source the bullets that way.

He flies to Georgia (first class) on November 5, where his friend not only supplies bullets—hollow points, or "dum dums" as they are called, bullets with real stopping power—but takes him out for target practice for a day until Chapman is proficient, firing 150 rounds in the process.[42]

Chapman returns to New York, but discovers that Lennon is not at home. The doorman at the Dakota—the famous "Rosemary's Baby" apartment building where the Lennons have bought an entire floor—tells everyone the same thing: they are not at home, they are away, they are abroad, don't know when they will be back. In fact, the Lennons are still at work on the publicity and promotional material for *Double Fantasy*.

Chapman goes to the movies, and sees *Ordinary People*. The film provides a kind of catharsis for him, and his desire to kill Lennon subsides. He calls his wife in Hawaii, tells her that he had contemplated killing Lennon, that he has given up on that idea and is coming home.

Chapman returns to Honolulu on November 12, believing he has won a great victory by not killing Lennon, telling his wife that from now on every-thing will be okay, everything will be fine, it's all over, he's found himself. Don't worry. Be happy.

Within weeks, he is back on a plane for the mainland. This is where the story becomes muddied, with conflicting evidence showing that Chapman either left Honolulu on December 2, 1980 or December 5, 1980; that he either switched planes in Chicago, or stayed in Chicago for three days; that he brought his grandmother from Hawaii to Chicago, or that he visited his grandmother in Chicago, or he didn't see his grandmother at all.

Bresler makes a very convincing case—based on evidence at the Honolulu police department—that Chapman left for the mainland on December 2 and stayed in Chicago for three days before traveling on to New York, intending to return to Hawaii from there on December 18; he did not purchase a direct flight from Hawaii to New York, even though that would have been the cheaper alternative. Instead, he booked a roundtrip Honolulu-Chicago ticket, and then in Chicago at some point purchased a ticket for New York.

What was Chapman doing in Chicago for the missing three days? Was his trip in December specifically for the purpose of killing Lennon, or was there another purpose entirely, something to do with Chicago? Did he make the decision to go to New York to kill Lennon only after his visit in Chicago, with whomever it was he may have met there? His good friend David Moore says that he did not see him in Chicago, which, Moore admits, was very strange because even if Chapman only had an hour layover in O'Hare Airport he would have phoned him anyway. What would have kept Chapman from phoning his friend from the Fort Chaffee and world-tour days?

Several reports have stated that Chapman was accompanying his grandmother back to her home in Chicago, although they conflict on how long he spent in Chicago. Oddly, this grandmother cannot be located. Even more incredibly, United Airlines—the carrier he used for the flight from Honolulu and the later flight to New York—no longer even has a timetable in their records for the period in question, much less any passenger manifests! So it has been impossible for Bresler to backtrack over Chapman's movements and pin them down.

The missing three days in Chicago is troubling, as is the fact that Chapman did not purchase his ticket for New York until after he had landed and spent some time there. What happened in Chicago to point Chapman back toward his target?

Regardless of the Chicago interlude, by the time Chapman lands in New York City on December 6, 1980 his plan has been reaffirmed. He books himself into the YMCA closest to the Dakota and begins immediately to hang out around the entrance, waiting for Lennon. When Lennon doesn't show up that first day, Chapman begins that strange odyssey around Manhattan with a single cab, making two quick stops uptown and offering the driver a hit of cocaine, which the driver evidently refuses. Chapman then gets off in Greenwich Village, at Bleeker and Sixth.[43] We don't know what he does there, or when he gets back to the YMCA.

The next day, he checks out of the Y and books himself into the Sheraton Center Hotel, an expensive place on 7th Avenue and 52nd Street, far south of the Dakota and not within easy walking distance, as was the YMCA. No one knows why the sudden change of venue.

Then, in the hotel room, he arranges the famous shrine.

This is a composition of symbolic meaning, and consists of his expired passport with all the immigration stamps of his world tour; the letter of recommendation from his friend at the YMCA, David Moore; a photo of himself at Fort Chaffee with the Vietnamese refugees; a photo of his old car from his Georgia days, a '65 Chevy; his air ticket showing only the Honolulu-Chicago round trip, nothing showing how he arrived in New York; a Bible, inscribed "Holden Caulfield"; and a still from the movie *The Wizard of Oz*, also inscribed, this time "To Dorothy."

We must wonder at this point if Chapman was trying to tell us something, a message that was never received. The passport, the letter from David Moore, and the photograph of the Vietnamese refugees can be seen as simply an indication of some of the high points of his life, like the photo of his old car, or it could be seen as pointing in another direction: a paper trail meant to suggest the spoor of an ulterior motive, a hidden agenda. These, packaged with the Bible and the movie still, sum up the story of the inner and the outer Chapman.

He then has a call-girl come to his room at the Sheraton, and after she leaves he phones his wife in Hawaii and assures her of his love.

The next day is Monday, December 8, 1980.

So worrying about whether Wall Street or the Apocalypse is going to come in the form of the Great Beast—is not going to do us any good today.... I am going into an unknown future...
—John Lennon, the last interview, December 8, 1980[44]

On Chapman's twenty-block walk north to the Dakota, armed and dangerous and carrying a copy of the just-released *Double Fantasy* album, he realizes something is missing. Frantically, he seeks out a bookstore and finds a copy of *The Catcher in the Rye*. Relieved, he goes on to his appointment with destiny with the familiar red paperback in his pocket. In it he has written, "From Holden Caulfield to Holden Caulfield," and "This is my statement."

He waits around outside the apartment building, without seeing Lennon. Around noon, he invites two girls who had also been standing around to go to lunch with him, and they do. After lunch he returns to the Dakota, and that afternoon meets John and Yoko's five year old son, Sean, and shakes his hand. But still no Lennon.

Finally, Lennon shows up, and Mark Chapman manages to get his autograph on the *Double Fantasy* album, as do all the others who had been hanging around. But he does not shoot. There are too many people, too many things could go wrong. And, anyway, maybe Mark isn't ready yet. Maybe actually seeing John Lennon in the flesh was startling; and he acts like any regular fan when he realizes that his picture had been taken by a photographer who had been watching the building, saying, "They'll never believe this in Hawaii!"[45]

Finally, at nearly 11 o'clock at night, John and Yoko arrive back at the Dakota after a long session in the recording studio. Mark Chapman is still there. There is a voice in his head, saying over and over, "Do it. Do it. Do it."[46] He says, "Mr Lennon," and John turns to see Mark David Chapman in combat stance aiming the .38 revolver at him, firing the five rounds in rapid succession, hitting his target with four of them.

Lennon falls. Yoko screams. The doorman picks up the phone to call the police.

Mark David Chapman sits there, pulls out his copy of *Catcher*, and begins to read.

The subway entrance was right behind him. He could have escaped easily long before the police arrived. He could have been back in Hawaii (or Chicago) before anyone could identify him as the shooter, if actually anyone could. In fact, one of the first New York police detectives to interrogate Chapman felt that the young killer had been programmed to kill.[47]

Chapman was duly arrested, strangely shouting at the arresting officers, "I acted alone!"[48] He became silent in the police station, would not answer questions, but seemed strangely calm and unworried. (This was, incidentally, the same opinion people had of Lee Harvey Oswald after his arrest for the shooting of Officer Tipitt and the subsequent charge of killing the President.) As the months progressed, and as psychiatrists began visiting Chapman to derive some insight into his mental state, he was given an attorney, who labored to prepare a solid defense of "not guilty by reason of insanity" for his client. He was examined by a battery of famous psychiatrists, including Dr. Bernard Diamond, who had interviewed Sirhan Sirhan, Dr. Daniel Schwartz, who interviewed David Berkowitz, and hypnosis expert Dr. Milton Kline. All of that became moot when, on June 22, 1981, Chapman told the judge he was changing his plea to guilty. He told the judge that God had told him to plead guilty. His plea was accepted, and there was therefore never a trial in the murder of John Lennon.

In mid-August 1981, Chapman suddenly went berserk. He began screaming at other prisoners, tearing up his Bible and attempting to flush it down the toilet in his cell, which caused it to overflow. He splashed the water from the toilet at the guards, tore off his clothes, and started screaming like a monkey. (Shades of the Sirhan Sirhan hypnosis session with Dr. Diamond!) It took six men to subdue him, and bundle him off to Bellevue, New York's famous mental hospital.

In the ambulance on the way, he spoke to his guards in two entirely different demonic voices, named Lila and Dobar.[49] They said they had been sent to him by Satan.

After he was injected with anti-psychotics, the demonic presences began to fade, but not disappear entirely. He was visited by clergymen and prison chaplains of various denominations; all were convinced that Chapman was possessed by demons, a claim that only made Chapman angry.

On August 24, 1981 he was sentenced to twenty-to-life at Attica.

In Attica, in 1982, he began to invoke Satan again. His wife visited him and tried to exorcise the demons herself, but to no avail. Eventually, Chapman's demons faded once again, and he became somewhat normal.

Then, in 1983, the demons returned. Chapman began to invoke Satan for eighteen straight months, composing hymns and praying to the demonic forces day and night. He became so violent, that he was taken to Marcy, a mental hospital for convicts. They used anti-psychotics again, and brought him back to Attica.

But the demons returned.

Finally, in 1985, the exorcism of Mark David Chapman began in earnest. A minister would stand outside the prison in the middle of the night and begin the ritual, while Chapman would try to cooperate inside his prison cell at the same time.[50] The exorcism sessions finally worked, and Chapman slowly began to recover after vomiting up six demons, fluids leaking from his mouth as he writhed on the floor of his cell, snarling in arcane languages unknown to him.

He was cured. He was little Regan, safe at last.

A Day In The Life

In June of 1989, a stalker named Robert John Bardo—armed with a copy of *The Catcher in the Rye* and a Charter Arms .38—walked up to actress Rebecca Schaeffer and blew her away. But he was not the first to imitate Mark David Chapman.

In the crowds gathered outside The Dakota to mourn the loss of John Lennon, as they still do every year on Lennon's birthday and on the anniversary of the day he was shot, another man joined the throngs outside the infamous apartment building; another man stared up at the building, gazed at the crowds of people around him, many of whom were openly weeping, and silently plotted his own desperate act. Standing on the street across from the entrance where John Lennon was gunned down that December was John Hinckley, Jr. To avenge the murder of John Lennon, and win the admiration of *Taxi Driver* star Jodie Foster, he would attempt to assassinate President Ronald Reagan.

...I made a list of 50 total coincidences, things that were pretty frightening because there was no way that they could have been planned, no way that I could have set them up. It was like the whole killing was set up by destiny, just something that was meant to be.... It was just eerie, like something more was going on than I had ever envisioned. Like it was out of my control.

*It was like all of those coincidences were not only confirmed, but they were
magnified a thousand times and enlightened and new angles and nuances and
the whole purpose was given to me to understand.*
—Mark David Chapman[51]

Coincidence or, as Jung would have it, synchronicity. It is the first layer of
evidence that what we are dealing with is something other than a normal,
linear, cause-and-effect dynamic underlying the warp and woof of creation;
it is the first level of experience that can be reliably expected to obtain when
occult practices are employed, or when violent acts are accompanied by religious fervor. It is what one sees when there is a strain in the fabric of reality,
when time or space stretches or contracts, when terrible deeds are committed
by little men.

Once again, we are forced to consider: are the coincidences that surround
Mark David Chapman evidence of a political conspiracy to murder John
Lennon? That would be the scientific view, accepting for the moment that
we reject the notion of "coincidence" as being itself unscientific. Or are
they evidence of the workings of another force in the universe? Is a coincidence simply the line of least resistance, the shortest distance between two
phenomenological points? As we will see, the ancients had a special way of
dealing with coincidences: they codified them into something they called
"correspondences," and consciously employed the phenomena to attain
specific goals.

Are there people—individuals, or organizations—that, consciously or
unconsciously, employ these techniques today?

It is not known whether Chapman ever saw *Taxi Driver*, a film that was
released in 1976 to much critical acclaim, and this at a time when he was
struggling with his relationship with his fiancée and his university courses,
months before he had cut and run to Hawaii. One wonders if he would have
found any resonance between the character of Travis Bickle and his own
situation. Travis Bickle is a desperately lonely man, a nobody, like Chapman.
He has a hard time with human relationships, as does Chapman. He has a
very ambiguous sexual identity, as does Chapman. He gorges on junk food
and alcohol, as does Chapman. He begins to develop a plan to assassinate an
important figure, as does Chapman. He buys weapons, conceals them on his
person, and goes out to commit an assassination. In Travis Bickle's case, he
does not manage to kill the political candidate, but is run off before he can
draw his weapon.

Taxi Driver was based, in part, on the George Wallace assassination attempt
committed by Arthur Bremer, and on Bremer's diary. Thus, it was a case of
art imitating life. Bremer had used a Charter Arms .38 revolver, the same
make and model as that later used by Mark David Chapman.

Bremer had attempted his assassination of Wallace on May 15, 1972. His Charter Arms revolver only held five bullets, like that used by Chapman eight years later. Yet, Wallace was struck by a minimum of four bullets, and possibly all five. Taking into consideration the fact that three other people were wounded in the same fusillade, it would appear that at least eight bullets had been fired, which immediately raises the ugly specter of a second shooter, and thus of a conspiracy. Wallace himself always claimed that he was the victim of a conspiracy that day.

In addition, Bremer's fingerprints were not found on the gun retrieved at the scene, even though the famous film footage of him shooting Wallace shows he was bare-handed and not wearing gloves. An FBI agent retrieved it, not from Bremer, but from the ground where the assassination attempt had taken place, and held on to it for hours. No one knows why.

Like Chapman, Bremer traveled extensively in the days leading up to the murder; this for a man whose jobs were as a busboy in a restaurant and as a janitor. In fact, Bremer had also flown to New York City (from Milwaukee) and stayed at the Waldorf-Astoria Hotel, the same hotel favored by Chapman on his original trip to New York.

In the days leading up to the Wallace attempt, Bremer had bought a second-hand car, took a helicopter ride around New York City, rented limousines, bought weapons, etc., all on a busboy's salary. Records of his hotel stays, bills, etc. were seized by the FBI and not made available to the press.

Bremer's half-sister—Gail Aiken—was a close associate of Reverend Jerry Owen, the man who befriended Sirhan Sirhan in the days leading up to the Robert Kennedy assassination: yet another minister of religion with mysterious ties to assassination and murder. Reverend Owen was believed to be one of the sources of income for Sirhan Sirhan, and one of the members of the assassination conspiracy, according to researchers Turner and Christian. The net draws tighter and tighter.

And so it goes.

On March 30, 1981, John Hinckley, Jr.—strongly influenced by *Taxi Driver* (based in part on Bremer) and by Chapman's murder of John Lennon—attempted to assassinate President Ronald Reagan, armed with a revolver and a copy of *The Catcher in the Rye*. A case of life imitating art imitating life. And, like the fictional Travis Bickle, he does not succeed in his assassination attempt.

From Bremer to Hinckley, by way of Chapman.

The Hinckley family knew the Bush family; both were in the oil business. Hinckley's father had an appointment the day of the Reagan assassination attempt with George Bush's brother in West Virginia. The net draws even tighter. This is either evidence of a political conspiracy or simply another coincidence ... but in our case, we must look at coincidence very carefully, for it usually represents the action of a deeper, more sinister force.

Diane, when two events happen simultaneously pertaining to the same object of inquiry, we must always pay strict attention.
—Special Agent Dale Cooper, *Twin Peaks*, pilot episode

The shooters are all invariably *nemo*s, nobodies. Stunted personalities. Easy to manipulate, either by government forces or by … other forces. They are attracted to conspiracies because they see in them an entrée into the working world, the world where things happen and where people are fully-realized personalities. They seek the missing piece of themselves, filling the emptiness with a gun. They seek spiritual transformation. They are told (either by a government agent, or by the very culture itself) that they can become whole by absorbing the life-essence of a great man, a great warrior whose blood they drink, whose liver they eat. As the Mass says, *Hic est corpus meum; hic est enim calix sanguinem meam.* It is the oldest ritual of the shamans, the consumption of a God.

And it is the most dangerous message of the sinister forces, that there is nothing behind the curtain or the icon screen; that the Wizard is a fraud; that there is, in short, no God but Man. What was meant to liberate has now enslaved, for its message has been perverted by Men who wish to be known as Gods — who reserve Godhead for themselves — filling the vacuum of belief with naïve faith and the fascist mantra that "there's no place like home."

Endnotes

[1] Jack Jones, *Let Me Take You Down*, Villard Books, NY, 1992, p. 216

[2] Fenton Bresler, *Who Killed John Lennon?*, St Martin's, NY, 1989, p. 312

[3] Russ Bellant, *Old Nazis, The New Right, and The Republican Party*, South End Press, Boston, 1991, p. 68

[4] August Strindberg, *Inferno*, Penguin, NY, 1979, p. 250

[5] Gary Sick, *October Surprise*, Times Books, NY, 1991, p. 210

[5a] Ibid., p.23

[6] Ibid., p. 75

[7] Steven Levy, *The Unicorn's Secret*, Prentice Hall Press, NY, 1988, p. 130

[8] Quoted in Paul Krassner, *Confessions of a Raving Unconfined Nut*, Simon and Schuster, NY, 1993, p. 215

[9] Ibid., p. 215

[10] Bresler, op. cit., p. 322

[11] Jones, op. cit., p. 125

[12] Ibid., p. 121

[13] Ibid., p. 122

[14] Ibid., p. 12
[15] Ibid., p. 123
[16] Ibid., p. 123
[17] Ibid., p. 125-6
[18] Ibid., p. 131
[19] Ibid., p. 131
[20] Patricia Cornwell, *Portrait of a Killer*, Little, Brown, London, 2002, p. 178-9
[21] Bresler, op. cit., p. 116-121
[22] Jones, op. cit., p. 209
[23] Bresler, op. cit., p. 125
[24] Jones, op. cit., p. 209
[25] Bresler, op. cit., p. 121
[26] Jones, op. cit., p. 204
[27] Bresler, op. cit., p. 125
[28] Jones, op. cit., p. 135
[29] Bresler, op. cit., p. 217
[30] Ibid., p. 150-151
[31] Ibid., p. 150
[32] Ibid., p. 151
[33] Jones, op. cit., p. 171
[34] Ibid., p. 220-221
[35] Ian Hamilton, *In Search of J.D. Salinger*, Vintage, NY, 1989, p. 128
[36] Ibid., p. 97
[37] Ibid., p. 97-98
[38] Ibid., p. 80
[39] Jones, op. cit., p. 194-195
[40] Bresler, op. cit., p. 184
[41] Bresler, op. cit., p. 163
[42] Jones, op. cit., p. 210
[43] Bresler, op. cit., p. 216-218
[44] Ibid., p. 224
[45] Ibid., p. 227
[46] Ibid., p. 231
[47] Ibid., p. 256-257
[48] Ibid., p. 232
[49] Ibid., p. 307
[50] Jones, op. cit., p. 240-242
[51] Ibid., p. 226

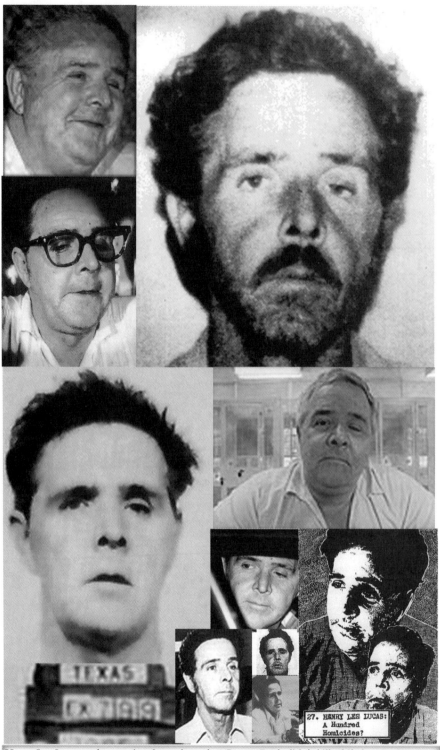

Henry Lee Lucas — the convicted murderer that George Bush didn't kill while he was Governor of Texas. Lucas is a confessed "cult" killer and has stated, "It's one of those things that I guess got to be part of my life, having sexual intercourse with the dead."

CHAPTER FIFTEEN

A VAST, RIGHT-WING CONSPIRACY

With political victory, the ideological conflicts that have swirled about this nation for half a century now show clear signs of breaking into naked ideological warfare in which the very foundations of our republic are threatened and we had better take heed.
    —Richard Mellon Scaife, Heritage Foundation rally, November 1994

This is the great story here, for anybody willing to find it and write about it and explain it: this vast, right-wing conspiracy that has been conspiring against my husband since the day he announced for president.
    —Hillary Rodham Clinton, *Today* show, January 27, 1998

If the... charge by the First Lady that the President is the target of a vast right-wing conspiracy is accurate, then nearly all the banking records point to one individual: Richard Scaife.
    —Keith Olbermann, "White House in Crisis," MSNBC, March 26, 1998

Richard Mellon Scaife, scion of the Mellon fortune and heavy financial backer of the conservative movement in America—including the campaign to discredit and eventually impeach Bill Clinton—made a most revealing remark when he addressed the Heritage Foundation in the heady days of the Republican Party winning control of Congress in the November 1994 election. He said that "ideological conflicts" had "swirled about this nation for half a century," i.e., since about 1945. Further, he warned that the nation was on the verge of breaking out into "ideological warfare in which the very foundations of our republic are threatened." This can not be understood without reference to the last days of the Second World War, and the polarization of the two most powerful American political parties on either side of the right-versus-left conflict, as Nazis were being recruited into the American intelligence, aerospace, medical and scientific establishments as a means of combating the Communist threat.

Deep into the Clinton presidency, a right-wing ideologue was giving voice to what a generation of conservatives and rightist Republicans feared most: that with the collapse of the Soviet Union and the demonstration that Communism was politically bankrupt, America would not take the initiative and extend its hegemony—even, according to some, its imperialism—over the rest of the world. To the Republicans, the Democrats were throwing away the one best chance America had to bring the entire world to heel. This conflict of opinions, of "true believers" from both sides, would result in the catastrophes of the early twenty-first century, and in particular, the invasion of Iraq under a Republican president who is the son and heir of former CIA Director George Bush.

As detailed in Book One, this was, indeed, an ideological conflict, and it was supported by powerful and influential individuals and organizations in the United States, with their ideology exported abroad in the support of vicious dictatorships of every stripe: essential elements of a "bulwark against Communism." Even as members of the American intelligentsia in science and medicine—notably space science and psychiatric medicine—were probing the far reaches of space and the deep secrets of the human mind, American political and religious leaders were leading the popular charge at home and abroad in the open forum.

Taken together, this was nothing less than a redesign of the American political and religious environment, an attempt to create a new country, one worthy of the mantle of global liberator, a liberator with its eyes on the domination not only of the world, but of space, as well. And, in order to create this new country, this new spiritual paradigm with new rules of engagement and a strange new morality in which some of the most brutal regimes the world has ever known—the Nazis and the Imperial Japanese—would become our allies against "godless Communism" and the "yellow peril," we had to take measures that were harsh and ruthless.

The war against Communism took more out of American society than the war against Nazism. For one thing, it lasted much longer and, as Communism was an "international" enemy and painted as more truly an ideological enemy than Nazism, anyone could be a Communist. Your neighbor, your boss, your employee, your brother, your senator and even—in the eyes of some—your president. America turned inward upon itself in its search for socialists, Communists, "reds" in general and their fellow-travelers. While Eleanor Roosevelt and Albert Einstein and Helen Douglas were in New York City raising consciousness and voice against the importation of war criminals under the Operation Paperclip program, the Dulles brothers and Richard Nixon were plotting an extension of that program to include thousands more. It was an ideological conflict that perhaps had its origins in American history decades if not centuries earlier, but which only became refined and fine-tuned during the war years.

We may say it was a Republican versus Democrat conflict, and in one sense this is true. The Republican Party had not been slow to support Nazism, as has been substantiated not only in Book One, but also in reports by other authors and in substantial documentation over the past fifty years. The Democratic Party has resisted this type of immoral *realpolitik* for a long time. In general, its leaders have supported human rights issues at home and abroad—whether in deed or in mere lip-service—and have resisted corporate America's attempts to give the country a make-over into its own, grey-flannel image. When critics of Democratic leaders itemize their complaints, they are generally in terms of political corruption (gerrymandering, pork barrel politics, bribes, and the like) and issues of sexual morality: character issues rather than policy issues. For example, Presidents Kennedy and Clinton have been pilloried in the conservative press because of real or imagined sexual adventurism.

Many consider this sheer hypocrisy: Kennedy was seen as dangerous to white hegemony in the United States with his, and especially his brother Robert's, support of integration; Clinton and (especially) his activist wife, Hillary Rodham, were seen as too popular among the black and Latino voters, and among women in general.

While it would be the grossest sort of hyperbole to suggest that Republicans are Nazis and racists, and that Democrats are loving humanitarians, there is some truth to the notion that the Republican Party is the party of corporate America, and this generally means white America. When attacks are made on Democratic leaders for purely political reasons, the attacks seem weak and unpopular. When attacks are made for social reasons—religion, sex, "character" issues—then the attacks become more confident, more virulent. Character issues are seen as spiritual ones, even theological ones.

Republicans are seen as the party of the corporation, big business, wealth. Democrats are seen as supporters of the labor unions, the poor, blue collar workers, racial minorities. It is, therefore, very difficult for many to view the Republican Party as anything but an oppressor of the poor, minorities and labor ... even though the large corporations that support the Republican Party are the source of jobs and technology that employ the workers. This is a simplistic view, but it is one that holds true for many people. The reinvention of the Republican Party in the last twenty years or so has been largely due to its hijacking of Democrat platforms and its *apparent* move towards the center under the neo-conservatives (to the dismay of old-line conservatives), just as the Democratic Party was losing the support of the very people it was supposed to defend against the rabidity of the Republicans. This took place against a backdrop of a frightening increase in crime, in the proliferation of drugs, illegal aliens (the terrestrial kind), unwed mothers, and AIDS. The American people—terrified at these domestic developments—turned towards the "law and order" Republicans to defend them against these threats to "homeland security." The taking of the hostages in Iran during Carter's Democratic administration was just one more indication that the Democrats were not the people to protect Americans and American interests.

We then had eight years of Ronald Reagan, and four of George H.W. Bush. Predictably, word of secret deals, guns-for-hostages, drugs-for-guns, and other skullduggery leaked out, and we had the spectacle of Iran-Contra and the rumors of an October Surprise. America learned that it was secretly arming drug dealers and guerrillas to fight against the Sandinista regime in Nicaragua, even though it was against the law to do so without the approval of Congress. America learned that people in positions of power and influence (non-elected positions) had nothing but disdain and contempt for the elected officials of Congress. America learned that it had agreed to sell arms to Iran, the same country that had taken Americans hostage in a humiliating orgy of nationalism. America learned that the White House operated on quite another level, one of *realpolitik*, one that did not respect Congress and the laws it had passed. But then, what did we expect of a Party that had held its 1980 National Convention in Dallas, not far from the spot where the most popular Democratic president of recent memory was assassinated?

And then there were the savings and loan scandals, in which even a Bush family member was indicted for his participation in a series of corrupt business practices that led to the collapse of the Silverado S&L. America was suddenly in debt up to its ears due to the S&L crisis, which was engineered by Ronald Reagan when he enacted sweeping banking "reforms" that opened loopholes in the practices of savings institutions large enough to drive police wagons through. It was business as usual. And it became too much. Too much business. Too much of the usual:

Item: May 1985. Reagan at the Nazi cemetery in Bitberg, Germany. Laying a wreath and memorializing the Waffen SS as "victims." Reagan also proclaimed April 10ᵗʰ as "Croatian Day" in the United States. April 10ᵗʰ, of course, is the anniversary of the day the Nazi Ustashi government under Pavelic took control in Croatia and began its reign of terror in the Balkans, including Catholic Father Kamber's establishment of a concentration camp at Doboj.[1] The entire Ustashi government, including Pavelic, managed to emigrate safely to Juan Peron's Argentina after the war.

Item: October 1987. The program for the National Republican Heritage Groups Council meeting lists, as co-chairmen, Anna Chennault (the Taiwanese lobbyist we came across during Nixon's 1968 "October Surprise" negotiations with Vietnam), and Laszlo Pasztor (former leader of the Hungarian Arrow Cross Youth Division, the Hungarian Nazi Party organ, during World War II). The Host Committee lists such notables as Romanian Iron Guardist (and supporter of Nazi war criminal Valerian Trifa) "Reverend" Florian Galdau; Italian fascist Phil Guarino, who was an associate of Licio Gelli and Roberto Calvi of Masonic P-2 fame; and even that doyenne of the cosmetics industry, Hungarian émigrée Christine Valmy.[2]

Item: September 1988. A flurry of news reports concerning a heavy concentration of Nazis on presidential candidate George Bush's newly-formed Coalition of American Nationalities, including the usual grouping of Romanian Iron Guardists, Ukrainian SS supporters, Croatian Nazis, and Holocaust-denial activists. This list includes Fred Malek, who, when working for the Nixon White House, compiled an enemies list of "Jewish sounding names." Malek resigned his position as Bush advisor immediately. He would eventually—and quietly—enter the administration after the election of George Bush.

The comfort of Republicans—and particularly the conservative wing—around Nazis and Nazism was (and is) unsettling.

But, hey... the Soviet Union fell. The Berlin wall fell. China became increasingly capitalist. Talks were held with Communist Vietnam with an eye towards trade. The enemies that the Republicans had warned about, sometimes shrilly, since 1945 were now disappearing. The Red Menace and the Yellow Peril were things of the past. We even witnessed the shocking scene of Brent Scowcroft in Beijing a month after the brutal Tiananmen Square massacre in 1989, toasting the Chinese leaders at the request of self-proclaimed China expert and former-Ambassador to China (briefly), President George Bush. Although America laid sanctions against China for the massacre (most Democrats were outraged at the wanton slaughter of students and pro-Democracy supporters), Bush ensured that his older brother—Prescott, Jr.—was still able to broker a deal between the Chinese government and Hughes Aircraft for the sale of communications satellites, when other American companies were barred from so doing. It was a New World Order, indeed. The Republicans had made the world safe for... well, Republicans.

And then along came Bill Clinton.

No matter what side of the fence you're on, you have to admit that there has never been as vicious, as concentrated a campaign to destroy a presidential candidate—and, then, a president—as there was with Bill Clinton. The emotions he aroused in his enemies were visceral, rabid, hysterical to the point of pathology. The fact that Clinton was re-elected and served his full eight years, even surviving an impeachment process, is testament more to his popularity among the rank and file American voters than it is to the lack of effort or focus of his enemies. During the Clinton administration, America prospered. That was supposed to be a Republican gimmick. Just as the Republicans tried to co-opt the Democratic Party platforms by loudly proclaiming a return to "family values" (this, in the Party of Newt Gingrich and his famous divorce from his hospitalized, bed-ridden wife), it seems the Democrats had taken a page from the Republican book and reminded themselves, "It's the economy, stupid."

When Governor of Arkansas Bill Clinton announced for the presidency, the scramble began to defeat him before he ever went to a single primary, much less the convention. Clinton, after all, had avoided the draft during the Vietnam War. Clinton was a Rhodes Scholar who went to Oxford. Clinton spoke German fluently. He was obviously the wrong person to have as the Commander-in-Chief of the Armed Forces, which title comes with the Presidency. He was brilliant; he opposed the Vietnam War; he had a famous photograph of himself shaking the hand of President Kennedy; he had an accomplished and attractive wife (who had actually worked for a Watergate investigator) and a young daughter; he was a friend of racial minorities; and ... he played the saxophone. He even admitted he had smoked pot, although he famously declared he "didn't inhale." Looking at the Clintons, one could not help but be reminded of the Kennedys. And there is nothing the Republican Party hates more than the Kennedy clan.

Clinton had to be stopped.

The story of the 1990s is that of how Clinton could *not* be stopped, no matter how much money and influence the Republicans and conservatives threw at the problem. It is not a story in which the Republican Party covered itself with glory. It is, in fact, the story of how the opposition to Clinton became so crazed that it didn't care how much America itself was humiliated in the process, giving rise to some speculation that the Republican Party has another agenda. Hillary Rodham Clinton was not spared the vitriolic character assassinations, either. An extremely intelligent and well-spoken First Lady, she epitomized the New Woman who could hold a prestigious job in law and still make a home for her husband and daughter, as well as find time to write a book on the problems of raising children in the new society: *It Takes a Village*. But as the Republican Party and especially the powerful Conservative wing mounted pressure on the Clintons both in personal as well as in policy terms, it was as if we were reliving that moment from the Vietnam War in which we heard that awful axiom: *we had to destroy the village in order to save it.*

It is also a story of how many Democrats lost their nerve and began to distance themselves from a President whose only crime—the only one ever proven after the expenditure of more than forty million dollars of taxpayer money and untold investigative man-hours over the course of more than eight years—was that of a sex act with Monica Lewinsky and his denial of same under oath. Essentially, it was the Profumo affair all over again, but minus the Communists.

In order to understand what happened to America during the Clinton administration—and without taking sides one way or another on Clinton's presidency, character, or accomplishments (or lack thereof)—we will see many of the same old faces reappear, like unsettled ghosts, in the American haunted house. We will have to look back once again to the first Nixon campaign and Nixon's mentor, Murray Chotiner. We have to go back and watch the slurry of Christian fundamentalists and charismatics around first Nixon and then Reagan and Bush, watch their influence over this story, and how they played true to form and supported some of the worst mass murderers in history. We have to remember how German Christians were duped and "played" by the Nazis into giving their support to the Third Reich (or, if not their support, then their studied neutrality) and watch the same strategy taking place again, in the America of the 1990s as—in the words of Sara Diamond—a famous televangelist "established for the Christian Right the standard message of tying one's personal redemption to a gospel of political participation."[3] We have to investigate the monied families of America, some of the same families who swirled around the séance tables of Andrija Puharich and Stephen Ward.

We have to evoke sinister forces.

GOING UP RIVER

"They were laying on hands," an American aid worker recalls, *"speaking in tongues and holding services while people were dying all around."*
——"Jewels for Jesus: Zaire, Mobutu and Pat Robertson" by Andrew Purvis, *Time* magazine, February 27, 1994

In Book One, we examined the development of the psychological warfare operations of the American military from World War II and extending through Vietnam. What we did not focus on then was the growing importance of evangelical Christianity as a venue for psychological operations against target nations, using resources that had "plausible deniability" written all over them. It was the influence of such Christian propaganda efforts as the Far East Broadcasting Company's radio stations beaming messages into Communist China (as one example) that led to a growing presence of the Christian Right within U.S. intelligence and psychological warfare operations around the world, often with chilling effect.[4] Although we described the cynical manipulation of Congolese spiritual beliefs by U.S. intelligence forces, we did not take that argument to its logical conclusion: the ability to manipulate *American* spiritual beliefs the same way, and for similar ends. We shall do so now, and with the prime example being Pat Robertson's Christian Broadcast Network (CBN) and his Christian Coalition.

In Book One, we cited in some detail a special report on African occultism prepared by the Special Operations Research Office (SORO) at American University, a paper commissioned by the US Army that was entitled "Witchcraft, Sorcery, Magic and Other Psychological Phenomena and Their Implications on Military and Paramilitary Operations in the Congo," by James R. Price and Paul Jureidini. This paper—prepared in 1964—was focused specifically on events in the Congo, where a young Army Chief of Staff tried to consolidate his power base and create a new country.

Previously, Patrice Lumumba had been the leader of the newly-independent Democratic Republic of the Congo, a country that had once been known as the "Belgian Congo" and which had gained its independence from Belgium officially on June 30, 1960. Lumumba was a charismatic speaker and firebrand, and largely believed to be a supporter of the Soviet Union and its brand of Communism. Of course, this *volte-face* had happened after Lumumba (in a replay of circumstances surrounding Ho Chi Minh's similar request of the United States in the 1950s) requested UN support to defend his country from an insurrection in southern Katanga province, a "native" insurrection bolstered by the sudden appearance of crack Belgian paratroopers. The UN turned him down, even though they had sent troops immediately to Leopoldville. Their mandate, Lumumba was informed, was to protect the new country from foreign aggression, but not from its internal problems. The fact that these "internal problems" also involved the presence of Belgian troops did not matter to the UN. Feeling betrayed, he was forced to go to Russia for help to prop up his administration, and the Soviets sent troops to help Lumumba put down the insurrection.

Thus, his government was seen as hostile to the United States. Long before the SORO paper had been prepared and digested, however, it had been up to another agency of the government to take steps to remove Lumumba from power, to terminate him with "extreme prejudice." This agency, of course, was the CIA, under orders from President Eisenhower. And the man who flew to Africa to put this plan into motion was none other than Dr. Sidney Gottlieb, the man in charge of MK-ULTRA.

Under orders from Richard Bissell, head of CIA Clandestine Services at the time, Gottlieb flew to the Congo in 1960, and hand-carried an infectious agent designed to kill Lumumba and make it look as if he had simply contracted a local, fatal disease.[5] His asset in the Congo—career CIA agent Larry Devlin—was unable (or unwilling[6]) to infect Lumumba in time, however; but the die—or the spell—was cast.

Mobutu—Lumumba's Army Chief of Staff—took over the country on September 14, 1960, barely two-and-a-half months after its independence from Belgium. Lumumba himself was mysteriously assassinated on or about January 17, 1961. His body was never found. According to one source, Lumumba—who had been arrested and taken to an out-of-the-way military base—was chopped into pieces and dissolved in acid, either by Belgian specialists who wanted to remove all traces of the assassination[7] or on the advice of Congolese shamans so that his spirit would not haunt Mobutu or the new republic.[8] By November of 1965, the psy-war witchdoctors—in concert with Mobutu's witchdoctors—had won the day and made the Congo (renamed Zaire) safe for democracy, and Zaire safe for Mobutu (like Papa Doc Duvalier of Haiti, and Augusto Pinochet of Chile, a "president for life") for another thirty-two years.

What happened next could have been predicted by anyone who has spent any time at all in Africa. Mobutu changed his name from Joseph Desire

Mobutu to Mobutu Sese Seko Kuku Ngbendu Wa Za Banga, "The All-Powerful Warrior Who Goes from Conquest to Conquest, Leaving Fire in His Wake." He re-instated African religious and cultural practices in his new nation, considering anything else to be the trappings of colonialism. (As an example, Congolese were banned from wearing neckties and western dress.) In the process he became a leader equivalent to the Duvaliers in Haiti or Marcos in the Philippines, stripping his country of its natural resources and hoarding the proceeds in Swiss and Belgian banks. (It was Mobutu's reign that inspired the creation of the term "kleptocracy.") Although accounts of his reign are largely concerned with his greed—his personal worth has been estimated in the billions of US dollars—most studies (such as Michela Wrong's otherwise entertaining *In The Footsteps of Mr. Kurtz*) ignore Mobutu's secret police, the torture of political dissidents, the ruthless extermination of the opposition, and the murderous events of 1990, when more than 200 students were gunned down by Mobutu's security forces at a pro-democracy rally at the University of Lubumbashi. They ignore his administration's support of the Rwandan Hutu rebels who massacred the Tutsi minority in one of the worst cases of bloodshed and genocide the African continent has known in the past century.

A man who claimed vicious Romanian president Nicolae Ceausescu as his personal friend, this was the African leader adopted by American Christian fundamentalist and right-wing demagogue televangelist Pat Robertson as his idol.

And business partner.

To come to grips with this story is to begin to understand the depth of human depravity in the face of wealth. It is written in the Bible that "the love of money is the root of all evil" (1 Timothy 6:10), and while that may seem like an overstatement to some, it is certainly close enough to the truth to get us home. We have to say that either the opulence of Mobutu's personal wealth blinded Robertson to the truth of his regime, or that Robertson simply didn't care. After all, he was no stranger to Africa and its problems. His business enterprises there involved everything from logging to diamonds, and it was diamonds that lured Robertson to Zaire, a country famous for the stones that are a girl's best friend. And, while diamonds may be forever, Mobutu certainly wasn't, and as his regime began to fail in the face of popular uprisings, invasions, a disaffected army, and waning support from the West, Robertson's fortunes in Africa also dried up; but not before rumors began to spread of his cynical exploitation of the humanitarian efforts in Zaire as a mask for his business activities.

This is the Christian minister who would throw his support behind the conservative movement to discredit the Clinton administration by accusing it of having masterminded the murders of 200 individuals over the course of the Arkansas politician's career: two hundred unproven, unverified, unsubstantiated homicides, which were more the product of feverish imaginations than crime scene evidence and grand jury subpoenas. Two hundred fictitious murders over a long political career, up against what his close personal friend Mobutu had actually accomplished in a single day with his army at the University of Lubumbashi.

We read previously of the Christian minister-turned-socialist Jim Jones, who led his followers to death in the Guyanese jungles. Only a few years later, Robertson would travel to Zaire in the midst of war, disease and starvation … and ignore the plight of the suffering to take care of his burgeoning business deals in the diamond mines. He would use his religious organization as a cover for his more material pursuits, taking whatever he could get out of Zairean jungles before the insurrections and corruption made it impossible to leave with his fortune intact.

One of the little known sidebars to the story of World War II is that of the war in Africa. Once Belgium had been occupied by the Nazis, its colony in Africa—the Belgian Congo—also should have come under Nazi control. While Field Marshal Rommel was busy fighting a hit-and-run campaign across North Africa, there was a more shadowy campaign being waged in the Congo, in the heart of Conrad's "heart of darkness."

The Congo was valuable to the war effort for two reasons, one obvious and the other not-so-obvious, at least at the time. In the first case, it was the diamonds. Diamonds are an important commodity during war, as they can be used in industrial applications to further the war machine: as cutters in machine tools, as abrasives, and in a variety of other uses such as guidance systems and other electronics. They are also, of course, a means of barter and trade when currencies collapse due to invasions and insurrections. The Congo has the world's largest diamond reserves outside of South Africa, and when the Nazis came into power in Belgium they foresaw coming into this large fortune as well … if they could secure it. Although they were nominally in charge of Belgium and made it part of the Third Reich, they did not have physical control of the African colony. The Nazi military had other problems in Africa of a more immediate nature, and were not there in sufficiently large numbers to invade the Congo in order to control the diamond trade; but they didn't have to.

There was a large black market in diamonds, and the American OSS saw this as their opportunity to work in concert with the South African diamond giant DeBeers to thwart the Germans and gain control of the world's diamond supply. DeBeers, for its part, intended to drain the Congo dry of diamonds with Allied cooperation, in order to protect its own native reserves in South Africa from premature depletion. At the same time, DeBeers was actively smuggling diamonds to the Third Reich and making money from both sides in the conflict, ignoring Roosevelt's repeated requests for a guaranteed diamond stockpile in the United States or, at the very least, in Canada. By the time the OSS had learned of the details of the DeBeer black market network, the war was almost over and the urgency declined.

It would be to these diamond mines that Pat Robertson would resort, fifty years after the war's end, in a botched—but expensive—attempt to make his own fortune.

At the same time, there was that other commodity in the Congo, one that made it of such importance that Albert Einstein would write a letter to Washington, begging the Roosevelt administration to do all it could to protect that country from Nazi invasion. This, of course, was uranium. The Manhattan Project was in full swing, and the weapons-grade uranium that would eventually be used to build the two atomic bombs that were dropped on Japan in August 1945 did indeed come from the Congo.

With the end of World War II came the end of the Nazi occupation of Belgium. The Congo remained in Belgian control, but the times were changing and the end of the period of colonialism was near. Great Britain was losing control in India and Malaya, and Belgium was on the ropes in Africa. By the 1960s, the colonies would be liberated ... but at the same time find themselves in the midst of tremendous internal struggles.

The Congo was no exception. Civil war was tearing the country apart, and into this madness stepped Patrice Lumumba. With his eventual arrest and assassination, the Congo was not entirely free of internecine conflict. Mobutu would not become leader of his country for another five years, years of intense fighting in the Congo's provinces ... and of intense spell-casting by government-approved shamans, if the above-mentioned SORO document is any indication. Into this nightmare of war and bloodshed many adventurers and entrepreneurs would find themselves a home. One of these was Siegfried "Congo" Mueller.

Shown in an East German film of the 1960s, *Der Lachende Mann* ("The Laughing Man"), Mueller was a former Nazi and present-day mercenary who found himself "defending civilization" in the Congo's civil wars. He was interviewed by two East German filmmakers, who pretended they thought favorably of the Third Reich, and he opened himself up to them, smiling and laughing, smoking cigarettes and drinking from a glass of Pernod as he described his enthusiastic contribution to the savagery taking place all around him. The film was released in 1967 to some critical acclaim, but it was an East German offering and received very little attention in the West, which, after all, was satisfied that Lumumba was dead and that Mobutu—an anti-Communist and friend of the United States—was safely in charge of the Congo, now renamed Zaire.

Africa has always been a haven for military adventurism, whether of the home-grown or the imported variety. The mercenaries taking part in insurrections in Angola, Rhodesia, Mozambique and Namibia are the stuff of legend. The Biafran conflict in Nigeria provided mercenaries with employment on both sides of that conflict. The famous Selous Scouts of South Africa provided another opportunity for blood and money, if not glory. Tribal conflicts became inflated to national conflicts; revolution became civil war, became independence, became civil war, became revolution, in a sickening spiral of violence and deceit and greed that would characterize African politics for generations. Add to that religious and ethnic rivalries, economic competition, foreign manipulation of all sides in every struggle, and you have an excellent laboratory for weapons, tactics, and psychological warfare experimentation.

The Nazis who escaped justice at the end of World War II wound up in Latin America, North America, and Australia in large numbers. Many of these were protected by Allied intelligence agencies, as has been covered at length and in depth in many other studies, including my own *Unholy Alliance.* That Nazi scientists and criminals wound up assisting the governments of the Arab world is also not in doubt. The activities of Otto Skorzeny, Hitler's commando, in Egypt, Syria and other North African and Middle Eastern countries are well-known. The assistance of these men in the development of Arab missile and weapons programs has changed the balance of power in that troubled region.

The presence of Nazi war criminals in Africa has rarely been addressed, if only because Africa itself is still a "heart of darkness" for most Americans and Europeans, a treacherous land of incomprehensible intrigue. That Nazis such as Siegfried Mueller would have found their way to the Congo comes as no surprise. The opportunities for war and the spoils of war were too numerous.

In addition, with the advent of Lumumba, the struggle became characterized as a war between Capitalism and Communism, between the "values" of the West versus those of the East. The renegade Nazis came down squarely on the side of the West and Capitalism, fighting their old enemy the Soviet Communists on the battlegrounds of Katanga province. Enlisted to assist the efforts of the United States, and of the Belgian forces in the region, Nazi mercenaries were only too glad to offer their expertise in torture, interrogation, and military drill. This is the dirty secret of the African wars of the 1950s, '60s and '70s. More attention has been paid to the presence of Nazi war criminals in Latin America, but the activities of Nazis in Africa, Asia and Australia are only now coming to light in the literature.

For instance, under Otto Skorzeny's leadership, the Middle East became a safe haven for Nazis on the run. Moving there in 1953, Skorzeny managed to find posts for a lot of his old friends. The Grand Mufti of Jerusalem, spiritual leader for thousands of Muslims in Palestine, had worked for Schellenberg's counter-intelligence division of the SS. King Farouk of Egypt had collaborated enthusiastically with the Nazis during the war years. Skorzeny became the "chief military adviser" to General Mohammed Naguib of the new republic in Egypt, selected and groomed for that position by an "unholy alliance" of former Nazi spymaster and now head of the CIA's anti-Soviet effort in Europe, Reinhard Gehlen, and the CIA's own Allen Dulles. Skorzeny began the happy task of recruiting as many former SS officers as he could find to fill the ranks of what would become Egyptian strongman Nasser's secret police, including some four hundred SS men as a special operations group involved in the training of Palestinian commandos for attacks across the Gaza Strip.[9] Members of Field Marshall Rommel's Afrika Korps were also located and turned over to Nasser's command and, it is said, that some of these men were involved in the quiet liquidation of Jews in Egypt in the 1950s.[10] Moreover, in addition to the rank-and-file SS criminals sponsored by the Skorzeny/Nasser/Dulles triumvirate, there were also the superstars.

These men included Adolf Eichmann, who sojourned in Egypt before moving on to Argentina; General Oskar Dirlewanger, the Butcher of Warsaw; Leopold Gleim, in charge of the SS in Poland; and, even more ominously, a gaggle of concentration camp medical men.

Dr. Hans Eisele was Buchenwald's medical officer, and he was recruited by Skorzeny together with Heinrich Willerman, his opposite number at Dachau. These men formed a core of specialists in interrogation and torture techniques, seconded to the Egyptian secret service.[11]

Thus, what is being revealed, slowly and painfully, is the degree to which psychological warfare, biological and chemical weapons, and mind-control experimentation have been exploited with reckless abandon throughout Africa, and with the connivance not only of renegade Nazis but also of British and American scientists and government experts from Porton Downs and Fort Detrick ... which implies, of course, the participation of both British and American intelligence agencies since these organizations are military bases operating under the tightest security measures in their respective countries. This CBW effort was not limited to Sid Gottlieb's aborted attempt to kill Congo leader Patrice Lumumba with a nasty virus in 1960.

The depth and degree of the homicidal intent reaches much further into our nightmares. The existence of these programs in African countries being targeted by American intelligence agencies, as well as courted by American right-wing Christian organizations led by men like Pat Robertson, gives us the opportunity to witness what such programs could do when they were being expanded outside American territory, far from the reach of Congress and a disinterested electorate. We can see what these programs were intended to do, as they developed, untrammeled, in the African bush. We can proceed behind the apologetic shrugs and embarrassed smiles of a Dick Helms or a Sid Gottlieb before Congressional investigators, and go right where the fruits of their labors were being harvested. How else to really understand what MK-

ULTRA and all those acronyms were all about unless we see them in action? How else to visualize the true nature of the "fifty years of ideological conflict" mentioned by Scaife unless we watch some of the combatants, the same people who would conduct pious crusades against Clinton and the Democrats for real or imagined wrongs?

We might as well begin with South Africa, therefore, a favorite destination of Nazis on the run, as the regime was eager to import as many able-bodied white men as possible, men who were not afraid to get their hands dirty. Or bloody. We might as well begin with the revelations of biological and chemical weapons use, which have poured out of that country in the years since the end of apartheid. We might as well begin with Project Coast.

PROJECT COAST

The image of white-coated scientists, professors, doctors, dentists, veterinarians, laboratories, universities and front companies, propping up apartheid with the support of an extensive international network, was a particularly cynical and chilling one.

> -- *Final Report*, Truth and Reconciliation Commission, Volume Two, Chapter Six, "Special Investigation into Project Coast," 29 October 1998

In June and July of 1998, hearings were held in Cape Town, South Africa to determine the extent of chemical and biological warfare programs in that country when it was under apartheid rule. One does not automatically think of South Africa when one discusses chemical and biological weapons, but during the era of apartheid and before Nelson Mandela was released from prison and became that country's first black president, the Republic of South Africa pursued a "weapons of mass destruction" campaign as serious as any other. In cooperation with foreign firms and agencies, the South African Defence Force (SADF) and its CBW project leader—Dr. Wouter Basson—developed an arsenal of poisons, both chemical and biological, for use against critics of the regime. The cabal in charge of this effort included the chief of staff of the defense force, the chief of staff of intelligence, and the surgeon general, as well as Dr. Basson. Thus, it was a program initiated and maintained at the highest levels of the South African military and intelligence organs and was not a rogue effort by lower-level staffers.

Ironically, the discovery of the true nature and scope of this program was made in virtually the same way investigator John Marks made his discovery of the MK-ULTRA documents: "The arrest of Dr. Basson and the seizure of four trunks containing documents related to Project Coast in January 1997 provided the Commission with proof that there was more to the programme than had initially met the eye" (*Final Report*, "Methodology"). Readers may recall that Marks' discovery of the MK-ULTRA documents was also based on four boxes of documents long thought destroyed, and, in fact, crucial evidence regarding Project Coast was likewise in the form of financial records..

This cornucopia led to a major reappraisal of South Africa's CBW program and revealed links to foreign assistance that would prove embarrassing; so embarrassing, in fact, that the Deputy Minister of Defence tried to pressure the Commission to hold its hearings *in camera* so that they would not "jeopardise international relations with countries which may have assisted the programme but with whom South Africa continues to have diplomatic relations" (*Final Report*, "Methodology"). This request was denied, and the hearings were held in open court.

The revelations were nothing short of sensational, in a perverse sort of way, e.g.,

> The discovery of a document which has become known as the 'Verkope lys' (sales list) and a list of SADF sponsored ('hard') projects conducted at Roodeplaat Research Laboratories provided the Commission with a clear indication that there was an intent to poison individuals, and that the front company, Roodeplaat Research Laboratories, was involved in the development of the toxins used for this purpose.

The toxins involved included "anthrax in cigarettes, botulinum in milk and paraoxon in whiskey—in the Commission's view clearly murder weapons." Even more bizarre was the baboon fetus.

> The inclusion of a baboon foetus on the list, dated late July 1989 (just prior to such a foetus being found in the garden of Archbishop Tutu's house), as well as a reference to chemical and biological operatives, indicated that the items may well have found their way, directly or indirectly, into the hands of operatives of the Civil Co-operation Bureau (CCB).

The CCB, of course, was the Orwellian-nomenclatured South African secret police, responsible for assassinations in other African countries as well as within South Africa, and which maintained offices in Europe for monitoring anti-apartheid activities and conducting operations against those who opposed white rule in South Africa. The CCB has claimed responsibility for numerous murders in Africa, many of which were committed with toxins developed under Project Coast.

Another front company for Project Coast and Dr. Basson was Delta G Scientific, which was involved in the development of street drugs such as ecstasy and methaqualone. This was admittedly used for crowd control, but also for assassinations in which prisoners were injected with muscle relaxants … and then dropped from planes. In addition, Basson was sent to Croatia in 1991 during a negotiation to buy 500 kg of methaqualone from the Croatians (including "high-ranking government officials"), which was brought back to South Africa. This is the deal that eventually led to Basson's arrest when he was discovered holding $40 million worth of *Vatican* bearer bonds. His involvement in Project Coast gradually became revealed after his arrest (in Switzerland) and the discovery of the four trunks of documents in his possession.

But Croatia was not the only country on Basson's list. He also visited Taiwan to meet with CBW specialists there, as well as the United States, where—according to the Commission documents—the South African surgeon general met in 1981 with "Americans who were part of the United States CBW programme"; these Commission documents "demonstrate their willingness to assist the South Africans." As a reminder, this would have been during the Reagan administration and during the time of the United States' boycott of trade with South Africa.

By 1993, both the American and the British governments were concerned about the South African program and approached the South African government with these concerns. The Commission found this approach "unclear." According to Basson, the governments were afraid that the CBW program would fall into the hands of the African National Congress after the 1994 election. The ANC was viewed by most Western governments as a Marxist front or, certainly, unfriendly to Europe and America. Whether the approach was made at the level of the US State Department and the British Foreign Office, or whether it was an approach from nervous intelligence agencies who feared that documentation would reveal the true extent of their support for apartheid and the assassinations carried out in its name, is not known. A chemical-weapons attack on Mozambican forces in 1992 by South African troops came dangerously close to exposing the true extent of South Africa's CBW program, and it is possible that the Fort Detrick and Porton Downs scientists rushed to cover up their involvement.

The trial of Dr. Basson is, at the time of this writing, still underway. He has been charged on numerous counts in connection with his Project Coast program, but the lack of direct evidence linking him specifically to murder and assassination may prove to be his salvation. Others were not so fortunate; members of the CCB are in prison in various countries under lengthy sentences for using the chemicals and toxins developed under Basson's aegis. Other former members have become mercenaries, or are running "executive security" organizations, providing bodyguards for executives and security forces for diamond mines, oil rigs, and other industrial concerns in Africa. We have not heard the last of this episode, nor of the CCB.

JEWELS FOR JESUS

In the 1980s Shaba emerged as a key strategic outpost for the Reagan Doctrine. Reportedly, the CIA used an airstrip in the remote Shaban town of Kamina in order to channel covert weapons into neighboring Angola. President Reagan hailed Mobutu as "a voice of good sense and good will." ... "Ethnic cleansing" was the term that Zaireans, diplomats,

and aid workers used to explain the cramming of tens of thousands of hungry and destitute
citizens into and around two fly-strewn railway stations in the mining towns of Likasi
and Kolwezi. They were refugees in their own country....

—Bill Berkeley, "Zaire: An African Horror Story," *The Atlantic Monthly,*
August 1993

Into this morass of murder and methaqualone, Nazis and neurologists, comes
one of the strangest white men ever to set foot on the Dark Continent. Less
than a year after the above lines appeared, *Time* magazine would print a story
that—taken in this context—is nothing less than shocking.

When I began writing this book—more than twenty years ago—I considered writing it as a novel, since I was certain that no one would believe
it as non-fiction. That was before revelations about Pat Robertson's business
dealings with President Mobutu and his cynical manipulation of relief efforts
in Zaire made the newsweeklies in the 1990s. Now, I am presented with an
embarrassment of riches. Truly, this is the stuff of fiction. Imagine Joseph
Conrad-meets-Thomas Pynchon. Or Paul Theroux-meets-Tom Robbins, All
this, and against the backdrop of an African Holocaust and a campaign to
destroy a sitting American president. The cinematic possibilities are endless,
but this story will never make it onto the silver screen. Too many reputations
would be ruined. Too many deaths avenged.

Pat Robertson, the creator of the Christian Broadcasting Network (CBN),
the famous televangelist who once ran for the American presidency, is perhaps the most prominent spokesman for Fundamentalist Christianity in the
United States. His *700 Club*—with its Bible-oriented spin on world events—is
watched by millions nationwide. As the "ideological forces" invoked by
Richard Mellon Scaife began to polarize even more strongly in the 1980s and
'90s, it began to appear as if the Fundamentalist Christian Right was hijacking the moral high-ground, even as it was making its bed with conservative
Republicanism.

Soon, it would be difficult to find a Democrat in a Fundamentalist Christian
congregation. Democrats, after all, supported a woman's right to choose in
the case of an unwanted pregnancy; Republicans were grudgingly supporting
the Right to Life movement of the anti-abortionists. That alone was enough
of a religious rallying point, enough to polarize a nation into those who supported abortion as an alternative to an unwanted pregnancy and those that
preached that abortion was murder.

Democrats also numbered many ethnic minorities among their constituen-
cies who professed Roman Catholicism—the Irish, the Italians, the growing
numbers of Latin Americans—as well as Buddhism, Taoism, Confucianism,
Hinduism, etc. Republicans, on the other hand, traditionally attracted their
numbers from high-church Anglicans and other so-called WASPs (White
Anglo-Saxon Protestants). That strategy was fine when neither women nor

minorities nor teenagers had the vote. With the change in American demographics, however, it behooved the Republican Party to find a power base that was large in terms of numbers and not just assets. The Supreme Court decision in Roe v Wade provided an excellent opportunity to drive a wedge between the Democratic Party—the party of the "people," after all—and white American Protestants who were beginning to feel disenfranchised by affirmative action, New Age mysticism, homosexual rights, crime in the streets, and bilingual education: i.e., the whole celebration of the "Other."

Further, with the waning of the Cold War in the advent of *perestroika* and *glasnost* and the eventual collapse of Soviet-style Communism, the Republicans needed another agenda. Another enemy. It was time to consolidate their winnings and take the show on the road. Waving Bibles and shouting, "In God We Trust," the post-Cold War bandwagon was just starting out of the gate when President George H.W. Bush was defeated in his run for a second term in office by the youthful, draft-dodging, womanizing Governor of Arkansas, Bill Clinton.

Governor Clinton did not come from old money. In fact, he didn't come from money at all. As the years of the Whitewater investigation demonstrated, the Clintons couldn't even successfully make money in real estate, not even illegally. They were not members of the Old Boy's Network of oil, manufacturing, or banking. They didn't understand what was at stake. They didn't understand how the game was supposed to be played. They were the poor relations, outside the Club, who should only be allowed to stare into the windows at the old men sitting in the cracked leather chairs and smoking Havanas while reading the *Journal*. Clinton hadn't even been in the military, for goodness' sake. How were you supposed to deal with someone like that?

This is not to suggest that Clinton was a saint, or that he was blameless in his pursuit of politics and the politician's dream job, the White House. Becoming an American president virtually guarantees a resume of dirty deals, backdoor negotiations, and accommodations with the less-than-savory. The spiritual state of politicians is one of cynicism and choosing the lesser of two (or more) evils. Yet, the accommodations made by the Clintons in their ascension towards the White House were like those of every politician in the country; they did not include guns-for-hostages, drugs-for-guns, Nazis-in-hiding, and all the other machinery of despair. There was no background of deals with oil-rich sheikhs, negotiations with mobsters, or "missing time" during the Kennedy assassination.

Hillary Clinton, the successful lawyer from Chicago suburbs, had no skeletons in her closet, try as they might to find some. (The best the Right could do was to promote a rumor of lesbianism! Another sexual angle. And even then, it was dropped for lack of any kind of evidence at all.) And as for Bill, there were only rumors of women, women, and more women. It was all they had on him, and even then it wasn't much. But sex seemed like the way to go; it was consistent with the strategy of the conservative Right to attack the Democrats in general—and Clinton in particular—on moral grounds. The sex issue seemed like a natural partner of the abortion issue, after all, and isn't the depth of feeling on the part of some anti-abortionists related to the idea that these unwanted fetuses are the product of frenzied, unlicensed sexual activity? Every sexual act, according to the most conservative element of the Christian Right, must be for the sole purpose of procreation. There-fore the existence of an unwanted fetus is—in the terms of this debate—an oxymoron. Every fetus is the result of a sex act, and every sex act must be for the purpose of making a fetus. Q.E.D. (The ancillary doctrine is, of course, that homosexuality, masturbation, anal sex, and oral sex are also forbidden according to this rubric.)

The ferocity of the conservatives' attack against Clinton was remarkable for its lack of attack of political substance; it seemed as if, early on, they had decided that a sexually-loaded campaign against Clinton would rally the Christian Right around their cause in sufficient numbers to have the President impeached. Sex, after all, is the great unspoken issue in American politics. Sex is used to sell a political candidate, and to dethrone him. We have no trouble imagining Democratic politicians having sex—the Kennedys in all their glory, Bill Clinton, even nervous Jimmy Carter had "adultery in his heart"—but the mere suggestion of a Richard Nixon or a Ronald Reagan or a George Bush having sex is likely to elicit either groans of horror or gales of laughter. The Grand Old Party does not produce party animals. Or so it did seem, until George W. Bush became president, and his documented background of drunk driving became a non-issue, as was the drinking and carousing (and arrest) of his underage daughters.

If we were to consult Foucault once again—as we did in *Unholy Alliance*—we would wonder if the dichotomy between Democrats and Republicans in general was that of sex versus blood, respectively, since the crimes of which the Democrats are accused are those of sexuality and its side-effects (love affairs, abortions, women scorned), and those of the Republicans are of blood (war, murder, and assassination). Love and death.

All of this is just a setting for what comes next; providing a spiritual or at least theological context for the spectacle of a cabal of conservative, right-wing industrialists and religious leaders waging war against an American president as if their lives depended on it, spending untold millions of US dollars in the process.

Pat Robertson is not only a Christian minister with a congregation composed of television viewers who donate heavily to his cause. Robertson is also a busi-nessman. There is nothing wrong with this, of course, and the argument could be made that if more ministers and priests were businesspeople, there would be less corruption in the churches and clergymen would be more understanding of the day-to-day stresses of dealing with jobs, employers, volatile markets, and the like. The concept of the "worker priest" was popular for a while in Europe in the years after World War II, although it gradually took on a Marxist tinge. Robertson, however, is no "worker priest." His business deals are routinely in the millions of dollars and involve the exploitation of the natural resources of developing nations, what used to be called "the Third World."

Investing heavily in Africa, Robertson created the African Development Corporation, or ADC. This was allegedly not connected in any way with his religious broadcasting operations, although it is hard to tell how these companies are financed. What is known for sure is that, in 1992, the ADC entered into negotiations with the Zairean government of President Mobutu for the development of the diamond trade in the southern mining town of Tshikapa, along with projects including logging in other areas of Zaire.

The idea, as touted by the Robertson organization, was that it had secured Mobutu's blessing to use some of the profits from these enterprises to boost humanitarian aid projects in Zaire. The fact that Mobutu had already plundered his country's economy, banking hundreds of millions—if not billions—of dollars in foreign accounts in Switzerland and Belgium, suggests the cynicism of this self-congratulation. It has been estimated that Mobutu could have single-handedly solved his country's economic and humanitarian problems with the funds he had salted away abroad while his countrymen's per capita annual income was something like $500, belying the necessity of a Robertson–Mobutu partnership.

Robertson, by no means a stupid man, must have known exactly what he was getting himself into by making deals with a long-term dictator as venal as Mobutu. Mobutu needed assistance in developing more of his country's natural resources, since the US French and Belgian governments were coming down hard on his human rights abuses—an about-face from the days of the Reagan–Bush administrations, which had unequivocally supported the dictator—and were putting the squeeze on his international financial deals. To Mobutu, Robertson was, well, a God-send; he represented not only new business potential, but also the quiet moral support of the Christian Right in America, which had just lost its election to the Democratic candidate, Bill Clinton. To Robertson, Mobutu was a friend of the United States, a stalwart foe of Communism, and a good business partner. It was a marriage made in hell.

Robertson initiated Operation Blessing as a tax-exempt humanitarian mission to help those less fortunate in Africa, buying three Caribou aircraft in the process, for the ostensible purpose of flying medical supplies and doctors to those areas of Zaire being flooded by refugees, both internal refugees as well as those from the growing Rwandan crisis across the border. The Caribou are designed for short-take-off and landing (STOL): Vietnam-era aircraft ideal for short runways in the jungle. Robertson went on the air in the United States extolling the virtues of his operation and showing how the poor Zaireans and Rwandans were being helped by the smiling Christian American efficiency of Operation Blessing.

Unfortunately for the poor Zaireans and Rwandans, Operation Blessing was largely a sham.

Pilots who had been employed by the organization revealed to newsmen that their job was not hauling medicine to Goma or the other regions where people were starving to death or dying from a host of treatable illnesses; rather, they were involved with moving mining and dredging equipment to Robertson's diamond mines. It got so bad that one of the pilots had "Operation Blessing" removed from the plane's tailfins. Out of forty flights that had been flown in Zaire for Operation Blessing, only one or two had actually had anything to do with humanitarian aid.

As the Rwandan crisis deepened in 1994, Robertson was on the air constantly trying to raise money for his humanitarian efforts to help the refugees. Where this money wound up is anyone's guess at this point. None of the pilots who have been contacted by investigators could come up with more than half-a-dozen humanitarian flights during the entire period Operation Blessing was in operation in Zaire, and even then the medical support was minimal. In a 1994 *Time* magazine article, alluded to above, one aid worker complained that the efforts of Operation Blessing in Goma—the town hardest hit by the Rwandan refugee crisis—were a joke: that they were heavy on transportation and light on aid; workers preferred to stand around and preach rather than get down and dirty with the dead and dying, and the organization pulled its people out after only short tours in the region.

Eventually, in 1995, Robertson pulled the plug on the African wing of Operation Blessing (possibly due to all the bad publicity), but continued with his business deals in other parts of Africa, such as in Liberia in support of President Charles Taylor, a man with a human rights abuse record at least as long as Mobutu's. Taylor's use of death squads, his support of mercenary groups who use Liberia as a staging area for attacks in other countries, and his involvement in arms trading made him a '90s equivalent to former Ugandan dictator Idi Amin; he had even been known to conduct torture and interrogation sessions in his own home, the Executive Mansion. Corruption was rife and unapologetic in Liberia, with Taylor and his cronies pocketing at least 20% of Liberia's annual budget, according to a 1998 US Department of State Country Report on Liberia.

In 1998 Robertson created a company called Freedom Gold for investment in Liberia. His focus remained roughly the same: the exploitation of Liberia's raw materials and natural resources—gold, diamonds, oil, lumber—with the expectation that profits would be plowed back into the Liberian economy for humanitarian efforts. Well, Liberia—like Zaire—certainly needs humanitarian aid, of that there can be no question. The problem arises when dictators, consumed with greed and the desire for personal wealth, make deals with Christian ministers-turned-businessmen. There is no earthly way that profits would have been re-invested in the poor of either Liberia or Zaire in any significant amount, when the leaders of those respective governments had control over the profits. It would have been naïve to think so. That Robertson himself would have been remunerated for his assistance to these regimes goes without saying; but that he would have been able to bring this money back to the people of Zaire or Liberia, untouched by the corrupt fingers of Mobutu or Taylor, was impossible. If nothing else, after the debacle in Zaire Robertson should have realized this (if, indeed, he was simple-minded enough not to know what was going on from the beginning). Why he would have turned around and gotten into bed with Taylor after the Zaire fiasco boggles the mind ... unless he knew exactly what he was doing, and that it had nothing at all to do with humanitarian aid.

Moreover, there may have been another benefit to all of this for Robertson and his Christian ministry. Mobutu—who always waivered between African animism and Christianity—began to talk up the Christian message (even as he was murdering his opponents). Taylor became fanatically Christian, at least on paper, proclaiming his administration blessed by God and making it mandatory for his government ministers to attend prayer services on pain of losing their jobs ... or worse. Yet, as late as December 2002, Taylor (and African diamonds) would be linked to the Al-Qaeda money-laundering system, and Liberia described as a safe haven provided for Al-Qaeda operatives after the September 11, 2001 attack on New York and Washington, D.C.[12] And so it goes.

Robertson also went on the record as supporting the regime of Frederick Chiluba of Zambia, another African country in dire need of real assistance. Chiluba, who declared his country a "Christian nation" in 1991, removed all vestiges of Muslim, Hindu and African native religions from the nation's school system, and approved a plan to have Christian fundamentalist ministers work with the police to identify and destroy anything they deemed obscene. This was in tandem with an anti-abortion and anti-pornography crusade, and the shutting down of radio stations and newspapers that did not toe the party line.

Another "Christian" ruler supported by Robertson on television and in his books is Jorge Serrano, the bizarre President of Guatemala who wanted to create a Pentecostal Christian government in Guatemala. The list goes on and on. Here is Robertson sitting down to dinner with notorious Salvadoran death-squad leader Roberto D'Aubuisson.[13] Here is Robertson raising two million dollars for Guatemalan military dictator General Oscar Humberto Mejia Victores.[14] Here is Robertson being saluted by the Contras at their base camp in Honduras.[15] Here is Robertson once again in Guatemala, this time in support of death-squad leader and eventual president Rios Montt, a born-again Christian who suspended his country's constitution and proceeded to murder thousands of his fellow citizens.[16] The eagerness of Fundamentalist

Christians in their support of vicious dictators simply because they pay lip service to Christianity is baffling.

Perhaps it all goes back to Martin Luther, the Father of the Protestant Reformation and the church that bears his name, who declared the Epistle in which James claims, "Faith without good works is dead" (James 2:26) to be an "Epistle of straw." If it is enough simply to believe, and not to act in accordance with those beliefs, then there is no moral imperative to leading a Christian life. One simply "takes the pledge," and then does what one likes. I don't believe Robertson seriously entertains this viewpoint, but it does seem he entertains a double standard. Even as he was supporting a range of sadistic political leaders in Latin America, Africa and elsewhere—men with the blood of thousands if not millions on their hands—he was simultaneously on the attack against the President of the United States.

The story of Iran-Contra as is generally known to most Americans omits one important aspect. Although the trail of deceit and treachery—especially against the US Congress and in violation of the Borland Amendment which forbade the government from giving military aid to the Nicaraguan rebels—stretched as far as North, Secord, McFarlane and others sworn to defend the Constitution, and whose names became household words (and in some cases, heroes) to Americans in the 1980s, the breadth of "private funding" of the Contra rebellion has never been deeply explored. The fact that the Christian Right raised millions of dollars in aid to the Contras has been "backburnered" in most histories of the affair. Indeed, Pat Robertson's Christian Broadcasting Network was only one source of aid and support to the Contras; in addition, we find the Unification Church of Rev. Sun Myung Moon as well as the Knights of Malta fraternal society involved in fund-raising and other efforts on behalf of the rebels.

The Knights of Malta participation is interesting because, at the time, its head was J. Peter Grace, an old friend of Pat Robertson and the godfather to his children. It was Grace who famously hired a Nazi scientist, Otto Ambrose, to work for the W. R. Grace Corporation even though his past as a chemist and director of I.G. Farben during WWII was well-documented. Grace seems to be another of those monied Americans who feel an investment in fascism is always good for business, and who support (sometimes secretly, sometimes openly) all manner of right-wing dictators and death-squad capos in the defense of Christianity, democracy, and white supremacy.

As for Reverend Moon and his Unification Church, this convicted felon (for tax evasion) has supported the extreme right in America for decades. The Unification Church itself fronts for the Korean Central Intelligence Agency, and when the author himself was approached by the Church in the 1970s they owned—in addition to a network of churches with a sophisticated marketing campaign aimed at scientists and other intellectuals—a rifle factory in Korea. Reverend Moon himself believes that Jesus will return to earth as a Korean, and he has let it be known that he believes this Second Coming involves his own person. Incredibly, with all of this clearly heretical belief openly promulgated, Christian ministers such as Pat Robertson have no problem at all in sharing a podium with Moon and enjoying the international reach of the Unification Church.

The main organizer of the private funding endeavor was Major General John Singlaub (retired), who came to brief prominence during the Iran-Contra investigation. Singlaub, a decorated Army veteran who had worked closely with the CIA over the years, took control of the World Anti-Communist League (WACL) in 1984. Although mention was made of the WACL during the Iran-Contra hearings, one did not hear of the constituent religious groups that provided important sources of revenue for the anti-Communist and specifically anti-Sandinista campaign.

The WACL is a notorious hotbed of Nazis, pro-Nazis, and neo-Nazis from every continent. The number of groups involved in the WACL is almost embarrassing in its composition of ethnic organizations devoted not only to the destruction of Communism, but to the advancement of a neo-fascist agenda. Singlaub was able to find support from the governments of Taiwan and South Korea, as well as from Saudi Arabia, in his globe-trotting mission: support that went to the Contras in their efforts to overthrow the Nicaraguan government.

President Reagan's support for both Singlaub and the WACL is also well-documented.[17] For instance, it was Reagan who, in 1983, told Yaroslav Stetsko, former Nazi premier of Ukraine during the War, "Your struggle is our struggle. Your dream is our dream."[18] At the time, Stetsko was a leader of the secretive Organization of Ukrainian Nationalists-Bandera (OUN-B), which collaborated extensively with the Nazis in their invasion of the Ukraine, and in 1983 was representing the Ukrainian Congress Committee of America (UCCA), part of the bewildering matrix of acronyms and ethnic subgroups that are the legs and arms of the WACL.

Diamonds and uranium. Christianity and Paganism. Black versus White. Capitalism versus Communism. While the Cold War was being fought famously in the streets of Vienna and Berlin, Moscow and New York, Hong Kong and Singapore, it was also being fought more savagely in Latin America and Central Africa and could hardly have been called a "Cold War," when all the heat of battle and bloodshed fueled the fantasies of the armchair warriors in Washington and London. It was, after all, to the Congo that Sidney Gottlieb brought his vial of death for use against a man who Washington decided would not be cooperative. That was Lumumba's death sentence: he was an inconvenient man, like Frank Olson and so many others on the CIA's "hit parade."

As the Cold War wound down, however, and enemies abroad became harder to find, Americans could take their time and identify enemies at home. The defeat of Communism was seen by many to be a victory for Christianity, at least for the homegrown Fundamentalist form of Christianity. It was now time to weed out the opposition.

American Swastika

If Christian people work together, they can succeed during this decade in winning back control of the institutions that have been taken from them over the past 70 years. Expect confrontations that will be not only unpleasant but at times physically bloody ...
– Pat Robertson, "Pat Robertson's Perspective," Oct/Nov 1992

Although civil religion has been degraded in this manner in domestic politics, the dangers of extremist versions have been most visible in American interactions with the rest of the world.... Some critics have argued that this sense of mission coupled with a tendency to view international politics as a clash of moral opposites, has undermined the development of an effective foreign policy.
– Kenneth Wald[19]

Not to be outdone, even by financial backer and moral supporter Richard Mellon Scaife, Robertson identified a struggle lasting *seventy* years rather than Scaife's mere fifty. Seventy years from 1992 gives us 1922, the era of post-World War I euphoria in America, the Roaring Twenties, and—of course—the League of Nations, forerunner of that right-wing boogey-man, the United Nations. In less than a decade, the stock markets of the world would collapse, and a president was elected who would remain in power for more than twelve years, a Democrat whose New Deal frightened the hell out of the Republicans: Franklin Delano Roosevelt.

It was Roosevelt who had wanted to go to war against the Nazis, but was virtually forbidden to do so by all the politicos around him, until that fateful day when Germany declared war on the US in the immediate aftermath of Japan's attack on Pearl Harbor. America, just starting to recover from nearly ten years of the Great Depression, had not wanted a foreign adventure and could not be convinced that a war against Germany held any margin for them. Many of the men around the President—and many others who held positions of power in America—were sympathetic to the Nazis. Henry Ford is perhaps the best and most famous example of an American who actually donated funds to Hitler from the earliest days of the Nazi Party, and who received the Third Reich's highest honor for a non-German, sharing that dubious distinction with none other than Benito Mussolini.

But another Republican whose support of the Third Reich nearly cost him his livelihood was Senator Prescott Bush. Yes, gentle Readers, the father of 41st President George H.W. Bush (former-Vice President under Ronald Reagan, former-CIA Director, former-Ambassador to China) and, of course, the grandfather of George W. Bush, the 43rd President of the United States.

Prescott Bush was an active Nazi supporter, whose company—Union Banking, a subsidiary of W. A. Harriman & Company—had its assets seized by the
US Government in 1942 under the Trading with the Enemy Act. This was
done by US Government Vesting Order No. 248, for those who think I am
making this up. The gist of the government's case was that, for many years,
Prescott Bush and George Walker (his father-in-law) had been actively raising
money to support the fledgling Nazi Party, laundering the funds through Harriman and its subsidiary Union Banking. According to Loftus and Aarons in
their *Secret War Against the Jews*, George Herbert Walker was "one of Hitler's
most powerful supporters in the United States," and was under Congressional
investigation as early as 1934, when it was believed that Walker's Hamburg-
Amerika Line "subsidized a wide range of pro-Nazi propaganda efforts both
in Germany and the United States."

Both in Germany. And the United States.

Of course, by 1942 when the US Government seized the assets of Union
Banking, America was already at war with Germany. The Bush family support
of the Third Reich, however, began when the Party was barely functioning.
Although Hitler enjoyed financial support from German institutions such as
manufacturing giant Thyssen, AEG, Siemens, I.G. Farben and other household
names, there was also extensive financial backing from wealthy and prestigious
American companies and individuals. We do know of Henry Ford's backing,[20]
and now of the Bush and Walker families' support.

Could Hitler have become as powerful as he did *without* American financial
support? That question is almost impossible to answer now, more than seventy
years after the fact. What is certain, however, is that the enthusiastic support of
Hitler by Ford, Bush and Walker entails a deep moral responsibility for what
happened, for the ravaging of Europe under the swastika and for the deaths of
millions of people in the Holocaust, as well as nearly twenty million Russian
citizens and countless millions more throughout the European theater.

We cannot, of course, hold former President Bush responsible for the sins
of his father; nor can we hold his son responsible. Yet, we can expect a higher
degree of moral responsibility in their actions as men and as political leaders. We can expect them to repudiate the Nazi sympathies of their forebear,
if not in word, ten at least in deed. Unfortunately, as we saw, in the 1988
Presidential campaign, George H.W. Bush was happy to accept support from
a range of Nazis and Nazi-sympathizers in his quest for the White House,
and was just as happy to keep them on in the administration even after they
had been identified as such.

Aarons and Loftus present a case that this was anti-Semitism, pure and
simple; and, to a certain degree, anti-Semitism in the pursuit of Middle
Eastern oil. I tend to take a different view. Anti-Semitism was certainly part
of the story of why these companies and individuals supported Hitler and
continued to support Nazism even after the end of the war. Money (and oil)

is certainly another, very powerful, motive. Yet, I believe that the entire racial theory of Nazism was a comfortable environment for these men. They were, after all, from privileged backgrounds: old money, power, prestige, the right companies, the right schools, the right fraternities (such as the infamous Skull & Bones at Yale, to which generations of the Bush family belonged). The Nazis embodied the secret dreams and unspoken loyalties of these men, the public acknowledgment of all that the American elite held dear.

Racial (or ethnic, or familial) superiority meant that they did not have to be particularly smart, particularly accomplished in their own right, but could rely upon the mere fact of their bloodlines to ensure the continued power of themselves and their families from generation to generation. After all, America is not a monarchy, yet there burns in the secret heart of almost every American politician and businessman a desire for royal prestige, for the trappings of nobility, for the accumulation of knighthoods and noble degrees. Skin was the uniform these men wore; the right color identified you as a friend rather than a foe. Family name was the battalion to which you belonged and owed allegiance: Bush, Walker, Mellon, Scaife, Morgan, DuPont, etc. Jews were not allowed, of course, but neither were blacks, Asians, Hispanics, etc. Eugenics was the new "science" of population control, which was a code word for genocide and "ethnic cleansing," and the Bush–Walker team provided logistical support for the Third International Congress of Eugenics that was held in New York on August 21-23, 1932, at the American Museum of Natural History, ensuring that Nazi eugenicists were present at the Congress by providing free passage aboard their shipping line, Hamburg-Amerika.

The flyer advertising this Congress is revealing. It shows a tree with a large root system. Each root is labeled with one of the sciences: anthropology, archaeology, etc. The slogans say, "Eugenics is the self-direction of evolution," and, "Like a tree, Eugenics draws its materials from many sources and organizes them into an harmonious entity." Among those sources, depicted as a root off to the right side of the drawing, is one labeled "religion." Another is "politics," and still others include "fecundity," "mate selection," "race crossing" and "eugenic forces" (whatever they are). Thus, the "science" of eugenics was seen as means of organizing the whole of human endeavor, while weeding out those who do not fit the paradigm.

But what are we to make of "religion" in this context? As heinous as we have come to see eugenics as a whole—as it was the science proclaimed by the Third Reich as an excuse (or a reason) for eliminating the mentally-ill, the physically-infirm, and eventually the Gypsies, the Jews, the Slavs, etc.—we have to wonder what the American organizers understood the role of religion to be. In America, eugenics was a code-word for the subjugation, sterilization and eventual elimination of the black race. In Germany, of course, it referred to the Jews as well as Gypsies, homosexuals, Communists, and whoever else was on Himmler's enemies list at the time.

Whatever the core beliefs of the Congress, it was enthusiastically supported by some of the most prominent industrialists and people of "old money" in the United States, and support was extended to their like-minded brethren across the seas in Germany. In 1932, Hitler was on the verge of taking power in Germany and eugenics was one of the Nazi Party's platforms, a kind of pseudo-scientific imprimatur for race hatred and the Final Solution. American financiers—such as W.A. Harriman and George Herbet Walker, founding members of Union Banking—were sending bags of money to Hitler to prop up his shaky political position, or successfully laundering that money through American and European banks. It is clear that some of the most important businessmen in America felt they had a vested interest in promoting the Nazi Party, and through their support of ancillary programs such as the Eugenics Congress, we can begin to put together a more complete picture of this interest: America for white people, Europe for the Nazis, forming a broad alliance of power stretching over both sides of the Atlantic and ensuring the enslavement of millions upon millions of people who were not members of the club. In America, it was nothing less than a repudiation of everything the Statue of Liberty stands for.

Fast forward to 1992.

There is a religious war going on for the soul of America.
-- Pat Buchanan, May 1992 [21]

We have seen how the son of Prescott Bush, George H.W. Bush, carried on his father's support for fascism by hiring numerous pro-Nazis, ex-Nazis and Holocaust-revisionists and by courting ethnic organizations that were run by former Nazis. We have witnessed Richard Nixon's support for specific Nazis, such as Trifa and Malaxa, in a pattern that goes back to the days of Allen Dulles and the early post-War years when the two men collaborated on hiding the smoking gun of government documentation that would have shown the Dulles brothers' involvement with Nazi war criminals and Nazi fund-raising. We watched Ronald Reagan place a wreath at the SS cemetery at Bitberg. And now, we are forced to witness another gathering of the Klans in their desperate effort to dispatch the Democratic Party's presidential candidate Bill Clinton.

The old money in the 1990s was represented by one of the wealthiest dynasties in the United States: the Mellon family. Mellons can be found sprinkled throughout the American experience over the last century. Heirs of a fortune built by a Pittsburgh industrialist, they were at one time considered *the* richest family in the United States. Although their money was not quite as "old" as that of the Astors, they traveled in much the same circles. We will find Mellons present at the birth of Timothy Leary's LSD crusade; we will find them involved in the Profumo affair in England in 1962; we will find them involved in the skullduggery around Resorts International in the

Bahamas, along with Richard Nixon and Bebe Rebozo; we will find them once again financing a vociferous campaign of print and broadcast media to unseat Bill Clinton.

WILD BILL HITCHCOCK

Why Hitchcock decided to throw his weight behind the psychedelic cause is still something of a mystery. Was he simply a millionaire acid buff, a wayward son of the ruling class who dug Leary's trip? Or did he have something up his sleeve?
—Acid Dreams[22]

One of the principal witnesses against [LSD chemist Nicholas] Sand and two co-defendants was William Mellon Hitchcock, an heir to the U.S. Steel fortune, who testified under immunity and acknowledged that he had bankrolled the operation.
—San Francisco *Examiner*, "Fugitive to face LSD charges," June 6, 1998

The Legal Attache, London, forwarded copies of memoranda prepared by Alfred Wells, Secretary to Ambassador Bruce, concerning various persons involved in the instant case. In a memorandum dated 11/6/62 Wells stated that he had attended a dinner the night before at which he had met Dr. Stephen Ward and that Ward had made loud statements that he had been the principal liaison between the Soviets and the British Government during the Cuban crisis.... By memorandum 6/18/63 Mr. Wells stated he had been to a luncheon on 2/13/63 with Thomas Corbally, Dr. Ward, Mrs. Robin Dalton, an Australian woman, and William Hitchcock.
—FBI Memorandum 65-68218, from W. A. Branigan to W. C. Sullivan, dated 7/1/63, "Re: Christine Keeler; John Profumo"

William Mellon Hitchcock was no stranger to that rarefied atmosphere where American politics and American money mingle in a fuzzy miasma of intelligence agents, crooked financiers, and secret agendas. He was one of the heirs to the Mellon fortune and to Gulf Oil (founded by his grandfather William Larimer Hitchcock) and nephew of Andrew Mellon (a Secretary of the Treasury for three Republican Presidents from 1921-32). He and his sister Peggy were close to both Timothy Leary (and Australian film producer Robin Dalton) on the one hand, and to people like Stephen Ward, Thomas Corbally, and the American Ambassador to England on the other.

The latter was natural, since David Bruce—the US Ambassador to the Court of St. James during the Profumo affair—was his uncle. A former and important member of the OSS during World War II, Colonel Bruce landed at Normandy with the head of the OSS: General "Wild Bill" Donovan. A roommate of Billy Hitchcock's father at university, Bruce had married (and later divorced) a Mellon. During the War, David Bruce's OSS network operated behind enemy lines in France, disrupting the German Army; at one point, Bruce had hundreds of French agents under his command.

315

Bruce would later go on to even greater glory, not only as US Ambassador to England, but also to France and Germany. He would also be involved, with Henry Kissinger, in the Paris Peace Talks during the Vietnam Era. Bruce's connections in Europe during the War included high-ranking Italian Masons who held influential posts within Mussolini's government.[23] We also discover that OSS staffer and future-CIA Counterintelligence Chief James Jesus Angleton was working in Italy at this very time with his father, Hugh Angleton, cultivating close relationships with Masons working within the Fascist Mussolini government to advance a somewhat different agenda.[24]

Thus do we begin to realize that the word "conspiracy" does not do justice to what is, after all, merely a group of people from similar backgrounds with similar goals, all working to a common purpose which is hidden from the world at large by virtue of a Great Wall of wealth, prestige, culture and power. We begin to see that what the rest of us call conspiracy is just business-as-usual for the people that operate above, behind and below what we know as consensus history, consensus reality. I believe that the word "conspiracy" is over-used and emotionally-loaded in this context. Let us instead, and rightly, use the word "cabal" to denote this gathering of sinister forces.

There were other Mellons on board at OSS: Paul Mellon (Treasury Secretary Andrew Mellon's son) served with the OSS Special Operations Branch in London, moving on to become commander of the Morale Operations Branch, based in Luxembourg. According to Richard Harris Smith, "Other Mellons and Mellon in-laws held espionage posts in Madrid, Geneva and Paris."[25] Further, as reported in *Acid Dreams*, "After the war, certain influential members of the Mellon family maintained close ties with the CIA. The Mellon family foundations have been used repeatedly as conduits for Agency funds. Furthermore, Richard Helms was a frequent weekend guest of the Mellon patriarchs in Pittsburgh during his tenure as CIA director (1966-1973)." In addition to the Mellons, members of the Morgan, Vanderbilt, and DuPont families were very active in the OSS making it essentially a "rich man's club." David Bruce himself was the son of a US Senator and a millionaire even before his marriage to Ailsa Mellon.

Thus, William Mellon Hitchcock's presence at dinner in London in 1962 with Thomas Corbally and Stephen Ward is highly suggestive of an intelligence angle. At the time of the Profumo affair, Hitchcock was flying back and forth between New York and London: in London, to hang out with Ward and Corbally (the latter will become important a bit later on), and in New York to hang out with Timothy Leary, who had just returned from an aborted LSD-commune experiment in Mexico and was looking for another site. He found one at Hitchcock's Dutchess County, New York, estate: Millbrook.

Hitchcock's involvement with all of these people—and many more besides—has always been suspicious. Even those around Timothy Leary—full of peace and love and lysergic acid—were sometimes, well, leery of Hitchcock. Hitchcock did not live at the Millbrook mansion with Leary and his other guests, but instead stayed at a much smaller cottage elsewhere on the grounds, where he conducted business (he has been described as a stockbroker) and had his own guests over. He was never fully part of the acid scene, except for the trips he took with Leary and company at Millbrook, and kept mostly to himself, not sharing in the mysticism and deep philosophical musings of the Leary operation.

As it turns out, Hitchcock had so many ties to the intelligence community—mostly through banking circles and money-laundering operations—that it raises one's paranoia level to a new ... high. As described in *The Nine*, LSD was introduced to the American public through the CIA, which wanted to test its effectiveness for everything from mind control to crowd control. We then discover Hitchcock's involvement with the CIA and CIA-front organizations, such as Castle Bank and Resorts International. We also see Hitchcock turning state's evidence against his old LSD chemist, Nicholas Sand, even though Hitchcock himself admitted he had financed Sand's operation for the manufacture and distribution of millions of hits of LSD.

Probably the most accessible history of this period is the book *Acid Dreams, the Complete Social History of LSD: The CIA, the Sixties, and Beyond* by Martin A. Lee and Bruce Shlain, which was originally published in 1985. In those pages, we read of the strange development of Harvard professor Timothy Leary. We read of his salad days as a clinical psychologist at the Kaiser Foundation Hospital in Oakland, California (the same hospital where Andrija Puharich got his start) in the period 1954-59, where he developed a personality test ("the Leary") which was used by the CIA human resources people to screen potential employees.[26] We learn of his growing awareness of the field of psychedelics during a vacation in Mexico in 1960, where he was urged by a friend to try hallucinogenic mushrooms (psilocybin) in Cuernavaca. He returned to Harvard—where by now he had a professorship—filled with the experience, and related it all to Dr. Harry Murray, with whom he developed a psilocybin research project. This was the same Murray who had been involved with the creation of personality tests for the OSS during World War II. (As we see, the field of early psychedelic research in the United States was heavily influenced by men who had more than a passing relationship with intelligence matters.)

By the time he met—first Peggy, and then—Billy Hitchcock three years later, Leary was well on the way to becoming an acid guru, having abandoned psilocybin for the more attractive pharmaceutical developed by the Sandoz laboratories in Switzerland, lysergic acid diethylamide, or LSD-25. Peggy Hitchcock was a New York City socialite with tremendous energy and an interest in everything. She introduced brother Billy to Timothy Leary, and it was the beginning of a fateful friendship.

Aside from renting his vast Millbrook estate to Leary's acid organization for a mere five hundred dollars a month, he wound up subsidizing various drug operations and secret laboratories (including that of convicted acid chemist Nicholas Sand), for which he would eventually come to the attention of US Customs and other government authorities, although he would not spend any time in prison. This is not surprising in view of the fact that he walked with the gods.

One of Billy Hitchcock's earliest recorded introductions to the world of intelligence was his presence at that fateful lunch with Dr. Stephen Ward (who would be convicted, unfairly, of living off the earnings of women in the nasty Profumo Affair, which threatened to pull down the British government if not also an American president) and Thomas Corbally. Corbally, a mysterious and elusive businessman who seems to live only in hotels on either side of the Atlantic, reported this lunch to the US Ambassador, David Bruce, Billy Hitchcock's uncle by marriage. There were important intelligence ramifications to what was eventually reported to the FBI by the State Department, including the fact that Stephen Ward had been a go-between during the Cuban missile crisis of 1962, carrying messages back and forth between the British and the Soviets. This was not empty bragging, although it would have been better had Ward kept his mouth shut; it was his loose lip that sealed his doom, for once his reputation had been ruined by the Christine Keeler prostitution scandal, he would not be believed on anything having to do with such lofty matters as intelligence activities relating to the one incident in the twentieth century that had, without question, brought us to the brink of nuclear holocaust.

Rumors had it that Dr. Ward was involved in occultism, and some have tried to link him (without documentation so far) to the Golden Dawn or to one of its offshoots in Great Britain. That he was involved in orgies that were attended by the rich and famous is beyond all doubt, however, and some of these gatherings may have been ritualistic in nature. He was evidently very interested in occultism and "black magic."[27]

Yet, the intimate lunch attended by Ward, Hitchcock, Corbally and Robin Dalton leads us to wonder what could have brought these four people together, for of that group at least three had intelligence connections: Ward, Hitchcock, and Corbally. Ward would commit suicide directly after his guilty verdict was returned. Corbally, according to his own account, was sniffing around Ward either at the behest of the CIA or of Ambassador Bruce (depending on which story one believes), even though he considered Ward a personal friend, one who had once treated him for a knee injury.[28]

When David Bruce did not report back to the United States on this vitally important information, FBI Director J. Edgar Hoover became suspicious that Bruce himself was involved in some kind of international vice ring.[29] Hoover suspected—as did others in the American intelligence community—that one of Christine Keeler's clients may have been John F. Kennedy himself. Hoover, whose distrust and dislike of the Kennedys ran deep, spun a nightmare scenario in which Keeler—bedmate of a Russian military attache in London—was sleeping with the American president, and exchanging one kind of pillow talk for another.

Hoover had reason to be nervous. A sex ring that had operated in New York City until 1961 (barely a year before the Profumo scandal was exposed)—and to which it was believed Keeler and some of her colleagues belonged at various times—was staffed by at least one Chinese woman of foreign birth and assorted other foreign nationals. When the police raided the operation, the ringleader—one Alan Towers—fled to a safe haven behind the Iron Curtain. One of his "employees," the prostitute Maria Novotny, reportedly told police that Alan Towers was a Soviet agent and was running an international sex ring for the purpose of entrapping prominent politicians and businessmen.

In spy parlance, this is known as a "honey trap," and today many suspect that Ward was doing the same thing with Christine Keeler, Mandy Rice-Davies, and the other women associated with Keeler (including, it is said, Mary Anne de Grimston of the Process Church of the Final Judgment) ... but not for Soviet intelligence. Instead, it is believed that Ward was working for British intelligence in an attempt to entrap such Soviet targets as Yevgeny Ivanov, the GRU (Russian military intelligence) *rezident* whose name turned up in the Profumo affair as one of Keeler's lovers, causing the scandal that rocked the British government. Thus, Keeler was simultaneously sleeping with both John Profumo—the British Minister of War—and Ivanov, the Soviet military intelligence officer assigned to Great Britain. And this, during the time of the Cuban missile crisis! If President Kennedy was also sleeping with Keeler or with one of her associates (as Hoover feared might be the case), Christine Keeler might potentially be considered one of the most important women in the history of the twentieth century.

As it was, Profumo resigned (after at first denying then admitting that he had slept with Ms. Keeler) and Ivanov was sent back to Russia. Ward, unable to deal with the scandal and embittered with the way his friends all abandoned him in his hour of need, committed suicide. (The cottage where he lived on the Astor estate of Cliveden was subjected to the ministrations of an exorcist, giving rise to more theories of Ward's occult involvement). Ms. Keeler herself survived the episode and was interviewed a few years ago in the American and British press after the release of a film about the affair entitled, naturally, *Scandal.* The former prize-fighter (and fiancé of Process Church co-founder Mary Anne DeGrimston) Sugar Ray Robinson had wanted to produce a film on the Profumo affair with Keeler playing herself, but nothing had come of the project. Thomas Corbally and William Hitchcock also survived, and each went on to greater glory (or infamy): Corbally to a disastrous relationship with Connecticut conman Marty Frankel, and Hitchcock to a disastrous relationship with LSD chemist Nicholas Sand. The British government prepared an official report on the Profumo Affair known as the Lord Denning Inquiry, which, in its essential whitewash of the episode and its focus on Keeler and Ward, was likely the inspiration for another such government inquiry a year later: the Warren Report.

Why did US Ambassador David Bruce not report the details of the Ward scenario to his putative masters in the United States? What was the role of his wealthy in-law, William Mellon Hitchcock, in the affair? Was Thomas Corbally actually working for Bruce (*via* Billy Hitchcock?) when he began spying on Dr. Ward? What was Corbally—at the time over fifty years old—doing hanging out in London with William Hitchcock, who was at that time only in his twenties? The suave, urbane international businessman Corbally with a hip, young stockbroker like Hitchcock? One imagines that money would be a passion they shared; another might be intrigue. Almost immediately after the Profumo affair, Hitchcock is back Stateside, being introduced to Tim Leary by his sister Peggy, and virtually donating his family's ancestral home to Leary and his gaggle of acid heads.

This might seem like just a bit of youthful folly—thumbing one's nose at the Establishment, as some have put it—if not for the fact that Hitchcock did not drop his "straight" life and become a drug-entranced hippy. He lived apart from Leary and his commune—eventually renamed Castalia in honor of the Hesse novel *The Glass Bead Game*, in which Castalia represents an institute of pure intellectualism—and remained very much in charge of his business interests… and, when the chips were down, turned state's evidence against the drug dealers he himself employed. One is tempted to believe that Thomas Corbally was a guest of Hitchcock's at his own, rather more modest, cottage at Millbrook, kept safely away from Leary, Richard Alpert, Ralph Metzner, Gunther Weil and visitors such as R.D. Laing, Andrija Puharich, and Maynard Ferguson. Leary's spiritual mentor, Aldous Huxley—whom he met in the early 1960s when he was still a clean-cut university professor—had already died on November 22, 1963 (!!), while tripping on LSD to ease his way to the Other Side.

One is tempted to believe that some of the LSD-25 churned out by Nicholas Sand and others working for Wild Bill Hitchcock wound up supporting an intelligence agenda. No matter; eventually the Millbrook commune was raided—and Timothy Leary arrested—by none other than future Watergate Plumber G. Gordon Liddy. Liddy and Leary would eventually go on the lecture circuit years later, Liddy representing the conservative, law-and-order viewpoint, with Leary as an amiable but unfocused foil for Liddy's sarcasm. (Both, of course, were convicted felons who had served prison time for their separate offences.) Needless to say, it was not a marriage made in heaven, and the road show did not last; Liddy wound up as a radio personality in his own right, while Tim Leary passed away, still convinced of the righteousness of his acid cause, and dropping unsettling hints that he had been working for the CIA at the time.

While William Hitchcock's intelligence role is not known to any degree of certainty except for the circumstantial evidence cited above, he certainly surrounded himself with spooks, mobsters and … Republicans. His deep involvement in Castle Bank and Trust is just one such instance. A CIA front in the Bahamas run by former OSS China hand (and former boss of E. Howard Hunt) Paul Helliwell, it was used as a personal bank by Richard Nixon, George H.W. Bush, and Robert Vesco, as well as by an assortment of Republican movers-and-shakers and the occasional drug runner and Mafia don. Those who enjoy wallowing in Watergate will recall Castle Bank, but perhaps not realize that Billy Hitchcock was an important supporter of the institution.

His similar involvement with Resorts International, a spook-front and private Republican vault, is also well-known. The history of Resorts International has been brilliantly detailed in Jim Hougan's *Spooks*, and we will not go into any great detail here, but it is enough to say that Resorts is in the middle of not only the Watergate affair but also a vast array of intelligence operations that include anti-Castro Cubans, Mafia bagmen, illegal campaign contributions, and money laundering. The Nixon and Rebozo involvement with Resorts is only the tip of a very old and very dirty iceberg, and Hitchcock has managed to stay quietly in the shadows of these infamous politicos.

Alas, the same cannot be said of his relative, Richard Mellon Scaife.

THE CLINTON CHRONICLES

Richard Mellon Scaife's antecedents were also intelligence-connected in World War II. His father Alan Scaife was a major in the OSS. The Mellon side of the family, of course, included all those OSS Mellons with their cozy relationships extending to the modern incarnation of the OSS, the CIA. While Bill Hitchcock's involvement with twentieth century American history seems divided between the LSD culture on one side and money laundering on the other—including a variety of intelligence and high-level Republican Party cooperative efforts—Richard Scaife's politics are worn on his sleeve for all to see.

He has been identified in the mainstream media as the treasure chest for the anti-Clinton campaigns of the 1990s, supporting a wide variety of efforts to destroy the Democrat. We learned of the Paula Jones scandal through Scaife's investigation into Clinton's private life, an investigation undertaken with private detectives and well-placed bribes, as well as with investigative reporters working for his own newspaper. It was Scaife who joined hands with Pat Robertson—he of the "jewels for Jesus" investments in Zaire—to promote a video cassette purporting to tell the truth about Clinton the mass murderer entitled "The Clinton Chronicles," a conspiracy theory wrapped in innuendo and basted with misdirection which, if anything, gives the very idea of "conspiracy theory" a bad name. (This did not stop Pat Robertson from promoting it through his own Christian Coalition, however.)

The story of Richard Mellon Scaife is clouded by Scaife's own reluctance to talk to reporters, even though he controls several media outlets including the *American Spectator*, a newspaper published in Pittsburgh that has been instrumental in the Clinton attacks. It was the *Spectator* that first published the Paula Jones story, early in the Clinton campaign for the presidency. When *Spectator* editors or journalists have been slow to go to press with an anti-Clinton story that was heavy on innuendo but weak in verifiable sources, they have been censured by Scaife or fired outright.

To do him justice, Scaife's paper was also one of the first to come out with an editorial demanding the resignation or impeachment of President Nixon during the Watergate scandal; those who watched from the sidelines, however, interpreted this as a man distancing himself from the exposure of some of the Republican Party's dirtiest secrets. Nixon, though an eager tool of the Right, was not cut from quite the same cloth-of-gold as his aristocratic buddies, and thus could not be expected to maintain (achieve?) any kind of dignity in the face of the ongoing revelations.

With Nixon, the Republicans learned a valuable lesson: the poor and the greedy can be manipulated far more easily than the wealthy, but that manipulation can come with a price. The poor and the greedy are hired help; they are not part of the cabal and cannot be expected to act with the appropriate—*je ne sais quoi?... noblesse oblige?*—in times of stress. With the Bush presidencies, a wealthy dynasty was put in place, one that could be relied upon to give the party line with aplomb; further, the Bushes were members of that exclusive club of oilmen which is a venerated sect of the cabal; even further, they had enough family members in important positions—Governor of Texas, Governor of Florida, two critical states during an election—to consolidate power at various levels of government. The Bush dynasty was the Republicans' answer to the Kennedys.

Thus, when Clinton made a run at the Oval Office, it shook the conservative Right down to its heels. The plan had been to have George Bush serve for two terms, during which a consolidation of power could take place: the "ideological forces" mentioned by Scaife in 1994. When Clinton threatened that, action was required. On one level, that action would be taken by the same dirty tricks faction that had served Nixon so well in his political campaigns.

Lucianne Goldberg had worked for Murray Chotiner, Nixon's first and virtually only campaign manager. Chotiner had worked for Nixon since his first run at a political office after the War, orchestrating the red-baiting and Jew-baiting whisper tactics that helped Nixon in his California campaigns. Chotiner's involvement with organized crime is no secret; his delight in dirty tricks was passed on to his student as a virtual religion. After Chotiner's death—in an automobile accident ironically in front of a Kennedy residence—his mantle was picked off the floor by one of his latest camp-followers: Lucianne Goldberg. Ms. Goldberg had worked to infiltrate the campaigns of the Democratic opposition in 1972, looking for specifically sexual dirt that could be used to embarrass or ruin an opponent. (This was also the year of the Watergate break-in.) In 1992, she dusted off these skills and once again began seeking sexual scandal in an effort to defeat another Democratic contender. She was, in a way, less successful this time. Her efforts in 1972 helped re-elect Nixon to office. Her efforts twenty years later did not stop or remove Clinton, but it did prove to be a nightmare for the United States nonetheless.

It was Goldberg's relationship to Linda Tripp—a well-traveled former Delta Force member—that helped to unravel what would become the Monica Lewinsky debacle. Goldberg, acting as a kind of literary agent (who would go on to represent former LAPD officer and O.J. Simpson-trial celebrity Mark Fuhrman), was scouting around, looking—once again—for dirt on the Clinton administration. Tripp had worked for the previous Bush administration, and the White House found her a job at the Pentagon (where she made more money, incidentally) in the days after the Vince Foster suicide.

The Vince Foster case, of course, became a *cause celebre* among the Right, as they were convinced that Foster had been murdered by the Clintons, in spite of the evidence to the contrary. Foster had worked for the Clinton White House, and when news of his death reached the administration they began a search of his office and, it is alleged, removed documents before the arrival of police. In the days that followed, there was a flurry of activity as White House legal staff began to assess the fallout from the suicide. Tripp became increasingly contemptuous of the Clinton people and of the way she had been sidelined during the transition. When she was finally transferred to her office at the Pentagon, she wasted no time telling people of her dissatisfaction with the way she had been treated. Even though she was working for more money and back in the Pentagon, it did not compare with the prestige of working at the White House, and she was bitter and angry at the Clinton administration.

Word of her state of mind reached Goldberg through another friend, and Goldberg approached Tripp for more information. About all Tripp could come up with on her own were the shenanigans that took place around the time of the Foster suicide, and a lot of gossip about various staff people and the lack of organization within the administration. Goldberg was not satisfied with that. It just wasn't enough to sell a book … or destroy a president. She wanted more.

Tripp eventually made the acquaintance of another White House staffer, a former intern named Monica Lewinsky. Monica claimed to have been having a love affair with Bill Clinton. This was just what Goldberg was looking for.

At this time, the Whitewater investigations had been going full-swing. The Whitewater affair has been covered in many other books and newspaper accounts, and a full narration here would be tedious and not add very much.

It is probably enough to say that there were allegations of the Bill Clinton's wrongdoing when he was still in Arkansas, long before he became president, which involved a suspicious real estate deal known as Whitewater. Whether this deal had any relevance at all to whether or not Clinton should have remained President is, of course, for people far more knowledgeable than I to conclude. In fact, it began as a fishing expedition by the Republican opposition to find something—anything—to hang on Clinton to force him to resign or, barring that, to prevent him from seeking a second term as President.

An independent counsel was named, was replaced, and finally Kenneth Starr took over the task of finding something illegal in Clinton's background. The Whitewater investigation was turning up nothing. While the real estate deal had gone badly, there was never any evidence that the Clintons profited by it; in fact, they lost money. There was also no evidence that the Clintons had been involved in anything illegal. Forty million dollars of the taxpayers' money had been spent on chasing a chimera, and Starr was desperate for an angle. *Cherchez la femme.*

Richard Scaife, who had been pressuring his people to find dirt on Clinton, had placed private detectives in Arkansas to sniff around. They came up with Paula Jones and the statements of some Arkansas State Police who claimed that they had, essentially, pimped for Clinton when he was Governor of Arkansas. Paula Jones claimed that she had been having sexual relations with Clinton for some time, a fact that was also supposedly known to the State Police who were the Governor's security detail. The fact that the dates and places given by Paula Jones were later shown to be inaccurate (in one instance, she gives as the date and time of her rendezvous with the Governor the same time that he was in front of a few hundred people giving a speech) was inconsequential to the strategy. It was enough to have Ms. Jones stand in front of cameras and claim that she slept with Clinton.

During Clinton's campaign for the presidency, another woman—Gennifer Flowers—had also come forward with a story that she had been sleeping with the Governor. It had almost been enough to capsize the Clinton riverboat until the Clintons—both Bill and Hillary—appeared on national television, holding hands, and telling the American people that if they had no problem with the "revelations," neither should anyone else. That well-publicized demonstration of matrimonial solidarity deflected the anti-Clinton torpedo… for the moment. Clinton was elected in 1992, but the allegations of extra-marital affairs did not stop. Scaife wanted more, and he found it in Paula Jones.

Jones would be called before Ken Starr as he fished for more evidence of wrongdoing, but there was a danger that Jones would not be enough. Her testimony had been challenged before. But with Monica Lewinsky, the Starr investigation took on new energy. Whitewater—in all its complexity and ultimate failure—was all but forgotten, but here was something the

American people could really get into. A sexual scandal, taking place in the Oval Office itself!

Monica had been tricked by her "friend" Linda Tripp into relating details of her meetings with the President over the phone ... and into Tripp's tape recorder. With that, Tripp and Goldberg could go to the Starr investigation. What had begun as a search through Clinton's balance sheets ended as a search through his bedsheets. Starr was happy that he finally had something to beat the President with, and at last the long-awaited impeachment proceedings were begun.

During this time, several other events were taking place behind the scenes. In the first case, the anti-Clinton lobby had worked itself into a frenzy with something called "The Clinton Chronicles." Financed by Scaife, this was an "exposé" of the Clinton mafia and its evil machinations—including murder—over the years. As mentioned before, the source material for the Chronicles was rather flimsy, largely based as it was on the "revelations" of a "disgruntled former employee," Larry Nichols. Nichols had been fired from his state government post in Arkansas because he had been using the office facilities to raise funds for ... the Contras. Embittered over what he perceived as his cavalier treatment by the governor—Bill Clinton—he became an easy mark for the intrepid private investigators hired by Richard Scaife. As in the case of Lucianne Goldberg and Linda Tripp, Scaife's people found Nichols to be a good source of gossip about the future president but they needed more.

Nichols began spinning tales of drug-running in Arkansas, of womanizing politicians, gun deals, and assorted Contra-related derring-do. He became the George Adamski of the Clinton administration: claiming he had been aboard that spacecraft and had seen the evil aliens at work, and was only too happy to go public with what he knew (or could invent).

In a bizarre twist, however, the core of the Arkansas revelations is the infamous Mena episode. A small town in Arkansas with an airstrip, it was used by the CIA to transport guns and drugs between Latin America and the United States as part of the Contra operation. In other words, it was the legacy of the *Reagan–Bush* administrations and had nothing to do with Governor Clinton; indeed, as a "black op," it was probably completely unknown to the Governor in the first place.

Although the taped interviews were not quite ready for prime-time, they were promoted heavily by televangelist Jerry Falwell and, later, by Pat Robertson's own CBN, and by the Christian Coalition he founded after his unsuccessful run at the American presidency in 1988. Also appearing on "The Clinton Chronicles" was Paula Jones, she of the purported sexual relationship with Clinton while he was governor. The Christian Right ate it up. It may not have been ready for prime-time, but it sure played well in Peoria.

But that was not the end of Richard Scaife's campaign to unseat the President. In order to ensure a most favorable outcome of the Kenneth Starr investigation, he funded a chair at Pepperdine University specifically for Starr when his role as special prosecutor was complete. Once this arrangement became public, however, everyone denied the connection, and Starr was forced to refuse the chair.

Scaife's hatchet man for the *American Spectator* was one David Brock. Brock's story is by now quite well-known. Famous as a muckraker on the trail of the Clintons for several years, he eventually balked at writing a story that would claim Hillary Clinton was a lesbian. Scaife wanted the story to be explicit in its claims; after all, he was donating heavily to the *American Spectator* from his own pocket and felt he owned the paper. In addition, Brock's pieces had always been on the mark. But when it came to Hillary as gay, Brock could not find the evidence, and he couldn't find the heart to go forward with the conservative program. Scaife demanded Brock be fired from the paper, and Brock went ahead and apologized to the Clintons publically for the hatchet jobs he had been doing at Scaife's insistence, admitting that they were created largely out of whole cloth.

There is no law against philanthropy, of course, and one should not hold Richard Scaife's donations against him. Yet, it is of interest to note that in addition to over $900,000 he donated to the 1972 Nixon Committee to Re-Elect the President (CREEP), he has substantially supported Conservative Republican causes steadily through the years since then. The fact is that the bulk of his largesse in the 1990s went to organizations that represent the core of the Conservative movement—including millions to the Heritage Foundation (a famous Conservative "think tank"), the Western Journalism Center and Accuracy in Media (two groups specializing in Vince Foster assassination theories), and the National Taxpayers Union (which produced yet another video "exposé" of the Vince Foster assassination theories)—is an indication of how much "old money" is allied to the "New Right" in American politics. Like the funding of the Nazi Party by wealthy German (and American) corporations in the 1920s, '30s and '40s, the presence of such tycoons as Scaife, H.L. Hunt, Nelson Bunker Hunt, and many others in the background of the Christian Right campaigns against Clinton reveals a deeper, darker purpose in the souls of these men, a moral conviction representing an entire constellation of religious, racial, social and cultural theories that the rest of the world might find abhorrent or even frightening.

In Weimar Germany there were dozens of political parties that could have used financial support from huge industrial concerns like Farben, Krupp, Siemens, and the rest; the fact is that these companies threw their backing behind Hitler and the Nazi Party. American companies such as Ford Motor, Harriman Brothers, ITT, and many others followed suit. Men like Allen Dulles, John Foster Dulles and Richard Nixon conspired to give aid and comfort to the enemy, pulling the strings necessary to ensure that thousands of war criminals escaped justice at Nuremberg; and that millions of dollars in German money found their way to safe haven as well.

In a sense, the young inheritors of Old Money were picking up where their parents left off. The elder Bushes, Mellons, Scaifes, Hitchcocks, etc. were dying off or fading into retirement. In one year alone—1994—the obituaries of the New York *Times* were reporting the demise of many old OSS men, their affiliations buried deep within the columns memorializing their contributions to society. Thus was even such a venerable institution as television chef Julia Child revealed to have been in the OSS, outed in her husband's 1994 obituary. Her husband, Paul Cushing Child was an OSS cartographer, whom she had met during her wartime OSS service.

The youth and energy of Bill Clinton posed a threat to the old way of thinking, the old right-wing power politics that many claim—and with much justification—built the United States in the first place. The Mellons, the Astors, the Morgans, the Carnegies, the Forbeses, the DuPonts, the Hunts, all made serious contributions to the strength and power of America. Their industries employed millions of Americans, even as they were building massive fortunes that would sustain generations of their own bloodlines long after they were dead. They also built monuments to themselves, of course, with stone blocks large enough to bury the corpses of the men, women and children who died for their sins. The Holocaust is but one example of what may happen when an almost religious zeal for racial and ethnic superiority is wedded to extensive wealth and connections in high places.

The wannabes—the Pat Robertsons, Jerry Falwells, and other spokesmen for the New Right, the Christian Right—were only too eager to use these connections and these funds to further the goals of their financial masters, meanwhile nurturing their own bank accounts. Whether it was tearing down an American president or building up a Third World dictator, the Christian Right had managed to instill in their followers the idea that—as sociologist Sara Diamond so eloquently put it—"one's personal redemption" was tied to "a gospel of political participation." Pat Robertson certainly exemplified that concept, as his track record of support for Mobutu, Taylor, Rios Montt, and the Nicaraguan Contras dramatically shows.

Americans in general do not have on-the-ground experience in the developing nations, especially not those regions in the midst of political struggle and military turmoil. They can't be expected to know how America is perceived abroad by the citizens of these countries whose only experience of America is either the politically-committed Christian missionary (like Robertson), the rapacious capitalist businessman (again, like Robertson), or the government spooks and saboteurs who support first one dictator and then another. If America is despised in some foreign countries, and if American humanitarian efforts are greeted with suspicion or scorn, it is largely due to the mixed signals sent out by a combination of American businessmen, American missionaries, and American foreign policy experts and in-country foreign service bureaucrats.

We may despise the Islamic promotion of a *jihad* against the West and specifically against America, but unrecognized by most Americans is the fact that their own most visible "ambassadors" to the East have been people like Robertson on the one hand, and agencies like the CIA on the other, complemented by a wealth of oil men, military advisers, and cultural emissaries in the food, entertainment, and fashion industries. If everyday Americans do not support, condone or participate in cultural or military colonialism, their overseas counterparts are not so innocent. Groups like the Christian Coalition, the Christian Broadcasting Network, the Heritage Foundation, and individuals like Pat Robertson and Jerry Falwell, have been busy creating a philosophical framework for the New Right in the absence of a credible Communist threat: the idea that personal spiritual redemption and political activism (of an approved, Conservative, variety) are mutually dependent.

The Christian Right took a page from the psychological warfare book. What is missionary work, after all, but psychological warfare by other means? Sara Diamond, who has written extensively on the phenomenon of Christian fundamentalist and evangelical political action, notes the relationship between humanitarian aid and psychological warfare, a relationship hinted at in Christopher Simpson's work on psychological warfare, *Science of Coercion: Communication Research and Psychological Warfare 1945-1960* (Oxford, 1994).

"Humanitarian aid" and "psychological operations" are two areas of "total war" where the Christian Right serves U.S. foreign policy objectives best. Acting either as "private" benefactors or as agents of the U.S. government, Christian Right "humanitarian" suppliers and promoters of anti-Communist ideology use religion to mask the aggressive, cynical nature of "humanitarian" projects.... It is doubtful, however, that counterinsurgency could be effective without the use of religion. Because the conduct of "psychological operations" relies on the successful interpretation and manipulation of a target population's deeply held beliefs and cultural practices, the functional use of religion simply must be addressed by anyone intending to understand and put an end to "total warfare."[30]

When Diamond first published her work, in 1989, Pat Robertson's "humanitarian" efforts in Zaire had not yet begun, and were not noticed by the media until 1993. As men, women and children were dying from the combined results of war and the Ebola virus, Robertson's "Operation Blessing" was flying dozens of sorties ... to a diamond mine far from the scene of the conflict. When they did manage to fly into Goma and other regions ravaged by refugees (both internal and external), they brought a few pounds of aspirin. No blood, no vaccines, nothing that addressed the real problems of the sick and dying. They prayed, said a witness, and spoke in tongues, and preached ... and then got the hell out of there.

At the same time, Robertson was running an anti-Clinton campaign on his *700 Club*, watched by millions, and raising money for his obscenely cynical African operations. With funding from right-wing zealots like Richard Mellon Scaife and H.L. Hunt, the Christian Right was simultaneously hailing Larry Nichols, Paula Jones, Linda Tripp, and Monica Lewinsky as political "heroes" while supporting dictators in Africa and Latin America, men with the blood of thousands of civilians on their hands. Islamic militants may be forgiven, therefore, if they see America as embarked on a "crusade" reminiscent of the worst excesses of the thirteenth century, promoting evangelistic Christianity with fire and sword abroad, and with rumor, paranoia and innuendo at home. The Christian Right has supported regimes that actively used chemical and biological weapons against their own people, that tortured and killed political opponents, all in the furtherance of dubious national interests. Can America accept that some of their most revered spiritual leaders may be moral imbeciles, praising Jesus on the one hand while financing terror on the other?

The involvement with the Nazis of the sainted forebears of these men should have told us everything we needed to know. But most Americans are completely unaware of this long, involved history when they go to a voting booth to select our national and local leaders. For one thing, this history is the stuff of thick, academic tomes that never find their way to a secondary school classroom. For another, the irrefutable evidence shown in these sources is relegated to the "crank" category by mainstream historians, since it does not fit neatly into preconceived ideas of the American historical experience. To integrate this information into our history books would be to rewrite history itself.

Thus, when Hillary Rodham Clinton went on the air with her mention of a "vast, right-wing conspiracy," no one was really listening. It did not sound like an objective read of the situation, but as a self-serving statement designed to exonerate her embattled husband. Now, with the benefit of years of hindsight, we may be able to see the outlines of this conspiracy more clearly. From the days of Prescott Bush, Allen Dulles, and Richard Nixon and their enthusiastic collaboration with Nazism to the days of Ronald Reagan and George H.W. Bush, the fascist "ethnic outreach" programs of the Republican Party courted the Nazi vote and employed hundreds of Nazis and Nazi war criminals in its political campaigns in the decades after World War II. In a more contemporary context, George W. Bush can be shown to have had connections with Islamic terrorists through his oil businesses. Thus the weight of the evidence is such that we are forced to realize that Richard Mellon Scaife, Pat Robertson, and Pat Buchanan were all correct: America is truly a land where two ideological forces have been battling each other for generations for stewardship over the American soul. And, as usual, the Devil is better-dressed, has better public relations, and quotes Scripture for his own ends.

BUSH AND GOD

We are in a conflict between good and evil, and America will call evil by its name.
—President George W. Bush, Commencement Address, West Point, June 1, 2002

Those who believe I am heavily overstating a case for which the evidence is circumstantial need only look at the cover of *Newsweek* for March 10, 2003, with a cover story entitled, "Bush & God: How Faith Changed His Life and Shapes His Agenda." While giving us a tale of how George W. Bush found Jesus in his forties, stopped drinking, and got serious, there is a deeper, more unsettling message that may be summed up in these lines:

> The presidential campaign was Texas on a grander scale. As he prepared to run, in 1999, Bush assembled leading pastors at the governor's mansion for a "laying on of hands," and told them he'd been "called" to seek higher office.[31]

The entire article—and series of accompanying, shorter, articles—describes the Bush presidency as a "faith-centered" administration. To further quote,

> ...this president—this presidency—is the most resolutely "faith-based" in modern times, an enterprise founded, supported and guided by trust in the temporal and spiritual power of God.[32]

It would sound mean and petty to complain about a presidential administration that was spiritual, if it were not for the fact that the Bush administration picks and chooses its scriptural texts with its own agenda in mind. The administration—as admitted in the *Newsweek* articles—has ignored the clergymen, the priests, the mullahs in coming to its current state of spiritual enlightenment. The combined voices of Protestants, Catholics, Jews and Muslims against war does not move George W. Bush at all. Obviously, he considers himself more spiritually enlightened than the professionals, and having a circle of Christian evangelical sycophants around him—and the backing of wealthy Fundamentalist political action groups hailing from the days of Robertson, Falwell, Scaife, and others—means that he never need hear a discouraging word.

There is no spiritual debate in the White House. Instead, what motivates and drives this president—at least, insofar as we are able to tell—is a belief in his own position (he claimed he was "called" to the presidency by God), a simplistic understanding of good and evil (Saddam Hussein is evil, those who do not support United States' foreign policy are evil, etc.), and the fact that he is now the leader of the world's last remaining superpower. If the Islamic world is afraid that Bush is on a Crusader-like rampage to Christianize the Middle East, though, they need not worry too much. When Saudi Arabia was being chastised by the US Commission on International Religious Freedom for its human rights abuses, especially in terms of its persecution of foreign Christian workers on Saudi soil who are thrown into prison for practicing their faith, they were not censured by the US government. The support of Saudi Arabia is considered too important to alienate in this fashion.

One must also remember the practical parameters of this brand of spirituality. When George W. Bush was Governor of Texas, the rate of executions of prisoners on death row was at an all-time high. This is the "old time religion" of a Savanarola or a Torquemada, molded to fit the *realpolitik* of twenty-first century global confrontation. It is the British film *The Ruling Class*, performed on a world stage with George W. Bush in, alas, the Peter O'Toole role: the wealthy scion of a moneyed dynasty who believes himself to be Jesus Christ and is battling against another mental patient—this time played by Osama Bin Laden or Saddam Hussein, take your pick—who believes he is the Creator God. In the film, the Peter O'Toole/George W. Bush character is "cured" of his delusion that he is Jesus Christ ... only to wake up one morning and "realize" he is Jack the Ripper.

And so it goes.

The utterances of the Divine Name, which was supposed to make the devils tremble and place them at the will of the Magus, was at least equally powerful, it was argued, to enforce their obedience for a purpose in consonance with their own nature. Behind this there lay also the tacit assumption that it was easier to control demons than to persuade angels. Then seeing that prayer to God and the invocation of the Divine Names presuppose a proper spirit of reverence, devotion and love as the condition upon which prayer is heard, it became a condition in Goetia. The first impossibility required of the adept in Black Magic is therefore that he should love God before he bewitches his neighbor; that he should put all his hopes in God before he makes pact with Satan; that, in a word, he should be good in order to do evil.

—The Book of Ceremonial Magic[33]

Endnotes
[1] Mark Aarons & John Loftus, *Unholy Trinity*, St Martin's Press, NY, 1991, p. 98

[2] Russ Bellant, *Old Nazis, The New Right and the Republican Party*, South End Press, Boston, 1991, p. 22

[3] Sara Diamond, *Not By Politics Alone: The Enduring Influence of the Christian Right*, Guilford Press, NY, 1998, p. 30

[4] Sara Diamond, *Spiritual Warfare: The Politics of the Christian Right*, South End Press, Boston, 1989, p. 6-8

[5] John Marks, *The Search for the "Manchurian Candidate,"* Times Books, NY, 1979,

p. 75

[6] Michela Wrong, *In The Footsteps of Mr. Kurtz*, HarperCollins, NY, 2002, p. 80

[7] Ibid., p. 82

[8] Ibid., p. 82

[9] Charles Higham, *American Swastika*, Doubleday, NY, 1985, p. 251

[10] Ibid., p. 251

[11] Ibid., p. 251-252

[12] As reported in the *Washington Post*, Dec 28, 2002

[13] Diamond, 1989, op. cit. p. 17

[14] Ibid., p. 17

[15] Ibid., p. 17

[16] Ibid., p. 164-168

[17] Bellant, op. cit., p. 65-68

[18] Ibid., p. 72

[19] Kenneth Wald, *Religion and Politics in the United States*, Washington DC, 1992, p. 65

[20] Peter Levenda, *Unholy Alliance*, Continuum, NY, 2002, p. 101-102

[21] Diamond, 1998, op. cit., p. 93

[22] Martin A. Lee & Bruche Shlain, *Acid Dreams*, Grove Weidenfeld, NY, 1985, p. 99

[23] Richard Harris Smith, *OSS: The Secret History of America's First Central Intelligence Agency*, University of California Press, Berkeley, 1981, p. 84-85

[24] John Loftus & Mark Aarons, *The Secret War Against the Jews*, St Martin's Griffin, NY, 1997, p. 82-87

[25] Smith, op. cit., p.15-16

[26] Lee & Shlain, op. cit., p. 73

[27] Phillip Knightley & Caroline Kennedy, *An Affair Of State*, Atheneum, NY, 1987, p. 48

[28] Ibid., p. 197

[29] Ibid., p. 201

[30] Diamond, 1989, op. cit., p. 161-162

[31] Howard Fineman, "Bush and God," *Newsweek*, March 10, 2003, p. 20

[32] Ibid., p. 17

[33] Arthur Edward Waite, *The Book of Ceremonial Magic*, Dover, NY, p. 142

Index

Blue Bird, The 259, 260
Blum, Howard 83
Blum, William 183
Blythe CA 92
Bogomils 163
Bois Caiman 24
bokors 25
bomoh 12, 14, 20, 21
Bond, James 23, 28, 247, 275
Bonet, Lisa 23, 24
Bon religion 6
Book of Ceremonial Magic, The 332
Book of Shadows 95
Book of the Law 134
Book of the Law, The 85, 99, 134
Boomer WV 192
Borland Amendment 309
Borneo 12, 256, 257
Born in Blood 156
Borobudor 12
Bosnia 58, 138
Bound Brook NJ 58
brainwashing 35, 133, 163, 170, 204-206, 211
Branch Davidians 191
Brand, Oscar 37
Brando, Marlon 25, 228, 229
Brandt, Steven 38, 102, 108, 116, 170
Branigan, W.A. 315
Brasilia 186
Bravin, Jess 127
Brayton, Georgina 91-95
Brayton, Richard Montgomery 91
Brazilian Workers Party 183
Breen, Walter 244, 245
Bremer, Arthur 254, 282, 283
Brenneke, Richard 241, 242
Bresler, Fenton 265-270, 275, 278, 284, 285
Brimley, Wilford 80
Bristow, Alan 242
Bristow Helicopters 242
Brock, David 326
Brooklyn Heights NY 37, 38, 101, 253
Brown, Edmund 39
Brownstein, Ronald 48, 83
Bruce, David 315, 316, 318, 320
Brunei 19
Brunner, Mary 90, 106, 111, 115, 123
Brussell, Mae 251, 252
Buchanan, Pat 314, 329
Buchenwald 299

Buckland, Raymond 95
Buckland, Rosemary 95
Buckley, William 87
Buddha 12, 176
Buddhism 6, 11, 90, 136, 162, 185, 303
Buffy, the Vampire Slayer 11
Buford, Terri 228
Bugliosi, Vincent 101, 120, 121, 126, 127
Bui Dem 68
Bujanovic, Father Josip 58
Bulgaria 66
Bureau of Aeronautics 43
Burlingame, Mildred 91, 94
Burlingame, Ray 91
Burnham, Forbes 181
Buruma, Ian 30
Busbey, Fred E 198
Bush family 44, 283, 290, 312, 313
Bush, George W. 135, 248, 283, 305, 311, 322, 325, 329-331
Bush, Neil 250
Bush, Prescott 311, 312, 314, 322, 329
Bush, George H. W. 67, 69, 240-243, 248-251, 265, 276, 288, 290-292, 304-306, 311-314, 321-325
Buzhardt, Fred 1
Byzantine Empire 50, 54, 55, 137, 140

C

Caddy, Douglas 71
Cafritz, Charlene 262
Cairo 99, 140, 141
Calaveras County CA 112
California Republican Assembly (CRA) 63, 64
caliph 134
Calvi, Roberto 290
Cambodia 34, 88, 229
Cameron, Ewen 82, 87, 98, 162
Canaris, Admiral 61
candomble 185, 255
Cape Town, South Africa 300
Caracas 182
Carlucci, Frank C. 207, 208, 235
Carpenter, John 112
Carter, Chris 71
Carter, Jimmy 67, 201, 206, 237-243, 254, 276, 289, 305
Carter, Rosalyn 201
Carusi, Ugo 66
Casey, William 241, 242, 247

serratia marcescens 196
Sespe Hot Springs, CA 119
Set 6, 28, 86, 99
700 Club 303, 329
Seventh Day Adventist Church 269
Seven Pillars of Wisdom, The 275
Shaba 302
Shah of Iran 182, 265
shamanism 10, 12
Shandruk, General Pavlo 58, 66
Share, Catherine "Gypsy" 104, 122, 123, 262
shariyah 21
Sharp, James 116
Shaw, Clay 88
Shaw, Joyce 208
Sheen, Martin 228
shen 153
Sheraton Center 277, 278
Shi'ism 21, 139, 238
Shinto 11, 271
Shlain, Bruce 126, 317, 332
Shu 86
Sick, Gary 242, 247, 284
Siegel, Bugsy 45
Siemens 194, 312, 326
Silver Tassie, A 74
Silverado Savings & Loan 290
Simon Magus 130, 157
Simpson, Christopher 50, 62, 83, 323, 328
Sinatra, Frank 73, 74, 100, 257
Sinatra, Nancy 100
Singapore 12, 14, 19, 30, 72, 271, 310
Singer, Margaret 227
Singlaub, John 63, 310
Sirag, Saul Paul 243, 246, 249
Sirhan, Sirhan Bishara 114, 118, 252, 254, 280, 283
Sitting Bull 191
Six Years With God 170, 189, 231
Skorzeny, Otto 67, 298, 299
Skull & Bones 313
Slater, Herman 253
sleep room 87
Slovakia 57, 73, 74
Smith, Joseph Jr, 154, 190
Smith, Reverend 210, 214
Smith, Richard Harris 316, 332
Solar Lodge of the OTO 91-95
Soledad prison 226
Solomon 132, 138, 149, 152, 153, 155, 161, 163, 185

Somerset Methodist Church 174
Son of Sam ii, 87, 89, 101, 112, 116, 117, 174, 179, 253, 254, 255, 268, 269
Sophia 157, 160, 166
South African Defence Force (SADF) 300, 301
South Dekalb County YMCA 263
Soviet Union 44, 52, 53, 66, 70, 81, 197, 219, 249, 265, 288, 291, 294
Spahn Ranch 89, 97, 98, 104, 106, 107, 109, 110, 114-117, 122, 123
Spandau 188
Speaking With The Devil 47
Special Operations Research Office (SORO) 293, 294, 297
Specter, Arlen 257
Spectra 244, 245
Spencer Memorial Church 37
Spiderman 40
Spielberg, Steven 150, 246
Spiral Staircase 104
Splendid Blond Beast, The 50, 62
Spooks 80, 176, 321
Spruitt, Herman Adrian 249
Spruitt, Mary 248, 249
Squeaky: The Life and Times of Lynette Alice Fromme 127
Srinagar 131, 151
SS Galicia Division 57, 58
SS Manhattan 194
stagecraft 125
Stalin, Josef 190
Stallone, Sylvester 144
Standard Oil 45
Stanford Research Institute (SRI) 188, 245
Stanislavsky, Constantin Sergeyevich 125
Stankievich, Stanislav 58
Stardust 38
Starr, Kenneth 324-326
Star Trek 246
Steal This Book 37
Stephenson, William 63
Stetsko, Yaroslav 57, 58, 310
Stevenson, David 156
Stockholm Syndrome 206
Stoen, Timothy 191, 200, 211, 213, 215, 216, 225
Straight Shooter 108
Straight Theater 103, 104
Stranger in a Strange Land 123
Strategic Defense Initiative (SDI) 250

CHAPTER HEADINGS FOR *SINISTER FORCES,* BOOK THREE, *THE MANSON SECRET*

SECTION FIVE: MAGIC IN THEORY AND PRACTICE

Chapter Sixteen: Psycho
Serial killers, the insanity defense, multiple personality disorder, dissociative identity disorder, and demonic possession. The Finders case. Schools for assassins. Shamanism and serial murder. The cases of Jeffrey Dahmer and Arthur Shawcross.

Chapter Seventeen: Voluntary Madness
Renaissance magician Giordano Bruno and the murder of Professor Ioan Culianu in 1991. Initiation and Interrogation. Magic, surrealism, and mind control: art imitating life imitating art.

Chapter Eighteen: Hollywood Babalon
The Stanislavski Method as mind control and initiation. Filmmaker Kenneth Anger and Aleister Crowley, Bobby Beausoleil, Marianne Faithfull, Anita Pallenberg, and the Rolling Stones. Filmmaker Donald Cammell (Performance) and his father, CJ Cammell (the first biographer of Aleister Crowley), and his suicide. Jane Fonda and Bluebird. The assassination of Marilyn Monroe. Fidel Castro's Hollywood career. Jim Morrison and witchcraft. David Lynch and spiritual transformation.

Chapter Nineteen: Am American Dream
David Berkowitz, the "Son of Sam", Maury Terry and The Ultimate Evil. The case for a Son of Sam cult. The Process Church of the Final Judgment returns. The Cotton Club murders. The Bluegrass Conspiracy. All connected, all lethal.

Chapter Twenty: Communion
Jack Sarfatti, Whitley Strieber, and the secret schools of the 1950s. The Stargate Conspiracy and the Nine.

Chapter Twenty-One. The Machineries of Joy
Nobel-Prize-winning physicist Wolfgang Pauli, Carl Jung and synchronicity. Quantum consciousness, the root of the "sinister forces". Remote viewing.

SECTION SIX: HUNGRY GHOSTS

Chapter Twenty-Two: Haunted House
The origins of evil. The return of fascism.

Chapter Twenty-Three: The Manson Secret
The technology of sociopaths. How to create an assassin. The CIA, MK-ULTRA and programmed killers.

Epilogue, Bibliography, Acknowledgments